Why Harry Met Sally

Why Harry Met Sally

SUBVERSIVE JEWISHNESS, ANGLO-CHRISTIAN POWER, AND THE RHETORIC OF MODERN LOVE

Joshua Louis Moss

University of Texas Press *Austin*

Publication of this book was made possible in part by support from the late Milton T. Smith and the Moshana Foundation, and the Tocker Foundation.

Requests for permission to reproduce material from this work should be sent to:

Permissions
University of Texas Press
P.O. Box 7819
Austin, TX 78713-7819
http://utpress.utexas.edu/index.php/rp-form

♾ The paper used in this book meets the minimum requirements of ANSI/NISO z39.48-1992 (R1997) (Permanence of Paper).

LIBRARY OF CONGRESS CATALOGING DATA
Names: Moss, Joshua Louis, 1973–, author.
Title: Why Harry met Sally : subversive Jewishness, Anglo-Christian power, and the rhetoric of modern love / Joshua Louis Moss.
Description: First edition. | Austin : University of Texas Press, 2017. | Includes bibliographical references and index.
Identifiers: LCCN 2016050504
 ISBN 978-1-4773-1282-7 (cloth : alk. paper)
 ISBN 978-1-4773-1283-4 (pbk. : alk. paper)
 ISBN 978-1-4773-1284-1 (library e-book)
 ISBN 978-1-4773-1285-8 (non-library e-book)
Subjects: LCSH: Jews in motion pictures. | Jews on television. | Jews in popular culture—United States. | Love in motion pictures. | Judaism—Relations—Christianity. | Interpersonal relations—Social aspects.
Classification: LCC PN1995.9.J46 M67 2017 | DDC 791.43/6529924—dc23
LC record available at https://lccn.loc.gov/2016050504

doi:10.7560/312827

For my daughter,
SHIRA EDEN MOSS

Contents

Acknowledgments

*E*VERY BOOK IS A COLLABORATIVE PROCESS THAT TESTS the patience and frays the nerves of everyone in the author's life. *Why Harry Met Sally* was no different. The sheer volume of material and numerous academic disciplines that I was required to research during this project often felt beyond my capabilities as an author, an academic, and a functioning human being. The time and effort it took me to produce the finished manuscript required years of forbearance, support, suggestions, and encouragement from my friends, colleagues, and loved ones. This book simply would not have been possible without their assistance and guidance. It is therefore with deep appreciation that I offer them my thanks.

First and foremost, I am enormously indebted to the five members of my dissertation committee at the University of Southern California: Akira Lippit, Michael Renov, Marsha Kinder, Steven J. Ross, and Aniko Imre. My dissertation chair, Akira Lippit, offered invaluable guidance when this book was nothing more than a vague notion proposed by a confused and overwhelmed first-year graduate student. I remain humbled by his support and am pleased to call him a friend. Michael Renov offered critical early input on this project and helped elevate my writing from opinion to structured analysis. Marsha Kinder's pull-no-punches passion for outside-the-box thinking and rigorous scholarship pushed me out of my comfort zone and forced me to take original and bold research paths. Steve Ross's emphasis on grounded, real-world facts and dates convinced me to dispense with much of my sometimes abstract jargon, historicize my work, and cut to the basic truths of my argument. Aniko Imre's daily encouragement, brainstorming sessions, and detailed scholarly feedback provided the backbone that held this project together. I am honored and grateful for the time and effort of each of these revered academics. I can think of no finer collection of scholars to have guided me during the years that it took to refine this research and to develop my literary voice.

In addition to my committee, I am deeply indebted to Vincent Brook for his many years of detailed peer review notes and invaluable advice in all aspects of my academic career. Vincent's passionate thinking and rigorous academic standards have helped me to become a better writer and academic. My editor at the University of Texas Press, Jim Burr, has been patient and supportive during the sometimes challenging rewrite process. Cristina Venegas and Janet Walker displayed unwavering support of my teaching and research over the four years that I was a visiting member of the faculty in the Department of Film and Media Studies at the University of California, Santa Barbara. Nathan Abrams, Benjamin Wright, Monica Champagne, Sally Furgeson, Lynne Chapman, Jennifer Holt, Sarah Lefton, Rob Kleinman, Fred Raskin, Jamison Newlander, Rea-Silvia Feriozzi, and Jim Hundertmark are just a few of the other friends and colleagues who assisted with the manuscript and provided encouragement, suggestions, and feedback. My mother, Barbara, my grandmother, Dorothy, and my wife, Melissa, also deserve thanks for their incredible love, patience, and support. Finally, I dedicate this book to my brilliant, rambunctious, and ever-curious three-year-old daughter, Shira Eden Moss. I can only hope it will someday inspire her to ask her own set of questions about the world as it is, the world as it imagines itself to be, and the truth that locates somewhere in between.

Why Harry Met Sally

INTRODUCTION

Sally's Orgasm

Had my dream again where I'm making love and the Olympic judges are watching. I'd nailed the compulsories, so this is it, the finals. I got a 9.8 from the Canadians, a perfect 10 from the Americans, and my mother, disguised as an East German judge, gave me a 5.6. Must have been the dismount.

HARRY BURNS (BILLY CRYSTAL), *WHEN HARRY MET SALLY*

You are a human affront to all women. And I am a woman.

SALLY ALBRIGHT (MEG RYAN), *WHEN HARRY MET SALLY*

THE ORGASM SCENE IN *WHEN HARRY MET SALLY* (1989) remains one of the most iconic and startlingly disruptive moments in the history of American film comedy. In the nearly three decades since the film's release, the sequence has been referenced or parodied dozens of times, including on *The Muppet Show* (1998), *The Office* (2005–2013), *Family Guy* (1999–), and on sketch comedy shows such as *Upright Citizens Brigade* (1998–2000), *Improv Everywhere* (2013), and *Saturday Night Live* (1975–).[1] Early test audiences reportedly roared with such sustained, cacophonous laughter that director Rob Reiner was forced to add thirty seconds of second-unit footage of New York streets just to provide time for them to recover. *Time* magazine described it as the exact moment when Meg Ryan became a movie star.[2] The iconography has become so entrenched in the public consciousness that when Keira Knightley and Judi Dench re-created the scene as part of a series of short films produced for *Vanity Fair* in 2015,

Sally Albright (Meg Ryan) and Harry Burns (Billy Crystal) in the famous "orgasm" scene in When Harry Met Sally *(1989).*

the sketch needed no titles or credits to identify it.[3] It remains instantly recognizable as a landmark in popular American entertainment.

The setting is a crowded lunch rush in Katz's Deli on New York's Lower East Side. Sally Albright (Meg Ryan) and Harry Burns (Billy Crystal), two young singles living in Manhattan, are attempting a long-term platonic friendship despite Harry's insistence that men and women can never truly be friends. Over lunch, the two begin to debate whether a woman can fool a man by faking an orgasm. The boastful, sexually arrogant Harry insists that he can always tell. In response, the usually uptight Sally begins to moan, gradually performing a loud demonstration of her ability to convincingly fake an orgasm. As her performance grows in intensity and volume, Sally causes the entire restaurant to stop and stare. The normally verbose Harry retreats into silence. Sally completes her faked orgasm, takes a breath, smiles, and returns to eating her lunch. The sequence then culminates with one of the most famous lines in popular American cinema. An older woman (Estelle Reiner, director Rob Reiner's mother), sitting at a nearby table, remarks, "I'll have what she's having."[4]

What made Sally's orgasm one of the most resonant moments in American film history? The popular understanding focuses on gender comedy. The sequence inverts traditional notions of masculine and feminine identity while staying true to the screwball battle-of-the-sexes comedy traditions that it references.[5] In claiming sexual visibility in a public space, Sally trumps Harry's normative role as the pursuer and sexual aggressor. This undercuts and undermines Harry's masculine power, revealing his boastful sexual confidence to be a fraud. Sally's unruly agency also comments on the genre in which it takes place. It literalizes the subtext of sexual titillation that locates beneath the hostile banter so entrenched in the screwball comedy form.

But to stop at this level of gender and genre analysis is to miss another contextual framework. The repressed, polite Sally exemplifies the blonde, blue-eyed Anglo-Saxon movie star beauty of postwar American cinema. Harry is her opposite, the familiar urbane, hyper-verbal, sexually compulsive New York Jew.[6] As Nathan Abrams observes, this Christian-Jewish culture clash was already embedded in the film's use of locations, backgrounds, secondary characters, and in the dialogue found throughout the film.[7] When Sally performs her orgasm, this already-established Jewish cultural context visibly informs the comedic inversion of her sexual exhibition. The two are seated at Katz's Deli, one of the most famous Jewish delis in New York. They are eating pastrami sandwiches and drinking Dr. Brown's soda, culturally Jewish identifiers. Sally's orgasm is therefore informed by a second layer of comedic inversion. Through a performative act of sexual agency, Sally upends not only the obvious gender stereotypes, but also an entrenched, embedded Anglo-Christian-Jewish power dynamic. Harry's subsequent smirk and Estelle Reiner's punch line coda confirm this second layer of comedic incongruity. In claiming the right of unruly, performative sexuality, Sally becomes the "Jew."

For more than a century in plays, vaudeville, literature, cinema, and television, Anglo-Saxon Protestant and Anglo-Catholic figures such as Sally have occupied the default position of idealized, chaste romantic desire. Visible Jews such as Harry function as their neurotic, boundary-crossing, and taboo-violating counterpoint. This entanglement has recurred in numerous historical, cultural, and industrial contexts. When Jack Robin (Al Jolson), a Jewish immigrant and cantor's son, puts on blackface to win the heart of the Protestant Mary Dale (May McAvoy) in the first sync-sound studio release, *The Jazz Singer* (1927), the romance served as an allegory for technological and industrial change. The love affair between Irish-Catholic journalist Kitty Fremont (Eva Marie Saint) and Israeli Jewish settler Ari Ben-Canaan (Paul Newman) in Otto Preminger's *Exodus* (1960) critiqued ethno-religious bigotry through stylized Hollywood romance. Dustin Hoffman's cross-swinging liberation of Katherine Ross in *The Graduate* (1967) and Barbra Streisand's affair with Robert Redford in *The Way We Were* (1973) challenged sexual boundaries during the rise of the American counterculture. In the 1980s, the quintessentially sheltered Jewish American Princess, "Baby" (Jennifer Grey), jumping into the raised arms of the working-class Catholic, Johnny (Patrick Swayze), in *Dirty Dancing* (1987) renegotiated transgression through the lens of Reagan conservatism.

Whether perceived as threat or triumph, these Anglo-Christian-Jewish couplings have provided a visceral, easily graspable template for understanding the rapid transformations of an increasingly globalized, modern world. When "Christian" and "Jew" overcome obstacles to achieve some form of union, issues such as nativism and xenophobia, European class systems, censorship, and the tensions of an increasingly globalized marketplace are navigated. It is a pattern that first emerged in nineteenth-century European politics and literature as emancipated Jews increasingly assimilated into bourgeois societies. A hundred and fifty years later, it remains intact as one of the most powerful and enduring cultural forums of the mass media age.

THE THREE WAVES

This book is structured chronologically and organized into three parts. Each part contains three chapters that collectively examine a distinct historical period in which Christian-Jewish literary, stage, and screen couplings emerged to grapple with political, industrial, economic, and social changes. "The First Wave: The Mouse-Mountains of Modernity (1905–1934)" explores how writers, artists, intellectuals, and filmmakers at the turn of the twentieth century developed Anglo-Christian-Jewish couplings as an exemplar of modernist sensibilities. Chapter 1 traces the emergence of Anglo-Christian-Jewish coupling fantasies by examining the personas, and marriages, of two polarizing public figures, British Prime Minister Benjamin Disraeli (1804–1881) and the persecuted French Captain Alfred Dreyfus (1859–1935). Disraeli, an effete dandy and successful romance novelist, used his marriage to prominent Protestant British aristocrat Mary Anne Lewis to mitigate his Jewishness for political advantage. Captain Dreyfus, whose 1894 conviction on false charges of treason in France led to the explosive Dreyfus Affair, married a young French-Jewish woman, Lucie Hadamard, in 1890. The intermarriage of the Disraelis and the Jewish marriage of the Dreyfuses serve as contrasting case studies for how the selection of one's spouse mediated public perceptions in the emergent popular media of the time.

Chapters 2 and 3 consider the impact of both the Disraelis and the Dreyfuses on late modern European literature and early American cinema. Authors such as Marcel Proust, Franz Kafka, James Joyce, and Leonard

Woolf seized on Anglo-Christian-Jewish couplings as a powerful allegory to champion a new form of cosmopolitan modernism. Early American cinema soon followed, featuring numerous immigrant Anglo-Christian-Jewish coupling narratives. This first wave of Anglo-Christian-Jewish love stories in popular screen media challenged the reactionary nativism of European anti-Semitism and American xenophobia seen in the anti-immigrant political movements of the time. Films such as *The Cohens and Kellys* serials and features (1904–1933), *Private Izzy Murphy* (1926), *The Jazz Singer* (1927), *Surrender* (1927), and *Abie's Irish Rose* (1928) soon followed.

In the second part, "Erotic Schlemiels of the Counterculture (1967–1980)," the second wave is located emerging in late 1960s New Hollywood cinema as a corrective to political conservatism and representational absences of the 1950s and early 1960s. Chapter 4 begins by examining the postwar impact of Israel and the rise of the counterculture in producing a new, visibly carnal form of Jewish sexual agency in the late 1960s. Two decades earlier, in the wake of the Holocaust and paranoia of the McCarthy years, a postwar decoupling of Jewish-Christian representation had taken place. By the early 1950s, Jews had become implicated by prewar socialist labor movements and were driven to the margins. It wasn't until Otto Preminger's 1960 *Exodus* that a new, potent postwar Anglo-Christian-Jewish sexuality was introduced through the on-screen coupling of actors Paul Newman and Eva Marie Saint. It was a redefinition that would take hold in American popular cinema seven years later in Mike Nichols's *The Graduate* (1967).

Chapter 5 examines the development of sexually explicit stand-up comedy and postwar literature in the 1950s and early 1960s. Young, politically engaged Jewish writers and comedians began to use ribald sexuality as a form of political resistance. In these early second-wave performances and texts, Jewishness was deployed to critique the desexualized conformity and ethnic-free representational landscapes of the postwar decades. The literature of Saul Bellow, Bernard Malamud, and Philip Roth and the stand-up comedy of Lenny Bruce, Mort Sahl, Nichols and May, and Stiller and Meara produced visible carnality as pushback on McCarthy-era Gentile domination. These parallel artistic movements recalibrated first-wave subversive Jewishness as a site of political and ideological resistance. They subsequently informed the myriad Anglo-Christian-Jewish love stories that defined New Hollywood throughout the late 1960s and 1970s.

Chapter 6 explores the second wave in Hollywood cinema. Beginning in 1967 with *The Graduate* and continuing in films such as *I Love You, Alice B. Toklas* (1968), *Bob & Carol & Ted & Alice* (1969), *The Way We Were* (1972), *The Heartbreak Kid* (1972), and *The Apprenticeship of Duddy Kravitz* (1974), a new wave of overtly Jewish performers in relationship with Anglo-Saxon partners became a framework for changing aesthetics and sensibilities. New movie stars such as Barbra Streisand, Woody Allen, Dustin Hoffman, Elliott Gould, Richard Benjamin, Richard Dreyfuss, George Segal, and Bette Midler represented a collective rejection of the white, Anglo-centric beauty standards of stars in the 1950s. Carnal sexuality was deployed as an allegory for historical revisionism, gay rights, civil rights, the feminist movement, and the taboo-shattering sexual politics of the hippie "free love" era. This second wave peaked in the late 1970s before receding under the conservative sensibilities of the Reagan years in the 1980s.

"Global Fockers at the Millennium (1993–2007)" locates the third wave emerging in television sitcoms, Broadway musicals, and "gross-out" film comedies of the 1990s and 2000s. This wave is understood as a response to both the Reagan era's rejection of identity politics and the subsequent economic globalism of the 1990s. Chapter 7 explores Jewish absence and Anglo-Christian dominance in popular media of the 1980s by considering how Art Spiegelman's two-volume *Maus: A Survivor's Tale* (1986/1992) and David Cronenberg's *The Fly* (1986) used metamorphosis and codes to explore residual Holocaust traumas and the historical context of both earlier waves. Chapter 8 examines how television shows such as *Seinfeld* (NBC 1989–1998), *Mad About You* (NBC 1992–1999), *The Nanny* (CBS 1993–1999), *Dharma & Greg* (ABC 1997–2002), and *Curb Your Enthusiasm* (HBO 1999–) reintroduced visible Anglo-Christian-Jewish love stories as safe, malleable formats for the revenue streams of the emergent global economy. Chapter 9 concludes by exploring how Broadway musical theater such as *Angels in America* (1993), *Rent* (1996), and *Hedwig and the Angry Inch* (1998) and Hollywood romantic comedies such as *American Pie* (1999), *Meet the Parents* (2000), and *Knocked Up* (2007) used Jewish-Christian couplings to explore transgressive experimentations with time and image.

In each of these waves, Anglo-Christian-Jewish couplings are understood as a response to nativist, reactionary political climates of the 1910s, 1950s, and 1980s. The emancipated literary, stage, and screen Jew—a reflection of real Jews emerging, en masse, from the shtetls of Europe—became aligned with the rapid popularity of the burgeoning American media industries. The Christian screen partner confirmed this emergence as an essential part of the fabric of cosmopolitan modernity by offering physiognomic, physiological, and gendered contrast. Together, through predominantly comedic interplay, these Anglo-Christian-Jewish couples pointed spectators toward a multicultural melting pot where the barriers of nationalism and the sexual mores of Victorian-era nativism could be safely negotiated. The model for this rethinking of popular media is called "coupling theory" and is the central theoretical intervention of this book.

COUPLING THEORY

Coupling theory proposes a methodology for reading relational configurations of literary, stage, and screen couples as single, rather than dual, identifiers. It argues that it is the interplay among subjectivities, representational polarities, and gendered binaries, and not within the individual figure, in which one of the critical generative processes of popular media locates. The imagined couple operates as a privileged rhetorical nexus. It produces a visceral binary for what political science scholars such as Walker Connor have defined as the emergence of "ethnonationalism," the problematic transitions and transformations brought about by technology, industry, and the new sciences in the mass media age.[8]

Ethnonationalism, as Connor argues, provides a way to visualize and articulate national identity through ethnic archetypes and stereotypes. But these national avatars are also informed by the new sciences and technologies.[9] Coupling theory calls for a rethinking of this ethnonationalist link among ethnicity, science, technology, and representation. It does this by relocating the tensions of the national-historical from individual figuration into a recognizable expression of romantic and/or erotic love—what Jacques Lacan calls the "affinity between the enigmas of sexuality and the play of the signifier."[10]

Coupling theory locates this tension by reading the literary, stage, and screen pairing as a single, entangled construction oscillating between holistic and fragmented perspectives. The obvious totems of gendered, sexual, and other representational discourses visualize this fragmentation. But coupling theory also proposes that this rhetoric expands beyond race, class, gender, and sexual embodiment into negotiations of history and absence, chronology and disruption, cohesion and dissonance. Body contrast and gendered oscillation manifest this heterodoxy in an easily palatable way. To the reader or spectator, the couple is an inevitable precursor to the family. The family operates as an extension of the nation. The successful or unsuccessful navigation of screen coupling mediates events at both the psychoanalytic and cultural-political spectrum points. Framed in genre forms such as screwball, romantic, or sex comedies or in romantic or historical melodramas, this negotiation is understood by the spectator through a reassuring, repeatable, easily graspable pattern. Coupling theory thus draws from both fields to propose a new historiography for understanding the evolving relationship among spectator, text, space, and industry.

The specific pattern examined in this book is the Anglo-Christian-Jewish coupling. The reason for this focus is the long historical link between ethno-religious Christian-Jewish rhetoric and the emergence of the modern nation-state. As Lilie Chouliaraki and Norman Fairclough, building on the work of Pierre Bourdieu, have shown, the impact of the rapid development of technologies and sciences in the early twentieth century is primarily understood through a discourse of holism and fracture.[11] The rapid invention and dissemination of radically transformative forms of media such as photography, radio, newspapers, and the cinema sparked a fundamental destabilization in the relationship among the individual, the apparatus, and the established cultural institutions of the nation-state. The European (Anglo-Christian) flâneur, struggling to understand the rapid changes taking place, sought out a visual identifier of this transformation. Decoherence, dissonance, and fracture were soon signified, and embodied, by "Jewishness." Cohesion, normativity, and premodern historical linearity were likewise defined as "Christian." Together, informed by the voyeuristic erotics of screen figuration, they became a central site for exploring myriad economic, transnational, and sociopolitical renegotiations across more than a century of books, theater, music, cinema, and television.[12]

Coupling theory locates this relational figuration as a single form represented by two related parts. The white, Anglo-European/American protagonist and/or romantic interest sits in the dominant position as a cohesive signifier of a linear, established, ethno-historical chronology. The Jewish deviant acts as a disruptor of this cohesion and is therefore often comedic. The meta-coupling provides a perpetual, ongoing nexus for subversive discourses and verboten subject matter across a wide range of topics and cultural pivot points.[13] Gender (Jewish men/Christian women vs. Jewish women/Christian men), queer formulations, religious sub-groupings (Jewish-Catholic vs. Jewish-Protestant) are each collectively understood as variations of the same figural meta-coupling.

This entanglement was certainly not new to the mass media age. Philosopher Jean-Luc Nancy argues that European Christian culture has always been defined by an ongoing, perpetual tension informed as much by what it is not (for example, Jewish, Islamic, polytheist) as by what it is. Nancy describes this incomplete doctrine as a "subject in relationship to itself in the midst of a search for self."[14] As early as the fourth century CE, sexual deviancy was identified by what historian Susanna Drake describes as the "Christian construction of the carnal Jewish subject."[15]

Richard Dyer, building on the work of Michael Lerner, argues that medieval Jews played a distinct role as the embodiment of European (Christian) structural instability.[16] Jewish threat took place in the "gentilizing" of images of Jesus and Mary in medieval Christian art. This process, as Dyer observes, positioned the Jew as self-denying entry into whiteness by rejecting Jesus. The "Jew" subsequently had racial visibility inscribed on his or her body as punishment for this rejection. Ethno-darkening of Jews in Christian art offered visual demarcation between European culture and the Jewish/North-African Orientalist origins of Jesus's historical past. Jesus (and therefore all Christians) was increasingly identified through blue eyes and blond hair, offering a visceral and easily recognizable physiognomic binary. This contrast became reinforced through centuries of medieval and Renaissance drawings, paintings, stained-glass imagery, sculptures, and other forms of art.[17]

By the early twentieth century, racial whiteness, the marker of European Christian purity, was reframed in biological terms.[18] In 1903, Otto Weininger (and others) argued that the modern Jew was a covert agent of sexual perversion akin to a biological infection.[19] Omer Bartov describes this reframing as drawing from the central foundational belief of anti-Semitism locating in the fear of the Jew as "master of transformation."[20] The nativist solution was to respond to the threat of the sexual Jewish pervert by preventing Anglo-Christian-Jewish or Nordic-Christian-Jewish couplings through the new eugenics-based race "mongrelization" laws.[21]

This contested binary quickly worked its way through literature and into the concurrent emerging mass media art forms of theater, radio, and cinema. Walter Benjamin, updating Baudelaire, described the emergence of privileged, bourgeois consumers as "flâneurs."[22] They became a newly empowered class of spectators able to cross oceans, cultures, and other societal boundaries through the products and imagery of an increasingly transnational world. But, as Anne Friedberg argued, this mobilization also produced psychological dissonance and transcultural fracture.[23] New forms of ontology and epistemology, both inside the academy and in popular art and literature, emerged to engage this intercultural scrambling. Scholars, artists, and politicians began to describe this climate through a rhetoric of dissonance rather than coherence, erosion rather than cohesion.

In arguing for this relationship among text, figuration, performance, and spectatorship, coupling theory requires a consideration of multiple written, live performance, and screen mediums. Vaudeville, theater, music, literature, poetry, film, television, and public couplings are considered as part of the same rhetorical and affective process. Literary, stage, and screen couplings allow for subversive discourses and taboo subjects to be negotiated across a wide range of subject matter and cultural pivot points. But in keeping with modernist fracture, the coupling pattern never fully resolves. It simply perpetuates a framework for additional exploration, thus explaining why so many examples are given in this book.

While this perhaps overlooks important distinctions of medium in reading these texts and representations, coupling theory proposes a transgeneric, transmedial intersectional model. In visualizing romantic, social, or carnal unions, couplings produce what Christian Metz calls "suture," the illusory signifier of cohesion in screen media.[24] Through familiar, recurrent interplay, ethno-cultural Anglo-Christian-Jewish couplings offered fantasies of progression. This coupling binary was flexible and adaptable. The couplings emerged at key historical moments to navigate the legacy of the Victorian era and champion the pluralism of an increasingly visible, libertine, modern world.

WHAT DO I MEAN BY "JEWISH"?

Nathan Abrams has identified three central and often competing methods for locating Jewish representations in popular media.[25] First, there is explicit textual identification. The "Jew" is identified either by an overt reference in the material or through clear cultural contexts. These can include the character having a Jewish name, living in New York, wearing a yarmulke, or being played by an identifiably Jewish actor. Books by scholars such as Abrams, Vincent Brook, Todd Gitlin, Lawrence Baron, Patricia Erens, David Desser, and Lester D. Friedman, among many others, focus on this form of textual reading strategy as their primary means of identifying Jewish representations in popular media.

Second, there is the implicit Jew, or what Abrams calls the "sub-epidermic." This form of Jewishness is harder to identify. It conceptualizes Jewish identity around subtler cultural and/or historical rubrics. This approach often focuses on the "Jewish" body locating outside of textual specificity. Sander Gilman's pioneering work in the 1980s and 1990s focused on how centuries of physiognomy stereotypes defining "Jewish" bodies were used to communicate crypto-Jewish biological "deviancy" without literal identification.[26] More recently, Henry Bial and Joseph Litvak have explored how Jewishness can locate in signifiers such as language, vocal tone, hand gestures, and other modes of performance. Bial identifies this process as unique to the insider/outsider duality of American Jewish identity and calls it "double coding."[27] Litvak agrees, noting that Jews of the 1950s performed "comicosmopolitanism," a comedic masquerade as the means of avoiding anti-Semitism during the Joseph McCarthy investigations.[28]

Finally, there is abstract, or ephemeral, Jewishness, a partial and subjective set of codes and signifiers that is completed through active spectator agency. Daniel Boyarin coined the term "Jewissance" to describe this ephemeral affect, arguing that Jewishness can locate outside of national, racial, or ethnic specificity, across both text and subtext, "rooted somewhere in the world, in a world of memory, intimacy and connectedness."[29] Identifying this Jewishness-without-Jewishness requires a complex reading of structuring absence rather than presence. For example, Erin Graff Zivin shows how "Jewishness" operates as a haunting specter in South American literature, describing it as a "symbolic container that is always embedded in the historical and the ideological . . . (a) negotiation between presence and absence."[30] It was precisely the slippages of this ephemeral Jewishness that led Vincent Brook to describe the Jewish figure as a "decentered, destabilized, postmodern subject par excellence."[31]

Boyarin, Brook, Abrams, Litvak, and Zivin are just a few of the scholars who have expanded or problematized the search for Jewish representations in popular media beyond obvious textual and/or performative cues. The rise of inter-ethnic historiography in the 1990s prodded scholars such as Hasia Diner, Deborah Dash Moore, Ella Shohat, and Karen Brodkin, among many others, to explore what Shohat describes as "permeable bounds of identity" that circulate among numerous ethnic, gendered, class, and racial configurations.[32] This approach argues that Jewishness operates as a stand-in for numerous discourses of alienation, ghettoization, and non-European absence. Postcolonial scholars such as Aamir Mufti have shown how minorities in India function as variants of the Jewish Diaspora by reproducing "Jewish" conflicts through forms of mimicry and performance.[33] British novelist Zadie Smith traces the Jewish subtext of Kafka's exile narratives through numerous transnational contexts and a variety of subaltern cultures.[34] Ruth Ellen Gruber explores how "virtual" Jewishness informs a variety of twentieth-century European art and culture even in the absence of a significant Jewish presence.[35]

Much of this theoretical reworking connects to the notion of late modernity as a fracturing process. In 2004, historian and cultural studies scholar Yuri Slezkine provocatively claimed that the entire twentieth century must be understood as the "Jewish Century."[36] According to Slezkine, the early twentieth century was the moment that "Jewish" modes of fractured, dialectical thinking usurped the dominant, holistic Christian model.[37] In *Anti-Judaism: The Western Tradition*, historian David Nirenberg agrees, tracing this tension back over nine centuries of European culture.[38] Nirenberg argues that the entire foundation of Western art, politics, and culture was expressed through a related dynamic between an idealized Christianity and Jewish demonization. Together, both constructions articulated the rhetorical and visual boundaries of normative civilization and the profane primitivity that threatened it.

Why Harry Met Sally contributes to this scholarship by proposing coupling theory as a relational model for locating this renegotiation beyond the specificities of a given text and a given medium. In coupling theory, both archetypes (and subversions of those archetypes) are repositioned as necessary conditions of the other. "Jewishness" is identified throughout this book in one of two ways. Either a character is recognizable as culturally or religiously Jewish through evidence in the text—such as dialogue, an obvious Jewish surname, or familiar ethno-religious stereotypes—or the performer playing the character is visibly and recognizably Jewish. This identification process requires a Christian "Other" to complete what I am arguing is a single rhetorical and/or figurative construction. Fully "Jewish" or fully "Anglo-Christian" worlds are not relevant to this model. It is in the dialectic between the two that coupling theory locates its critical negotiation between text and context.

I am certainly not the first to propose a re-examination of society and culture based on Christian-Jewish intersubjectivity. In his famous 1843 essay, "On the Jewish Question," Karl Marx critiqued the entire framework of Christian power and Jewish resistance as a fraud that perpetuated the bourgeois state.[39] In 1948, Jean-Paul Sartre's *Anti-Semite and Jew* revived Marx's binary to argue that the relational interplay between Jewish alterity and Christian power informed the fragmentation of late modern European holism that led to the Holocaust.[40] Marx saw Judaism as a false form of resistance to Christian power. He argued that both religions formed an illusory choice within a framework of collective imprisonment. Sartre read this binary tension in the nativist backlash of Nazis reacting to a phantasmic threat of their own creation. In the 1950s, Frantz Fanon extended this dialectic into what became the foundations of postcolonial theory. Fanon argued that the unresolved binary of "Jew" and "Christian" became the originary template for the fractured tensions of the postcolonial subject.[41] By the 1980s, Gilles Deleuze and Félix Guattari had expanded Fanonian fracture into a study of late modern capitalism, observing how ethno-religious fault lines between "Jew" and "Christian" produce a form of economic modernism in which consumption is understood as "becoming-Jewish." The philosophers argued that this transformation of market system economics "necessarily affects the non-Jew as much as the Jew."[42] These foundational scholars explored Christian-Jewish intersubjectivity in figuration, text, and rhetoric as a critical component of understanding the entangled economic and social relationships of the contemporary world.

I recognize and acknowledge that coupling theory methodology is inherently subjective. It requires a selective curation of texts and performances in which judgment calls must repeatedly be made. To eliminate as much of this bias as I can, I have endeavored to pick only texts, performances, and star personas that feature established and recognizable Anglo-Christian and Jewish identifiers. In locating Jewishness, this can be an actor whose Jewish background is known either as a central component of a performer's star construction, via paratexts such as magazine profiles, or through obvious, visible codes in their performances. Hollywood stars who qualify for this study made visible Jewish identity central to their star personas and performances. Examples include George Jessel, Al Jolson, Dustin Hoffman, Barbra Streisand, and Ben Stiller. Fictional characters performed by these identifiably Jewish stars are treated as default "Jewish" unless the text specifies otherwise. For example, Dustin Hoffman as the culturally unidentified Benjamin Braddock in *The Graduate* (1967) is treated as a Jewish character because of Hoffman's physical and performative codes. Non-Jewish actors with "Jewish" star personas acquired through playing numerous identifiably Jewish roles—such as Irene Wallace in *The Heart of a Jewess* (1913), John Turturro in *Barton Fink* (1991), or Jason Biggs as Darren Silverman in *Saving Silverman* (2001)—also qualify as Jewish examples. Identifiably Jewish actors playing non-Jewish characters, such as Hoffman as the Italian Catholic Enrico "Ratso" Rizzo in *Midnight Cowboy* (1969), are examined on a case-by-case basis in which a determination must be made as to whether a thematic Jewishness remains present in the performance.[43]

Performers and public figures born to either one or two Jewish parents who did not make their ethno-religious background a visible element of their public personas are removed from this study. This includes actors such as Hedy Lamarr, Kirk Douglas, Lauren Bacall, Michael Douglas, Harrison Ford, and Winona Ryder, to name just a few. These stars rarely identified as Jewish in either performances or public activities. I have therefore removed their work from consideration.[44] These absences are not meant to argue that their filmographies are irrelevant. There are many other examples of literary, stage, and screen media that fit the premise of this book and are worthy of examination under the coupling theory model. It is simply a matter of supporting my thesis with those texts and performances that can most credibly be understood as generating a dichotomy between "Christian" and "Jewish" partners.

Author intent and auteur theory are also deemphasized in this study. I do not view work produced by Jewish-born writers, directors, musicians, and other artists as "Jewish" simply because of their personal biographies. If the media artifact or performance does not engage a tangible and foregrounded sense of Jewishness and Anglo-Christian dynamics through text, performance, casting, or cultural allusions, then it is not considered here.

These curation choices can and should be critiqued. Numerous texts, performances, images, public figures, and rhetorical contexts not introduced in this book can be understood as articulating subtler, nuanced forms and signifiers of Jewishness, Anglo-Christianness, and Jewish-Christian interplay. Others can and should challenge this book for these absences. But I have endeavored to focus only on widely disseminated and recognizable materials, star personas, and texts. This is for the purpose of introducing a wide-ranging historiography that rethinks the relationship among representation, spectatorship, industry, and culture through a rereading of popular literary, stage, and screen couplings. It is my hope that this macro-topography will lead to a subtler and more nuanced rethinking of how coupling formations intertextually generate meaning beyond the specifics of a given plot, narrative, text, and performance.

WHAT DO I MEAN BY "CHRISTIAN"?

"Christianness" is identified throughout this book primarily through physicality and star persona with an emphasis on European-Christian figuration. Characters inhabited by actors with identifiably Anglo-Saxon, Nordic, European-Catholic, or German-Teutonic looks are presumptively given a default identity as "Christian." This process of identification draws from centuries of European art traditions. Beauty standards established throughout British, Polish, French, Scottish, Irish, German, and Scandinavian figuration have defined a distinct physiognomy as an aesthetic European-Christian ideal. These characteristics are defined by features such as fine hair, light brown or blue eyes, pale skin, and thin, aquiline noses.[45] Recognizable body types empowered by the Hollywood star system in the 1930s firmly established the range of Anglo-Christian types. From Jimmy Stewart and Katharine Hepburn to Meryl Streep and Matt Damon, screen "whiteness" carries with it an inherent underlying Christianness rooted in Anglo-European traditions. This is recognized and presumed by spectators to occupy the privileged representational position, the default normativity of American screen culture.

The second identifier of Christianness locates in the absence and/or repression of visible sexual desire. The notion of chaste, repressed, and/or withheld sexuality has defined a virtuous form of Christian identity for millennia. After the Roman Emperor Constantine summoned the Council of Nicaea in 325 to inculcate Christianity as the dominant religion of Europe, the national and the religious became fused. Christianity taught that the body was a vessel for temptation and sin.[46] The virginal status of Jesus had established asexual purity and dedication to God as directly at odds with the desires of the flesh. Convents in which virginal women (nuns) pledged themselves to Jesus further established this mind/body tension state. This gender essentialism became desexualized, as George L. Mosse explains, in service to the national (Christian) interest.[47] Anti-sexuality rituals were quickly elevated as an extension of Christian dogma. This subsequently informed a construction of "whiteness" as an extension of sexless morality—what Richard Dyer describes as an ethno-religious rhetoric defined by sexual containment, erasure, and absence.[48] But this "absence" also produced "presence" in the form of the carnal Jewish Other.

This conflation of sexuality purity, European-Christian institutions, and "whiteness" is essential to understanding how the Anglo-Christian figure is routinely identified in screen culture fantasy. The libidinal, deviant Jew, defined by centuries of Euro-Christian blood libel as the embodiment of amoral impulse, became the figural rope in this late modern tug of war. Emerging in the late nineteenth century, the constructed literary, stage, and screen Jew, informed by the new sciences of Marx, Freud, and Einstein, was a complex construction that oscillated between the new cosmopolitanism and the residual sexual mores of the Victorian era. But it was the Anglo-Christian who negotiated this tension point by acting as the gatekeeper for socially codified erotic and romantic desires.

This identification process should not be confused with actual Christian practices, histories, cultures, or regions. It ignores numerous permutations of Christian identity and religious and cultural practice around the world that are not defined in this corpo-figural way. This includes myriad Latino, black, and Asian nations, cultures, and subcultures that strongly identify as Christian. The purpose of their exclusion here is not to deny or erase the importance of these cultures to global Christianity. It is simply due to the fact that American and European literature, theater, and screen media over the past hundred and fifty years created an ethno-corporeal link between Christian representations and white, European, Anglo/German/Saxon/Celtic identities. The use of "Christian" in this book only refers to this specific representational definition in popular media. It does not refer to historical or geographical Christianity as a set of cultural codes and practices.

Central to this post-structuralist reading is a theoretical term called "Christonormativity." I first introduced the concept of Christonormativity as part of my analysis of the comedic protagonist archetype in the films of Woody Allen.[49] Building off Michael Warner's concept of "heteronormativity," I argued that a metatextual framework exists across Western screen texts that can only be seen or noticed when positioned in opposition to deviations, disruptions, and taboos. Drawing from race, gender, sexuality, and humor studies, the concept of Christonormativity suggests that there is an inherent link among sexual, historical, and physiognomic norms. This privileged default is occupied by a distinct European, Christian Anglo-Nordic, Anglo-Saxon, and/or Anglo-Catholic identity.[50] But Christonormativity expands race, gender, and sexuality figuration to consider the impact of myth and archetype. The Christonormative is informed by the repetition of narratives, rituals, imagery, literature, and artwork developed over a millennium of Christian European art and culture. Concepts such as angels, devils, heaven, hell, and sinner/saved moral quandaries are just a few of the ideological constructions that communicate this lineage. Christonormativity argues that these artifacts are embedded throughout texts, figuration, rhetoric, and iconography in the mass media age.

Christonormativity, and coupling theory more generally, do not presume any essentialist gender conclusions. For example, couplings such as Barbra Streisand and Robert Redford in *The Way We Were* (1973) and Charles Grodin and Cybill Shepherd in *The Heartbreak Kid* (1972), to pick two examples (discussed in chapter 6), are read in this book along ethno-cultural, not gendered, models. In both examples, Jewish subjects (Grodin and Streisand) gaze at Christian beauty objects (Redford and Shepherd) as an externalized expression of the international tensions of youth culture alienation. I argue that both examples offer the same rhetorical and figural pattern despite the gender reversal of the couplings. This is not to say that important gendered distinctions do not remain. It is only to argue that the variations of Anglo-Christian-Jewish couplings discussed in this book are collectively engaging the same figural pattern regardless of gender. The conflicting relationship between the established hierarchies of European institutions in the Victorian era and the fractured pluralism of an increasingly visible, sexually libertine inter-ethnic modernism operates similarly whether it is an Anglo-Christian male and a Jewish female, an Anglo-Christian female and a Jewish male, or some homosocial variation of either pattern.

The majority of my research inevitably focuses on the more prevalent Jewish male/Anglo-Christian female couplings. However, two historical periods of Jewish female presence are examined in this book: the eroti-cized "Jewess" as temptress figure in the ghetto love story films of the 1910s and 1920s (chapter 3) and the unruly Jewish housewife in television sitcoms of the 1990s (chapter 8). Jewish females in both periods embodied sexual agency in a way that the chaste, Christian Victorian-era female could not. However, I position these texts as variations on the same macro-thematic coupling binary of Christonormative power and disruptive Jewish alterity. Scholars such as Judith Plaskow, Joyce Antler, Judith Baskin, and Hasia Diner, among many others, have addressed the myriad reasons for Jew-ish female screen absence and Jewish male presence that began in the late 1920s and carried through the contemporary era.[51] Daniel Boyarin, Jona-than Boyarin, Sander Gilman, and Eve Kosofsky Sedgwick, among many others, have also explored the relationship among Jewishness, queerness, transgender, and transsexuality.[52] Their important work responded to the glaring historical absences of Jewish women and Jewish queerness in terms of both academic study and textual representation. These distinctions are underexplored in this book and deserve more consideration under the cou-pling theory rubric. I plan to revisit both of these subjects in future work.

Part One

THE FIRST WAVE:
THE MOUSE-MOUNTAINS
OF MODERNITY (1905–1934)

I would like to be transformed into a mouse-mountain!

WALTER BENJAMIN

*I*N 1931, GERMAN-JEWISH PHILOSOPHER WALTER
Benjamin's journal featured a simple proclamation: "I
would like to be transformed into a mouse-mountain!"[1] The statement was not mere fancy. Benjamin was in the process of recording his every emotion and thought while exploring the effects of
hashish on his mind. This may seem like a moment of little importance in the larger body of Benjamin's work. He was, like many of
his contemporaries in the early 1930s, experimenting with drugs as
the means of seeking out new forms of inspiration and insight. But
Benjamin's fanciful desire for an impossible, paradoxical transformation between mouse and mountain cannot be easily dismissed
from his more widely acclaimed philosophical treatises.[2] His me-
thodical approach to drug experimentation was authored in tandem with his literary criticism exploring the work of Baudelaire,
Proust, and Kafka.[3] His seemingly absurdist epiphany was inti-
mately connected to this analysis.

Throughout the 1920s, modernists and futurists had argued
that art, science, culture, and philosophy could only be expressed
through collision imagery, incongruities, and paradoxes. The impact of technology, impressionist art, and the new sciences had
shattered established traditions and cultural norms throughout
Europe. The invention and dissemination of photography, the discovery of electricity, the integration of lightbulbs, radio, cars, wire-

less telegraphy, and early cinema had all transformed how nations, cultures, and individuals understood themselves. This new cosmopolitan sensibility privileged science over religion and mobility over the cohesive boundaries of the nation-state. As Philip Brey describes it, "technology made modernity possible."[4]

Hybridity, what Zygmunt Bauman calls "ambivalence," became the means of negotiating this massive intercultural transformation. In art, Marcel Duchamp's so-called readymade art projects—including his famous mounting of an upside-down bicycle wheel on a stool (*Bicycle Wheel*, 1913)—offer one such example. Another is René Magritte's 1928 painting, *The Treachery of Images*, which depicts a pipe with the words "Ceci n'est pas une pipe" (This is not a pipe) written below it. As with deconstructionism in art, Benjamin tried to free himself of overdetermined bourgeois philosophy.[5] To locate this expansive model of thinking, cause and effect had to be scrambled.

Read in this context, Benjamin's imagery of the mouse-mountain was not merely fanciful poetics. The collision of "mouse" and "mountain," a Kafkaesque play with animality and metaphor, exemplified the contradictory rubric of modernism as represented in art, philosophy, and the new sciences. Benjamin's search for playful, impossible juxtapositions was the means of locating the modern self. It used paradox to grapple with the increasing schizophrenia of the mass media age.[6]

The mouse-mountain can also be understood as an expression of Bauman's late modern ambivalence. At first, it appears to be apropos of nothing more than drug-inspired imagery. Nor does it appear to be a reference to Benjamin's Jewish background or emancipated European-Jewish identity more generally. But the hybrid form contains an embedded referent to a distinct cultural transformation taking place. It conflates both posthuman transformational aspiration (man-into-mountain) with the pathetic animality of the rodent (man-as-mouse). The interplay between both extremes carried with it a distinct European Jewish allusionism.

In 1931, two years before Hitler's rise to power, Germany was increasingly focusing on emancipated Jews as the embodiment of the new modernist sensibility. After centuries in ghettos and shtetls, assimilating Jews from Europe and Russia had begun to play an increasingly visible role at the vanguard of the new arts and sciences. This backlash saw the Jew as a transgressive hybrid figure able to scramble existing hierarchies and national-historical boundaries. The modernist response was to amplify and champion this scrambling. The nativist pushback was to condemn it.

Benjamin, an emancipated German-Jewish philosopher, was one of the leading public intellectuals of the period. Yet, he denied any Jewish specificity in his work. His close friend and confidant, the German-Jewish philosopher Gershom Scholem, critiqued Benjamin for this denial of what Scholem saw as the Jewish origins of Benjamin's philosophy.[7] In Scholem's view, the emancipated European Jew, now both insider and outsider, was distinctly positioned to comment on the fractures of late modernity. To deny this connection was to deny what Scholem argued was the unique role that Jewish philosophers occupied in mainstreaming the ambivalences and paradoxes of modernist thinking.

If, as Scholem argues, Benjamin's entire work was Jewish philosophy dressed up in code for non-Jewish acceptance, the mouse-mountain emerges as an example of coded Jewish hybridity in modernist metaphor. In linking inferior-superior paradox to animal-object fusion, it spoke to the emergent debate between nativists and modernists.[8] Written on the eve of World War II and the Holocaust, it offered a succinct summation of how ephemeral Jewishness could circulate more easily through the secular codes of hybridity. The mouse-mountain was an easily graspable metaphor. It visualized the cosmopolitan debate over identity politics at the heart of late modern European Jewish assimilation. Could the cosmopolitan (Jewish) figure lead Europe into the modern world? Or would the new hybrid modernism collapse into dissonant fracture?

To understand the mouse-mountain as both the culmination of a fifty-year transformation in thinking and a metaphor for the new Jewishness, we need to trace the origins of Benjamin's coding technique. Two influential political figures of the late nineteenth century, British Prime Minister Benjamin Disraeli (1804–1881) and French Captain Alfred Dreyfus (1859–1935), offer comparative case studies for how emancipated Jewishness circulated as transgressive hybridity. Both demonstrated the allegorical relationship between assimilated secularism and an emergent modernist, transnational shift. Disraeli, a Jewish-born raconteur, dandy, and romance novelist turned unlikely British prime minister, provided an early road map for how the emancipated Jew could successfully navigate the tensions of the media age. The French-Jewish Captain Alfred Dreyfus, convicted on false charges of treason in 1894, serves as a tragic counter-example. In both examples, coupling—the selection of marriage partner—played a critical role in navigating anxieties of Jewish hybridity. In 1839, Disraeli married an Anglo-Saxon widow, Mary Anne Lewis, tempering debates over his Jewishness through the visible role of his Christian wife. Despite playing an important role during her husband's trial and retrial in the late 1890s, Dreyfus's Jewish wife, Lucie, failed to win over the majority of the French public to her husband's cause. In both examples, the marital coupling became the lens for Christian Europe to both perceive and debate national identity. The threatening figure of the outsider Jewish Other could be either tempered or amplified. Marriage selection emerged as a critical methodology for this negotiation in the public sphere.

This debate was informed and amplified by the technologies of the mass media. Disraeli's literary background and political acumen enabled him to understand what Dreyfus could not. The most visceral way to temper the threat of Jewishness (and modernity) located in the foregrounding of intermarriage as an act of national fealty.[9] His marriage to Mary Anne Lewis exemplified a figural mouse-mountain, the inferior Jew transformed into non-Jewish exemplar. The Jewish Dreyfus located no such tempering performative caveat. His Otherness resulted in his public condemnation and exile from French society for more than a decade.

These case studies provide contrasting archetypes for the subsequent emergence of Anglo-Christian-Jewish couples in twentieth-century literature, art, and screen media. Disraeli's deft manipulation of popular media and the subsequent crisis of the Dreyfus Affair had a profound impact on writers, artists, filmmakers, and public intellectuals in the early decades of the twentieth century. Marcel Proust, James Joyce, Franz Kafka, and the writers of the Bloomsbury Group recognized and expanded on the Anglo-Christian-Jewish coupling metaphor that Disraeli had introduced in his mid-nineteenth-century romance novels and political life. This outlined the figural cartography for an emergent transnational, secular cosmopolitan ethos. Inter-religious couplings could be rendered as hopeful, star-crossed exemplars of the modern age. Or they could be infused with sexually graphic, carnal panic as a byproduct of the dissolution of the nation-state. But whether hopeful or tragic, the Anglo-Christian-Jewish coupling solidified into one of the most popular templates for exploring what Friedrich A. Kittler describes as the disintegration of "love's wholeness," the crisis of romance and sexuality brought about by the impact of the new technologies in the machine age.[10]

Early American cinema also recognized the potency of this template. Pre-Hollywood and early Hollywood films of the 1910s and 1920s unabashedly championed Anglo-Christian-Jewish love stories as waves of émigrés, chased out of Europe by various ethno-religious and racial demonization laws, began to champion the United States as an aspirational melting pot. In depicting young first- and second-generation American Jews and Anglo-Christians coming together on screen, a secular American ideology was understood as defeating the class divisions of European nativism. This emerged primarily in two popular genres of the pre-sound era in the 1910s: slapstick Irish-Jewish family comedies and melodramatic ghetto Jewess love stories. By the late 1920s, when Hollywood transitioned to sound, the first wave of Anglo-Christian-Jewish love stories reached its pinnacle. Wide-release studio pictures such as *The Cohens and Kellys* (1926), *Private Izzy Murphy* (1926), *The Jazz Singer* (1927), *Surrender* (1927), and *Abie's Irish Rose* (1928) each featured variations of young Catholic-Jewish or Protestant-Jewish romances winning out over the prohibitions of the older, European generation. These successful Anglo-Christian-Jewish screen unions were understood as exemplifying the assimilationist sensibilities of the 1920s. In depicting the union of romantic Christian-Jewish love, this first wave championed the liberal pro-immigrant politics and technological triumphs of America's Jazz Age.

CHAPTER I

Disraeli's Page

PERFORMATIVE JEWISHNESS
IN THE PUBLIC SPHERE

I am the blank page between the Old Testament and the New.

BENJAMIN DISRAELI

*B*ENJAMIN DISRAELI WAS A DANDY, A RACONTEUR, AND
a theatrical rogue. He was also the embodiment of contradiction. He was a second-generation British Jew who also identified as an
assimilated nobleman and a populist romance novelist turned conservative politician. He proudly celebrated his Jewish ancestry while also championing his conversion to Protestantism and frequently attending masses.
Such eccentricity and flamboyance in the climate of the Victorian era
should have ended any hopes of an ambitious political career. Yet, despite
all odds, Disraeli remarkably ascended to prime minister briefly in 1868,
and again from 1874 to 1880. How was it possible for a strange, short, unconventional Jewish dandy with an odd last name to rise to the top of late
colonial British politics? The answer locates in Disraeli's embrace of these
very paradoxes. He was not just a savvy politician, but also the first major
nineteenth-century political figure to recognize the power of mythic Jewishness as an allegory for European transition into the modern age.

From early in his career, Disraeli's political strategy was to view his
weaknesses as strengths. He did not try to mimic or kowtow to British
class distinctions or to the bureaucratic rankings of title. Instead, he embraced his outsider status as exemplar of the new sensibilities of the modern age. He deftly navigated ethno-cultural tensions over the role of British
Jewry in genteel English society through flamboyance, theatricality, myth
building, and the clever manipulation of the power of the emergent popular press. His Jewishness was central to this manipulation. Disraeli de-

fined his Jewish identity through absence rather than presence, refusing to allow the often openly anti-Semitic British press to pin him down. When asked if he identified more as a Christian or a Jew, Benjamin Disraeli famously responded, "I am the blank page between the Old Testament and the New." The quip was considered yet another clever comeback by one of the most famous wits of his generation. But this "blankness" was central to Disraeli's success. Pastiche, performance, and perpetual redefinition presented a figure explicitly at odds with the fixed hierarchies of the Victorian era. Even the quote was appropriated: Disraeli had stolen the line from a play by Richard Brinsley.[1]

In his forty-year political career, Disraeli reveled in producing duplicitous states fraught with apparent contradictions. As he rose through the House of Commons in the 1850s and 1860s, he faced daily, vicious anti-Semitic attacks from the British press. The papers called him everything from a money grubber to an ugly "Jewboy." He responded, as Geoffrey Wheatcroft describes it, by alternating between ironic self-deprecation and thunderous arrogance.[2] When it was advantageous, Disraeli was happy to embrace his lineage as a member of an exoticized, ancient Jewish tradition. He did not change his overtly Jewish last name. Nor did he downplay his "Jewish" mannerisms, acerbic wit, or long friendship with the most powerful Jewish family in Europe, the Rothschilds.[3] But, when needed, Disraeli just as easily pivoted to his new identity as a British Protestant. He made frequent references to the fact that he had voluntarily converted and was in good standing with the Church of England.[4] Disraeli's "blank page" thus produced an exemplary metaphor for Britain's passage from the Victorian era.[5] It also gave him the mechanism for his unlikely political survival. It visualized his own personal Jewish-Englishman contradictions as a way for Anglo-Saxon Britain to see itself from the outside. In Disraeli's various dichotomies, Britain began to understand the post-colonial context of an increasingly globalized and spatially fragmented world.[6]

Amidst all the theatricality, Disraeli's fanciful biographical ambiguity was belied by one immutable fact. In 1839, the longtime bachelor had married the Anglo-Saxon widow, Mary Anne Lewis. Without the aristocratic stamp of Lewis, all of Disraeli's political skills, oratory techniques, and raconteur skills would likely have fallen short of his ambitious goals. Mrs. Disraeli played a critical role during the next three decades of her husband's career. Theatricality and ambiguity may have mitigated Disraeli's Jewishness by positioning it as a metaphor for the modern state. But it was not sufficient to reassure the majority of Britons that he was trustworthy enough to become a significant political leader. As both his wife and political partner, Mary Anne Disraeli tempered these concerns. Her aristocratic background (and numerous estate homes) cemented his ability to navigate the complex world of nineteenth-century British parlor politics. Together, they embodied a new form: Jewish-Anglo-Saxon partnership as an emerging template for the New Britain in an increasingly cosmopolitan world.

MRS. DIZZY

In 1839, the unmarried Disraeli reached an epiphany. He was in his early thirties and nearly a decade into an increasingly frustrating political career. Struggling with the barriers of anti-Semitism and facing daily innuendos about both his masculinity and his sexuality, Disraeli had become nothing more than a spectacle and a curiosity in Parliament.[7] Perhaps drawing inspiration from his early romance novels, he hatched a plan. He began to court the much older, wealthier, aristocrat Mary Anne Lewis. Disraeli had known Lewis for seven years after befriending her first husband, a politician and member of Parliament, Wyndham Lewis. The Lewis marriage had lasted for twenty-two years until Wyndham's untimely death in 1838. By the time Mary Anne Lewis had become a widow, she was already established as a well-known and often outspoken spouse among the British political class.

Disraeli's pursuit of the childless widow a year after her husband's death began as a calculated career move. Lewis was nearly forty-five at the time of the marriage, twelve years older than Disraeli. She was already defined by her impolitic language, challenging the notion of the taciturn Anglo-Saxon dowager.[8] This made her another kind of insider/outsider. It also may have explained her appeal. In a letter during his courtship year, Disraeli wrote, "I was influenced by no romantic feelings . . . (but) I was not blind to worldly advantages in such an alliance."[9] His use of the word "alliance" shows a keen awareness that his Jewish identity in Parliament required assistance to overcome institutional anti-Semitic biases.

By comparison, the Rothschilds, the most famous and wealthy Jewish family in England, had refused to intermarry for generations. Despite their enormous wealth, they were unable to advance past certain barriers of entrenched British life. As he was technically a Protestant since the age of twelve, Disraeli could already move into politics in ways that even the Rothschilds could not.[10] But he still faced significant obstacles. Perhaps his experience as a romance novelist had opened him up to the power of myths in overcoming these cultural barriers. Mary Anne Lewis represented a display of loyalty to the British crown that the Rothschilds had refused to demonstrate. Her acceptance of Disraeli's proposal not only helped to neu-

Early portraits of the Disraelis before their marriage: Benjamin at age thirty-five (1840) and Mary Anne in her early twenties (1820s).

tralize accusations of disloyalty but also drew a clear distinction between Disraeli and his fellow assimilated British Jews.

Disraeli may have initially married his wife with career ambitions as the primary motivation. But their detailed letters over their four decades of marriage reveal a partnership at once both professional and enduringly intimate.[11] "Mrs. Dizzy," as Mary Anne referred to herself, became a powerful partner for the ambitious politician. She was on her second political marriage and fully aware of Disraeli's machinations. She was also conscious of her importance in the public sphere as his wife. When the couple met Queen Victoria for the first time in 1845, their shared loud and theatrical style stood out from the crowd. The queen was entertained by the unusual partnership, taking a liking to both the Jewish-born politician and his strangely flamboyant wife.[12] Matching his theatrical countenance but mitigating his Jewishness, Mrs. Dizzy provided a critical stabilizing political influence to Disraeli's career.[13] Her loyalty to her husband preserved the legitimacy of his political ambitions, even as he teetered on the edge of bankruptcy and conducted numerous sexual liaisons in the years before his unlikely ascent to prime minister.[14]

Four years after their first tea with the queen came the first example of Mrs. Dizzy's value to Disraeli's political career. In 1849, he began his campaign to convince Lord Edward Smith-Stanley, the Earl of Derby, that he was capable of leading the Protectionist Party (soon to become the Conservative Party). The "Jewish Question" played a critical role in this debate. Disraeli had supported the "Jew Bill" of 1849 that was debated upon the election of Lionel de Rothschild to the House of Commons. Rothschild refused to be sworn in on a Christian Bible. The Jew Bill, explicitly designed to allow Rothschild to take political office, removed the requirement that members of Parliament had to be willing to swear loyalty to the Church of England. Disraeli had made the case for the bill by reminding Parliament that, like Jesus, he was a Christian and that both he and Jesus were Christians who came from Jews.[15] Disraeli's rhetorical entanglement sought to merge Christianity and Judaism into a shared cultural narrative.

However, the fear that Disraeli, despite his powerful oratory skills, was still a Jew looking to help other Jews—in this case, Lionel de Rothschild—became one of the biggest obstacles to his goal of leading the Protectionist Party. His supporters neutralized this in two ways. The first was by highlighting Disraeli's frequent criticisms of the Jewish religion. He began to refer to Christianity as "completed Judaism" in press and in speeches.[16] The second approach located in increased references to Disraeli's baptism, thereby highlighting his renewed dedication to the church. This PR campaign lasted for a decade. In the early 1860s, when Disraeli's role as opposition Tory leader in the House of Commons was gaining strength, he proudly advocated for the importance of the Church of England and began attending church services more frequently.[17] But these gestures were not enough to convince the Protectionists that Disraeli was an appropriate choice as their leader. Many assimilated Jews had committed similar acts of fealty to the Church of England. Disraeli needed one more element to assuage the structural anti-Semitism that was holding back his career.

That solution came in the form of his wife. Disraeli's frequent appearances with Mrs. Dizzy at social functions privileged Mary Anne as the final sign of his unwavering commitment to a Protestant England. Their increasing emphasis on taking tea at the country estates of various political friends (and foes) was a necessary element of the performance of private social functions as an extension of the public sphere. The Disraelis relied on their unusual and flamboyant charm to win over the necessary votes to help Benjamin ascend to Leader of the House during a fractured period in 1851. Mary Anne offered the critical social counterbalance that Lionel de Rothschild had lacked. Mrs. Dizzy supported Disraeli's rejection of his Jewishness at critical political moments when he had to assuage fears that his Jewish identity would not undercut the political goals of the emerging Conservative Party.[18]

By 1852, despite continuing anti-Semitic attacks from their foes, the Disraelis had become fully entrenched in the upper echelons of British political power. This was confirmed when Queen Victoria famously invited the couple to a private dinner reception at Buckingham Palace. Despite the queen describing Disraeli's looks as "most singular," the political power couple was ascending to heights unimaginable for a second-generation Jew even a few years earlier.[19] When Disraeli briefly became prime minister as leader of the Conservative Party in 1868, it was viewed mostly as a fluke. After the retirement of Lord Stanley, Disraeli formed a coalition government pushed through by Victoria's unwavering support. But his career seemed over after he lost the next election.

With nothing to do after leaving office at the end of 1868, Disraeli made an unprecedented political decision. He returned to writing romance novels. A little more than a year later, on May 2, 1870, he published *Lothair*, his first novel in decades. The romantic story focused on a young, naïve, Protestant Scottish nobleman named Lothair, who finds himself pursued by three young women. The women were obvious metaphors for the three dominant branches of Christianity in England at the time, Protestantism, Catholicism, and progressive Christian radicalism. Lothair begins his journey as a clueless idealist. At first, he navigates his romantic desires as an extension of his naïve idealism, favoring the female representing the Protestant upper class and rejecting all other variations of the Christian faith. But after meeting Clare Arundel, a young Catholic woman, Lothair begins to view Catholicism through what Robert O'Kell describes as an erotic, sensuous lens.[20] Lothair gradually begins to compromise his ideological purity by accepting both Catholicism and Protestantism as equal parts of the greater good.

Lothair's romantic progression from naiveté to realistic compromise thematized Disraeli's career-long emphasis on Anglo-Christian-Jewish relativity. Lothair begins the novel as intellectually incurious and ideologically rigid. It is only through romances with women of different religious backgrounds that he learns that compromise and collaboration are more important than the preservation of ethno-religious demarcation. This is also reflected through Lothair's experiences entering various secret Christian societies, such as the Freemasons, the Jesuits, and the Illuminati. These side journeys gave the novel a salacious conspiracy theory appeal, as readers presumed that the former prime minister was letting them in on the hidden secrets of British society.[21] While Jewishness is not directly addressed in the novel, the revelation of secret Christian societies operates as a thematic "outing" of hidden identity. Lothair's discovery of the Carbonari and the

Mary Anne societies (no relation to Mary Anne Lewis) in particular hinted at Jewish cabals hiding in plain sight.

Lothair's Catholic-Protestant eroticism worked as a powerful metaphor for the increasingly multicultural Europe emerging in the late nineteenth century. It reinforced what George A. Kennedy describes as Disraeli's life-long emphasis on multi-religious and multi-class identity at the heart of the political philosophy of new conservatism.[22] The book was an enormous and immediate best seller. The original print run of two thousand sold out in days, forcing Disraeli's British publisher to fast-track another six thousand copies to meet demand.[23] Despite poor critical reviews, the novel sold well across Europe.[24] The novel was also a smash in the United States, selling more than eighty thousand copies in a year. The semi-ironic tone, romantic melodrama, and deft musings on changing religious identities in the modern era all spoke to the theatrical "blank page" that Disraeli himself had performed for decades. *Lothair* championed religious intermixing. While it focused on Catholicism, Protestantism, and other lesser-known branches of Christianity, the point was clear. The book's success resonated across British society, reinvigorating Disraeli's fame and his political career. Four years later, in 1874, after the defeat of William Ewart Gladstone, Benjamin Disraeli was finally elected prime minister of the United Kingdom. With his unlikely ascension, the United Kingdom proclaimed itself ready and able to engage a newly mobile, increasingly multicultural, post-Empire world.

THE DANDY ISRAELI

The road map for Disraeli's link between the personal and public persona in his political career can be traced directly to his romance novels. Beginning with *Vivian Grey* in 1826, Disraeli, then only twenty-three, used the tropes of romantic melodrama to champion an inclusive, pro-Jewish British society.[25] Disraeli continued to write novels even after he launched his political career, repeatedly using his fiction to champion his ideology and ambitions. Examples appear in two novels published at a critical moment in his political career, *Conigsby, or The New Generation* (1844) and *Sybil, or The Two Nations* (1845). In the former, Conigsby, an ambitious young Protestant British politician, finds himself caught in a love triangle with two young British women. One woman represents Conigsby's romantic love. The other represents his political ambitions. His struggle in choosing served as one of two stand-ins for Disraeli's own political battles. The other was the character of Sidonia, a Sephardic Jewish political activist who appears in numerous Disraeli novels, frequently reciting speeches directly cribbed from Disraeli's political career. Ostensibly modeled on Lionel de Rothschild, Sidonia is presented as a rationalist, unapologetically Jewish to the point of advocating Jews as a racially superior ethnicity, despite his childhood conversion to Catholicism.[26] The Protestant Conigsby and Jewish Sidonia reflected the two sides of what Robert O'Kell describes as the alienated schism within Disraeli.[27] This tension was then explored in numerous romantic and melodramatic scenarios in which sexual desire manifests each character's internal struggle. Conigsby experiences romantic love for Edith, despite his practical engagement to another, more politically advantageous woman. This tension between the heart and the mind reflected the political conflict experienced by the young Disraeli as he navigated genteel British culture as an emancipated Jew.[28]

In *Sybil, or The Two Nations*, the love story between the Catholic Sybil and Protestant Egremont provided yet another example of Disraeli's idealized Anglo-Christian-Jewish coupling template. It presented inter-religious love as the means of transcending the antiquated divides of the British class system. While Judaism is not textually present in the novel, it informs the tensions in the courtship and romance of Sybil and Egremont. This approach was familiar to readers of Disraeli's novels. Catholicism served as what O'Kell calls "metaphorical Judaism" at numerous points throughout Disraeli's published work. The titular "two nations" refers textually to the rich and poor classes of Britain. But religious allusions expand this division to one of ethno-religious identity. The book contains frequent references to the "Hebraeo-Christian" traditions of the Church of England as a reminder that exclusion of both religion and class works against Christian ideals.[29] Disraeli used the empathy of a romantic love story to make a political point. Lack of rights for Jews, Catholics, and other recent immigrants was an extension of the same struggles faced by the British working class.[30]

Disraeli's life story was also a tableau for his inventive writing skills. He claimed that the insertion of "Israel" in "Disraeli" was intentional on the part of his brave Jewish ancestors. This was done, according to his imaginative retelling, so that no one would forget his family's proud Jewish lineage.[31] He also claimed to be a Sephardic Jew from Spain. In reality, and obvious to many Brits, Disraeli was Ashkenazi (Eastern European), not Sephardic. His last name was almost certainly given to the family by non-Jewish officials in Eastern Europe as a Jewish identifier. But these mythic backstories only served to heighten his larger-than-life public persona. By rewriting his lineage from the realities of Ashkenazi Eastern Europe to a fanciful, exotic Spanish Sephardim, Disraeli had become an extension of the melodramatic emotional excesses of his well-known literary characters.[32] Both art and life became parcels of the same story of individual transformation, what Werner Sollors defines as "consent"-based ethnicity, an identity formed through choice rather than actual lineage.[33] This successful suturing of ethnic and class divisions offered Disraeli, and, by mimetic association, all British subjects, entrance to a modern world defined by personal choice rather than by bloodlines and titles.

Disraeli's embrace of a protean transnationalism was also an extension of his childhood conversion. His father, Isaac D'Israeli, had baptized the young boy when he was twelve years old.[34] Isaac had little religious inclination. He was happy to embrace baptism as the means of advancing the careers of both himself and his children. Benjamin immediately became a Protestant in good standing with the Church of England. He was subsequently able to use this baptism to serve in the House of Commons when other politically inclined Jews such as Lionel de Rothschild could not. But Isaac also had insight into the value of maintaining a visible Jewish identity in tandem with this conversion. In 1833, as his son was well into his political career, Isaac wrote, "In Judaism we trace our Christianity, and in Christianity, our Judaism."[35] Rather than demarcate the two religions, Isaac merged them. This Christian-Jew amalgam produced a conceptual malleability in which both identities supported the other. Isaac's insight was to understand that Judaism could not be negated. Instead, a new possibility existed: hybridity. Like his father, Benjamin sought a way to exploit this relational Anglo-Christian-Jewish pattern. If performed correctly, Jewishness could be perceived as both British and not-British, at once both an ancient religion and a sign of the emerging modern secularism. Isaac hoped this amalgam would allow him to work freely as a businessman. Benjamin made the leap into the realm of politics. But both father and son embraced hybridity.

Benjamin Disraeli's amplification of his father's protean religious duality also took place in the performative realm. The younger Disraeli co-opted the style of the dandy, theatrically performing Anglo-Christian-Jewish entanglement through the mannerisms of the effete, flamboyant raconteur.[36] His selection of fourteenth-century Spain, the legendary center of intellectual Jewish thought, had a specific motivation. His (fictional) ancestors were identified as Sephardic intellectuals who had suffered persecution and expulsion from a nation (Spain) unable to appreciate the gifts of emancipated Jewry. The metaphor was clear. Spain had decided to expel or kill its Jews under the Spanish Inquisition. Over the ensuing centuries, Spain had ceded global power to the rise of colonial Britain. Disraeli was performing political theater by self-identifying as the fatal flaw of Spanish history. By embracing Disraeli, Britain, clinging to power on the global stage, would not make the same mistake.

Disraeli's decision to marry Mary Anne Lewis was another critical step in this mythic reinvention.[37] The British emphasis on nobility, titles, and the class system relied on the notion of marriage as a political and contractual exchange. Romantic love rarely played a role at the upper levels of the British aristocracy. Families, titles, and estates transferred, consolidated, and expanded power. Disraeli critiqued this tradition through his own background as a literary romantic and flamboyant Jew. The Protestant-Jewish coupling, whether in Disraeli's life or art, offered an easily graspable road map for the link between the personal and the political in the emergent mass media age. Baptism had mitigated Disraeli's Otherness enough to get him elected to the House of Commons. But it was not enough to assuage larger concerns about his ultimate loyalty to the crown. Mrs. Dizzy was the final chess piece. Her Anglo-Saxon privilege successfully diminished the cloud of mistrust that a potential Jewish prime minister represented. Disraeli had found a way to transcend the barriers of Otherness that his Jewishness had carried into the House of Commons. His mannerisms might be questioned. His sexuality mocked. His looks derided. But his loyalty was no longer in doubt. The Jewish dandy was a viable figurehead for the New Britain. But this was true only so long as he was accompanied by his sign of fealty to the crown: an Anglo-Saxon wife.[38]

AFFAIR AND *L'AFFAIRE*

In 1894, an obscure French-Jewish captain named Alfred Dreyfus faced a military trial on false charges of treason for selling state secrets to Germany. Over the next few years, Dreyfus's conviction, retrial, and eventual reconviction would captivate and divide France on an unprecedented level. Even when clear evidence exonerated Dreyfus after his initial conviction, the societal uproar and anti-Semitic suspicion directed at the most powerful Jew in the French military led to reconviction. This early example of a mass media feeding frenzy turned the Dreyfus prosecution into the proverbial "trial of the century." Polarizing and captivating, it was steeped in what historian Venita Datta describes as the codes of a grand theatrical melodrama.[39] Accusations, counter-accusations, suicides, and betrayals scandalized and polarized France for the next decade until Dreyfus was finally officially exonerated in 1905. Major players in the scandal were cloaked in literary allusions drawn more from Greek tragedy than from historical fact. The affair was real-world theater. It played out, in near real time, on an increasingly image-based public stage dominated by the printing press and early cinema.

Dreyfus scholar Susan Rubin Suleiman describes the affair as the moment in which artists and writers first collectively mobilized art, literature, photography, and cinema with the intent to influence a single public debate.[40] This mobilization cut both ways. Debates over whether Dreyfus was a Jew or a Frenchman, and not the facts of the case, produced a war of imagery rather than evidence. Newspapers and photography printed propaganda caricatures of Dreyfus as either a hook-nosed Judas betrayer of France or a persecuted Jesus figure innocent of all charges. The new pseudo-science of eugenics was also engaged. Centuries of blood libel accusations settled around breakthroughs in genome studies to mark Jews (and, by extension, Dreyfus) as biologically deviant. Dreyfus's physiognomy became the contested template for this new form of public debate. He was often compared to a medical disease infecting the national body of France.[41] The distorted visages of him on anti-Semitic caricatures on the covers of *Le Pilori* (January 6, 1895) and *La Libre Parole* (July 11, 1895) used stereotypes of the Jewish body to indict Dreyfus as a traitor to the French nation.[42] A depiction of Dreyfus's most visible public defender, the non-Jewish writer Emile Zola, depicted Zola as a pig covered in excrement.[43]

Dreyfus's identity as a Jew became the litmus test for his loyalty, and, by proxy, the loyalty of all French Jews. As the *Harvard Law Review* summarized Dreyfus's retrial in 1899, "Alfred Dreyfus, a Jew, captain of the French artillery, in December, 1894, was convicted of a charge of treason by a court-martial, proceedings of which were not made public."[44] The emerging power of technology-driven visual media such as the reprinted illustration, the reprinted photograph, and early cinema "actualities" of the events of the trial all focused on Dreyfus's (Jewish) body and face.[45] When the respected Grand Rabbi of Paris J. H Dreyfuss (no relation) vociferously defended Dreyfus, it was the tonality of his Yiddish accent, not the facts of his argument, that was mocked by the anti-Dreyfusards.[46] This nativist anger could not be countered by logic. It was part of a primal fear spreading across Europe over new discourses of sexuality, psychology, and biology. Dreyfus's betrayal of the "body" of France echoed the emerging connection among Jewishness, sexual perversion, and biological distinction.[47] Dreyfus was no longer an individual. He was a contagion, hiding in plain sight, accelerating the breakdown of the cohesive purity of the French nation state.

One of the most important subjects in which this figural contestation took place was Dreyfus's wife, Lucie. After a brief courtship, Alfred Dreyfus married Lucie Hadamard in a wedding held at the synagogue on Rue de la Victoire on April 21, 1890.[48] He was thirty-four. She was twenty-five.

Both the bride and groom were assimilated French Jews. Born into a prominent bourgeois French-Jewish family of wealthy diamond merchants, Lucie had been educated by tutors and was an excellent pianist. The Hadamards owned numerous country houses and estates.[49] Lucie's last name carried weight long before her marriage to Alfred.[50] The marriage took place just one year after Alfred had become the first Jewish captain to be accepted into the French army. He was, on many levels, marrying up.

At first, the marriage of Alfred and Lucie exemplified the new freedoms of La Belle Époque. Both moved easily in both French-Jewish and French-Christian circles. Unlike Disraeli, Dreyfus felt no concerns about identifying as Jewish in either his personal life or in his choice of a marriage partner. Their assimilated Jewish world was untroubled and consistent with the libertine climate of urban French culture in the 1880s and 1890s. The barriers of anti-Semitism appeared to be giving way to the utopian ideals outlined in Disraeli's *Lothair*. Given these new freedoms, Dreyfus's selection of a Jewish wife was hardly inevitable. A rising star in the military, he likely had plenty of opportunities to court Christian women. Yet, as historian Piers Paul Read notes, there is no evidence Dreyfus considered marrying outside his faith.[51] Lucie and Alfred were secular but their Jewish identity remained culturally strong. Dreyfus did not find that his selection of a Jewish wife posed any impediment to his ambitions in the French military. In 1890, the future must have appeared to the newly married Jewish couple to be free of the cultural barriers that Disraeli had faced in England.

By 1894, the political climate had rapidly changed. Anxieties of another impending Franco-Prussian conflict had begun to trigger a nativist backlash. When evidence came to light that Germany had acquired top secret military files, suspicions fell on Dreyfus precisely because he was not "fully" French. He was arrested, given a secret military trial for the high crime of treason, and accused of selling highly classified weaponry secrets to Germany. Despite no evidence at the trial, Dreyfus was hastily convicted on January 5, 1895. He was sentenced to life in prison on Devil's Island and taken away in chains. The case initially received little attention. Yet, between Dreyfus's initial conviction and Emile Zola's famous intervention during the retrial in late 1898, the proud, assimilated, former Lucie Hadamard played a critical role in bringing public attention to the case.

LUCIE'S CRISIS

With Dreyfus silenced and in exile, Lucie was the scandal's public face as the affair entered the French national consciousness. As with Mary

Anne Lewis, she was not directly implicated in the political debates that surrounded her husband. But her presence in the controversy played a critical factor in the court of public opinion. As early as January 1895, months after the conviction, Lucie began to play a highly visible role in the first press accounts, demanding a retrial for her husband. In September 1896, she submitted the official petition to the Chamber of Deputies to reconsider the conviction.[52] Her evidence of Dreyfus's innocence was incontrovertible. After his initial conviction, secret handwritten files had been discovered by the new head of French Intelligence, Lieutenant Colonel Georges Picquart. They revealed that the act of treason attributed to Dreyfus was likely done by another military officer, Ferdinand Walsin Esterhazy. Esterhazy, deeply in debt at the time, had been in contact with the Germans for some time. His handwritten notes appeared directly on the documents used to convict Dreyfus. Esterhazy was clearly the real culprit.

Lucie used Picquart's discovery to shame the court into giving Dreyfus a retrial. Along with Dreyfus's brother, Mathieu, Lucie had managed to convince the Jewish poet, literary critic, and anarchist Bernard Lazare to help them publicize the injustice of the case in the popular press. Lazare's incendiary pamphlet, *A Judicial Error: The Truth About the Dreyfus Affair*, cited the Dreyfus conviction as a distillation of the dangers of French anti-Semitism.[53] Lazare made the case that the repugnant history of anti-Semitism marshaled against Dreyfus could not be ignored as part of the larger debate in French society. Modernism itself was on trial. The cause célèbre inspired the non-Jewish Emile Zola, one of the most important literary voices of the Left Bank, to risk his career.[54] Zola authored "*J'Accuse! . . . ,*" a savage critique of the French government that appeared on the front page of *L'Aurore* on January 13, 1898. Dreyfus was granted his retrial at Rennes in 1899.[55] Bernard Lazare had inspired numerous modernist thinkers and artists to rally to Dreyfus's cause. But it would be Lucie, as much as Alfred, who would become the contested face/body by which the trial was debated in early visual mass media forms.

This visibility peaked during Dreyfus's retrial at Rennes in 1899.[56] Newspapers, photography, and early cinema captured numerous images of Lucie's stoic figure standing in symbolic loyalty with her husband outside of the tribunal. She remained outside the courthouse nearly every day. This led to drawings, photographs, and early Kinematoscopes of Lucie as the "face" of the trial. Her visage appeared in newspapers, either by photograph or sketch. Nothing about her character was impeachable, even by the anti-Dreyfusards. She was seen as either a tragic wife standing loyally by her innocent husband or a blindly loyal dupe, just another victim of Dreyfus's malfeasance and duplicity. Either way, Lucie played a central role in how

Press footage of Lucie Dreyfus leaving Rennes during Alfred's retrial, late 1890s.

the case was perceived. She was one of the first public figures whose countenance was visceral and immediate, disseminated by the new mass media technologies that had rapidly overtaken France.

Christian iconography provided a rhetorical framing device for this image war. Two years before "*J'accuse . . . ,*" Lucie's petition to the president of the Chamber of Deputies on behalf of her husband was reprinted by nearly all the major French newspapers, including *Le Figaro*. Lucie's plea, written in first person, described her husband as suffering under a cruel form of proto-Christian martyrdom.[57] Lucie established herself early on as an active advocate expressing clear agency. This stood in stark contrast with the passive role played by "traditional" French wives. Hoping to temper Lucie's aggressive visibility, writers such as Zola began to reframe Alfred and Lucie, using iconography drawn from the Christian Passion Play.[58] Dreyfus was depicted as a suffering Jesus figure with Lucie as his loyal companion, a crypto-Mary. This argument was tailored as an appeal for Christian empathy. It depicted Alfred as being subjected to a modern-day crucifixion.[59]

This belated attempt by the pro-Dreyfusards was in response to the anti-Semitic backlash directed at Alfred. From the outset of the trial, Dreyfus had been described as a "French Judas" and the betrayer of the Christian body of the French nation.[60] The mob screamed "Judas!," "Traitor!," and "Kill the Jew!" at the young captain during his public shaming in the courtyard of the École Militaire on January 5, 1895.[61] The effort to produce a retroactive "baptism" of Alfred and Lucie in the court of public opinion was a creative act of re-appropriation. The schismatic public debate shifted from facts to iconography. Dreyfus-as-Jesus lost out to Dreyfus-as-Judas. Lucie-as-Mary lost out to Lucie-the-Jew.[62] She found herself tarred by the same suspicions of dual loyalty that stuck to her husband. Dreyfus was re-convicted and returned to Devil's Island in 1899. It would take another seven years before the conviction was finally overturned.

The image battle was illuminating in what it revealed about Jewishness and performance in the mass media age. To the economics of the new media industries, it did not matter whether Dreyfus was hero or villain. Profit located in the contestation between the two. France's exploding newspaper

Pro-Dreyfusard rendering of Dreyfus as Christ/victim by Henri Gabriel Ibels, approximately 1898.

and yellow journalism had found value in cultivating a potent, polarizing, real-life melodrama. Disraeli's performance of Jewish theatricality as modernist meta-fiction proved prescient. The Dreyfuses were unable to corral the contested signifier of figural Jewishness in their favor. But the nascent French mass media industry had discovered the power of mythic, visual provocation as a way to produce a new form of political theater.[63]

Fourteen years after Disraeli's death, the Dreyfus Affair became the first major European political crisis of the screen media age. Disraeli's dandyism had neutralized British suspicions by scrambling Jewish stereotypes as a literary trope and theatrical myth-making. The stoic Dreyfuses had no such performative talents. Dreyfus's masculinity was conventional.[64] He was, for all intents and purposes, a classic, loyal French military officer. He did not convert to Christianity. Nor did he attempt to placate his superiors by expressing fealty toward the church when it may have been advantageous for his career. This created an untenable paradox. In remaining a Jew but exemplifying French bourgeois culture in all other ways, Dreyfus was caught. His very conventionality ironically amplified suspicions that he was, as a Jew, hiding something from view.

Would the trial have been received differently if Dreyfus, like Disraeli, had chosen a Christian wife? Given the myriad historical, political, and cultural differences between Disraeli and Dreyfus (England vs. France, 1860s vs. 1890s, among others), no easy conclusions can be drawn. The complexities of the Dreyfus case push back on any simplified parallels. Dreyfus was not a politician. He certainly could not have foreseen the forces of history that would marshal against him in the mid-1890s. It is just as possible that French hysteria over Dreyfus would have reached a fever pitch regardless of his choice of spouse. But the public tug-of-war over the role of both wives offers at least a basic comparison point. Lucie was as important to Dreyfus's trial as Mary Anne Lewis was to Disraeli's political career. Both examples offer insight into the link among marriage, coupling, Jewishness, and modern identity at the beginning of the screen media age. Both cases also reveal the influence of visual media to arbitrate these ethno-religious affiliations and the national-cultural fault lines that this arbitration exposed.

The malleability Disraeli located in embracing a "blank page" between old world and new and between Jewishness and Christianity relied on his skills as a savvy performer in the public sphere. Alfred and Lucie Dreyfus demonstrated the limits of this form of agency. This was ironic. Dreyfus was a brave, stoic, handsome, conventionally masculine French soldier. Disraeli was a foppish, implicitly queered dandy with a widowed, much older Anglo-Saxon Protestant wife. Disraeli was the cultural outlier, not Dreyfus. Yet, Disraeli's mastery of theatricality and myth gave him an ability to perform queered Jewishness as anticipatory self-deprecation. Disraeli did not attempt to conform to a normative masculinity he could never ultimately access. By emphasizing difference, Disraeli had solved the emancipated Jewish paradox. The solution was not to blend. It was to stand out. Dreyfus's indistinguishable persona from the French Catholic ironically made him even more suspect of covert, hidden betrayal.

The virulent nativist anti-Semitism provoked by the Dreyfus case shook the utopian ideals of modernists not just in France, but also in England, Germany, Spain, and other nations throughout Europe. Dreyfus's reconviction so disturbed Theodor Herzl, an apolitical Hungarian-born playwright, that he reversed his assimilationist philosophy. Herzl joined Max Nordau to become the leading proponents of Zionism, the movement to convince Jews that they had no choice but to leave Europe and establish a nation in Israel. From the beginning, Zionism made Dreyfus the center of its argument. Nordau's 1897 address at the First Zionist Conference in Switzerland argued that if an assimilated, honorable Jew such as Dreyfus could not succeed in convincing France that he was a patriot, then there was little hope for the rest of Europe's Jewry.[65]

Despite eventually being exonerated, Dreyfus never recovered. He died quietly in France of natural causes in 1935. Lucie would not be so lucky. She lived until 1945, long enough to see the fears of Zionists such as Theodor Herzl confirmed.[66] The cracks exposed by Dreyfus four decades earlier eventually reached nativist fruition. Alfred and Lucie's granddaughter, Madeleine Dreyfus Levy, paid the price. She perished in a Nazi concentration camp in 1943.[67]

COUPLING AND MODERNISM

In 1946, Hannah Arendt drew a direct connection between the anti-Semitism of the Dreyfus Affair and the Holocaust.[68] In *The Origins of Totalitarianism*, she argued that the Dreyfus scandal was an early test case for the subsequent Nazi mass extinction, describing it as "a huge dress rehearsal for a performance that had to be put off for more than three decades."[69] Jean-Paul Sartre's *Anti-Semite and Jew* followed the next year. In this 1947 work, he attributed Jewish sexual desire for the Christian to the reactionary anxiety at the core of Nazism. As Sartre argued:

> We must understand this world of extremes, this humanity cut in
> two; we must see that every Jewish sentiment has a different qual-
> ity depending on whether it is addressed to a Christian or a Jew. The

love of a Jew for a Jewess is not of the same nature as the love he may feel for an "Aryan" woman. There is a basic doubling of Jewish sensibility concealed beneath the exterior of universal humanism.[70]

This was the Dreyfus paradox. If he truly assimilated, for example, by taking a Christian wife, he was violating the nation-state sexually. If he married a Jewish wife, as he did with Lucie, he was untrustworthy and suspicious of disloyalty to the nation-state by maintaining his Jewishness. This paradox was at the center of a relational interplay among ethno-biological alterity, European Christian traditions, and the schisms of modernism brought about by the new sciences.[71]

Arendt and Sartre recognized the destabilizing role of visible Jewishness in navigating the purported "universal" arguments of both nativists and modernists. Arendt's use of the terms "dress rehearsal" and "performance" described anti-Semitism as a form of public theater. Sartre linked the struggle to define "universal humanism" through differing (European Christian) receptions to Jewish-Jewish and Anglo-Christian-Jewish couplings. This conflict can be seen in both the Disraeli and Dreyfus examples.[72] Disraeli countered Otherness by embracing the theatrical and ambiguous nature of public Jewishness. He did this preemptively before his Jewishness could be used against him as a marker of difference. Alfred and Lucie Dreyfus were not capable of this proactive approach. Despite Lucie's best efforts at adopting Christian iconography during Alfred's trial, they lacked the requisite theatrical skills to give the performance required to assuage the masses in the theater of public opinion.

Despite his lack of critical respect as an author of merit, Disraeli, with his "blank page" metaphor, offered an important template for linking the lived experience to the creative process. By the early 1900s, numerous European writers and intellectuals continued Disraeli's metaphorical intersubjectivity.[73] Proust, Joyce, Kafka, and Leonard Woolf were just a few of the authors who began to explore in their work how malleable Anglo-Christian-Jewish interplay thematized the transgressive, utopian aspirations of their lives. These writers broke down formal structures to transgress the divide between author and reader, whether literal or in code, to posit new forms of literary modernism. They did so to argue for an emancipated, enlightened secular European modernism.

But the recurring template continued to return to the sexual realm. Jews who sought to assimilate through intermarriage exemplified a transcultural, cosmopolitan, fully secular modernism. Jews who did not desire the non-Jew provoked the same threat of nation-state betrayal as Alfred and Lucie Dreyfus had in France.[74] Just as Disraeli had predicted, the template of the new transnational politics was explored through constructed notions of a biologically distinct body. Political suspicions of disloyalty now ran through the twin prisms of sexual desire and prohibition. Disraeli's page had provided the literary template for what would become one of the central areas of ideological contestation in the mass media age.

CHAPTER 2

Kafka's Ape

LITERARY MODERNISM, JEWISH ANIMALITY, AND THE CRISIS OF THE NEW COSMOPOLITANISM

When I was handed over to my first trainer in Hamburg, I imme-diately recognized the two possibilities that were open to me: zoo or vaudeville.

RED PETER THE APE, "A REPORT TO THE ACADEMY"

IN 1917, AT THE AGE OF TWENTY-FOUR, FRANZ KAFKA enjoyed his first major publishing success. Martin Buber, a leading German-Jewish intellectual and author, agreed to publish two of the young author's short stories in Buber's German-language monthly mag-azine, *Der Jude* (*The Jew*). Established in 1906, *Der Jude* was one of the leading European forums for modern Jewish thought. It published on a wide range of subjects pertaining to German intellectual and creative life. But it was also explicitly Jewish in both form and mission statement. When it did engage Jewish themes, the journal published debates among Buber, Her-mann Cohen, Viktor Jacobson, and other Jewish intellectuals over Zionism and the role of emancipated Jews in Europe.[1] It was one of the first print forums to explicitly engage the contested, problematic role of Jews in post-Dreyfus Europe.

Read on a textual level, both "A Report to the Academy" ("Ein Bericht für eine Akademie") and "Jackals and Arabs" ("Schakale und Araber") ap-pear only to offer early examples of Kafka's interest in animality and alien-ation. The word "Jew" does not appear in either text. But Kafka's meta-phorical play with Jewish stereotypes is unmistakable. These were not solely universal parables. They were direct commentaries on the link among Jew-ishness, metaphor, and modernity.

"A Report to the Academy" consists entirely of a speech delivered by a talking ape named Red Peter to a roomful of unidentified (and silent) academics. Red Peter explains that he has been asked to give a report on all that he has learned as an educated ape living and studying in modern European society. After living happily as an ape for many years, he was captured from his native habitat in Africa and educated by his European captors. Despite keeping him locked in a cage, Red Peter's captors eventually taught him language, cultural refinement, philosophy, and art. He proved himself a capable student and quickly became a refined intellectual.

But enlightenment came with a cost. The power of consciousness forced Red Peter to confront his undeniable biological alterity. He was a perfect mimic of the academic. But he was also an animal. No elocution, education level, clothing style, or performance could solve the immutable truth of his hybridity and Otherness.[2]

Red Peter's animal-human hybridity was not just a stand-in for the contradictory impulses of the id and superego in a dream-like scenario, as is the dominant understanding of much of Kafka's work. Nor was he simply a satire of colonized, subjected African cultures grappling with the influx of European "civilization." Kafka's ape-intellectual was rooted in the obvious codes of Jewish specificity. Red Peter satirized post-Haskalah charges against Jews for "aping" non-Jewish culture by becoming a literal manifestation.[3] His subsequent confusion invoked the conflicting stereotypes of Jews as both hyper-intellectual academics and carnally deviant, compulsive animals.

When understood in context with Buber's journal, Kafka's tale ridiculed the core paradox surrounding emancipated Jewish visibility that had begun to circulate across Europe, influenced, in part, by the popularity of the notorious anti-Semitic forgery, *The Protocols of the Elders of Zion* (ca. 1905). *The Protocols*, a "secret" guidebook purportedly written by rabbis as a how-to guide for international Jewish control of world governments, simultaneously positioned Jews as international masterminds and intellectually inferior deviants.

Kafka's animal-human hybrids mocked the ludicrousness of this accusation without once explicitly mentioning Jewishness.[4] His indictment of these Jewish stereotypes works by taking them to their cartoonish extreme. Despite apparent freedom to interact with the Fully Humans, the Verbal Ape remains trapped in a conceptual prison. This rhetorical confinement is enforced by the spectators to whom he delivers his report. On his stage, a simultaneous zoo, prison, and academic institution, Red Peter becomes a performer. Yet, this performance remains in a state of perpetual tension. He occupies a dual space of both superiority and inferiority. This duality is witnessed by the Fully Human (European Anglo-Christian) spectators using Red Peter as a test case to locate a distinction between human/self and animal/other. Red Peter's efforts at entering their society through intellectual acumen alone are ultimately ineffective.[5] No matter how articulate or profound his mimicry, he will always be perceived as part alien.

Kafka's retort to Disraeli's aspirational performative dandy suggested a far gloomier future for European Jewry. Red Peter's "blank page" between worlds old/new and animal/human serves only to entertain the normative (Christian) witness. His efforts are ultimately doomed. They reinforce the primal, reactive, nativist divisions that lurk beneath the veneer of modern thinking. No redefinition of the self and no performance of humanity can change the fact that the (Anglo-Christian) human masses will eventually reject the non-human (Jewish) mimic. Red Peter will always remain as they first defined him: a sexually compulsive animal.[6]

"Jackals and Arabs" was even less nuanced about its allusions and geopolitical allegory. The (unnamed) narrator describes witnessing a desert confrontation about to take place between sleeping Arabs and the bloodthirsty desert jackals that hope to eat them. The jackals are logical and highly verbal, but their bestial qualities ultimately betray them. The Arabs trick the jackals into feasting on a camel carcass by exploiting instincts that the jackals cannot control. As with Red Peter, Kafka was parodying wellknown anti-Semitic stereotypes. One of the main anti-Zionist arguments of the time was that amoral Jews were preying on Arabs by taking their land in Palestine. Kafka's satirical invocation of blood libel imagery was then taken to its ludicrous extreme.[7]

Kafka's modernist animal metaphors place the role of the witness/reader at the center of both stories. The academics in "A Report to the Academy" and the privileged observer/narrator of "Jackals and Apes" both appear to be detached from the spectacles they witness. But this act of observation was also an act of participation. The gaze of the spectator/reader was essential to defining both animal-human and Christian-Jewish intersubjectivity. In Kafka's Hegelian entanglement, the European Christian could only locate himself through a subjectivity defined by what he was not. The stage animal (Jew) provided that definition.

Kafka's satirical use of animal-human hybridity as sociological critique suggests why Martin Buber championed the young, then-unknown writer's short stories in Der Jude. Kafka's fanciful, comedic animal metaphors were a literary and poetic extension of Buber's own work. Beginning in 1914 and up to the official publication of I and Thou in 1923, Buber combined theories from Jewish philosophy, Kabbalah mysticism, poetry, and the emerging field of linguistics to develop the theory that became his seminal work. Over this decade, Buber introduced a new approach to philosophy rooted in relational subjectivity and the hidden meanings of linguistic dialectics. He combined the study of words, language, and religion with the nascent field of cultural studies to explore how presumably innate identity is actually informed by social experience and cultural influence. His central insight was to focus on relational meanings. The text offers a phenomenological framework for exploring how the individual relates to the world. This can be located by focusing on the schisms, fragments, and paradoxes lurking beneath seemingly cohesive words and concepts:[8]

> The basic words are not single words but word pairs. One basic word is the word pair I-You. The other basic word is the word pair I-It; but this basic word is not changed when He or She takes the place of It.[9]

I and Thou was one of the first major texts to propose networks of intersubjectivity at work within systems of communication. It built on the emphasis on interiority inspired by both Freudian psychoanalysis and the modernist turn in art. It offered a plea for acceptance of difference through the notion of dual entanglement. It did this by mining the shared traditions of both Christian and Jewish messianic thought without explicitly championing either one.[10] Buber's "philosophy of dialogue" argued that Christianity and Judaism were essentialist, intrinsically linked building blocks within all of modern philosophical thought. This gave the book transnational and transcultural appeal. Contemporary Christian philosophers such as J. Coert Rylaarsdam and Karl Thieme understood *I and Thou* as a way to link Jewish and Christian theology under a single philosophical umbrella. Christian clergy adopted the I/Thou duality as a way to understand Jesus's struggles as both God and man. Buber's work was seen across Europe as a malleable approach that sought to maintain the ephemeral codes of religion within the secular emphasis of the new sciences.[11]

Kafka made the same point through the satirical allegory of inter-species couplings. But whereas Buber saw intellectual emancipation in locating religion within secular modernism, Kafka's vision was far more cynical. His entanglement of "I" and "Thou," whether the verbose jackals or the self-aware Red Peter, operates as an appeal to a universality that never quite arrives. It is held back by the tribal limits of humanity's basest impulses.

A decade later, Kafka's last published short story, "Josephine the Singer, the Mousefolk," made Buber's I/Thou subtext even clearer. Published mere months before his untimely death in 1924, the childlike tale offered a thematic coda to Kafka's career-long exploration of metamorphosis and animality as allegories for the tensions of modern identity. The story's protagonist is Josephine, a talented songstress who also happens to be a field mouse. Josephine's unique talents are praised by an unnamed mouse observer who serves as the story's narrator. As with the ape concept, the notion of a mouse as a metaphor for a Jew would have been easily recognizable to readers of the 1920s.[12] Kafka's interest in European Jews attempting (and failing) to hide their Jewishness permeated much of his correspondence with his close friend and confidant, Max Brod. In one letter, written in 1921, Kafka described his fascination with young Jewish authors attempting to write in German to hide their backgrounds. He used the metaphor of a "glue mousetrap" to describe this tension. In this excerpt from his private correspondences, originally observed by Sander Gilman, Kafka revealed his allegorical thinking.[13] In fiction, Kafka relocated the desired transformation from the young Jew writing in German to Josephine's aural talents. She aims to use her voice to elevate her above her mouse-specific identity. But like those young Jews whom Kafka described to Brod in 1921, and like Red Peter and the Jackals a decade earlier, Josephine's self-identified transformation is not enough. Despite her clear agency, she remains trapped in a fixed state of animality placed upon her by the imposition of the (European-Christian) spectator-witness.

This use of animality was not confined to Kafka. In his study of philosopher (and Kafka contemporary) Martin Heidegger's interrogation of the world of the animal, Akira Lippit depicts Heidegger as on a quixotic quest to resist and reject the complexities of modernism. Lippit describes Heidegger's compulsive need to define and locate a clear distinction between the "animal" and the "human" as an example of philosophy's "last stand against the swelling tide of psychology and technology."[14] Heidegger's goal was in direct opposition to the intertextual work of Martin Buber. Heidegger aspired to clearly demarcate the worlds of the human and the animal through the function of speech. For Heidegger, the moment of speaking conjures not only an awareness of death but also an awareness of the self as distinctive from the wordless (and deathless) animal.[15] If the human and the animal could be clearly differentiated, the modernist artistic and philosophical emphasis on subjectivity could be resisted.

While Heidegger wouldn't publish his significant work on this subject, *Being and Time*, until 1927, more than a decade after Kafka's talking apes and jackals, these works existed on oppositional sides of a central philosophical debate. Three decades earlier, Nietzsche had advocated for the ascension of the individual mind over the institutions of culture and society, as well as the primitive "animal" instincts that lurked within them.[16] The subsequent Dreyfus crisis and debates over the new sciences relocated Nietzschean debates from the philosophical human/animal binary to the political tensions of European-Christian/Emancipated-Jew. Critics of Heidegger recognized the danger of his post-Nietzschean form of hierarchical classification. They claimed his anti-modernist stance was actually just anti-Semitism recoded for the philosophical realm.[17] These criticisms were amplified when Heidegger joined the Nazi Party in 1933.

Kafka's talking animal-Jews had offered a conceptual pushback that aligned with Martin Buber. Coded Jews-as-animals mocked the racial underpinnings of emerging proto-fascist eugenics theory by blurring Heidegger's animal/human distinctions.[18] Whether making fun of the Jewish blood libel (in "Jackals and Arabs") or Jewish cosmopolitan intellectualism (Red Peter), Kafka scrambled the arbitrary boundaries of eugenics to the point of becoming an absurd Jewish joke.

Kafka had located a literary solution that extended Disraeli's blank page slippages into a critique of the emergent racial-biological sciences. But Kafka's satirical parables also indicted the spectator/reader for complicity. The (European-Christian) reader/witness, unable to accept the mutability and fractures of modern thinking, inadvertently commits violence against the animal-human subject. This is done when Kafka's reader (and the proxy spectator/narrator located within the story) experiences an impulse for narrative resolve. Despite occupying a presumably passive position, the reader desires an either/or identity to emerge at the conclusion of the story (ex: animal or human?). When Kafka denies or problematizes this resolution, late modern paradox is sustained rather than resolved. Those able to empathize with the animal-human on its own terms could, through the power of mutable figuration, understand the complexities of an increasingly cosmopolitan mass media age.

But, as Kafka's bleak parables repeatedly and satirically conclude, most could not. The (Jewish) animal-human had become the privileged allegory for European Christian transformation into the modern age. But the animal-Jew (and modernity itself) remained an impossible object for the European Anglo-Christian to fully accept.

CHARLES SWANN AND ODETTE

Kafka was not the first modernist writer to recognize the potency of Christian-Jewish intersubjectivity. Marcel Proust's experimentations with form destabilized the authority of the narrator by emphasizing the power of subjectivity and the unreliability of memory. But Proust also recognized the role of Anglo-Christian-Jewish coupling as an expression of this renegotiation. Prior to Dreyfus, the twenty-something Proust was an apolitical socialite, ambitious columnist, and aspiring novelist. By the time Emile Zola went on trial for treason after penning *"J'Accuse! . . ."* in 1898, Proust had experienced a political awakening.[19] He began to make daily appearances in court in visible support of Zola.[20] Whether this tentative entrance into hot-button French politics was out of ideological commitment or self-preservation remains debatable. Despite his Catholic upbringing and lack of religious practice, Proust's Jewish background was an inimitable part of his public life.[21] Like Disraeli, he had no choice but to address his public recontextualization. After the Dreyfus Affair "outed" him as a Jew, Proust began to both embrace and subvert his Jewishness through modernist techniques. His technique relied on meta-fiction and intertextuality, blurring the line between his fictional characters and his public persona.

Although their public personas were radically different, Proust and Disraeli shared notable similarities. Both were short, frail, and physically distinct from their fellow countrymen. Both were baptized by assimilated parents (Catholicism for Proust, Protestantism for Disraeli). Both dabbled in the codes of effete dandyism and remained disinterested in any religious aspects of their Jewish backgrounds. But, most notably for the purposes of this book, both were authors who recognized the power of ephemeral "Jewishness" as a literary metaphor for the crisis of European modernism. Both authors highlighted this slippage through interplay with its opposite: erotic desire for the Christian partner.[22] Disraeli linked his theatrical Jewishness to the blank page of modernity. Proust extended this corporealization into the form of the modernist novel. In Proust's episodic, dream-like meditations on the imprecise nature of memory, the suffering of repressed homosexuality and hidden Jewishness became twin manifestations of the crisis of subjectivity within the modern self.[23] Assimilation was no longer defined by bourgeois taste culture or mimicry. It was defined through the sublimation of alienation and transference into erotic desire.[24]

This is one of the themes of the first volume of Proust's most famous work, *Remembrance of Things Past, Vol. 1: Swann's Way* (published in chapters between 1913 and 1927).[25] Begun as early as 1905 but published in 1913, *Swann's Way* foregrounds the connection between Jewish erotic desire for the Christian and the residue of the Dreyfus Affair through the story of an erotic affair between Charles Swann and Odette de Crécy.[26] Swann, Proust's semi-autobiographical protagonist, is an assimilated, "half-Jewish" member of the French bourgeoisie with little interest in politics. He pays scant attention to the events of the Dreyfus scandal, remaining preoccupied with his thoughts and desires. Yet, Swann begins to feel political stirrings at the precise moment he experiences libidinal desire for the embodiment of hyper-sexualized female French fantasy, the former prostitute, Odette.[27]

Odette is introduced in chapter 2 as a "demi-monde," the Belle Époque term for a sexually libertine prostitute or mistress. Her low class standing serves as ironic counterpoint for Swann's assimilated French-Jewish bourgeois.[28] Swann is seeking out "vulgar" sexual pleasures as a release from his class constraints. But this also has a political bent. He begins to advocate for Dreyfus's innocence as an extension of this erotic awakening. Swann's sexual epiphany is also a recognition of his own inexorable status as a Jew.

Swann's erotic desire for Odette is built as much on sexual compulsion as romantic love. This transgression of both class and the sexual mores of the bourgeoisie are presented by Proust as a novel within the novel. This creates a distancing effect. The Anglo-Christian-Jewish coupling emerges in the realm of both politics and inter-class conflict as an extension of literary modernism itself. A second degree of alienation is required to create the idealized plateau for Charles and Odette to couple. This labyrinthine, challenging literary structure visualized the same end point that Disraeli had in Britain a generation earlier: the blank page of modernism was directly aligned with the boundary-crossing iconography of Christian-Jewish entanglement.

In Proustian fashion, no easy corollaries can be determined. Swann is both an embodiment and a rejection of Dreyfus. Unlike Dreyfus, Swann is both Jewish and not-Jewish, French bourgeois and alienated outsider. Daniel Karlin argues that Proust's fracturing of French national identity can also be located in his deft interweaving of English and French. Karlin describes Proust as intentionally producing a merging of two languages into "Franglish."[29] Linguistic hybridity reflects Swann's dual state. He is torn between his desire for acceptance and his erotic boldness. This coalesces around his semi-forgotten Jewish ancestry. Swann's desire for Odette focuses him on an erotic cipher as the perceived solution to this internalized tension. Odette represents an idealized French female object of carnality. His desire to conquer her sexually is triggered by his obliviousness to the Dreyfus crisis. Swann's eventual confusion and feelings of inadequacy toward Odette represent an irreducible facet of alienation that Swann himself cannot grasp. Mimicry will never be enough. Erotic union with the Other offers only an incomplete salve in dealing with the fractured self of modern identity.

In volume four, *Sodom and Gomorrah* (1921), Proust again finds Swann grappling with the complexities of the Dreyfus Affair. Proust describes his character's internalized tensions with the following:

> Tempering the burning conviction of the Israelite with the diplomatic moderation of the man about town, whose habits he had imbibed too deeply to be able this belatedly to shed them.[30]

Swann finds himself in perpetual conflict between two identities. He contains both the "burning conviction" of the Israelite and the skillful ability to mimic and ingratiate as an urbane Franco-Christian sophisticate. The Dreyfus Affair had revealed this fault line within Swann. It was a tension state that could not be resolved. The cultural divide between bourgeois atavism and the emerging cosmopolitanism was insurmountable both within Swann and within France. Whichever path Swann chose, he would remain fractured.

Lynn Wilkenson provides another example of Dreyfus's impact in Proust's work. In volume three, *The Guermantes Way* (1920), the non-Jewish Robert de Saint-Loup finds his position on the Dreyfus Affair as a direct result of his sexual desire for the Jewish prostitute, Rachel. Wilkenson notes that Albert Bloch, the narrator's childhood friend and vicarious observer of this story, is a Jewish pro-Dreyfusard. Bloch serves as another alter ego for the malleable Proustian narrator figure who weaves through all seven novels. He joins Robert de Saint-Loup on a journey to the Palais de Justice where they observe one of the Dreyfus trials.[31] Like Swann, Bloch both evokes and subverts a number of Jewish clichés as he witnesses and narrates Saint-Loup's sexual desire for Rachel. Bloch highlights the reductive power of anti-Semitic stereotypes as commentary on the larger political backdrop in which the story locates.[32]

Dreyfus recurs throughout the novel as a central structuring totem. Proust does this without directly engaging the political events of the trial. Reactions to Dreyfus, both pro and con, exert influence on the various erotic and homosocial couplings taking place in Proust's multiple pairings. Just as Swann discovered his desire for Odette at the same moment of his political awakening, Saint-Loup becomes a supporter of Dreyfus as part of his attempt to seduce Rachel. The distinctions among Jewish male and Christian female (Charles/Odette), Jewish female and Christian male (Rachel/Robert), and Jewish male and Christian male (Albert/Robert) are not important. All three Christian-Jewish couplings schematize political fracture. The romantic, sexual, social, and political are all inextricably linked.

Proust was one of the first writers after Disraeli to recognize the slippages of Christian-Jewish intersubjectivity as a template for literary modernism.[33] Numerous French artists, writers, and intellectuals followed. Jacques de Lacretelle's *Silbermann*, an enormously popular period-piece novel on the impact of the Dreyfus Affair, captivated France in 1922. Similar to Proust, de Lacretelle privileged the entanglement of Anglo-Christian-Jewish desire as a sublimated expression of the fault lines of French society.[34] The novel's narrator is a nameless Protestant schoolboy obsessed with a sullen, artistically talented Jewish classmate named David Silbermann.

Their friendship blossoms during the rise of intense anti-Semitism as Dreyfus's retrial was taking place in the late 1890s. Both schoolboys form an intense homosocial friendship. This crypto-love story allows the non-Jewish protagonist/narrator to serve as empathetic witness and confidant to the troubles of French anti-Semitism.

Silbermann was one of the first major French novels after Proust to directly connect the crisis of later modern French national identity to the mutual entanglement of Christian and Jewish desire.[35] All we know of the biographical background of the anonymous schoolboy relating Silbermann's story is that he is Protestant. He is therefore under none of the threat and pressures that Silbermann's family experiences. The novel furthers this relational interplay by introducing a third schoolboy, Philippe Robin, a Catholic. Despite myriad differences between Catholics and Protestants in French society, they collectively gaze at the Jew to form a subjective tripartite. The titular Jewish outsider of de Lacretelle's novel ends up as both fetishized and demonized.

The traumatic dénouement, Silbermann's exile to the United States, gave de Lacretelle's novel an even more pessimistic view than that of Proust. Like Proust's characters, de Lacretelle's characters internalize and sublimate the political tensions of Dreyfus into the crypto-erotic realm. The narrator's admiration of Silbermann is both an inversion and a continuation of Swann's desire for Odette. Yet, the narrator is unable to protect his friend. In the novel's conclusion, the Silbermanns are forced to flee France and move to America to become diamond merchants. It was a grim reminder of the continuing hopelessness of postwar French Jewry to successfully integrate.[36] By the 1920s, Disraeli's utopian hopes seemed more and more like the fantasies of nineteenth-century antiquity.

LEOPOLD BLOOM'S WANDERLUST

Dozens of symbolists, artists, writers, and intellectuals of the early 1900s followed Proust's lead in arguing for political activism through dream-like fantasies of Christian/Jewish interplay.[37] Writers such as Bernard Lazare, Marcel Schwob, and Gustave Kuhn used absurd, often eroticized Jewish symbols, fragments, and evocations. Like those of Kafka, these images were often based in animality and other anti-Semitic stereotypes. These acts of reclamation commented on the political through the lens of the emerging sensibilities of subjectivity, impressionism, and the impact of the subconscious. This approach was not just confined to French

Jews. Non-Jewish French pro-Dreyfusards such as Emile Zola and poet Stéphane Mallarmé used modernist metaphors to make similar arguments.

But, arguably, the most influential example of this emergent metaphor of Christian-Jewish intersubjectivity took place not in France or England but in Ireland. It was the centerpiece of what is considered the most influential novel of the twentieth century, James Joyce's *Ulysses*.

Ulysses (1918–1920) primarily (but not exclusively) focuses on the story of Leopold Bloom, a wandering, middle-aged, Irish Jew. Like Proust's Charles Swann and Kafka's Red Peter, Bloom is a hybridity of competing, seemingly contradictory identities rooted in Jewish emancipation and assimilation. He is the product of a Jewish immigrant father and Irish-Catholic mother. This makes him at once both Catholic and Jewish.[38] But because Bloom's mother was not Jewish, he was technically not Jewish according to Jewish law. This secondary level of alienation, the Jew who is not a Jew, feeds into the novel's segmented, meandering, disconnected narrative form.

Bloom's Jewishness begins as a joke. The title of the novel appropriates the epic poem of the ancient Greek hero, Ulysses (the Latin name for Odysseus) in Homer's *The Odyssey*. That a hyper-masculine hero has been replaced by an impotent, weak, wandering Irish Jew offered an ironic metacommentary on the crisis of masculinity and heroism in the modern era. *Ulysses* focuses on Leopold Bloom's picaresque, meandering wanderings through the streets of Dublin over the course of one single day, June 16, 1904. Bloom suffers from insecurities, impotence, and a general sense of middle-age malaise. He is incapable even of stopping his wife, Molly Bloom, from her impending affair with Hugh "Blazes" Boylan, a somewhat sleazy Irish events promoter. Bloom is figuratively castrated. He is a complete inversion of the Western traditions of masculinity and heroism. This is embodied by a stubborn Jewishness that clings to Bloom despite his secularism and Irish assimilation. Joyce fuses Proustian memory with open-ended Kafkaesque parables to locate a crisis of identity in the form of the protean, fragmented Jew.

Like Proust, Joyce plays with the unreliability of the narrator. Bloom's record of his thoughts and the events of the day give way to contradictory accounts from his wife, Molly, and his friend, Stephen Dedalus. Bloom's memory is rendered suspect and unreliable. Joyce's hapless Jew made a serious point. Ulysses was cursed by the gods to wander for twenty years despite his noble goal of returning home to Penelope. Bloom wanders Dublin over the course of a single day without a clear purpose. Ulysses fought numerous physical threats on his epic journey. Bloom's battles are primarily internal and concern jealousy, insecurity, and self-loathing, all visibly Jewish traits. Where once-potent Greek warriors battled gods and monsters, in the modern world, there was only the schlemiel.[39]

Why did Joyce choose a Jew to embody modern Ireland? Neil Davison argues that the crisis over Jews in European discourse of the late nineteenth century had a profound influence on the young Joyce, who visited Paris in 1902 when the Dreyfus Affair was still raging.[40] Witnessing the debates over Dreyfus's loyalty may have convinced the young writer that Jews were the embodiment of the crisis of the nation-state. Bloom's neurotic debates over his role in Irish society reflected Joyce's take on the European Jew as metaphor for the breakdown of national cohesion. Joyce makes this explicit when Bloom enters the Hungarian Jewish butcher shop, owned by Moses Dlugacz. Dlugacz is a proud Hungarian Zionist who nonetheless sells unkosher pork. Bloom is a baptized, non-Jewish Jew who eats unkosher pork. He is also, as Davison observes, an Irishman who does not drink. His lack of participation in the pub culture of Ireland amplifies his alienated Jewishness.[41] In these paradoxical desires, he embodies the contradictions of the modern age. It is impossible to reduce Bloom's identity just as Joyce's novel itself rejects the established literary traditions of cohesive sentence structure and plot-driven narrative. The stereotype of rootless, nationless Jewish Diaspora was an ideal metaphor for the fractures of Irish identity under British rule.[42] But the hybrid Jew was also an exemplar of the new art.

Benjamin Disraeli also likely played a significant role in influencing Joyce's creation of Bloom. Joyce's father, John Joyce, was active politically in the Irish Parnellites movement of 1880, a direct response to Disraeli's policies toward Ireland.[43] As Joyce grew up, the residual spread of anti-Semitism during the Dreyfus Affair revealed how the alienated European Other easily mapped onto the crisis of the accused, wandering Jew.[44] Leopold Bloom internalized Dreyfus as a metaphor for the wandering, alienated Ireland of the modern world.[45] This notion that the Irish and Hebrews shared common cause was a folkloric tradition. The Celts of Ireland were frequently suggested to be one of the lost tribes of Israel.[46] Joyce's insight was to introduce the key central figure of late modern Irish alienation not as an Irishman but as an Irish Jew oscillating between both identities and without the ability to resolve either one.

This is also reflected in the character of Leopold's wife, Molly Bloom. Like Leopold, Molly is "half-Jewish," but unlike him, she is fully Jewish under Jewish law. Her father is Irish and her mother, Jewish (Spanish Sephardim). This distinction may seem incidental. But it directly links the crisis of gender, sexuality, and power in an increasingly secular Europe directly to the Jew/not-a-Jew question hanging over both Leopold and Molly.

Both hold uncertain identities. This is offset by tensions of their coupling. This destabilization of character reflects Joyce's own liberties with the novel's subjective shifts. The meandering narrative structure and frequent allusions to the story of the Greek Ulysses privilege intertextual allusion and referents over any textual specificity. At the core of all of these formal destabilizations circled the unstable coupling of two "half-Jews."

The final episode of the novel makes this fragmentation clear. It places Molly and not Leopold in the privileged position of narrator. The episode is titled "Penelope," but is often referred to as "Molly's Soliloquy." It is an uninterrupted stream of consciousness delivered by Molly as she lies in bed next to Leopold. Her internal monologue is presented almost entirely without punctuation. It is written in long run-on sentences, eight total, that are an amalgam of Molly's repressed passion and sexualized longing for her youth. They do not describe the reality of her current life. Her hopefulness is directed backward at a memory that is informed as much by imagination and whimsy as it is by truth. Molly rewrites her impotent husband lying in bed next to her into a powerful, heterosexual, carnal beast. Her subjectivity rebuilds Leopold's problematic transnational Jewish hybridity into a mouse-mountain, a totem of desire and a phantasm of liberation.[47]

In this final passage, Joyce privileges Molly as the authorial voice. Leopold's un-heroic journey of passivity and meekness has cost him the privileged position of narrator itself. Molly has taken hold of the voice of the novel and all its inherent privilege. She is a Jewish daughter born to a Jewish mother and is therefore self-actualized in ways that the alienated Leopold cannot be. Through this coupling binary, Joyce scrambles both gender and sexuality to produce what Joseph Allen Boone calls a celebration of "the womanly man."[48] This power struggle locates in Molly's carnal desire. Her descriptors of her "breasts all perfume" and her repeated cries of "yes," some capitalized in midsentence, reveal the emergence of a newly explicit sexuality simply by acknowledging the female orgasm.[49] The meandering, everyday journey of *Ulysses* is purportedly driven by the impotence and confusion of Leopold, a wandering Irish Jew. But it ends in the orgasmic memory-fantasy generated by Molly.[50]

In scrambling the codes of subjectivity, authority, gender, and identity, Leopold and Molly respond by articulating the same "blank page" that Disraeli had once performed in the House of Commons in the 1850s. Jewishness operated as a slippage between worlds. This fracture offered a conceptual bridge to the (non-Jewish) reader. In an entangled Christian-Jewish hybrid state, the Blooms operate similar to Kafka's ape, emerging to take center stage and give his report on the tensions of modernism. Bloom was Kafka's animal-human reconfigured as Irish-Jewish, the antihero-as-new-hero transformed by the very modernist break with form that the novel exemplified. The episodic intersubjectivity of literary modernism transformed the Blooms into a new form of heroism. This new "Ulysses" was a comedic inversion, an impotent, alienated half-Jew as epic conqueror. In appearing to fail, the "feminized" Leopold Bloom actually transcends the written word. He became the harbinger of the new, entirely modern, self-aware sensibility.[51]

Joyce's intersectionality among carnality, transnational Jewishness, and the modernist literary form offered a direct indictment of Europe's nativist and xenophobic backlash after the Dreyfus Affair. To anti-Semites, Jews were sexually libertine, amoral, and perverse Fagins and Shylocks. Disraeli had performed theatrical Jewish dandyism to circumvent this anxiety. Proust had used cascading subjectivities and novel-within-novel distancing effects to allow Jewish sexuality to circuitously emerge. Kafka introduced the metaphor of the carnal animal and the active role of the reader/observer as a satirical form of voyeuristic pornography. Joyce brought all of these modes of resistance together. He satirized the fear of Jewish perversion by embracing it as irony. Leopold and Molly's sex life was entirely dormant. They have not had sex in more than a decade. Yet, both express carnal thoughts and desires throughout the novel's episodic form. This link between Jewish thinking and literary interiority reflected the mythic power of modernism to transgress European Christian prohibitions on externalized forms of sexual deviancy. Just as Disraeli transformed the British nobleman into the theatrical Jewish dandy, *Ulysses* transformed the mythic Greek hero into the figure of the sexually confused nebbish.[52]

LEONARD WOOLF'S VIRGIN

The Bloomsbury Group, a loose affiliation of intellectuals, artists, and writers in Edwardian England, quickly expanded on Joyce's modernist allegory. Bloomsbury was founded in 1905, an important year for the development of new artistic and literary sensibilities emerging across Europe. The movement began as an informal series of academic and philosophical debates led by writer and intellectual Leonard Woolf and the then-teenage Virginia Stephen. Debates took place among dozens of young, ambitious artists and writers over the changing relationships of art, philosophy, and sexuality in the machine age. By 1911, Bloomsbury's dedication to radical thinking led a number of the participants to challenge the chaste codes of married life and monogamy as a by-product of Britain's fading empire.[53] While the members of the group never slipped into outright orgies or lib-

Virginia and Leonard Woolf shortly after their marriage in 1912.

ertine hedonism (as far as we know), one of the central organizing philosophical principles was the challenge to the conventional boundaries of sexuality.

One of the pivotal moments in the growing influence of Bloomsbury took place in 1912 when Virginia Stephen married Leonard Woolf. Despite numerous affairs, sexual ambivalence, and clinical depression, the often anxious Virginia had made a decision more political than romantic. She rejected her middle-class, Anglo-Saxon background and agreed to marry the "penniless Jew."[54] Both were ambitious writers who saw the lived experience inextricably tied to their art. Leonard and Virginia Woolf were also literary partners. In the first few years of their marriage, they produced a number of literary works that reflected a connection between sexual transgression and political rebellion. In the case of Leonard, this was drawn through what was becoming a familiar literary metaphor: Anglo-Christian-Jewish coupling.

Leonard's second novel, *The Wise Virgins* (1914), offers insight into how the Bloomsbury Group approached the idea of Jews marrying Christians. Leonard began work on *The Wise Virgins* while on honeymoon with Virginia in 1912, drawing direct inspiration from their relationship. The novel focuses on an angry, libidinal Jewish protagonist, Harry Davis, struggling to overcome the constraints of living under the chaste class system of early twentieth-century London. The autobiographical elements were unmistakable. Leonard's barely coded protagonist, Harry, struggles to resolve his alternating desire for and repellence from seemingly asexual British females. Harry's frustrated sexual desire also works as an extension of post-emancipated Jewish cultural alienation. Harry's confusion codifies around his alternating erotic desires for Katherine, an intellectual British Anglo-Saxon elite, and her younger sister, Camilla. His thwarted desires for both sisters exemplified Leonard's understanding of the psycho-sexual blockade that prevented any true transgression of the British class system.

Harry's angry, sexualized assaults on the sisters both invoked and subverted the anti-Semitic, Fagin-esque stereotype of Jews as carnal seducers of innocent Christian virgins. "Virginity" in *The Wise Virgins* is thus indicted as an ignoble artifact of class control rather than an idealized embodiment of Christian virtue. Harry's carnal assault on Camilla's innocence exemplifies, by the end of the novel, the beginning of the end of the Victorian era.[55] Male Jewish desire for female Christian "purity" formed an intergenerational transgression. Leonard and Virginia Woolf's marriage informed their work, embodying the seeds of creative, cultural, and political revolution to which Bloomsbury aspired.

This theme was even clearer in Leonard Woolf's 1917 short story, "The Three Jews." Published in the book *Two Stories* alongside Virginia Woolf's first officially published story, "The Mark on the Wall," Leonard again uses Anglo-Christian-Jewish coupling as a metaphor for the breakdown of Victorian-era class control. The story concerns three Jewish men who sit down for tea and eventually discuss their struggles in the changing world. One of the men reveals that he disowned his son for marrying a Christian servant who worked in their house.[56] While all three are religious skeptics and assimilated British Jews, it is the notion of Christian-Jewish intermarriage that sparks a sense of cultural crisis among the men. Woolf's *The Wise Virgins* had directly invoked the metaphor of Christian-Jewish carnality. "The Three Jews" suggested the residual effects that such a coupling would signify to the Victorian generation.

Like Disraeli, Proust, Joyce, and Kafka before them, the Woolfs grasped the transgressive allegory of Christian-Jewish coupling as a rejection of class divides. To the Bloomsbury Group, the bourgeois boundaries of the Victorian era had to be challenged in life as well as in art. Virginia's emerging talent as an author of a new form of literary modernism was also amplified by her selection of a Jewish husband. Their literary marriage, in *Two Stories* and elsewhere, was a reflection of the boundary crossings of their actual marriage. They founded Hogarth Press together in 1917 and used it to publish their writings for the next two decades.[57] The meta-form of their Anglo-Christian-Jewish coupling allowed discourses of masculine power, feminine subjugation, and the mostly unspeakable possibility of gay female desire to emerge as subtext throughout their work. This nuanced interplay among tropes of gender, sexuality, and the coupling of religions crossed the boundaries of work and life. It eventually extended into the manic, volatile relationship of Leonard and Virginia themselves.

THE BACKLASH

The works of Proust, Joyce, Woolf, Kafka, and de Lacretelle offer just a few examples of how authors had built on Disraeli's "blank page" template to advocate the cosmopolitan ethos in the 1900s, 1910s, and 1920s. But there were numerous other literary examples following the same topography. American expatriate authors gathering at Gertrude Stein and Alice B. Toklas's famous salons at 27 rue de Fleurus expanded on the allegory in the mid-1920s. Then-twenty-seven-year-old Ernest Hemingway's *The Sun Also Rises* (1926) explored the fallout from an affair between a sexually compulsive, twice-divorced, Jewish former boxer, Robert Cohn, and an aristocratic WASP divorcee, Lady Brett Ashley. The affair is perceived through Cohn's friend and the novel's central protagonist, the Anglo-Saxon aristocrat, Jake Barnes.[58] F. Scott Fitzgerald's Jewish gangster, Meyer Wolfsheim, in *The Great Gatsby* (1925) and Jewish studio executive Monroe Stahr in his unfinished *The Last Tycoon* (published posthumously in 1941) produced similar notions of Jewish alterity at work within Christian power structures. In the former, Wolfsheim's disgust with the WASP elites with whom he is forced to deal causes him to embrace the ugly image of stereotypical, amoral Jewish greed. In the latter, as Sander Gilman notes, Jewish success in Hollywood is tied to the power of Stahr's erotic magnetism and potent sexuality.[59] The novel's narrator, a teenage Irish-American daughter of one of Stahr's colleagues, is mesmerized by Stahr's Jewish physicality and his superior intellectual acumen.[60] Like de Lacretelle with his unnamed Protestant boy in *Silbermann* and Kafka with his anonymous witnesses of crypto-Jewish animality, Fitzgerald positioned the power of an eroticized Euro-Christian gaze produced by witnessing the deviant carnality of Jewish sexual desire for the non-Jew.

But there was an unintended flip side to this recurrent use of Christian-Jewish erotic entanglement. The categorization of Jews as uncontrollable, carnal animal-humans could just as easily be stripped of irony and nuance and reframed into the very propaganda that Proust, Joyce, Kafka, Woolf, and so many others had worked to problematize. Nativists and eugenicists recognized the double-edged sword of this duplicitous metaphor. They began to use the same tropes to articulate a prohibitive pro-nationalist retrograde argument against Christian-Jewish miscegenation. This inverted the allegory. Rather than arguing for cosmopolitan emancipation, it condemned the constructed "Jew" as a biologically deviant animal-human whose amoral sexual promiscuity represented an existential threat to the purity of the nation-state.

One of the most notable early examples of this pushback can be seen in the work of Otto Weininger. The twenty-three-year-old Jewish-born Catholic convert published his study of the deviant nature of Jewish sexuality, *Sex and Character*, in Vienna in 1903.[61] The book created an enormous scandal after its publication by noted academic Wilhelm Braumüller Verlag. Weininger had placed Jewish sexuality at the center of the violent biological rhetoric of the nascent eugenics movement. Not just a malevolent cultural threat, the "Jew" also represented biological disease based in his flawed masculinity and deviant physiognomy.[62]

Weininger became the public face of an emergent post-Dreyfus, biology-based anti-Semitism. But he was not the first to make this connection. As early as 1899, French nativist Édouard Drumont began critiquing Jews as sexual conquistadors corrupting France with amoral vice.[63] Drumont held a particular fascination for the Svengali-like power of the seductive Jewess. Two years later in London, Joseph Bannister's *England Under the Jews* expressed a similar fear of fifth-column conquest from within through the potent power of Jewish sexuality. Conversely, British writers—including George Bernard Shaw, Arnold White, and Austin Freeman—condemned Jews as complicit in anti-Semitism for their refusal to intermarry.[64] Throughout these texts, the Jewish body was not seen as just deviant physically. It was also suspected of a corrupting, libidinal carnality directed at the chaste, pure Christian.

Weininger, suffering from intense depression, committed suicide mere months after the publication of *Sex and Character*. But the impact of the book was significant. By 1905, most countries in Europe had caught on to the fear of Jewish carnality as an extension of the backlash against modernism and the new sciences. The anti-Semitic forgery, *The Protocols of the Elders of Zion*, was officially published in 1905 in a government-sanctioned first edition in Russia by Sergius Nilus.[65] It was a crude adaptation of a political screed written in 1864 in France by Maurice Joly that originally had nothing to do with Jews. Once adapted for anti-Semitic propaganda, the document purported to reveal how global Jewish cabals withheld loyalty to the nation while pretending to culturally assimilate. For those who suspected Dreyfus (and Disraeli) of carrying hidden treasonous Jewish agendas, the book was "evidence" that the conspiracies were true. The forgery is believed to have been assembled by expatriate Russian propagandist Mathieu Golovinski, then living in France, in 1898.[66] The year was not coincidental. Golovinski's political goal was to save Tsarist Russia from revolutionary threats brought about by the Marxist philosophy of the Bolsheviks. Marx's Jewish background was a ripe target. If Jews could be marked as suspicious—as had happened with Dreyfus in France—then to reject the "International Jew" was to pledge allegiance to the political status quo (in this case, the reign of Nicholas II).

The Protocols had an even broader impact than *Sex and Character*. Amateurishly printed copies were passed around in small, often incomplete forms for nearly a decade. The book received keen interest everywhere, from France, Germany, and Britain to Russia and the United States. But with Nilus's publication in 1905, the book was now seen as legitimate evidence of Jewish disloyalty and hidden agenda throughout Europe. Nilus wrote a preface to his edition claiming that *The Protocols* were notes taken from a secret meeting of rabbis held in Basel, Switzerland, in 1897 during the First Zionist Conference. Copies soon appeared in France, England, and, eventually, the United States.[67] Between 1911 and 1913 in Kiev, Russia, the trial and conviction of Russian Jew Menahem Mendel Beilis for the ritual murder of a young Ukrainian teenager, Andrei Yushchinsky, became a media sensation. The "Beilis Affair" operated as a thematic Dreyfus redux. The Beilis investigation and subsequent trial was built almost entirely on suspicions of Jews as secret practitioners of the blood libel. Popular leaflets of the time drew from the biological pseudosciences of *Sex and Character* and the conspiracy theories of *The Protocols of the Elders of Zion*, producing waves of anti-Semitic backlash throughout Russia and the Ukraine, even as the case collapsed and Beilis was ultimately acquitted.

Adolf Hitler, a young art student in Vienna when *Sex and Character* was published, synthesized the conspiracy theories of *The Protocols* with Weininger's thesis by linking the survival of the nation-state to the purging of the carnality of Jewish animality. This expanded anxieties over a hidden, global Jewish cabal by linking political power to the sexual realm. As Hitler wrote in *Mein Kampf* in 1922:

> The religious teaching of the Jews is principally a collection of instructions for maintaining the Jewish blood pure and for regulating intercourse between the Jews and the rest of the world.[68]

While Hitler praised Jews for maintaining a purity of bloodline, it was "Jewish" thinking that was identified as a form of intellectual, cross-cultural, carnal threat.[69] Hitler's reactionary nativism used the emergent post-*Protocols* anti-Semitism as a motivating force. But he was hardly alone.

By 1918, the Bolshevik revolution in Russia had inspired a new round of mistrust for Jewish "intellectualism" as the source of the revolution. In late 1918, the national quarterly *The Literary Digest* published "Are Bolsheviki Mainly Jewish?"[70] The notion of a hidden, global Jewish cabal working through mass media had taken root. The United States saw similar reactionary movements take hold. In 1922, Henry Ford's weekly newspaper, *Dearborn Independent*, began to publish excerpts connecting *The Protocols* to what he saw as the power of "Jewish" Hollywood. The goal was to force the film industry to purge what Ford saw as a direct link between European Marxism and immigrant Jewry.[71] The "Jew" in early screen culture became associated with hyper-intellectualism, shysterism, and a general betrayal of Christian mores.

This anxiety was not confined to the United States, Europe, and Russia. Literary scholar Erin Graff Zivin has shown how "Jewishness" quickly became a metaphorical body representing disease, prostitution, and vice that traveled throughout Latin American literature at the turn of the twentieth century.[72] Novels such as Jorge Isaac's *Maria* (Columbia, 1897), Ruben Dario's *Los raros* (Nicaragua, 1896), and the short stories of Argentinean author Jorge Luis Borges played with the idea of an ephemeral, transnational "Jewishness" as the conduit by which an emerging global media spread throughout Latin America.[73] Argentinean Jewish newspaper editor Jacobo Timerman made this point in his autobiography when he noted that Marx, Freud, and Einstein were at the core of an irrational and sudden spike in anti-Semitism. Timerman offered his reasons as to why:

> Karl Marx, because he tried to destroy the Christian concept of society; Sigmund Freud, because he tried to destroy the Christian concept of the family; and Albert Einstein, because he tried to destroy the Christian concept of time and space.[74]

Timerman's quote led popular cultural theorist Christopher Hitchens to describe Marx, Freud, and Einstein as three members of an "anti-Trinity," a triptych modernist Jewish assault on the core institutions and concepts that defined European Christian power.[75] Together, Freud, Marx, and Einstein provoked anxieties of recolonization throughout South America. Citing author Rebecca West, Hitchens described how a culture war emerged between the reassurance narratives offered by postcolonial Christianity and the "disintegrating ideas of skepticism" that became embodied by the figural Jewish Other.[76] As early as 1919, Albert Einstein was aware of how his biography played a role in adjudicating reception to his work:

By an application of the theory of relativity to the taste of readers; to-day in Germany I am called a German man of science, and in England I am represented as a Swiss Jew. If I come to be represented as a bête noire, the descriptions will be reversed, and I shall become a Swiss Jew for the Germans and a German man of science for the English![77]

Einstein's joke about his "relative" identity as Jew/German, depending on where one stood on his physics, foregrounded the slippages of emancipated European Jewishness. For those who accepted the theory of relativity, Einstein was viewed, like Benjamin Disraeli before him, as an exemplar of the modern nation. For those upset by what Einstein had revealed about their cosmos, he would be marked, like Alfred Dreyfus, as a rootless member of a disloyal Diaspora.[78]

Both the Jew and science became twinned as entangled transmissions of biological deviancy via the expression of sexual neuroticism. Marx, Freud, and Einstein were disparate social and physical scientists, working in different fields and in different national contexts. Their work was unconnected, save for one critical distinction. The merits of their work were informed by the perceived link between Jewish Otherness and late modernism. Jews were increasingly being understood as the spreaders of an intellectual pathology informed by the biological sciences. For the champions of these scholars, the solution to this anxiety was privileging entanglement itself as a new form of being. If Christianity and Judaism could be reconfigured as relational, codependent forms, fears of the "anti-Trinity" could be overcome. For the nativists, modern thinking fractured European-centric holism. It was a form of intellectual debasement that could only lead to carnality, vice, and spiritual decay.

This reactionary panic had direct literary antecedents. Citing Julia Kristeva's work on anti-Semitic fantasy, Judith Halberstam argues that the psychology of Gothic horror texts—such as Mary Shelley's *Frankenstein* (1818) and Bram Stoker's *Dracula* (1897)—was responding to anxieties of a supernatural Jewish body haunting Anglo-Christian society.[79] Frankenstein's new-science monster and Dracula's blood-sucking predator both pull from blood libel, the Golem myth of Prague, and understandings of European Jewry as diseased parasites lurking within the nation-state.[80] This can also be seen in the character of Fagin in Charles Dickens's *Oliver Twist*. Fagin's interest in corrupting young Christian children, and especially his desire for the Anglo-Saxon idealized innocence of Oliver, operates as a barely coded metaphor for child molestation.[81] By the time of George Du Maurier's enormously successful *Trilby* (1894), which features the hypnotic Jewish character named Svengali, European writers were expressing both fear and desire over the erotic power of supernatural Jewish mind control.[82] The monstrous Jewish body had become a corporeal road map to express anxieties of emergent biological theory and the new sciences.

Mein Kampf updated this threat by emphasizing the notion of the national body politic as a metaphorical human body. Hitler's insight was not to reject the figural metaphors of modernism and the new sciences but instead to reappropriate them. As Daniel Boyarin points out in his reading of Freud, modern psychoanalytic discourses on race were infused with a hidden binary between "Aryan" and "Jew."[83] Hitler embraced this binary while simultaneously recalibrating it from emancipation to threat. Once the nation-state was a "body," the removal of Jewish thinking was an extension of the purging of the physical Jewish body, a corporeal extension of psychoanalytic relief. Hitler repeatedly used poisonous body terminology in *Mein Kampf* to describe Jewish assimilation, writing that Germans must fight for the "elimination of the Marxist poison from our national body."[84] This updated the carnal, vampiric Jewish predator of European Gothic tradition through the metaphors of the new sciences. Buber's I/Thou Christian-Jewish hybridity was still at work in Hitler's reframing. But it was recalibrated. Buber had outlined the path to an inclusive modernism through the acceptance of intersubjectivity. Hitler's marriage of vampirism and biology represented the nativist response without denying the premise. His eliminationist rhetoric collapsed Charles Swann and Odette, Leopold and Molly Bloom, and Leonard and Virginia Woolf into un-ironic versions of Kafka's jackals, apes, and mice. Instead of avatars of modern complexity, the erotic-taboo desire of Anglo-Christian-Jewish coupling became the central iconography of national-cultural decay.[85]

Hitler's anxiety also extended to the rapid spread of mass media technology as an extension of this carnal miscegenation, writing in *Mein Kampf*:

> Our whole public life today is like a hothouse for sexual ideas and stimulations. Just look at the bill of fare served up in our movies, vaudeville and theaters.[86]

Stage and screen entertainment was the emerging battlefield between nativism and modernism. Jews, once maligned as predatory vampires, perverts, and prostitution peddlers intent on corrupting Christian purity, were reframed by Hitler as carnal embodiments of the most powerful mass media tool of the day: the cinema itself. The American media industries quickly recognized this. Their response was to embrace the very cohabitation that Hitler rejected as a way to envision the ideological clash between nativism and the emerging American "melting pot" ethos. The Anglo-Christian-Jewish coupling in early cinema quickly became an identifiable figuration of this debate. It also ascended, in the 1920s, into one of the most popular entertainment archetypes of the early Hollywood era.

CHAPTER 3

Abie's Irish Rose

IMMIGRANT COUPLINGS,
UTOPIAN MULTICULTURALISM, AND
THE EARLY AMERICAN FILM INDUSTRY

Father Whalen: Now if the Jews and the Irish would only stop fighting, and get together, they'd own a corner of the world!
Rabbi: You're right, Father, and I think they ought to start getting together right here!

ABIE'S IRISH ROSE: A COMEDY IN THREE ACTS (1924)

W ITH MILLIONS OF NEWLY ARRIVED AMERICAN IM-
migrants seeking entertainment in the early 1900s, representations of assimilation through intermarriage provided an obvious, appealing, pro-melting-pot allegory. European literature had already forged the path. The literary couplings depicted by Disraeli, Proust, Kafka, and Joyce easily adapted into the storytelling apparatus of American mass media. But while those authors tempered their hopes in response to an increasingly nativist, divided Europe, American cinema of the 1910s and 1920s was far more utopian. Early American cinema repeatedly depicted the platonic, romantic, and erotic couplings of Jew and Anglo-Christian as untempered, unbridled joy, a celebratory marker of the ascendant Americanism triumphing over the European nativism that so many immigrants had left behind. The economic benefits were also clear. The union of Jews and Anglo-Christians offered the American media industries a clear template for a multi-ethnic, industrial self-inscription.

These early screen coupling fantasies emerged primarily in two popular genres: slapstick Irish-Jewish romantic immigrant screwball comedies and melodramatic "ghetto Jewess" love stories. Both genres contained literary and stage antecedents. European Jews and Irish Catholics had already been established as familiar comedy teams in popular vaudeville sketches that had toured the country for decades. Irish-Jewish culture clash comedy had broad appeal, serving as ethnic stand-ins for numerous immigrant subcultures including Italians, Poles, Russians, and other Eastern European minorities. In its most familiar form, exemplified by *The Cohens and Kellys* serials (1904–1933), Irish and Jewish families are brought together when their children decide to get married. Both ethnic groups mine comedy by alternating between their similarities (immigrant status) and differences (religion). The comedy of manners and riffs on stereotype are brought into further relief when both families face the recognition that the next generation has little interest in continuing the ethnic practices of the old world.

These comedies of intermarriage played off a culture clash not only along the Irish/Jewish axis, but also of a European/American binary. The successful marriage of Irish Catholic and Jew didn't just exemplify a new America. It also rejected European classicism while satirizing the desire of non-Anglo ethnics to reach the same level of power as the entrenched Brahmin American aristocracy. The early American film industry, at first centered in New York, discovered the economic value in catering to these emerging audiences. One- and two-reeler Anglo-Christian-Jewish love and friendship gag-based sketches offered a populist salve for immigrants at the nickelodeon. They articulated a clear break with the nativist backlash taking place in both Europe and the United States. But they also provided a response to the institutions of repression from which millions of newly minted Americans had fled. In the emerging urban ghettos of major American cities such as New York, Chicago, and Boston, early American cinema provided an ideological salve.

Throughout the 1900s, 1910s, and early 1920s, American English and Yiddish cinema was replete with examples dramatizing the assimilationist American immigrant experience through Anglo-Christian-Jewish intermarriage. One- and two-reelers, mostly gag-based sketches that trafficked in obvious ethnic stereotypes, were screened in nickelodeons, penny arcades, storefront movie theaters, and throughout numerous vaudeville circuits. Films such as *The Yiddisher Boy* (1909), *Judith of Bethulia* (1914), and the Cohen serial films and features (1904–1933) exemplified the transformative journey of the immigrant ethnic into assimilated American. Both genres also showed remarkable resiliency as cinema began to transition from actualities and spectacles into a developed, cohesive narrative grammatology.

The pinnacle of this first-wave ascension occurred in concert with the height of the Jazz Age from 1926 to 1928. The most famous example can be seen in the widespread critical and cultural impact of *The Jazz Singer* in 1927.[1] The iconic sync-sound film remains the most famous legacy of the Anglo-Christian-Jewish love story in early screen culture.[2] But it was

Film promotional poster for Abie's Irish Rose *(1928).*

hardly alone. Five major Hollywood films, each released within eighteen months of the other, built their narratives around established Anglo-Christian-Jewish coupling templates. In addition to *The Jazz Singer*, *The Cohens and Kellys* (1926), *Private Izzy Murphy* (1926), *Surrender* (1927), and *Abie's Irish Rose* (1928) all featured visibly Jewish protagonists struggling to either assimilate or transcend institutional barriers and obstacles. In each of these texts, the marker of final ascension into American life featured a variation of either intermarriage or a thematic Anglo-Christian-Jewish coupling. Jewish protagonists caught between worlds (European/American or American Jewish/American assimilationist) sought out the love of the Anglo-Christian partner to resolve conflicting loyalties between old world (ghetto Jewish) and new (assimilated Christian). Their successful union had to overcome both generational and sociopolitical objections to intermarriage. In so doing, the Anglo-Christian-Jewish coupling forged an ideological argument that also championed the cultural importance of the American film industry itself.

THE IRISH-JEWISH COMEDY TEAMS

Patricia Erens argues that 1909 was the first year that Jewish-themed films began to link Jewish moral codes with the Gentile majority culture in which they took place.[3] *The Yiddisher Boy*, a three-minute short produced and directed in Philadelphia by Sigmund Lubin, provided a remarkably complex portrayal of early American ghetto life. The short depicted a tale of friendship between two children, one Jewish and the other Catholic, over many years. The film begins as the story of a boy named Moses. Moses works to support his family by selling newspapers. When another newsboy tries to rob him of his money, an Irish boy named Ed helps to save him. To thank him, Moses invites Ed for Shabbat dinner. The detailed set design featured in the subsequent Shabbat dinner sequence features one of the most overt early screen examples of first-generation immigrant Jewish life. The tableaux then shifts to twenty-five years later when the adult Moses, a successful merchant, runs into Ed, who is down on his luck and in desperate need of help. Moses returns the favor he received as a child by hiring Ed. The film ends with Ed and Moses, non-Jew and Jew, going into a successful business venture together.

But *The Yiddisher Boy* was also a more nuanced version of an already popular series of one-reelers that paired Irish and Jewish immigrant families in hapless, comedic partnerships. One of the earliest examples can be located in 1903. Mutoscope & Biograph Company released a filmed version of an ethnic vaudeville sketch called "Levi and Cohen, the Irish Comedians." Early New York film production had just begun marketing Anglo-Christian-Jewish couplings to appeal to the multi-ethnic urban penny arcade markets. These storefronts were dominated by first-generation immigrant customers. The profit motivation was an obvious one. The one-reeler *Levi and Cohen, the Irish Comedians* featured two comedians entering a vaudeville stage in front of a painted storefront. The two figures, one in a bowler hat and the other in a top hat and ill-fitting tuxedo, represent the easily identifiable stereotypes of an immigrant Irishman and Jew. The two get into an argument and proceed to hit each other, emulating the popular "knockabout" vaudeville comedy teams of the era. As the film progresses, it becomes clear that Levi and Cohen are not good entertainers. The off-screen crowd begins to pelt both actors with eggs, interrupting their clownish slapstick antics. Both are forced to flee the stage in shame.

The film's physical comedy was consistent with much of the slapstick excess that Tom Gunning defines as central to the attraction strategy of early cinema.[4] But a second layer of meaning exists underneath the obvious slapstick and ethnic stereotypes. By placing the audience into the events on screen, the film foregrounds a self-reflexive awareness regarding the offensive stereotyping taking place on stage. This inverts the comedic address, satirizing the over-reliance on ethnic stereotypes in vaudeville while demonstrating how the episodic format had inadvertently given rise to exhaustive, overplayed tropes. The Irish had dominated vaudeville comedy as early as the 1860s. Jewish immigrants of the 1880s and 1890s subsequently filled vaudeville theaters with similar stereotype comedy. This led to creative inter-ethnic mixing decades before the one-reelers of the nickelodeon era. By the time early filmmakers began to capture vaudeville performances on film, Irish-Jewish stereotypes were a well-entrenched and easily recognizable trope. *Levi and Cohen, the Irish Comedians* indicts this form of ethnic comedy as hacky by depicting an audience in revolt.

In 1904, the innovative director Edwin Porter released a one-reeler based on a popular vaudeville sketch called "Cohen's Advertising Scheme." Similar to *Levi and Cohen, the Irish Comedians*, *Cohen's Advertising Scheme* at first trafficked in obvious stereotypes. Cohen is presented as an obvious immigrant Jew and a clownish, greedy shop owner. He tricks a passerby into purchasing a large coat. When the customer is distracted, Cohen hangs a sign advertising his store on the back of the coat. *Cohen's Advertising Scheme* was the first of many "scheming merchant" comedy shorts to play in the urban markets.[5] It was also one of the first to identify a simple form of comedy: the stereotypical Jew engaging, and subverting, the Gentile world in which he lived. Three years later, in *Cohen's Fire Sale* (1907), the now hat-selling Cohen nearly goes bankrupt when his hats aren't selling, so he creates an "accidental" fire in his shop to collect insurance money.[6] This depiction of the immigrant Jewish shopkeeper as amoral and willing to do "anything for a buck" was a popular comedic trope.

In 1907, the same year of *Cohen's Fire Sale*, "nickel madness" was breaking out in New York and other major cities. Unofficial reports claimed that one nickelodeon in lower Manhattan was generating nearly two thousand dollars in a week.[7] Irish, Italian, Polish, and Jewish immigrants made up the vast majority of paying customers. Catering to this audience became a matter of representation. Jewish representations proved particularly popular with Jewish and non-Jewish audiences alike because Jews were easily identified through stereotypical garb, clichéd "Jewish" hand gestures, beards, hats, and overcoats. These sorts of overtly stereotypical Jewish representations define the humor of *Levi and Cohen, the Irish Comedians, Cohen's Advertising Scheme, Cohen and Coon* (1906), and the D. W. Griffith–scripted *Old Isaacs, the Pawnbroker* (1908).[8] However, whatever humor was mined through stereotype was tempered by the nobility of cohabitation. Stereotypes produced the laugh. But in acknowledging the shared, collective plight of all immigrants, these films advocated for a universalism that belied the specificities of ethnic humor.

When *The Yiddisher Boy* was released, in 1909, a shift in Jewish representation emerged that established Jewish-Christian intersubjectivity as an ideal within pro-immigrant American cinema. The film's depiction of a successful Christian-Jewish business "marriage" expanded on the comedic Jewish-Catholic interplay developed in the Cohen serials. In *Cohen Saves the Flag* (1913), Mack Sennett's Keystone Company embarked on a lavish Civil War spectacle that rivaled D. W. Griffith's work of the period. This time Cohen, played by pre-Chaplin Keystone star Ford Sterling, finds himself a sergeant in the Union army. While Sterling's portrayal continues the stereotypes of the period, Cohen's heroic role in saving the infantry marked the first of an emerging complexity of depiction found outside of crass stereotype.

Like the modernist writers of Europe, early filmmakers had stumbled on a potent totemic binary. The transgressive generational break of Jewish desire for Christian partnership exemplified the crumbling barriers and changing social mores of ghettoized Europeans transformed into multiculturalist Americans. But ghetto-busting Anglo-Christian-Jewish partnership also served as an argument for the acceptance of early cinema itself. If Jews and Christians could successfully overcome the barriers of entry institutionalized by the ethnic enclaves of the Victorian era, then so too could the expansive industry of early screen entertainment. By 1909, the pattern was firmly established. The nascent pre-Hollywood cinema industry recognized the value of Anglo-Christian-Jewish couplings as an ideologically emancipatory meta-text. One that argued for an inclusive "melting pot" Americana explicitly at odds with the European divisions simultaneously taking place in the old world that so many millions had left behind.

THE GHETTO JEWESS

If the early Irish-Jewish screwballs focused primarily on economics as assimilation, the other popular genre of the era, the ghetto Jewess love story, thematized the same idea through carnal sexuality. Throughout the 1910s and 1920s, the erotic seductress identified as the "ghetto Jewess" was a unique representation of female sexuality. The most common representation of the (white) female was that of a passive victim under assault from rogue, prurient men, but ultimately saved by the noble, virtuous, fully masculine hero. This chaste, innocent icon of female passivity, victimhood, and sexlessness was primarily emodied by the white, virginal Christian female of European art traditions.[9] This idealized Anglo-Saxon virginity was often seen in a racial context. By the late 1910s and early 1920s, black, Latino, and Asian men were presented as either rape-inclined savages or swarthy seducers overcome with primal lust for the highest currency of femininity—the innocent, white Christian virgin.

Cecil B. DeMille produced numerous shorts in the 1910s depicting the struggles of young, white Christian males to control their sexuality in the face of desire for the white Christian female. If sexual desire was consummated in these early screen narratives, it inevitably led to the end of civilization.[10] Two films in 1915 racialized this dynamic. The hour-long urban melodrama directed by Cecil B. DeMille, *The Cheat*, and D. W. Griffith's *Birth of a Nation* both depicted the dangers of unconstrained ethnic sexuality to entrenched Anglo-Christian society. In one of most famous sequences in *Birth of a Nation*, a period piece examining the chaos after the end of the Civil War, a young, virtuous, chaste, Southern white female comes under attack from the uncontained sexuality of a newly freed African-American former slave. His lascivious pursuit drives the young woman to kill herself by jumping off a cliff rather than submit to rape. Similarly, *The Cheat* depicted the attempted rape of a married white woman (Fannie Ward) at the hands of a wealthy Japanese businessman, played by silent film heartthrob Sessue Hayakawa. When she resists his advances, Hayakawa's character holds her down and brands her shoulder with a hot iron, defiling her skin and declaring that she is now his property.

Despite the differing settings and historical contexts, Griffith's indictment of African-American sexuality and DeMille's exoticized fetishization of Japanese savagery located the white, Christian female as the ultimate sexual prize. Both films also trafficked in the spectatorial titillation of revealing transgressive and deviant sexual desires. Six years before Rudolph Valentino emerged in the Jazz Age to embody a swarthy icon of ethnic, libertine sexual freedom, both Griffith and DeMille were exploring the fears (and desires) of unconstrained "ethnic" sexuality. They did this by locating the virtuous state of the Christian virgin at the heart of numerous dramatic tableaux.

The ghetto Jewess archetype functioned in direct contrast to this construction of an idealized, chaste Christian female. She was a glamorous, eroticized figure, explicitly carnal, sexual, and unconstrained by modesty. The archetype first emerged in the United States as an erotic figure of sexual agency in dime novels of the 1850s.[11] But the character was biblical in origin. In the Bible, Jewish women such as Eve, Tamar, Judith, and Queen Esther each used their power of sexuality to express various forms of political agency, personal ambition, or erotic desire. For millennia, Jews had been identified in Christian literature, art, and theater as the embodiment of deviancy, carnality, and exotic temptation.[12] Screen Jewesses extended this tradition to early cinema.[13] They offered a solution for early filmmakers who desired to depict female sexual agency without crossing the Victorian-era sensibility that required white Christian women to remain in a state of virginal purity.

But there was one caveat. In expressing female sexual desire, the Jewess was required in nearly all cases to direct that erotic impulse at the requisite Anglo-Christian male.[14] This implicitly (or perhaps explicitly) rejected the notion of Jewishness as a distinct, hermetic Diaspora. Thematically paralleling the Jesus of the New Testament, the Jewess's selection of the Christian partner was also an act of de-selection. It rejected her Jewish past in favor of a new identity in the future. The visualization of Jewish sexual agency was empowered precisely because it ultimately acquiesced to the modern Anglo-Christian world.

Between 1910 and 1915, dozens, perhaps hundreds, of one- and two-reeler ghetto Jewess love stories were produced and distributed to urban nickelodeon halls, fairground theaters, and vaudeville houses. D. W. Griffith's *A Child of the Ghetto* (1910) echoed his earlier *Romance of a Jewess* (1908) to privilege the Jewess as an agent of sexual emancipation. The earlier film's protagonist, Ruth, ultimately chooses a practical Jewish husband over the romantic temptations of the non-Jew. But her rejection of her religious family's efforts at an arranged marriage represents what Joyce Antler calls an early thematic Americanization process.[15] *A Child of the Ghetto* was even more explicit in its championing of intermarriage as an emancipatory act. Despite its infantilizing title, the film portrays the sexual awakening of a young Jewish woman through a mixture of thematic and literal intermarriage. The titular child of the ghetto is a young Jewish woman also named Ruth (Dorothy West). An orphaned teenager, she runs away from the Lower East Side ghetto after being accused of a crime. She ends up in the country where she falls in love with a young Anglo-Saxon American farmer. The warm embrace of the farmer's love helps to heal Ruth's traumatic experiences in the ghetto. It offers her new hope of a better life in rural America.

Griffith's championing of rural America as an idealized end point to a fairy tale structure emancipates Ruth. The film's utopian perspective on Anglo-Christian-Jewish intermarriage also stands in stark contrast to Griffith's depiction of miscegenation as rape a few years later in *Birth of a Nation* and DeMille's Orientalist fetishization in *The Cheat* (both 1915). It also proposed the Jewess as a liminal quasi-white ethnic construction given a sexual freedom that other ethnicities, such as black and Japanese, were denied. Interracial intercourse remained the great fear of Victorian-era Anglo-Saxon institutions. But the Americanized Jew was allowed erotic entrance, with one caveat: the Jew had to leave Jewish culture (and Jewish partners) behind.

In 1913, Yiddish film director Sidney Goldin produced three of the most complex portrayals of Anglo-Christian-Jewish ghetto love stories with *The Sorrows of Israel*, *The Heart of a Jewess* (both for Universal Studios), and the most successful ghetto melodrama of the early 1910s, *The Bleeding Hearts, or Jewish Freedom Granted by King Casimir of Poland*. Both *The Sorrows of Israel* and *The Heart of a Jewess* presented young Jewesses struggling with both erotic desire for non-Jewish men and their desire to immigrate and assimilate in the United States.[16] Another film released that year, *The Jew's Christmas*, codified the ultimate act of assimilation, the Jewish acceptance of Christmas. A year later, both *A Passover Miracle* and *Faith of Her Fathers* linked the temptation of the non-Jewish (Christian) male as an extension of a religious quandary. In each of these shorts, spatial movement, ethno-religious transformation, and American assimilation were linked through Anglo-Christian-Jewish couplings. So long as the "Jewess" sought an Anglo-Saxon partner, her agency was upheld.

In 1914, Griffith's *Judith of Bethulia* marked his first significant foray into the biblical epic. It also tested the grounds for the multi-narrative complexities that would define *Intolerance* in 1916. Like many of Griffith's films, *Judith of Bethulia* is biblical in origin. Judith, a young Jewish woman living in a small village, finds her community under siege from an invading Assyrian army. She must use her sexuality to seduce the army's general, Holofernes, to save her town from annihilation.[17] Judith's expression of sexuality creates what Miriam Hansen terms a "fiction of erotic reciprocity." The threat of death and self-sacrifice inform the erotic tantalization of the onscreen coupling. Judith's submission to Holofernes is exoticized and fetishized.[18] Griffith's Jewess expresses an empowered female sexuality under the safe narrative confines of performing a noble, self-sacrificial goal. Denatured of any alignment with the crisis of American Anglo-Saxon institutional power, Jewish females such as Judith offered Griffith what the Christian female could not: the ability to perform voluntary acts of sexual

The Ghetto Jewess as erotic temptress in Judith of Bethulia *(1914).*

agency. Griffith did not, apparently, object to the notion of the sexualized female seeking at least a variation of miscegenation coupling.[19]

The Jewess-as-seductress was not confined to American cinema. In his analysis of the 1920 German silent film *The Golem: How He Came into the World* (*Der Golem, wie er in die Welt kam*), Omer Bartov notes that the character of Miriam Loew (Lyda Salmonova) uses the specifics of the Jewess archetype as a metaphor for generational change taking place in Weimar Germany. Her erotic desire for the Christian/Aryan male is once again the forbidden fruit at the center of a generational break. Miriam is the young adult daughter of the Rabbi Loew (Albert Steinruck), the legendary Prague rabbi who invented the Golem to save the Jews from annihilation. Mitigating the Jewish-specific nature of the Golem as avenging, proto-Frankenstein monster, Miriam seeks out and seduces the Aryan knight, Florian (Lothar Müthel), the embodiment of non-Jewish masculinity. Their coupling humanizes and universalizes the Jewish specificity of the narrative, allowing non-German spectators to identify with Miriam's journey.[20]

But perhaps the most pervasive image of the seductress ghetto Jewess was the cartoon character of Betty Boop. Fleischer Studios, founded by Jewish cartoonists Max and Dave Fleischer in New York in 1921, introduced Betty

Boop as their first "talkie" cartoon in 1930. Fleischer Studios was a fledgling animation studio set up in direct competition with the then-emerging Walt Disney Studios. Despite eventual struggles with the Hays Code in the mid-1930s, Fleischer Studios designed Betty Boop as a raunchy, sexualized cartoon depiction of the ghetto Jewess fantasy meant to appeal to the urban nickelodeon and vaudeville markets. Boop's design reflected the short-skirt stereotype of the libertine Jazz Age flapper. Her Jewish background was communicated through her squeaky, accented voice and the frequent use of Yiddishisms in the various characters of her world. The teeming tenements depicted in the urban, presumably Lower East Side locations solidified the Jewish specificity of the cartoon milieu.[21]

Boop's family was explicitly identified as Jewish in the episode titled "Minnie the Moocher" in 1932. Early in the twelve-minute short, Betty is berated in pseudo-Yiddish by her yarmulke-wearing father for not finishing her sauerbraten (a German pot roast). Upset and in tears, Betty runs away with her best friend, Bimbo the dog. Betty and Bimbo are then subjected to a series of leering skeletons, ghosts, cats, and other horrific creatures, depicting the savagery of the urban streets. Betty and Bimbo eventually end up watching as a walrus voiced by Cab Calloway sings the warning tale of "Minnie the Moocher." Fleischer's depiction of the leering, sexual horrors of Boop's journey outside the Jewish home took on the same satirical form

Betty Boop is berated by her father in Yiddish for not finishing her sauerbraten in this still from the 1932 episode, "Minnie the Moocher."

as Kafka's jackals and apes. But, in Fleischer's inversion, the non-Jews be-came the monstrous predators, targeting the sexual appeal of the volup-tuous Jewess.

Ghetto Jewess love stories did not reflect the statistical realities of actual ghetto life. Intermarriage rates in 1912 between Jews and non-Jews were only 1.17 percent, barely higher than that of interracial marriages, which were only legal in some states at the time.[22] This disparity suggests the ghetto Jewess love story operated as idealized tableaux. When the ghetto Jewess was empowered to express sexual agency toward the non-Jew, the trans-gression thematized the generational shift taking place in first-generation Americans. These tensions were as much about class as ethnicity or reli-gion. Ghetto Jewesses were invariably securing their exit from the ghetto. Romantic love for the non-Jew expressed desired economic emancipation. The narrative crisis is ultimately not on the romantic desires of the Jewess or her love interest, but instead on the Jewish patriarch who must accept his daughter's intermarriage at the cost of his cultural traditions.[23] The agency of the Jewish female to determine her own life also acted as an intergenera-tional act of negation. After successful coupling, she could consider the old world officially over.

Representations of empowered female Jewish sexuality also had an in-dustrial function for the nascent U.S. film industry. The radical potential for early cinema to portray and disseminate a form of sexual deviancy was being connected by numerous government investigations to the ubiquity of Jewish media ownership of the nickelodeons. As in post-Dreyfus Europe, American Jews were also being accused of spreading Communist ideology as a form of corruption of white, Anglo-Saxon purity.[24] Ghetto Jewess love stories subverted both these accusations. The sexually desirable but also no-ble and virtuous ghetto Jewess relocated anxieties of Jewish masculine per-version into the less threatening realm of female sexuality. When the Jewess sought love with the non-Jewish (Christian) male partner, she denatured any threat of Jewish sexual deviancy. This performed both a political and an industrial argument. The ghetto Jewess rejected stereotypes of Jews as contemptuous of non-Jews. But, perhaps even more importantly, she also rejected the notion of the Jewish male as a desirable sexual partner when a superior (Christian) form of masculinity presented itself as a viable option.

IRISH ROSES AND JEWISH JAZZ SINGERS

Two decades of popular Irish-Jewish immigrant comedies and ghetto Jewess love stories had firmly established the ideological and economic benefits of the Anglo-Christian-Jewish coupling in popular American cinema. The peak of this first wave occurred in the late 1920s when five major studio productions, all released between 1926 and 1928, updated the familiar elements of both genres within big-budget narratives of Jazz Age libertine emancipation. In *The Cohens and Kellys* (1926), *Private Izzy Murphy* (1926), *The Jazz Singer* (1927), *Surrender* (1927), and *Abie's Irish Rose* (1928), visible Anglo-Christian-Jewish love stories moved to the center of Hollywood cinema at the height of the country's roaring 1920s political and cultural liberalism. *The Cohens and Kellys* and *Private Izzy Murphy* offered updated big-budget variations on the hundreds of screwball Catholic-Jewish immigrant shorts and features screened throughout the 1910s and early 1920s. *The Cohens and Kellys* followed the popular Cohen comedy shorts that dated to as early as 1904, recreating standard vaudeville-era family cultural clashes in which stereotypical Irish and Jewish families struggle to cohabit as a result of the impending marriage of their children. The film's massive popularity led to the quick production of five successive travelogue sequels. In *The Cohens and the Kellys in Paris* (1928), *The Cohens and Kellys in Atlantic City* (1929), *The Cohens and the Kellys in Scotland* (1930), *The Cohens and the Kellys in Africa* (1930), and *The Cohens and Kellys in Trouble* (1933), the vaudevillian sketch pattern was repeated to diminishing box-office success.

Private Izzy Murphy introduced a new wrinkle into this familiar Irish/Jewish screwball configuration. For two decades, Irish-Jewish coupling comedies were contemporary, meant to reflect the experiences of the immigrant audiences that paid nickels or bought tickets to see them. *Private Izzy Murphy* was a period piece. Distributed by Warner Bros. in October 1926, the film was a comedy about the ethnic tensions in the military during World War I. It starred popular stage entertainer George Jessel as Izzy Goldberg, a Jewish store owner living in an Irish neighborhood in New York City. Playing off the stereotype of the Jewish shop owner as economically unscrupulous, Izzy decides to change his name to the Irish-sounding "I. Patrick Murphy" to help his business flourish. Izzy/Patrick subsequently meets the Irish Eileen Cohannigan (Patsy Ruth Miller), setting up a familiar vaudevillian comedy framework of mistaken identity. Eileen falls in love with Izzy/Patrick, assuming he is Irish. He is eventually drafted and then wounded in France after fighting heroically in World War I. The experiences of the war trigger guilt in Izzy/Patrick, who decides to write Eileen from his hospital bed and reveal that he is actually Jewish. After returning home to receive a military parade, Izzy/Patrick sees Eileen standing with his rival for her affections, an Irish-American named Robert O'Malley (Douglas Gerrard). Izzy assumes that his fears have come true: his revelation of his Jewishness has apparently cost him Eileen's love. But the film concludes with the familiar successful transgression of cultural barriers. Eileen declares her love for Izzy, despite their religious differences. The final image is Izzy and Eileen heading toward the marriage bureau to get married.[25]

Even with its period setting, *Private Izzy Murphy* was a cash grab made partially in an attempt to mine the theatrical success of *Abie's Irish Rose* on Broadway and in tandem with that play's upcoming film adaptation. The casting of Jessel, the originator of the role of Jack Robin in *The Jazz Singer*, furthered the circulation of Jewish performers at work in the popular intercultural religious films of the era. The unapologetically overt Jewish-Irish hybrid name of the titular character, Izzy Murphy, demonstrated the fearless nature of Irish and Jewish subject matter in 1920s Hollywood. It also offered a proud miscegenation of two immigrant cultures, playing up the notion that ethnic stereotypes were nothing more than cultural masks. Izzy has no problem passing as "Patrick," both in the American military and in Eileen's eyes. But the period piece also suggested an increasing exhaustion with the format. The familiar template of Irish-Jewish coupling had become so ingrained in American popular media by the mid-1920s that it was also quickly becoming a historical relic.

While *The Cohens and Kellys* and *Private Izzy Murphy* trafficked in familiar genre tropes, the enormous cultural impact of *The Jazz Singer* in 1927 elevated Anglo-Christian-Jewish coupling to its most visible status as arbiter of mass media cultural transformation. Jakie Rabinowitz (Al Jolson), the son of an orthodox cantor in a synagogue, is torn between his loyalty to his Jewish culture and his desire to become a jazz singer on Broadway. Jakie's duality is symbolized in a number of ways. His name change from Jakie Rabinowitz to Jack Robin suggests the de-Judaizing process as required by assimilation. His donning of blackface externalizes this transformation through the minstrel show traditions of racial mimicry.[26] Jakie/Jack's transformation is also marked through the film's technological breakthrough. When Jolson began speaking off the cuff while playing piano early in the film, the sync-sound era famously began. This act of crossing from silent to sync-sound cinema was thematized by the ethnotransformative shift from the Jewish Jakie to the American Jack. As Jakie/Jack finds his metaphorical voice as an American, he also finds his literal voice through the film's introduction of sound. Warner Bros. used a familiar genre template to connect Jewish assimilation to the rapidly developing technologies of early sound cinema.

The play, written by Samson Raphaelson, had been a hit on Broadway for George Jessel beginning in 1925, playing in tandem on the Great White Way with the box-office-shattering *Abie's Irish Rose*. The film's link between

Still from The Jazz Singer *(1927), in which Jack Robin's (Al Jolson) identity crisis as an assimilating Jew is mediated by performative blackface, the love of Mary Dale (May McAvoy), and the introduction of the film's breakthrough synchronized sound.*

the performative nature of ethnic identity and the new technology of sync-sound also worked in a unique way to visualize what Michael Rogin and Vincent Brook describe as the unique insider/outsider duality of American Jewish identity.[27] The film was therefore both universally relatable in its technological spectacle while remaining ethnically distinct in its subject matter.[28]

This tension informs the aesthetics of *The Jazz Singer*. The film is only partially synchronized. The sync-sound sequences, when they appear, are deliberate elements of the narrative.[29] Jolson's synched talking/singing voice and the film's silent sequences each represent different moments in the problematic transformation of Jakie Rabinowitz into Jack Robin. This is also reflected in Jakie/Jack's transition between his presumed Jewishness/whiteness and his black minstrel performances on the stage.[30] The use of blackface occurs, as Matthew Frye Jacobson notes, not only to "change the race of the Jew, but also to eradicate race from *Judaism*."[31] Together, minstrel/whiteness and silence/sound are both externalized oscillations of Jakie/Jack's internal transformation from ethnic Jew to fully white American.

Decades of scholarship have focused on the film primarily in terms of its technological and ethno-representational perspectives on Jolson's use of blackface. But there is a third element at work that links technology to ethnic transformation. Jack's first spoken lines famously occur in an off-the-cuff riff as he sits at the piano and sings to his doting Yiddishe mama. But his affections gradually shift from his Jewish mother to his love interest, the secular, presumably Protestant Mary Dale (May McAvoy). The two women form the third metaphorical duality that expresses Jakie/Jack's journey. As Rogin notes, Jack loses the power of synchronized speech at specific moments when he is torn between his loyalty to his Jewish culture and his desire to enter the Jazz Age.[32] Jolson's reclamation of his voice occurs in the film's penultimate scenes, as he gets closer to joining Mary Dale, free of the (Jewish) family burdens and loyalties that he carries. It is only after the death of his father that Jack finds his metaphorical (and literal) voice long enough to verbalize both his love and his completed journey of becoming American.

This occurs in two musical sequences at the end of the film. Jack's performance as a Jew singing "Kol Nidre" for his father in temple operates as dual requiems for Jack's father and Jack's former Jewishness. His triumphant version of "Mama" on Broadway, which he sings to his mother in the audience, marks his ascent into the American popular culture mainstream. Jack's mother simultaneously approves of Jack's transformation and his selection of a Christian wife. As Mary Dale watches from the wings, it is through her spectatorial gaze that Jakie finally becomes Jack, Jack becomes American, and silent cinema fully turns to sound. The shift from Mama to Mary Dale performs a mimetic transfer for the presumably immigrant audience. Mary Dale is the Anglo-Christian witness, the proxy spectator who allows Jolson's stage Jewishness to embody the film's and, by extension, the country's transformation.

As Patricia Erens notes, the "shiksa" stereotype exemplified by Mary Dale and soon to be codified across the next nine decades of popular literature, theater, cinema, and television, emerged fully formed for the first time in *The Jazz Singer*.[33] Irish-Catholic love interests had been paired with Jews for years. But the Irish were perceived as loosely equivalent to Jews in immigrant class status, if not religious identity. Mary Dale marked a different level of assimilation. While the film is never explicit on this point, her already assimilated, Anglo-Saxon status reconfigured her as the embodiment of elite, Brahmin, WASP aristocracy. Like Disraeli's Mary Anne a half-century earlier, Jack's Mary Dale provided a final step for acquiescence to the ethno-racial political power structure he sought to enter. The film's technological and generational "voice" championed familiar ideas of cultural pluralism, romantic desire, and the secular nature of the Jazz Age. But it also introduced a next-level marker of assimilation: the Jewish male's acquisition of the final prize, the idealized, privileged, all-American, Anglo-Saxon female.

One other major studio release of 1927, *Surrender*, focused on a Jewish-Gentile coupling. But this was the rare film of the era to offer a historical rather than a contemporary perspective. A sweeping Jewish ghetto melodrama set in historical Austria, the film combined the themes of Goldin and Griffith's ghetto Jewess love stories from a decade earlier with the emergent big-budget Hollywood spectacle. The title of the film offers a distilled reminder of the appeal of ghetto Jewess love stories. A young Jewess, Lea (Mary Philbin), must decide whether she is willing to surrender sexually to Constantine (Ivan Mozzhukhin), a non-Jewish Russian general, in order to save her shtetl from annihilation. Like Jack's father in *The Jazz Singer*, Lea's father is a rabbi, making her sexual choice both a transgressive act of sublimated desire and a direct refutation of the religious component of Jewish cultural life. Lea acquiesces to sleep with Constantine to save her village from destruction.

But the film frames this scopic pleasure in the context of witnessing the erotic charge of female sexual agency. Like the ghetto Jewesses of the 1910s, Lea's eroticism is embodied by the nature of her ability to make a sexual choice. Her submission to the hyper-masculinity of Constantine also affirmed the normative nature of non-Jewish, white masculinity. Constantine, obsessed by her beauty to the point of madness, embodied the carnality of brute masculinity exemplified by "exotic" male stars of the 1920s, such as Valentino. He was a direct rejection of the singing, dancing, urbane Jewish masculinity depicted by George Jessel and Al Jolson. Jewish men were free to be clowns, dancers, and entertainers. They could win the heart of the chaste, Christian female through talent and ambition. But the Jewess found erotic charge in cohabiting with a different form of masculinity. The transgressive nature of Anglo-Christian-Jewish coupling had developed its own taboo: Jewish-Jewish love.

Surrender presented an unusual counterpoint to *The Jazz Singer*, *Private Izzy Murphy*, and *The Cohens and Kellys* serials and features. The lavish and expensive production values of the sweeping melodrama contained many details of nineteenth-century Russian Jewish shtetl life re-created in exacting detail.[34] This re-creation of a lost Jewish cultural life was one of the film's main selling points. The screen shtetl offered a nostalgia for many first-generation immigrants longing to see realistic re-creations of the world they'd left behind. But the imagery also operated as a thematic critique for the urban ghettos of contemporary American Jewish life.

Unlike the smash Broadway-to-Hollywood success of *Private Izzy Mur-*

phy, *The Jazz Singer*, and *Abie's Irish Rose*, *Surrender* was not a box-office success. It lacked the reassurances of screwball comedy or the triumphant modernism of contemporary (voluntary) couplings. Perhaps because of this darkness, its themes of rape and ambiguity regarding assimilation found little success in the aspirational climate of the late Jazz Age. The age of sound cinema was rapidly replacing the erotic Jewess of the silent era with the fast-talking Clara Bow "It Girl" flapper. The film marked the budgetary pinnacle but also the creative end point for the ghetto Jewess as romantic avatar.[35] The visible Jewish female, with a few notable exceptions, would remain absent from American screens for the next four decades.

Abie's Irish Rose was the last major success of the period to cash in on the familiar archetypes of Irish-Jewish interplay.[36] The 1928 film may be less historically heralded than *The Jazz Singer*, but it was also one of the first talkies and a significant box-office hit in its own right. It was based on the surprise Broadway smash of 1922 authored by Anne Nichols. The comedic beats broke no new ground, trafficking in the broad slapstick Irish-Jewish stereotypes so familiar to audiences of the 1910s and 1920s. The familiar narrative is a star-crossed love story between two young adult children of immigrants, the Jewish Abie Levy (Charles "Buddy" Rogers) and the Irish-Catholic Rosemary Murphy (Nancy Carroll). Like the ethnic comedies that preceded it, *Abie's Irish Rose* was entirely familiar. Abie and Rosemary both struggle to convince their families, her priest, and his rabbi to accept the union. However, the film's innovative use of sound continued the link between Anglo-Christian-Jewish coupling and technological transformation first introduced in *The Jazz Singer*. In one synchronized sound sequence in the film, the events play chronologically as well as generationally. Abie's father chants the kaddish for a non-Jew over the objections of other Jewish elders.[37] Like Jolson's jazz, Abie's kaddish transgresses the insular world of Jewish life to connect with the non-Jew. Synchronized sound signified the universalization of Jewishness through Anglo-Christian-Jewish connection. Even more than *The Jazz Singer*, *Abie's Irish Rose* represented what Erens calls "the definitive statement on intermarriage and assimilation."[38] But each of these films celebrated the assimilationist iconography of Anglo-Christian-Jewish couplings and marked a collective peak of the first wave in Hollywood cinema.

THE PUSHBACK

After the stock market crash of 1929, the backlash against the visibility and perceived economic power of Jews in popular entertainment reached a political tipping point. This pushback had been building for decades. The anti-Semitic canard of Jewish trade merchants as transnational peddlers of sexual filth had been directed at the nascent Hollywood media industries as early as the first years of the twentieth century. This accusation had its origins in the blood libel, the infamous European anti-Semitic myth that argues that Jewish families kidnapped, killed, and then drank the blood of innocent Christian children as a wine substitute in Sabbath rituals.[39] The success of nickelodeons and vaudeville had revived fears that new technologies could operate as an extension of carnal-necrotic Jewish perversion. The fact that so many of these early entertainment halls were Jewish-owned and featured Jewish-produced proto-Hollywood material meant an alignment between anxieties of technology and anxieties of anti-Victorian sexual perversity.

As early as 1909, the year that *The Yiddisher Boy* was released, New York Mayor George B. McClellan Jr. shut down more than five hundred and fifty movie theaters and nickelodeons in a series of raids meant to ferret out deviancy and sexual corruption.[40] Cultural historian Lary May notes how the news of these shutdowns of the mostly Jewish-owned nickelodeons—and specifically the arrest and prosecution of theater owner Jacob Weinberg—was seen among the Jewish immigrant class as a form of pogrom. McClellan's actions were perceived as Catholic antipathy toward the amorality of Jewish-owned and Jewish-produced media product. This perception took hold despite the fact that many of the owners of early cinema production companies, including Biograph and Vitagraph, were not Jewish. Yet, McClellan ignored the larger (non-Jewish-owned) film companies in favor of targeting the Jewish-owned nickelodeons. Just as Hitler eventually critiqued the influence of Jews in screen media in *Mein Kampf,* American nativists cultivated suspicions that Jews were using the nickelodeon to corrupt the purity of white Christian virtue.

A second development in 1908–1909 was the massive cross-cultural success of British playwright Israel Zangwill's *The Melting Pot.* Zangwill used a familiar ghetto love story narrative in his play, unabashedly championing Anglo-Christian-Jewish intermarriage as an essential component of the emerging American melting pot, although at the time, as previously noted, actual intermarriage rates were quite low. The narrative focused on a young adult Russian-Jewish immigrant composer named David Quixano, who aspires to write a distinctly "American" musical. His talents as a composer and his desire to create a new form of uniquely American music thematized much of the changing forms of immigrant-influenced entertainment of early twentieth-century vaudeville. This was especially true as ragtime and early jazz music were just then reaching mainstream popularity.

David's artistic goals are presented in tandem with a love story that drives most of the narrative. David meets and falls in love with Vera, also Russian but Christian and the daughter of an anti-Semitic father. As David and Vera struggle to overcome the entrenched cultural barriers to Christian-Jewish marriage, David also begins to locate his distinctly American form of music in his compositions. Zangwill's link between creative expression and American melting pot cultural pluralism found articulation through the romantic melodrama of David and Vera's courtship.

Zangwill's formula was instantly recognizable. It spoke to the immigrant dreams of millions of newly Americanized young men and women in the first decade of the twentieth century. The figural embodiment of this prosaic metaphor was an interfaith romance story. *The Melting Pot* opened in Washington, DC, in 1909, performing to adoring crowds just a few months after McClellan's nickelodeon shutdowns in New York. It quickly became a key text in the emerging culture wars between nativist and multiculturalist ideologies, the latter being championed enthusiastically by President Teddy Roosevelt. McClellan's vice squads resisted Roosevelt's ideological multiculturalism. They saw the generative function of the new cinema's influence as sexually and defiantly at odds with established American-Christian values. Whatever deviancy and eroticism the new medium offered, it would thereafter frequently be framed by these critics as produced and distributed by an amoral and deviant Jewish merchant class. Zangwill's immigrant drama directly took on this debate. The play popularized the metaphor of America as a mixing of many European cultures, and it did so by aligning the American assimilation journey with romantic love rather than with sexual amorality.[41] But American-Christian nativists were not the play's only critics. It also provoked a backlash in the Jewish community against the play's blatant support of Christian-Jewish intermarriage.[42] Like Proust before him (and Disraeli before Proust), Zangwill used Anglo-Christian-Jewish entanglement to challenge nativist fears of immigrants as disloyal infiltrators. In Zangwill's depiction, David was not the money-grubbing Jewish stereotype. He did not have a large beard, talk in a comedic Yiddish dialect, or engage in clownish antics. David was the embodiment of a new form of Americanism. As both Jew and assimilated American, he was directly at odds with McClellan's anxieties about Jewishness as purveyor of prurient filth and sexual deviancy. The romance between Christian and Jew in the text overcame this nativist ghettoization by privileging the healing power of romantic love. But Zangwill's Anglo-Christian-Jewish miscegenation narrative also signified the ascendance of the mass media age. David's professional desire is to become an entertainer. His reinvention from member of the wandering Diaspora to integrated American is exemplified by his ability to compose music for Broadway. This link between Jewish transformation and the popular arts would, of course, crystallize a decade later in popular Hollywood cinema. But this message was already resonating for Jewish and non-Jewish audiences alike in Zangwill's play. The transformative power of Christian-Jewish love emerged as a figural endorsement of the power and value of mass media to transform the immigrant into the American.

The success of *The Melting Pot* in 1908 and 1909 was an early demonstration that representations of Anglo-Christian-Jewish couplings held appeal far beyond Jewish markets. Likewise, the popularity of McClellan's vice raids among American nativists suggested unease with this increasing visibility. The parameters of the conflict were clear.

By the 1920s, as Zangwill's melting pot ethos continued to find expression in the nascent but burgeoning American film industries, nativist backlash grew. Suspicions of Jewish-owned exhibition halls as dens of iniquity reached a fever pitch by the time Henry Ford was publishing excerpts from *The Protocols of the Elders of Zion* in the *Dearborn Independent* in 1922. Between 1920 and 1940, dozens of well-publicized prosecutions, raids, and arrests of Jewish New York book merchants took place around the country.[43] These vice squad investigations were engineered by self-proclaimed Christian government officials, most notably, "vice crusader" John Saxton Sumner, an Episcopalian and a Son of the American Revolution. Like McClellan before him, Sumner believed that Jews were smut merchants. He spent nearly a decade leading a series of prosecutions aimed at the predominantly Jewish bookstore owners and distributors who sold European literature to American audiences via mail-order catalog.[44] His prosecution of Samuel Roth for the distribution of books, including D. H. Lawrence's *Lady Chatterley's Lover* and James Joyce's *Ulysses*, eventually led the increasingly powerful Catholic lobby in Washington to pressure the post office to crack down on mail-order distribution methodology.[45] American Jews were increasingly understood as peddlers of a new form of sexual deviancy that was concurrently emerging from modernist European art and literature, with the Jewish male stereotyped as an amoral sexual libertine spreading illicit material out of both prurient and political motivations.[46]

The police raids on vice halls of the 1910s and 1920s were just a few public examples of the emerging conflict between the perceived Jewishness of America's burgeoning media industries and the American Protestant and Catholic cultural anxieties it provoked. Protestant-led pushes for censorship of media in Washington were less overtly anti-Semitic.[47] But the effort was grounded in the same binary. Both offered examples of how emerging theories of race had fundamentally changed understandings of the "Jewish Question." The perception that assimilated Jews had power over mass media fueled fears of rampant sexual promiscuity in the emerging Jazz Age. The popularity of visual entertainment had congealed into a collective existential threat on the traditions, mores, and values of entrenched Anglo-Christian power.

At the core of this reactionary movement was the pseudoscience of eugenics. Despite the centrality of biological race theory to the Nazi movement in Germany in the 1920s and 1930s, eugenics actually originated as an academic movement among some leading biologists in the United States. Scholars of the new science of biology, inspired by Darwin's theory of evolution and breakthroughs in chromosome isolation in the breeding of farm animals, began to propose regulating human reproduction on moral, physical, and cultural grounds. In 1904, a Harvard professor of zoology, Charles Davenport, received a ten-million-dollar grant from the recently endowed Carnegie Institution of Washington to found an organization focused on the experimental study of human evolution.[48] Davenport's research institute, founded in Cold Spring Harbor, New York, focused on the genetic heredity of diseases and deformities over generations, with an emphasis on the racial makeup of each group studied. In his widely read 1911 book, *Heredity in Relation to Eugenics*, Davenport credited his most positive biological analysis to white Anglo-Saxon Protestants. His "research," made up mostly of anecdotal case studies, likewise found negative, racial characteristics in the Polish, Irish, and Italian groups, with an emphasis on the newly biological category of "Hebrews." Racial mixing constituted, according to Davenport, a "threat from within" to the very fabric of the United States. Were "Hebrews" to have children with white Protestants, their children would be, as Davenport termed it, "more given to crimes of . . . murder, rape, and sex-immorality."[49]

Davenport was at the forefront of negative eugenics, an anti-immigration movement that sought to indirectly influence the genetic makeup of future American generations by limiting "undesirables" from entering the United States. Anxieties about uncontrolled carnality underwrote this racial panic. The first forced sterilization laws, passed in 1907 in Indiana, were a response to the "scientific" study of young men suffering from the perceived degeneracy of excessive masturbation.[50] While the forced sterilization movement in the South primarily targeted blacks, the eugenics movement in the North focused on Jews. As with miscegenation, their fear was Jewish-Christian sexual congress. Eugenicist Madison Grant, author of *The Passing of the Great Race* (1916) and leading voice in New York's virulently pro-eugenics Galton Society, repeatedly focused on the threat of Jews and Catholics "diluting" the genetic purity of white, Anglo-Saxon Protestant stock.[51] Grant described Jewish-Christian procreation as genetic "mongrelization."[52]

The rising influence of the eugenics argument fueled a political backlash in the early 1920s. Coming off a spike in anti-Semitic and xenophobic mistrust in Washington, DC, Congress passed the Emergency Quota Act in 1921. It was the first law to place direct limitations on European immigration by using ethnicity as a guideline.[53] To halt the influx of new ethnicities, the bill linked the annual admission number of new immigrants of any ethnic group to 3 percent of the total population of that ethnic group already in the country. Signed into law on May 19, 1921, by President Warren G. Harding, the law caused a sharp decrease in European immigration, especially Jewish immigration. Still not satisfied, the Catholic-led Immigration Restriction League convinced Congress and President Calvin Coolidge to pass the Johnson-Reed Immigration Act in 1924, which altered the percentages of the 1921 bill using a new breakdown: quotas of "desirables" and "undesirables." Immigrants from Western Europe (England, Germany, and the Netherlands) were free to continue to immigrate to the United States. Eastern European immigrants—mainly Catholics and Jews from Italy, Spain, Poland, and Russia—were barred from entry in any meaningful numbers. Immigrants from Russia were reduced from 16,270 to 1,792 under the restrictive quota law.[54]

A number of prominent news stories featuring Jews engaging in acts of sexual deviancy also fueled this crisis. One notorious case was the trial, conviction, and eventual mob lynching of Jewish Southerner Leo Frank in Georgia in 1915. Frank, a factory owner, was accused and convicted of molesting and killing Mary Phagan, a thirteen-year-old Christian girl who worked in one of his factories. Frank's conviction on deeply flawed evidence had originally led to the commuting of his death sentence by a court of appeals. This set off outrage across Georgia. The yellow press stoked this fury by printing lurid accusations about Frank's long history of rumored sexual deviancy. The commuting of Frank's death sentence prompted the formation of a late-night mob that dragged the factory owner out of jail and lynched him on a nearby tree. The fact that a likely innocent Jewish "sexual deviant" was hanged in the manner of so many African-Americans was not lost on the American public. This was also the same year of the release of Griffith's notorious nativist paean, *Birth of a Nation*. The Frank trial gave new ammunition to American proto-eugenicists who equated black and Jewish sexuality as a threat to the purity of white, Christian America.

In an even more notorious murder trial, two wealthy young Jewish teenagers, Nathan Leopold and Richard Loeb, were charged in 1924 with the abduction and subsequent murder of fourteen-year-old Bobby Franks. Although they ostensibly kidnapped Franks for ransom, Leopold and Loeb were eventually accused of having no motivation other than a "thrill" killing. The facts of the case soon gave way to national hysteria over what Leopold and Loeb signified. They became the twin (Jewish) faces of the libertine amorality of the Jazz Age amplified by the innuendo and subtext that they were actually gay lovers.

The subsequent trial captivated the nation, quickly becoming known as "the crime of the century." Legendary defense attorney Clarence Darrow managed to save the two from the death penalty by introducing psychoanalytic profiling as evidence. The irony was not lost on nativists. What Hitler was calling the "Jewish" science in *Mein Kampf* was being deployed as the last line of defense for the depravity of sexually perverse Jewish murderers. Details of the personal lives of Leopold and Loeb exploded in the press. Salacious gossip spread about the pair's homosexual habits and youthful amorality that had now, apparently, been taken to its most frightening conclusion.[55] Sexual perversion, not the murder, was at the core of the story's appeal. Leopold and Loeb were seen as Jewish intellectuals turned Nietzsche-inspired philosopher-murderer predatory vampires. Details of their close, possibly intimate relationship only furthered the link between Jewish sexual deviancy and depravity that had fueled vice raids for decades.[56]

The Leo Frank and Leopold and Loeb cases also dominated the true crime pulp novel market for a decade. They operated as a thematic continuation of the conspiracy theories introduced in *The Protocols of the Learned Elders of Zion*. Both cases appeared to confirm the suspicion that Jewish men, while appearing normal in public, harbored secret sexual perversions and deviant desires at odds with Christian, nationalist values. Their notoriety fueled the anti-Semitism of Henry Ford, media critic and Episcopalian minister William Sheafe Chase, and other public figures who had been speaking out against Jewish influence in the media for years. Studio films of the 1920s had fought against this xenophobia through the utopian haze of happily-ever-after intermarriage. But by the late 1920s, it was not enough to stem the nativist tide. The emerging power of anti-immigrant fervor in Washington had became clear.

Jewish studio moguls faced an ideological dilemma. The Jewish backgrounds of Adolf Zukor, Carl Laemmle, William Fox, Louis B. Mayer, Samuel Goldwyn, and the Warner brothers were well known. Their response manifested in a collective desire to produce Hollywood films that would reject suspicions of Jewish vice and instead be bathed in pro-American patriotism.[57] Apocryphal tales of Jewish studio heads rejecting actors for looking "too Jewish" inform the legend.[58] Hollywood's founders were seen as either afraid to sell overtly Jewish stories to non-Jewish America or as self-hating Jews who wanted nothing to do with their Diaspora past.[59] As anti-Semitism increased during the Depression years, Hollywood moguls, desperate to prove their Americanism, began to reject their film characters' Jewish identities and European roots.[60] By the early 1930s, even the massive lingering success of *The Jazz Singer* wasn't enough to continue Jewish-themed subject matter.[61] With the country's eventual descent into the Great Depression, the first wave of Christian-Jewish love stories in American cinema was effectively over.

THE RISE OF WHITENESS

As Karen Brodkin has shown, the oscillation between Anglo-Christian acceptance and rejection of Jews as fully "white" was a product of the ebb and flow of political forces of the 1920s and 1930s.[62] Depression-era anti-Semitism had shattered the confidence of immigrant Jews that what was happening in Europe would not happen in the United States. By 1937, the emerging censorship power of the Catholic-run Production Code Administration and the success of the Immigration Restriction League to ban "undesirables" diminished ethnic visibility throughout popular entertainment.[63] Advocacy for an American cultural mosaic in screen media gave way to a reactionary sensibility that aligned non-Anglo-Saxon identity with the threat of fifth-column infiltration.[64] Outside of *The Cohens and Kellys* featurettes and the popular radio program *The Rise of the Goldbergs*, nearly all depictions of Jews on radio and screen were that of acculturated, fully assimilated Americans.[65] Even Horace Kallen, the respected New York Jewish intellectual who had advocated a melting pot argument that he called "cultural pluralism" throughout the 1910s and 1920s, began pushing religious Jews to seek a more reformed, inclusive lifestyle.[66]

Jewish characters still existed. But they relocated from the text to the recognizable codes of performance. The comic ethnic "disguises" of the Marx Brothers offer one of the most prominent examples. They satirized this ethnic coding by embracing it. Groucho, with a greasepaint mustache and an ill-fitting suit, critiqued the same cliché of hidden Jewish masquerade as Al Jolson had in blackface in *The Jazz Singer*. In films such as *Animal Crackers* (1930), his deft weaving of Yiddishisms (Crowd: "Hooray for Captain Spaulding! The African Explorer!" Groucho: "Did someone call me *schnorrer*?") and sly references to the family's Jewish background ("This program is coming to you from the House of David") used the comedic ruptures of linguistic wordplay to maintain Jewishness in an easily identifiable but safe code.

Other exceptions also persisted. The link between Jewish transformation and technological innovation introduced in *The Jazz Singer* continued in films such as *Disraeli* (1929), *The Kibbitzer* (1930), and *Street Scene* (1931). *Disraeli* famously starred the real life (non-Jewish) married couple George and Florence Arliss as Benjamin and Mary Anne Disraeli. George Arliss, a renowned British stage actor, had originated the role of Disraeli in the London theater production of *Disraeli* in 1911. The plot of the film adhered closely to its British theater origins, focusing mostly on the politics of Parliament and ignoring Disraeli's Jewishness. *The Kibbitzer* and *Street Scene* were more overt in their Jewish subject matter. Both were tenement films that followed *The Jazz Singer* in merging familiar historical re-creations, Jewish-Irish tenement love stories, and early sound technology. Each focused on the romantic interplay of young Irish and Jewish lovers and concluded with a generationally distinct shift in dialect from the Yiddish of the parents to the "American" accent of the fully assimilated next generation.[67]

The 1934 Academy Award–nominated *The House of Rothschild* was probably the most notable studio outlier of the period. A historical biography set in the late eighteenth and early nineteenth centuries, it was the rare Hollywood film of the 1930s to directly engage the notion of Jewish power and political influence. The plot concerns assimilated, wealthy British Jewish patriarch Nathan Rothschild (George Arliss) and his troubled relationship with his daughter, Julie (Loretta Young). Julie is being courted by the dashing but non-Jewish Captain Fitzroy (Robert Young). Nathan's initial resistance to his daughter's marriage to a Gentile changes as the political events of the Napoleon era unfold. In the film's conclusion, Nathan experiences a familiar epiphany. His daughter must be allowed to marry for love rather than out of religious obligation.

As in *The Jazz Singer*, the assimilation of Rothschild's daughter was reflected in the film's aesthetic and technological innovations. Next-generation Anglo-Christian-Jewish coupling was celebrated as the film transitioned from black-and-white into a four-minute sequence shot in Technicolor, one of the earliest examples of three-strip color cinema in a studio release. This final scene depicts a grand ballroom celebration of Julie and Captain Fitzroy's intermarriage despite Nathan Rothschild's misgivings over the union. Nathan directs his wife, Hanna, to observe how happy their daughter and her new husband are at the exact moment the color sequence begins. Moments later, still in color, Nathan is knighted as a baron. His metaphorical transformation, from Jewish immigrant to British noble, is represented in the film's literal transformation from black-and-white to color.[68]

Three years later, Warner Bros. produced *The Life of Emile Zola* (1937), a film based on the Dreyfus Affair.[69] The representational shift is dramatic.

As Nico Carpenter points out, the hero of the film is not Dreyfus, but the French-Catholic character of Emile Zola (perhaps ironically played by Jewish actor Paul Muni).[70] The film contains almost no references to Alfred and Lucie Dreyfus's Jewish identity. Dreyfus is sent to the margins of the narrative, while Zola is presented as a noble, benevolent Christ figure. By the end of the film, Dreyfus is redeemed, France is healed, and anti-Semitism is mostly ignored.[71]

Responding to this cultural pushback, an iconography of a new Hollywood movie star quickly emerged: white, with a vaguely British surname, and entirely free of any ethnic identifier other than an Anglo-Saxon continentalism.[72] A new escapist form of romantic coupling narrative—the screwball comedy—replaced the ethnic interplay of immigrant love stories. Fast-talking dames and gold digger archetypes defined a new female ideal. The continental accents and Anglo-Christian body types of Katharine Hepburn, Ginger Rogers, Irene Dunne, and Barbara Stanwyck embodied what Elizabeth Kendall describes as a vibrant, idealized notion of (Christian) white femininity produced as a response to the crushing realities of the Depression.[73] For male movie stars, handsome ethnic-free whiteness—as seen in the star personas of Gary Cooper, Errol Flynn, James Stewart, and Henry Fonda—presented a genteel masculine resolve. Even Cary Grant and Clark Gable's swarthy hints of ethnicity were playfully hidden behind their highly constructed, affected personas. Stars of the 1920s, such as Paul Muni and Edward G. Robinson, began to hide their Jewishness behind a more general "ethnic" classification that included Irish, Italian, and other ethnic codes.[74] Jews were increasingly identified as both biologically deviant and amoral, secular Communists.[75] In the escapist cinema of the late 1930s, as World War II beckoned, a fully white world offered respite from these messy ethno-religious complications.

When Hollywood produced yet another film on the life story of Benjamin Disraeli, *The Prime Minister* (1941), no references were made to his Jewish identity. Disraeli was even played by noted British actor and embodiment of genteel Anglo-Saxonism, John Gielgud. As in *The Life of Emile Zola*, Jewishness shifted from text to subtext.[76] The emphasis on cultural pluralism of the 1920s had been replaced by an idealized fantasy of whites defined by continental accents and Anglo-Saxon physiognomy. Overtly identifiable Jewish performers such as Al Jolson, George Jessel, and Fanny Brice began to appear in the less lucrative Yiddish cinema market, or they returned to stage, theater, and radio. Jewishness was deemphasized in all popular mediums. Jewish-centric radio programs of the 1930s, such as *The Eternal Light*, reframed Jewish spirituality as a universal belief that was no different from its Christian counterpart.[77] Gertrude Berg's lucrative and popular two-decade radio comedy-drama, *The Rise of the Goldbergs* (and later, the retitled TV show, *The Goldbergs*), emphasized the assimilationist impulses of the Goldberg family. Except for a brief revival in the late 1940s, the postwar House Un-American Activities Committee years and conservative political climate of the 1950s created what Matthew Frye Jacobson describes as an increasing emphasis on the value of whiteness.[78] Screen Jews moved away from Christian partners and to the margins of popular screen media. They would remain there for another twenty-five years.

Part Two

THE SECOND WAVE:
EROTIC SCHLEMIELS OF THE
COUNTERCULTURE (1967–1980)

*A bird may love a fish, but where would they build a home
together?*

TEVYE, *FIDDLER ON THE ROOF* (1964)

*As far as a certain school of shikse is concerned . . . [her]
knight turns out to be none other than a brainy, balding,
beaky Jew.*

ALEXANDER PORTNOY, *PORTNOY'S COMPLAINT* (1969)

*I*N A 1967 ARTICLE IN *NATIONAL REVIEW* TITLED
"Who Are the Hippies?" columnist Will Herberg criticized the then-burgeoning "free love" counterculture movement
as an impulse of narcissism, indulgence, and the breakdown of
moral codes.[1] Speaking for what he claimed was the "silent (conservative) majority" that would soon elect Nixon, Herberg wrote,
"it would be hard to find anything so rancid as the love-unction
of the hippie love mongers." The movement, brought to popular attention by the politically radicalized "Summer of Love" in
San Francisco in summer 1967, rejected the sexual inhibitions and
bourgeois standards of the postwar decades. For the youth culture
of the late 1960s, sexuality was also an act of political resistance.

Herberg's "rancid" condemnation of hippie sexuality soon became central to Nixon's election campaign. Rumors of casual sex,
orgies, and wife swapping and an embrace of both homosexuality
and bisexuality produced tremendous cultural anxiety. Conten-

tious issues—the war in Vietnam, civil rights, abortion legalization, and women's rights—were increasingly contested in popular media through the allegorical landscape of the individual body. Nixon's pushback against what he perceived as the youth culture's moral relativism and promiscuous sexuality was built around championing a return to 1950s-era gender and sexual "normalcy." This repairing of postwar moral standards was visualized in the values and sensibilities of the nuclear, white American (Christian) family archetypes drawn directly from popular media during the Eisenhower years.

At the same moment that sex and politics were clashing in the political realm, Hollywood experienced a creative renaissance. As the legend tells it, the postwar collapse of the studio system and the mid-1960s replacement of the Production Code with a ratings system opened the door for a new generation of film savvy auteurs.[2] In the thirteen-year period from 1967 to 1980, these filmmakers revitalized the studio system by introducing the aesthetic influence of the French Nouvelle Vague, the pop music of the British New Wave, the self-reflexive irony of Warholian pop art, and the new sensibilities of hippie-powered youth culture.[3] This period, now referred to as either "New Hollywood" or the "Hollywood New Wave," has been lauded by scholars and critics alike as one of the major peaks of creative output for American cinema.[4]

But this hagiography overlooks an important rhetorical and figural revival at the center of this creative revolution. In film after film, New Hollywood navigated the new sexuality and identity politics of the counterculture by reviving and recalibrating the familiar archetypes of the 1910s and 1920s, the Anglo-Christian-Jewish love story.

In films such as *The Graduate* (1967), *I Love You, Alice B. Toklas* (1968), *Funny Girl* (1968), *The Producers* (1968), *Goodbye, Columbus* (1969), *Bob & Carol & Ted & Alice* (1969), *Where's Poppa?* (1970), *Getting Straight* (1970), *Straw Dogs* (1971), *The Heartbreak Kid* (1972), *Sleeper* (1973), *The Way We Were* (1973), *The Apprenticeship of Duddy Kravitz* (1974), *Annie Hall* (1977), and *The Rose* (1979), awkward, overtly Jewish nebbishes coupling with Anglo-Christian love interests both embodied and parodied the visceral angst and confusion of the counterculture. On television, situation comedies such as *He and She* (1967), *All in the Family* (1971–1979), *Bridget Loves Bernie* (1972–1973), and *Rhoda* (1974–1978) introduced either coded or textual young Jews romancing and marrying Anglo-Christian partners as icons of the new generation. Jewish character actors, who in earlier decades would have been relegated to the comic margins, suddenly became the unlikely faces of New Hollywood stardom. Dustin Hoffman, Barbra Streisand, Gene Wilder, Dyan Cannon, Elliott Gould, Mel Brooks, Charles Grodin, Woody Allen, Richard Benjamin, George Segal, Richard Dreyfuss, and, in the late 1970s, Bette Midler, Carol Kane, and Madeline Kahn each signified the usurpation of Anglo-Saxon norms by performing a new, comedic ethnic visibility as an amalgam of white and not-white, straight and queered, immigrant and American.

This resurgence of unapologetic Anglo-Christian-Jewish screen couplings in the New Hollywood cinema was influenced by the confluence of three developments over the preceding two decades. The first was the emergence of a raunchy, sexually provocative, highly political form of comedy produced by a new generation of stand-up comedians in the late 1950s and early 1960s. Mort Sahl, Lenny Bruce, Allan Sherman, Woody Allen, Joan Rivers, and the comedy teams of Mike Nichols and Elaine May and Jerry Stiller and Anne Meara deployed unapologetic Jewishness, often a comedic but carnal form of compulsive Jewish sexuality, as a response to the politically conservative and sexually repressed norms of the 1950s. Second, a new wave of critically lauded American literature was codified. Like their comedian counterparts, Jewish authors such as Arthur Miller, Saul Bellow, Bernard Malamud, and Philip Roth focused on the specificity of the American Jewish experience—neurosis, compulsive sexuality, and the breakdown of the nuclear family—as a response to the marginalization of Jews in the 1950s and an allegory for the alienation of postwar suburban malaise. Third, the growing awareness of the military power of Israel reconfigured and re-masculinized the Jewish Diaspora, peaking with Israel's shocking military victory in the Six-Day War in 1967. Seemingly overnight, Israel created a new origin story for American Jews. The end of the Production Code in 1966 opened up the possibilities for visible sexuality in mainstream American cinema. It was the screen Jew, comedically safe yet suddenly infused with mythic power, potency, and a rhetorical manifest destiny narrative, who stepped in as the familiar face to navigate this uncertain terrain.[5]

Described as the "Jewish New Wave" by J. Hoberman and the moment when "Jews became sexy" by Henry Bial, this unapologetically Jewish generation of stars embodied a collective generational break from the Doris Day and Rock Hudson hyper-masculine and ultra-feminine conventions of the first two postwar decades.[6] Anglo-centric movie stars found themselves replaced, or wooed, by performers with unusual faces, kinky hair, atypical bodies, and a highly neurotic verbosity.[7] Yet, these archetypes were also familiar. Streisand and Midler revived the Ghetto Jewess as sexual temptress. Hoffman, Grodin, Allen, Segal, Gould, Dreyfuss, and Benjamin encapsulated the untethered boundaries of the hippie generation through the familiar iconography of the neurotic Jewish schlemiel. These horny nebbishes were defined by their often (but not always) comedic libidinal neuroses as screen exemplars of generational change. However, as with the first wave in the 1920s, unconstrained Jewish carnality was mitigated in nearly every case by the pursuit, and acquisition, of the Anglo-Christian partner.[8]

The second wave reached critical mass consciousness in 1967 with the release of Mike Nichols's *The Graduate*. It was codified, two years later, with the runaway success of Philip Roth's novel about Jewish sexual compunction, *Portnoy's Complaint*. The movement began to fade a decade later with the election of Ronald Reagan and the New Conservatism of the 1980s. This was manifest in depictions of Christian-Jewish divorces and breakups in films such as *Kramer vs. Kramer* (1979), *Manhattan* (1979), and *Modern Romance* (1981). But this second wave left a lasting impact. The neurotic second-wave Jew was at once both uncontrollably carnal and comically safe. As in the first wave, the Anglo-Christian partner, nearly always an idealized screen beauty, served as both the fantasy object of acquisition and the acquiescent confirmation of successful cultural transformation.[9] Together, these second-wave couplings offered a transitional figuration between the sexually repressed Anglo-whiteness of the 1950s and early 1960s and the new ethnic and sexual visibility of the 1970s.

CHAPTER 4

Benjamin's Cross

ISRAEL, NEW HOLLYWOOD, AND THE
JEWISH TRANSGRESSIVE (1947–1967)

My unconscious was making this movie . . . it took me years before I got what I was doing, that I was turning Benjamin into a Jew.

MIKE NICHOLS ON DIRECTING *THE GRADUATE*, QUOTED IN
MARK HARRIS, *PICTURES AT A REVOLUTION*

*I*N 1967, TWO SEEMINGLY UNRELATED EVENTS OC-
curred. In June, Israel achieved a surprising and dominant military victory over the combined forces of Jordan, Egypt, and Syria in what
is now generally referred to as the Six-Day War.[1] The nascent Jewish nation
not only survived its existential war for survival, but it also doubled its land
size, taking control of the Golan Heights, Gaza Strip, East Jerusalem, and
the West Bank. Modern-day Israel was only nineteen years old at the time,
but this powerful military triumph had profound global reverberations. Diaspora Jewry had been seen in the postwar era as passive, meek, and acquiescent victims of the Holocaust. After Israel's military triumph, Jews were
suddenly recast as modern-day Davids, heroic and powerful fighters willing to risk all for their survival. Conversely, in much of the Arab world
and among hardcore political leftists throughout Europe and the United
States, Israelis (and Jews more generally) were increasingly reviled as violent
colonizers, occupiers, and usurpers, a transnational occupying force continuing the legacy of the British Empire in the Arab world.[2] Both perspectives participated in a reconfiguration. Whether by supporter or by critic,
global Jewishness was reframed from powerless Diaspora to geographically
emboldened.

The impact of this event on world Jewry was profound. In a March 2009
profile in the *New Yorker*, French playwright Yasmina Reza tells how her

immigrant Jewish father first "introduced the word 'Jew' into the house in an uncompromising, mythical way" only after learning of Israel's victory.[3] Reza, eight years old at the time, was a French Jew born to Eastern European parents who had emigrated from Hungary. Aware only of her Hungarian background, the young Reza did not know that she was Jewish until that moment. This recalibration of Jewish Diaspora transformed Reza's family from a place of historical origin (Hungary) to an imagined alternative lineage (Israel). It also fractured the young Reza's understanding of her own identity. Both Hungarian and French, Reza was now also, apparently, a Jew. She describes feeling that she had "no roots, no native soil, no sense of place, no nostalgia for one."[4] This became one of the central themes of her literature and plays for the next forty years.

Reza's memory exemplifies what Nurith Gertz describes as the "conflict between the two narratives—Israeli Zionist narrative and that of the Holocaust survivor raised in the Diaspora."[5] The original body of Diaspora, defined in the Western imaginary as the cosmopolitan, rootless Wandering Jew, became retroactively transformed. The hyper-masculine image of the Israeli settler was the "new Jew" with whom Reza's father suddenly identified. This identification replaced the clownish shtetl migrant who had defined Jewish passivity in both pre- and post-Holocaust contexts. In this understanding, the Six-Day War was not only a transformative geographic victory in the Middle East, but also an act of historical rewrite that resonated throughout the Jewish Diaspora.

Homi Bhabha describes the ongoing process of rewriting of diasporic identity as the central method of resolving the tension of displacement. The individual searches for an ironic compromise between one's new country of origin and the mythic cultural past, and between the dominant and repressed. This fractured duality posits a solution to the schizophrenia of existing both inside and outside the dominant understanding of the nation-state. Bhabha describes this process as a search for "a subject of a difference that is almost the same," in which double articulations are the only way of coping with the fractures of diasporic identity.[6] Reza's experience of her father suddenly becoming two people at once describes this diasporic duality. His retroactive transformation located an empowered Israeli Jewishness cloaked within his prior articulation as a disempowered member of the global Jewish Diaspora. The Six-Day War performed this profound rearticulation around the world. It reframed Jews from a wandering, transnational identity to a culture with a retroactive country of origin and military power.

Reza's experience offers just one anecdote of the profundity of trans-

Benjamin Braddock (Dustin Hoffman) interrupts the wedding of Elaine Robinson (Katherine Ross) to Carl Smith (Brian Avery) in the final scene of The Graduate *(1967).*

formation taking place in 1967. In the United States, historian Lawrence Grossman notes, there was an unprecedented surge in Jewish pride.[7] For the first time since the late 1940s, American Jews began to assert their Jewish identities publicly. This movement, in tandem with the civil rights and women's movements of the late 1960s, presented an ethnic awakening of Jews in popular media not seen since the first-generation immigrants of the 1910s and 1920s.

In December 1967, six months after the Six-Day War, director Mike Nichols's *The Graduate* was released in American movie theaters. It became a breakout sensation, lauded for its frank depictions of sexuality, innovative Nouvelle Vague techniques, and encapsulation of the ennui of the youth culture of the late 1960s. The film's first image, a long-take close-up of actor Dustin Hoffman's passive, emotionally confused face, announced that a new aesthetic sensibility had entered mainstream Hollywood. By the end of the film, a sequence in which Benjamin Braddock, Hoffman's character, breaks into a church to rescue Elaine (Katherine Ross) from a semi-conscripted marriage to a blond, blue-eyed WASP, Carl Smith (Brian Avery), a complete reconfiguration of youth culture gender and sexuality had taken place. The soundtrack by Simon and Garfunkel, the graphic language, and the frank discussion of sexuality all marked clear breaks with Hays Code Hollywood.

But it was the casting of Dustin Hoffman that humanized and visualized the transformation in gender, sexuality, and movie star archetypes represented by the New Hollywood counterculture. This casting decision remains one of the most unorthodox choices in Hollywood history. Benjamin Braddock was one of the most coveted roles in Hollywood. The studio originally slated the part for Robert Redford. Nevertheless, director Mike Nichols, a young, German-Jewish, theater-trained, stand-up-comedian-turned-director, made the nearly impossible choice to turn Redford down and cast the unknown Hoffman instead. In a 1999 interview with *Film Comment*, Nichols explained his motivations:

> And yet the parts of me that did identify with Benjamin predominate in what I did with the movie. By that I mean, I didn't cast Redford. Dustin has always said that Benjamin is a walking surfboard. And that's what he was in the book, in the original conception. But I kept looking and looking for an actor until I found Dustin, who is the opposite, who's a dark, Jewish, anomalous presence, which is how I experience myself. So I stuck this dark presence into Beverly Hills, and there he felt that he was drowning in things, and that was very much my take on that story.[8]

At first, Hoffman declined the role, rejecting Nichols's request to fly out from New York to Los Angeles for a screen test. Years later, Hoffman recalled the conversation in which he explained his reticence to Nichols:

> I said, "I'm not right for this part, sir. This is a Gentile. This is a WASP. This is Robert Redford." . . . And Mike said, "Maybe he's Jewish inside. Why don't you come out and audition for us?"[9]

After reluctantly flying to Los Angeles and screen-testing with non-Jewish actress and model Katherine Ross (Elaine), Hoffman recounted feeling even more alienated from the role. He could not comprehend how audiences would accept a nebbishy Jewish man successfully romancing a beautiful shiksa in a major motion picture. Hoffman described his thoughts thusly:

> (t)he idea that the director was connecting me with someone as beautiful as her. . . . became an even uglier joke. It was like a Jewish nightmare.[10]

But after viewing the screen test, Nichols became fully convinced of the necessity of the unusual casting choice. Years later, he explained his logic:

> (Benjamin) couldn't be a blond, blue-eyed person, because then why is he having trouble in the country of the blond, blue-eyed people? It took me a long time to figure that out—it's not in the material at all. And once I figured that out, and found Dustin, it began to form itself around that idea.[11]

What Hoffman saw as a "Jewish nightmare" and Nichols described as an "anomalous presence" became the unruly element that infused the film with its sense of purpose in channeling the generational break taking place. Hoffman was not only the new face of youth culture confusion, but he also broke with the previous generation's postwar beauty standards. As with Reza's father, he communicated a duality as both *Hoffman* and *not-Redford*. This twin signification signaled a screen transformation that did not exist in the novel or screenplay. It became a scrambled marker of mass culture transformation, an ethno-religious "coming out" applicable to the rising visibility of the civil rights movement, the women's rights movement, and the sexual revolution. The embedded absences and ethno-cultural marginalization of the previous two decades of postwar American screen culture were instantly critiqued. The counterculture of the 1960s had sought disruptive totems to mark its break with the postwar generation. In Hoffman's star turn, youth culture found the face of generational revolution. It emerged in the unlikely visage of a short, big-nosed, nebbishy Jew.

GENTLEMEN'S DISAGREEMENT

The unapologetic Jewishness of the second wave had antecedents in the Jazz Age. In the 1920s and early 1930s, a performer's ethnic background was often a celebrated element of their star persona. Jewish characters in particular were rarely cast with non-Jewish actors.[12] Jewish-born performers from the 1910s and 1920s such as Sophie Tucker, Paul Muni, Edward G. Robinson, Jack Benny, Molly Picon, George Jessel, Al Jolson, and Fanny Brice had celebrated their Jewish identity as part of the progression narrative of immigrant American assimilation. As discussed in chapter 2, screen representations of Jewishness had undergone a near total erasure of that visibility by the late 1930s. Thomas Doherty credits this to the impact of the increasingly powerful Catholic-led Production Code. Michael Rogin ascribes it to Jewish studio moguls fearful of rising anti-Semitism.[13] Whatever the motivations, by the time of World War II, this disappearance was almost complete.[14] Hollywood was increasingly defined by a valuation and emphasis on what Steve Cohan calls the "currency of whiteness."[15] Jewish performers hid in plain sight through what Joseph Litvak calls the comedic codes of "archaic comicosmopolitanism."[16] But textual Jewish specificity in mainstream American entertainment was nearly completely gone.

This is not hard to understand. Hitler's propaganda ministry, run by Joseph Goebbels, had seized on the argument that Jewish bodies were biologically distinct.[17] Photography and films were introduced as evidence. This display of Jewish "physiognomy" was a central tool in the arsenal of Nazi mass media propaganda. The eugenics argument had led to enormous, incomprehensible tragedy. The shock of World War II and the revelation of the depths of the horrors of the Holocaust caused a postwar reevaluation of how Jews could, and should, identify themselves. The logical response was to decouple Jewish identity by shifting it into the realm of performance. This was noble in its intent. If Jewish faces and bodies had operated as a tool for biological racism, then Jewishness needed to be denatured from any physical indexicality. The assumption of a fixed Jewish body was redefined as the province of the anti-Semite. The solution was to liberate screen Jews by untethering the very idea of Jewishness itself.[18]

This decoupling of Jewishness from the Jewish body was articulated through two frameworks of representation. The first was the empowerment and championing of non-Jewish actors to play Jewish characters. The second was to emphasize the notion that Jewish bodies were not identifiable through physical or genetic difference. Any attempt to do so was portrayed as a form of embedded violence, bigotry, and racism. To counter the legacy of Nazism, Jewishness must not be physically identifiable. The postwar American ideology was clear. Anyone could be Jewish. And Jews could be anyone.[19]

In 1947, two films, released mere months apart, *Gentlemen's Agreement* and *Crossfire* (1947), established this new postwar reclassification. Both films defined anti-Semitism as a psychological disease. It was triggered by a fantasy of difference. The anti-Semite saw Jewish Otherness as corporeally and biologically distinct. Both films offered a well-intended response. They condemned the anti-Semite as delusional and ignorant, unintentionally buying into the Hitlerian eugenics framework. The anti-Semite held a pathological desire to lash out at people who were, in actuality, no different from anyone else. Jewishness was reclassified in these films as an arbitrary result of birth. The Jew was simply a non-Jew with different parents.

Crossfire, a B-picture from RKO Studios, was an inexpensive noir thriller about an anti-Semitic crime of passion taking place between soldiers during the war. A Jewish soldier, Joseph Samuels (Sam Levene) is murdered after having drinks with a woman. Police captain Finlay (Robert Young) investigates the crime, only to learn the anti-Semitic underpinnings of the violence. The narrative unfolds through the subjective recollections of Samuels's platoon.[20] These flashbacks repeatedly emphasize that Samuels is just like every other member of his platoon in every way. His Jewishness was entirely incidental, overshadowed by his complete military commitment and unbridled love of America.

Gentlemen's Agreement took the benevolent universality argument of *Crossfire* into American suburbia. This Academy Award winner for best picture focused on a non-Jewish journalist, Phil Green (played by non-Jewish actor Gregory Peck), who decides to write an article on the dangers of anti-Semitism by pretending to be Jewish. Green is able to pass as Jewish because of the ambiguity of his last name, perhaps a shortened version of Greenberg, and his general physical look. The film's well-intended ideological argument that Jewishness is not corporeally distinct locates in its emphasis on sameness, not difference.

In one key exchange between Green and his son, Tommy (Dean Stockwell), these universalization terms are made explicit:

> Tommy Green: What's anti-Semitism?
> Phil Green: Well, uh, that's when some people don't like other people just because they're Jews.
> Tommy: Why not? Are Jews bad?
> Phil: Well, some are and some aren't, just like with everyone else.
> Tommy: What are Jews, anyway?
> Phil: Well, uh, it's like this. Remember last week when you asked me about that big church and I told you there are all different kinds of churches? Well, the people who go to that particular church are called Catholics, and there are people who go to different churches and they're called Protestants, and there are people who go to different churches and they're called Jews, only they call their churches temples or synagogues.
> Tommy: Why don't some people like them?
> Phil: Well, I can't really explain it, Tommy.[21]

Judith E. Doneson argues that the film's ideological intervention locates in its relocation of the vantage point of who gets to determine who is and is not a Jew.[22] Green's ability to easily pass as both Jew and non-Jew dismisses any notion that biological lineage and cultural experiences are nec-

Dave Goldman (John Garfield) and Philip Green (Gregory Peck) present competing versions of postwar Jewish identity in Gentlemen's Agreement *(1947).*

essary. But it is the non-Jew, not the Jew, who is ultimately empowered to make this determination. Henry Bial notes another element of Jewish denaturing taking place in the film. Green's cooptive language and actions reframe postwar Jewishness as a performance rather than as ethno-racial biography.[23] Jewishness is redefined as a conscious choice at once accessible by Jew and non-Jew alike.[24]

This universality argument is counterpointed by the depiction of the two Jewish characters in the film. The first is Phil's Jewish secretary, Elaine Wales (June Havoc). Phil tells Elaine that she is complicit in anti-Semitism because of her desire to hide her identity by changing her last name.[25] The second is Phil's good friend, Dave Goldman, played by notable Jewish movie star, John Garfield. Garfield was the most famous openly Jewish movie star of the postwar era.[26] His celebrated sex appeal, working-class "ghetto" mannerisms, and unapologetic Jewishness made him a unique movie star at the cultural crossroads of the late 1940s. Garfield first became famous in the late 1930s for his portrayal of a seductive, young working-class musician in *Four Daughters* (1938). But his stardom reached its peak opposite Lana Turner in the noir thriller, *The Postman Always Rings Twice* (1946). His working-class persona was built around a feral, carnal sexuality.[27]

Even after becoming a movie star, Garfield did not shy away from his Jewish background in his acting choices. As Samuel J. Rosenthal observes, three roles that Garfield chose at the height of his career were either overtly or plausibly Jewish characters: the emotional violinist Paul Boray romancing WASP aristocrat Helen Wright (Joan Crawford) in *Humoresque* (1946), Lower East Side boxer Charlie Davis in *Body and Soul* (1947), and the watershed role of Dave Goldman in *Gentleman's Agreement*.[28] This was highly unusual. Other postwar Jewish-born movie stars such as Kirk Douglas, Lauren Bacall, and Judy Holliday avoided any overt Jewish identity in their roles. Perhaps due to his pugnacious star persona, Garfield felt no such concerns, playing Jewish roles without hesitation. This fearlessness was despite rising anti-Semitism in Washington, DC, the most notable example being Congressman John Rankin infamously reading a list of Jewish-born Hollywood actors, revealing their birth names, on the floor of Congress in November 1947.[29] Garfield's role as Dave Goldman in *Gentlemen's Agreement* represented his peak Jewish visibility at the exact moment an anti-Semitic backlash was building in Washington.

Matthew Frye Jacobson describes the tension between Goldman and Green's understandings of Jewishness as that of the philosophical clash between prewar and postwar constructions of identity.[30] In playing the non-Jew-as-Jew, Phil Green embodied what was an emancipatory liberation for Jews tarred as genetic deviants in the demonization that reached apotheosis in the Holocaust. Green solves this crisis by liberating Jewishness from biology. He is able to pass easily between Jewish and non-Jewish identities. When Green reflects on what a "Jew" is, he stares into a mirror searching for physical distinctions between his face and Dave's, yet finds none.

The film celebrates Green's performative Jewishness over Dave's indexical Jew, producing what Henry Bial calls "selective visibility."[31] Selective visibility identifies Jewishness as a voluntary act of self-selection, thereby countering the eugenics argument that Jews were defined by physical attributes. Garfield-as-Goldman embodied Jewishness as physiognomy rather than as choice. Dave Goldman refuses to hide or apologize for his Jewishness to the point of confrontation with anti-Semites. He accepts the inevitable conflicts that his visibility produces. Phil Green's universalist non-Jew-as-Jew countered and trumped Goldman's Jew-as-Jew. It explicitly rejected Garfield's (and Goldman's) embodiment of immutable Jewishness as dangerous to both Jew and non-Jew alike. Postwar Jewishness had become an act of performance, not biology.

Three years later, in 1950, despite no evidence that he had joined the Communist Party in the 1930s, Garfield was blacklisted by the House Un-American Activities Committee (HUAC) in their publication, *Red Channels: The Report of Communist Influence in Radio and Television*.[32] He was barred from working at any studio and was immediately unemployed and unemployable. During his testimony before HUAC, in April 1951, Garfield adamantly refused to name names. He subsequently became an active participant in the Committee for the First Amendment, a challenge to HUAC formed by numerous Hollywood luminaries including Myrna Loy, John Huston, and William Wyler.[33] His working-class nature gave his public statements an arrogant, defiant quality. But it did little good. By late 1951, Garfield's movie career was over. Although married, he was a notorious womanizer and, on May 21, 1952, he died of a heart attack in the apartment of a mistress. His death took place only one day after Clifford Odets had refused to name Garfield as a member of the Communist Party during Odets's HUAC testimony. Garfield died while awaiting his second round of HUAC testimony.

The end of Garfield's career (and life) cannot be solely ascribed to his Jewish visibility in Hollywood. But neither can this connection be dismissed. Eugenics theory had emphasized Jewish sexual deviancy and Communism as related perversions at work in the Jewish plan to erode nations from within. Fear of covert messaging in Hollywood had fueled the rise of McCarthy and HUAC in the late 1940s.[34] By the early 1950s, this crisis reached fever pitch. Congressman Rankin, a notorious anti-Semite, made this connection clear in a speech in 1952:

> They (Jews) whine about discrimination. Do you know who is being discriminated against? The white Christian people of America, the ones who created this nation. . . . Communism is racial. A racial minority seized control in Russia and in all her satellite countries, such as Poland and Czechoslovakia . . . they (Jews) have been run out of practically every country in Europe in the years gone by, and if they keep stirring race trouble in this country and trying to force their communistic program on the Christian people of America, there is no telling what will happen to them here.[35]

Garfield was not alone in bearing the brunt of implied Jewish-Communist associations. The trial and execution of Julius and Ethel Rosenberg on espionage charges in the early 1950s provoked a spike in accusations of Jewish disloyalty similar to the Dreyfus Affair. With their faces and Jewish last name plastered all over newspapers and on early television broadcasts, Julius and Ethel became allegorical Judas figures, the embodiment of national betrayal hiding in plain sight under the guise of suburban normalcy. Their very average-ness, a seemingly typical suburban, assimilated American couple, only furthered fears of a hidden Communist invasion. Like Alfred and Lucie Dreyfus, they were indicted as fifth-column traitors breaking down Christian society through hidden moral and spiritual deviancy.[36]

The Phil Green argument in *Gentlemen's Agreement*—that Jews were no different from Christians—offered at least a partial solution to this xeno-phobia. Numerous Jewish performers, directors, and writers in Hollywood subsequently attempted to conceal themselves beneath a veneer of Anglo-American whiteness to prove their inoffensiveness, assimilation, and loyal patriotism.[37] By emphasizing Jewishness as universally accessible to non-Jews, Jews could remain at least partially visible. But the connection be-tween Jewish characters and Jewish actors had to be severed. Jewish char-acters, when they did (infrequently) appear on-screen in the 1950s, were primarily performed by non-Jewish actors, following Peck's lead. In 1951, Peck himself was cast to play the title role of the Jewish King David in *David and Bathsheba* (1951).[38] Five years later, Charlton Heston performed as Moses in *The Ten Commandments* (1956), with almost no effort made to en-gage the Jewish specificity of the tale.[39]

The Young Lions (1958) was the first major film to confront anti-Semitism in a decade. But the soldier protagonist's Jewishness was mitigated through the casting of the non-Jewish Montgomery Clift.[40] Conversely, Jewish-born movie stars such as Judy Holliday, Kirk Douglas, Lauren Bacall, and Lee J. Cobb rarely played Jewish characters, each having changed their last names to Christian-sounding surnames.[41] Even the 1958 remake of *The Jazz Singer* featured Lebanese comedian Danny Thomas, albeit one of the most "Jewish-looking" non-Jewish actors in Hollywood, in the role of Jack Robin.[42] The intersubjective pattern was firmly established.

In 1947, *Gentlemen's Agreement* and *Crossfire* had proposed a new under-standing of Jewishness-as-performance, denaturing Jewishness from eth-nicity and biology. By the late 1950s, this well-intended postwar argument had brought unintended consequences. It had implicitly indicted the visi-ble screen Jew-as-Jew as a disruptive signifier and an ideological threat to the cohesion of the nation during the peak of the Cold War. Yet, it was this erasure that planted the seeds for the New Hollywood response to come.

THE RECASTING OF JAKE GOLDBERG

The Goldbergs (originally called *The Rise of the Goldbergs*) was one of the rare texts to continue past the end of the first wave. A massive radio hit that began during the Jewish heyday of the late 1920s, the show main-tained popularity throughout the 1930s and 1940s. The television version of *The Goldbergs* (1949–1956) began airing on the nascent CBS network as one of the very first structured fiction programs.[43] A huge success, it turned the already-famous creator/writer/star, Gertrude Berg, into one of the first tele-vision superstars.

The premise of the television show focused on Molly's Yiddishisms, puns, and stories of old world versus the new world technology and urban living in the postwar era. It embraced its Jewishness as a vehicle for this universal story of next-generation American assimilation. In the late 1940s and early 1950s, as early television began, this was a logical transition. Early television was dominated by Jewish Catskills comedians from both vaudeville and radio backgrounds. Catskills and Borscht Belt comedians such as Milton Berle, Jack Benny, Danny Kaye, George Burns, Sid Caesar, and Carl Reiner had, along with Berg, brought Jewish-style comedy into the nascent screen medium with shows such as *Burns and Allen* (1950–1958), *Texaco Star Theatre* (1948–1956), *Your Show of Shows* (1950–1954), and *The Phil Silvers Show* (1955–1959). But *The Goldbergs* was the most overtly and unapologetically Jewish television show to emerge in the 1950s.

Like John Garfield, Gertrude Berg as Molly Goldberg was a clearly identified Jew-as-Jew. She inhabited her character as a form of casting-to-performance truth claim. Like her character, Berg emerged from an unapologetically immigrant Jewish world. Her matronly, immigrant ghetto Yiddishe Mama was comically confused by American modernity. But this confusion gave her the old world gravitas to dispense Yiddishkeit-infused wisdom to both her family and the audience. This allowed *The Goldbergs* to be accessible to Jewish and non-Jewish audiences alike. It offered a revival of first-wave ghetto humor by playing with the same Yiddishisms and malapropisms that had defined *The Jazz Singer*, *Abie's Irish Rose*, and *Private Izzy Murphy* a generation earlier. In the linguistic double entendre of Molly Goldberg's "Mollypropisms," television used radio, theater, and vaudevillian comedy traditions to soothe the transition to a new medium.

By the mid-1950s, television found itself under attack. The same transformative ethnic whitewashing that had occurred in cinema began to take place on television. *The Goldbergs* was no exception. As Thomas Doherty notes, the "nascent suspicion of the American Jew as an alien intruder in Christian America" fueled a deep mistrust of the program, and, by proxy, early television itself.[44] HUAC began what would become a two-year tug-of-war between Berg and the General Foods Corporation, the sponsor of the show, over the political activities of actor Philip Loeb. Loeb played the patriarch, Mr. Goldberg, an important but supporting character. The accusations that the genial, innocuous Loeb was some sort of closet Communist were a stretch for a show that was so innocent, popular, and politically benign. But even a flimsy excuse led to extensive investigations in the charged political climate. The pressure on Gertrude Berg became too much. Initially supportive of Loeb, but with the fate of her show hanging in the balance, Berg was forced to fire him in 1951. She quickly replaced Loeb with the non-Jewish actor Robert H. Harris.[45] For Loeb, as with John Garfield, the McCarthy/HUAC investigations would prove not only to be a career ender, but a life ender as well. Isolated from Hollywood and with little public support, Loeb committed suicide in 1955.[46]

The recasting of Jake Goldberg was just one of many efforts the program made to denature its Jewish specificity. As Vincent Brook has shown, once *The Goldbergs* transitioned to television, it placed a growing emphasis on universal family values, integration, and, eventually, a move to suburbia that reflected the core tenets of the Eisenhower-era assimilationist project.[47] Frank Rich describes one startling moment when Molly Goldberg refers to the upcoming "Thanksgiving and Christmas," but makes no mention of Rosh Hashanah, Yom Kippur, or Hanukkah.[48] Working-class labor themes that had permeated the radio show became increasingly mitigated by what George Lipsitz calls the emergent domination of product consumerism.[49] By the time of its last season, in 1955, the increasingly desperate show relocated from New York's Lower East Side to "Haverville," a bland American suburb. The show's name was changed to the less ethnically overt *Molly*, a systematic process of transformation that Donald Weber describes as "ethnic erasure."[50] In the end, Molly Goldberg was there to sell Sanka, not Jewishness, to the American public.

The replacement of Philip Loeb with Robert H. Harris, a "Jewish-looking" non-Jew, on *The Goldbergs* codified the emergent postwar ideology of Christian/Jewish interchangeability. The locus of this debate between reactionary nativists in Washington and creators in Hollywood was not just about Philip Loeb, the actor, or Communism more generally. It was over the political threat of visible ethnic subcultures in popular screen media. The new Jake Goldberg demonstrated the only remaining solution. If television was going to be the dominant mass medium, then it would have to play according to Phil Green's rules.[51]

When *The Goldbergs* was canceled in 1956, ethnic comedies had mostly been driven off the air. They were replaced by fully white suburban counterparts on shows like *The Adventures of Ozzie and Harriet* (1952–1966), *Leave it to Beaver* (1957–1963), and *Father Knows Best* (1954–1960).[52] Vaudeville stars, such as Milton Berle, Sid Caesar, and Carl Reiner, who had successfully transitioned to television were, by 1958, barely hanging on as game show and talk show hosts.[53] Jewish-born performers such as Jack Benny, Phil Silvers, and Danny Kaye still thrived with a Catskills-era comedic style. But overt references to Jewish identity were removed.

The persecution of Philip Loeb was one of the clearest examples of the anti-Semitic anxieties underpinning the HUAC investigations.[54] David Zurawik describes how the near-complete absence of Jewish representations on television from 1955 to 1972 was intentional on the part of fearful studio executives responding to this anxiety.[55] Jewish characters became reconfigured as either coded Jews or simply recast as Anglo-Christians—what Neal Gabler describes as television's attempt to turn "every ethnic into a white, middle-class American."[56] References to Christmas and Easter increased in otherwise Jewish scenarios and comedy frameworks.[57]

This shift in post-Holocaust Jewish representations from the John Garfield peak in 1947 to the mid-1950s was overwhelming and swift.[58] These tensions were exacerbated not only by HUAC, but in the real-world drama of the 1951 trial and 1953 execution of the Rosenbergs. With the rise of television, this fear aligned with anti-Semitic traditions of Jews disguised within the larger population and working through media to undermine American (Christian) virtue. Loeb's potential left-wing political background and his role as a genial patriarch on a popular television show amplified this anxiety of hidden threat. The Peck/Garfield tension of *Gentlemen's Agreement* reemerged in the casting debate over Loeb's character of Jake Goldberg. Berg's concession was not just to fire Philip Loeb. It was also to recalibrate the "body" of her Jewish husband. Despite appearing Jewish in his performative style, Robert H. Harris was not just an actor replacement for Loeb. He also represented an argument for Phil Green's universalized Jewishness presented on the most Jewish show on television.

By the time of the 1962 film *A Majority of One*, the process of Jewish erasure had reached an ironic coda. The ghetto love story had been a huge hit on Broadway for post-*Goldbergs* Gertrude Berg. Written by Leonard Spiegelglass, the stage play relied on language puns and ethnic stereotypes drawn from the familiar world of 1920s-era immigrant culture clashes. The story focused on an unlikely love affair between an elderly Jewish mother, Bertha Jacoby, and a Japanese businessman, Koichi Asano. But it updated the comedic set pieces by infusing the narrative with unexpected pathos. The (mis)communication comedy of errors between the Yiddishisms of Bertha and the broken English of Asano eventually gives way to reveal a story of mutual loss. It is finally revealed that both characters lost children in World War II, a tragic unifying coda of shared loss.

Yet, Hollywood's period of erasure even applied to a text that built its entire premise on ethnic specificity. When *A Majority of One* was adapted for film, the characters of Bertha and Asano were played by the non-Jewish Rosalind Russell and non-Japanese Alec Guinness, who performed in Japanese eye makeup. Russell delivers a series of Jewish "*dahlinks*" that historian Joel Samberg describes as an obvious and offensive attempt by a non-Jew to "sound Jewish."[59] In 1947, *Gentlemen's Agreement* had introduced the postwar argument that all could play Jewish and, by proxy, other ethnicities, such as Japanese. In 1952, HUAC had removed a Jewish Jake Goldberg from the most visible Jewish family on television. Ten years later, in 1962, even Gertrude Berg's ironclad claim to the "Yiddishe Mama" archetype was open season for actresses like Rosalind Russell. But the pushback to this erasure was also beginning to build. It began to emerge in the discourse and rhetoric surrounding a small nation in the Middle East. The rise of Israel had a ripple effect on American Jewish representation that would soon emerge in the New Hollywood revolution of the late 1960s.

EXODUS AND THE MASCULINE RETURN

From Shakespeare's Shylock in *The Merchant of Venice* to Dickens's Fagin in *Oliver Twist*, Jewish sexual deviancy had been depicted for centuries throughout European art and literature through the linking of erotic fetishization, finance, and money. This connection between Jewish carnality and economics produced what Erin Graff Zivin describes as an iconographic "scene of the transaction."[60] In this taboo fantasy, sexual prostitution, corrupt financial stereotypes, and Jewish amorality are conflated in literary fantasies as an expression of deviancy denied to the Christian reader. By the time of the publication of Hitler's *Mein Kampf* in 1922, the rootless, cosmopolitan stereotype of the sexually deviant Jew became reconfigured by biological constructions of a perverse, flawed, and highly sexualized Jewish body. The expression of this taboo anxiety/fantasy was to identify the Jew seducing the Christian as an attempt to alleviate their Jewish impurity through sexual conquest. Seduction of the Christian became, as George L. Mosse argues, what first provoked the young Hitler in Austria: the fear of, as Mosse puts it, "Jews waiting to catch Aryan girls."[61]

Zionism began in the 1890s as a response to these fears. The acquisition, settlement, and foundation of a distinct Jewish land would, as Theodor Herzl argued at the First Zionist Conference in 1897, finally allow Jews to reclaim both the economic and gendered agency denied to them by centuries of demonization as rootless seducers and con artists. Zionism explicitly made this link between the national "body" of a future Israel and the agency of the emancipated Jewish individual. To Herzl, a Jewish Israel offered a structuring metaphor for the reclamation of Jewish masculinity. It could transform Jewish men from flawed deviants into conquerors and colonialists long defined in the Western Christendom tradition. As Daniel Boyarin describes it, Zionism was an effort "by German-speaking Jews in the nineteenth century to rewrite themselves, and particularly their masculine selves as Aryans, and especially Teutons."[62]

With the successful 1948 founding of Israel in the wake of the Holocaust, this process of gendered reinvention took on added urgency. Israeli
media of the 1940s and 1950s aimed to assist Holocaust survivors in replacing, as Moore and Troen argue, "Diaspora Jewish identity for a Hebrew-
Israeli one."[63] The goal was to couch the increasing militarism of Israel
within a progression narrative template as already defined by European colonial hero myth archetypes. Jews were no longer positioned as discursively
distinct. If Jewish men could be reconfigured as "conventionally" masculine and Jewish women as "conventionally" feminine in Israel itself, sus-
pects of duplicity in the Jewish Diaspora could be muted. Zionism became
understood throughout the world primarily through this gendered discourse in which the new Jewishness mimicked the Anglo-European power
structures from which it had successfully escaped.[64] Zionism became, as
David Biale describes it, an "erotic revolution for the Jews."[65]

Leon Uris's *Exodus*, a best-selling novel released in 1958, was one of the
first major texts to depict this link between the erotic and the geographic at
work in the formation of Israel. The novel told a factually grounded story
of the *Exodus*, a boat filled with European Jewish Holocaust survivors determined to find their way to Israel. But in the character of heroic Jewish freedom fighter Ari Ben-Canaan, it also reintroduced a new form of
potent, unapologetic Jewish masculinity to the American mainstream. In
Otto Preminger's film version, released in 1960, Ben-Canaan was played
by movie star Paul Newman. Newman's glamorous, idealized hero was a
representation of the rugged Jewish masculinity that Theodor Herzl and
Max Nordau had described as one of the central goals of the Zionist movement. No longer the purportedly embattled and weak Communist schlemiels hunted by Hitler in Europe and McCarthy and HUAC in the United
States, this new Israeli Jew offered what Yosefa Loshitzky describes as a
transnational recoding of the Jewish Diaspora, a "Zionization of the American Jew."[66]

But despite his idealized placement as a masculine icon at the center of
the narrative, Ari Ben-Canaan is not the protagonist.[67] The growing awakening of his American Anglo-Saxon love interest, Kitty Fremont (Eva Marie Saint), is the core character arc at work in both the novel and the film.
Kitty oscillates between assimilationist and outsider perspectives, alternately aiding and blocking the path between Ari and the unfettered ideals of the Zionism that he pursues. Her role as a blonde Christian from
Indiana is essential in the film's presentation of Ari as a new form of hyper-
masculinity. She serves as the non-Jewish spectatorial entrance point. But
she is also a tempering device. Her love for him universalizes the Jewish

American Anglo-Saxon nurse Kitty Fremont's (Eva Marie Saint) love for European Jewish settler Ari Ben-Canaan (Paul Newman) helps humanize the historical progression narrative of the creation of Israel in Exodus *(1960).*

specificity of Ari's Zionist ambitions. His love for her ultimately rejects the Jewish cultural purity inherent to the Israel project.

This recalibration of Zionism was essential to the film's success. It replaces Zionism with an ideology of American multiculturalism. This point is made clear just before the first kiss between Ari and Kitty as they debate the essential differences between Jews and Christians.

> Kitty: All these differences between people are made up. People are the same no matter what they're called.
> Ari: Don't ever believe it. People are different. They have a right to be different. They like to be different. It's no good pretending that differences don't exist. They do.
> Kitty: You're wrong, Ari. There are no differences.
> (They kiss)

As with Phil Green in *Gentlemen's Agreement,* Kitty is the idealized non-Jewish witness of Jewish suffering. The Jew's erotic desire for the non-Jew contradicts Ari's insistence on Jewish exclusivity. Their romantic liaison is ideological in nature. Ari's acquiescence to Kitty's kiss produces mutual Anglo-Christian-Jewish sexual desire as the final act of utopian transgression over the artificial barriers of race, religion, and ethnicity. If Ari and Kitty can successfully find love, the boundaries between Jew and Gentile—and, by proxy, European nativism and the modern world—are defeated.[68]

As Omer Bartov notes, Newman's "half-Jewish" biographical background, highly publicized in the film's press materials of the time, allowed *Exodus* to further temper any claims to Jewish distinction.[69] Newman's "perfect Aryan looks," counterpointed by his prominent Star of David necklace, merged a half-Jew-as-Jew star persona with the ideals of masculine/muscular Zionism.[70] The Zionist/Diaspora duality of Newman-as-Ari exemplified the two conflicting identities of post-Israel Jewish masculinity, the feminized Diaspora schlemiel and the hyper-masculine conqueror.[71] This liminal status hybridized both the "Peck" and "Garfield" arguments of *Gentlemen's Agreement* into the single body of Newman-as-Ari. The notion of Jewish/non-Jewish masquerade is seen in the film when Ari successfully impersonates a British naval officer by blending in with non-Jewish British crewmen. Newman's ability to "pass" as non-Jewish remains as unquestioned as that of Gregory Peck in *Gentlemen's Agreement.* Yet, in publicizing his Jewish lineage, Newman-as-Ari also signified the newly visible and proud Zionist Jewish masculinity emerging in the 1960s. Ari was thus both Jew and non-Jew, a hybrid, tenuous solution to the twentieth-century Jewish crisis that Daniel Boyarin describes as the long search for a "Jewish political subject who will find a place in modernity."[72]

The importance of the Ari/Kitty love story to this geopolitical renegotiation was a direct response to the premium placed on Anglo-Saxon beauty throughout the 1950s. The idealization of blonde and blue-eyed Anglo femininity had become what historian Steven Cohan describes as "the fifties' primary trope for female sexuality."[73] This physiognomy and gender template can be seen in everything from Hitchcock's "icy blondes" (Doris Day, Grace Kelly, Kim Novak, Tippi Hedren) to Brigitte Bardot as the idealized female in European art cinema such as *And God Created Woman* (1956). Cohan, via Richard Dyer, notes how reassuring narratives of WASP beauty helped quell anxieties brought about by the ethnic unrest of the American civil rights movement.[74] Yet, the artificial construction of idealized Nordic beauty was just as quickly coming apart. Marilyn Monroe was satirizing this cliché as early as 1953 in *Gentlemen Prefer Blondes.* In her real life, the quintessential blonde of the 1950s made headlines with her rejection of her storybook marriage to the icon of Italian-American athletic masculinity, Joe DiMaggio. Monroe left DiMaggio to marry the older, bespectacled, Jewish intellectual, Arthur Miller, in 1956. Monroe's choice suggested the value of the Jewish intellectual/artist at a time when Jews were operating on the margins of popular culture and through code. This permeability was further enhanced with Monroe's conversion to Judaism before her marriage to Miller.

Monroe was not alone. Elizabeth Taylor, Debbie Reynolds, and Janet

Leigh all married Jewish men in public ceremonies. Taylor, born a Christian Scientist, even converted to Judaism in 1959, taking the Hebrew name "Elisheba Rachel."[75] It was rumored in the popular press of the time that Taylor was forced to convert because of the demands of either her Jewish husband Mike Todd, or, after Todd's premature death in 1958, Taylor's next husband, Eddie Fisher. Taylor denied converting for any reason other than her affection for the Jewish people. The notion that Monroe and Taylor, two idealized exemplars of Hollywood beauty and glamour, would both actively decide to convert suggested a different sort of malleability. Instead of the Jew acquiescing to Gentile culture, the Gentile was choosing to be Jewish. Kitty's love for Ari's passion brought this shiksa-Jewish scrambling to the silver screen under the safe confines of a geopolitical progression narrative.

Ari's untempered conviction and fearless masculinity exemplified what David Biale describes as the sexual and gendered motivations of Zionism as a response to the European notion that "Jews lived a disembodied existence in exile."[76] Traditional male Jews found their virility not by physical accomplishment but by intellectual achievement in Torah study.[77] The energy purportedly demanded by God to be spent on Torah study has been described for centuries by rabbis as a form of erotic intercourse akin to a marriage between the Jewish male and his academic work. After the Dreyfus Affair, Zionists recognized that there had to be a restoration of externalized masculinity for the Jew to physically survive. The act of land conquest in Palestine offered a way to reclaim this virility. Ari Ben-Canaan was an action hero, not a scholar. His masculinity was defined in physicality, rather than in intellectual achievement. His acquisition of Kitty was the first step in reintroducing American Jewish men of the 1960s as newly remasculinized and emergent.

The Ari/Kitty love story also reflected the very real shifting demographics of the 1960s. The rate of intermarriage between Jews and non-Jews, at only 9 percent in 1965, rose to as high as 26 percent by 1974.[78] Ari's successful leadership of his fellow Jews into Palestine conveyed a spatial journey of conquest as an update to the iconography of the wandering Jewish schlemiel. But the character's emotional journey represented the nascent generational and political changes taking place in the United States in the early 1960s. Ari begins as a Jewish isolationist. Kitty's love convinces him otherwise. His eventual acquiescence to love from the non-Jewish Kitty with the blonde hair and blue eyes also communicated a universal coming together soon to be codified by the Summer of Love and the ascendant American counterculture in the late 1960s.

Seven years after *Exodus*, *The Graduate* problematized the transnational utopianism of the Ari/Kitty coupling by relocating it into an American suburban milieu.[79] In privileging Dustin Hoffman as the new face of youth culture masculinity, it became the first film of the second wave to establish a clear link among deviant Jewishness, taboo sexuality, and the liberation of Christian repression. This is not an obvious reading of the film. *The Graduate* appears to be a poetic parable of generational transformation and youthful angst set in white, upper-middle-class American suburbia. There are neither recognizably Jewish events nor specific Jewish subject matter in the film. But the triangular framework linking the characters of Benjamin, Elaine, and Mrs. Robinson produced an oedipal version of what Marjorie Garber describes as one of "the most fundamental courtship narratives of Western culture": the love triangle.[80]

It is within this triangle that the film's coded Jewishness, in the form of Benjamin's flawed masculinity and taboo sexual urges, first locates. The sexual freedoms and emerging gender empowerment of the women's rights movement of the late 1960s are embodied not by the daughter, Elaine, but by the mother, Mrs. Robinson (Anne Bancroft). As the sexual aggressor, Mrs. Robinson mitigates and problematizes simplified notions of sexual liberation. It is the *previous* generation that is rebelling against sexual norms. The new generation ultimately desires a classic courtship romance. The love triangle's ability to scramble and visualize cultural boundaries is, as Garber argues by way of René Girard, a narrative device that offers a complex intersubjective reading on the modalities of erotic discourse.[81] Benjamin's disruption is one of taboo presence. As with Benjamin Disraeli's romance novels a century earlier in England, the entrance of the Jew scrambles, inverts, and dissolves the utopian fantasies of entrenched Anglo-Saxon power.

The film's coded Jewishness also locates in physiognomy. A second love triangle eventually emerges that counterpoints Benjamin with Elaine's fiancé, Carl Smith (Brian Avery). Carl is introduced as Benjamin's physical and emotional opposite, a doppelganger of Robert Redford himself. After Benjamin travels to Berkeley to woo Elaine, he follows her on a bus to the zoo, where she is meeting Carl by the monkey house. As Carl approaches the monkey house to greet Elaine, he is immediately identifiable as a confident, pipe-smoking, blond, Teutonic-looking, Ivy League "frat boy," an almost cartoonish definition of the normative, postwar, Anglo-Christian masculine archetype.[82] Benjamin's sarcastic crack—"He sure is a good walker!"—upon seeing Carl for the first time has the ironic humor of the post–Lenny Bruce comedians. But Benjamin's alienated Jewishness as the embodiment of generational confusion is cemented as Elaine and Carl walk away. Benjamin turns and stares into the monkey house. His gaze is met by the uncanny stare of a gorilla. Like Kafka's ape before him, Benjamin's sexual desires have cast him out of normative society.[83]

The final sequence solidified this meditation on thematic historical religious-cultural taboo. Hoffman, as both the character of Benjamin and the disruptive signifier of not-Redford, breaks into the sanctity of Elaine's idealized, Christian church wedding to Carl. The division between the two worlds is made literal within the aesthetics of the sequence. Benjamin enters the church and rushes to the second floor, where he begins banging on an upper-level church glass window. His sweaty, dirty face and full-throated screaming of "Elaine!" over and over operate as direct counterpoint to the formal, clean wedding on display below. Benjamin is excluded from the Christian world below. But he is also positioned in the crucifixion pose as he bangs on the glass, an ironic coda to the idealized Christian world he is witnessing. Nichols's experimental, avant-garde use of subjective sound confirms this division. A sequence of shots shows the various wedding attendees becoming increasingly angry at Benjamin's disruption. Their faces, including those of Carl and Mrs. Robinson, stare directly into the camera, breaking the fourth wall. Yet, their voices are not heard. Only the sound of Benjamin permeates the scene. The silent world around Benjamin is only broken when Elaine responds by crying out, "Ben!" Her vocal response affirms the intrusion and marks the moment at which Benjamin, as the Jewish interloper, is validated over the normative, Anglo-Christian church fantasy embodied by Carl.

The subsequent chaos in the church entrance makes the symbolism of Jewish alterity rupturing Christian power even more explicit. Benjamin grabs a giant cross off the wall of the church and swings it at Elaine's rioting family, keeping them at bay. He then uses the cross to barricade the church doors as he and Elaine escape. He has become the triumphant Jewish transgressive, inverting the institutional power of Christianity through the use of an actual cross. The sequence concludes with the film's iconic final shot of Benjamin and Elaine's confused, nervous facial expressions in the back of a public bus.

In transgressing the barriers of the church to rescue Elaine, Hoffman-as-Benjamin operates both inside and outside the text as the embodiment of youth culture rebellion overthrowing the fantasy sensibilities of 1950s Gentile gentility. He saves the WASP princess from her conscripted fate. But the couple also enters an uncertain future. The chaos of the late 1960s is transposed onto the anxious, confused face of a nebbishy, neurotic, newly sexually empowered Jewish schlemiel and his equally unsure Anglo-Christian partner. The film's aesthetic sensibility was attuned to the cultural anxieties of the late 1960s. But the coupling of a young Jewish man with a Christian woman over the objections of older family members was also straight out of the first-wave immigrant love stories of the 1920s. In this reclamation of first-wave archetypes, the long history of the unruly Jew as a signifier of sexual transgression swung back from liability to asset. With one swing of the cross, Benjamin and Elaine had broken with postwar (Anglocentric) tradition and forged a new, uncertain path. The second wave of New Hollywood Jewish-Anglo-Christian love stories soon followed.

CHAPTER 5

Portnoy's Monkey

POSTWAR LITERATURE, STAND-UP
COMEDY, AND THE EMERGENCE OF
THE CARNAL JEW (1955–1969)

*Doctor, I had never had anybody like her in my life, she was the ful-
fillment of my most lascivious adolescent dreams—but marry her,
can she be serious? You see, for all her preening and perfumes, she has
a very low opinion of herself, and simultaneously—and here is the
source of much of our trouble—a ridiculously high opinion of me.
And simultaneously, a very low opinion of me! She is one confused
Monkey, and, I'm afraid, not too very bright.*

ALEXANDER PORTNOY, *PORTNOY'S COMPLAINT* (1972)

IN 1964, TWO SEEMINGLY UNRELATED BOOKS BECAME
national best sellers. The first, Saul Bellow's acclaimed 1964
novel *Herzog*, was about a middle-aged Jewish professor suffering from a
nervous breakdown after he discovers that his wife has been cheating on
him with his best friend. The second, *Call It Sleep* by Henry Roth, told the
story of David Schearl, a young Jewish immigrant learning to survive on
the Lower East Side in 1907.

Both books were unlikely texts for mainstream popularity. *Herzog* was
the latest novel by an already acclaimed postwar novelist who was about to
turn fifty. It was immediately hailed by both critics and audiences alike as
a masterpiece, remaining a best seller for nearly a year and making Bellow
a millionaire.[1] *Call It Sleep* was an anachronism, a thirty-year-old book that
suddenly reemerged to become a sensation to an entirely new generation of
readers. It was originally written by twenty-eight-year-old Henry Roth (no
relation to Philip Roth) and published with little fanfare in 1934. While it
received critical praise, the novel's dark tones of Lower East Side Jewish
slum life made it a tough sell at the peak of the Great Depression. It quickly

went out of print, and Henry Roth was forgotten.[2] Yet, when *Call It Sleep* was republished by Avon Press, in hardcover in 1960 and then in paperback in 1964, it became an unlikely publishing sensation. Paralleling the runaway success of *Herzog*, Roth's novel sold more than one million copies, eventually being named by *Time* magazine as one of the one hundred greatest English-language novels published after 1923.[3]

A domestic melodrama about an immigrant Jewish family, *Call It Sleep* focuses on the relationship of young David, his loving mother, Genya, and his cruel, distant father, Albert. The dark realities of 1907 and urban New York ghetto life are told through David's eyes. His struggles to adapt to his new country eventually transform his story into what Stanislav Kolar describes as a modernist redemption narrative.[4] David rebels by rejecting his Jewish culture. He becomes attracted to rosaries and crucifixes. He befriends a young Polish Catholic boy, Leo Dugowka. But perhaps most importantly, David's bildungsroman journey involves the gradual reconstruction of his mother's long-ago love affair with Ludwig, a Gentile with whom she fell in love in Galicia. David may or may not be the product of his mother's affair with Ludwig. The hostility of his father is revealed through this act of original Anglo-Christian-Jewish sin. David's Jewish-Gentile hybridity becomes a forbidden fruit, a mythic rewriting of his origin story with the potential to liberate him from his conscripted Jewishness.

The novel wove its unusual episodic narrative through the familiar ghetto love story and immigrant comedy tropes that had dominated vaudeville and early Hollywood in the 1910s and 1920s. Like the characters in those first-generation texts, Roth's David rebels against the cultural divisiveness of the parental generation. He longs to escape the Jewish ghetto and journey forward into a multicultural America made up of Christian and Jew alike. But it is David's sexual compulsiveness that continues to mark him as "Jewish" even as he assimilates. Roth drew from the graphic depictions of James Joyce's *Ulysses*, using sexuality to depict what Roth called the "obscene modernism" of the 1910s and 1920s.[5]

Unapologetic Jewish subject matter, clear Zionist overtones, and graphic language associated with the avant-garde of Europe were ahead of the times in American literature at the end of the first wave. From Israel Zangwill's 1908 play, *The Melting Pot*, through *The Jazz Singer* in 1927, other pre-WWII assimilation fantasies had focused on the first-generation American breaking bonds with cultural ghettoization. *Call It Sleep* problematized this progression narrative. David's exploration begins by focusing on his early childhood desires to expand his world by sampling American Christian culture. He becomes fixated on the habits of Christian children in his neighborhood. But as he matures, David begins to reject this outward focus. He instead traces his generational rebellion backward and into his own specific family history. His alienation is both from the greater Christian-American culture in which he resides and from the assimilationist, albeit repressed, background of his mother's journey to America. The novel eventually reveals that it is Genya, David's mother, who first transgressed the Jewish-Gentile divide in her sexual life back in Germany. This "original sin" for immigrant Jews suggests that Jewish-Christian erotic entanglements may not be an American invention after all.

This achronological generational revisionism narrative was one reason for the novel's massive next-generation popularity in the mid-1960s. Upon its initial release, Roth's novel with its Jewish focus found little acceptance in an increasingly anti-Semitic, anti-immigrant climate suffering under the Great Depression. But by the mid-1960s, *Call It Sleep* held the alluring power of a rediscovered, resurrected artifact of the lost world of Lower East Side Jewry. It became one of the most notable examples of what Matthew Frye Jacobson describes as an upsurge in interest in ethnocentric prewar Jewish life that began in 1960 with the hugely successful republishing of Abraham Cahan's 1917 novel, *The Rise of David Levinsky*.[6] The harsh truths of American immigration had become whitewashed into assimilationist fantasies in the postwar years. Youth culture was increasingly curious about the real immigrant origins of their parents and grandparents. The lost world of Roth's American Jewish ghetto offered a clear counterpoint to the emphasis on white, Anglo-Saxon suburban normativity as an idyllic, aspirational quest. It revealed the violence, sexual and otherwise, that lurked at the margins of the great diasporic movement at the turn of the twentieth century.

Roth's emphasis on carnality, not love, as the expression of generational break was central to the novel's potency. The novel's bleak depiction of Lower East Side tenement life was visceral, graphic, and raw. It was also unabashedly sexual. Alan Gibbs notes that the erotic themes conflate an oscillation between sexual pleasure and shame with the straddling between Jewish and Gentile worlds.[7] Roth's emphasis on carnality—not love—as the expression of generational break saw Jewish/Gentile lust as the problematic and flawed reality of the new American multicultural experience. Crossing this implicit taboo provided an allegory for the inchoate impulses of youthful anger and rebellion.

This had obvious appeal in the early days of the emerging counterculture of the 1960s. As the veneer of Eisenhower-era whiteness began to lift and the buried traumas of World War II began to surface, a process of historical reappraisal began. A sharp nostalgia for the prewar era emerged. Flapper girl fashion from the 1920s began to dominate fashion runways of the

1960s. This peaked in 1967 with the impact of Faye Dunaway's 1920s-era fashion in *Bonnie and Clyde* and culminated in 1971 with *Life* magazine's cover story, "Everybody's Just Wild about . . . Nostalgia." The *Life* cover featured six 1930s-era starlets on the cover, articles about Art Deco, fashion trends of the 1920s, and an article on the Broadway revival of the 1925 musical comedy, *No, No, Nanette.*[8]

As a forgotten literary gem of the period, *Call It Sleep* offered its own nostalgia. The book's anti-assimilationist Jewish pride and celebration of Jewish carnal desire over romantic love were both at odds with the receding immigrant visibility of the 1930s. But, by 1964, David's erotic yearnings for Christian women and his subsequent discovery of his mother's own dalliance with a German Catholic offered a reconfigured immigrant narrative far more complex than the simplified idealism of *The Melting Pot* and other assimilationist fantasies of the 1910s and 1920s. For the second-generation postwar reappraisal taking place, this honesty spoke to the new complexities of an increasingly uncensored and graphic mass media age.

Bellow's *Herzog* was not a reclaimed historical artifact like *Call It Sleep*. But it contained a similar reframing of moral sensibilities. As with *Call It Sleep*, it focused on the breakup of a Jewish family grappling with biographical secrets.[9] This tension is expressed not through the eyes of a child but in a story of midlife crisis. Bellow's protagonist, Moses E. Herzog, is a meek, passive, Canadian-Jewish academic who lives primarily within his own thoughts and is suffering through the breakup of his second marriage. His wife, Madeleine, a Jew who has converted to Catholicism, is pursuing her graduate studies in Slavonic languages. Similar to David's oscillation between Christian and Jewish identities in *Call It Sleep*, Madeleine operates as the idealized assimilationist Jew: secular, emancipated, and no longer tethered to her cultural past. She is seen by Herzog as an enlightened secular modernist but also as the "personification of the essences of romanticism and Christianity."[10] Yet, like *Call It Sleep*, *Herzog* indicts this American Jewish assimilationist fantasy by locating carnality and self-hatred as the destructive impulses lurking within the Jewish Diaspora. Madeleine's conversion to Christianity allows her the freedom to cheat on Herzog and, eventually, to leave him. Herzog, the Jew-as-Jew, is left behind with his ideals and his morals, but not his wife. His subsequent crisis of identity positions the problematic Jew as the traumatized outsider, struggling with America's postwar emphasis on cultural (Christian) sameness.

Herzog is depicted as both creatively and physically impotent; his Jewish ex-wife, transformed into a Catholic, symbolizes this failure. He becomes obsessed with revenge, buying a pistol and attempting to murder her. Failing to summon the courage to go through with the act, he instead begins to write voluminous reams of letters, which he never sends, to contemporary politicians and dead philosophers such as Spinoza and Nietzsche. His subsequent act of agency, an affair with his student, Ramona, seeks to use sexual taboo as a solution to this sense of impotence. The inappropriate use of his academic status as a respected professor becomes his one act of rebellion.

This use of transgressive sex as a coping mechanism for Herzog's post-divorce alienation is revealed by the class that Herzog teaches, "The Roots of Romanticism." Romanticism was, as Pauline Kleingeld notes, an early nineteenth-century corrective to the emphasis on individualism and rationality introduced during the Age of Enlightenment.[11] European Christian artists and philosophers, most notably in Germany, began to emphasize irrationality and emotions as guiding principles of a new nationalist pride. Romanticism was also a corrective to the secular rationality associated with cosmopolitanism. In Bellow's novel, this translates as a Christian/Jewish schizophrenia at work within Herzog himself. Romanticism was an emotive form of nationalism produced by European Christian modernists. Cosmopolitanism, with its emphasis on logic and individualism, was the province of the alienated, intellectual Jew. The irony of Herzog's academic life is that he teaches the very privileged Euro-Christian emotional freedom model that he himself is incapable of experiencing.

Bellow eventually traces Herzog's cascading ironies of alienation into the "Jewish" science of psychoanalysis. His therapist, Dr. Edvig, is a Christian, not a Jew. As L. H. Goldman points out, Herzog scorns Edvig's abilities as a psychoanalyst precisely because he is not Jewish.[12] His contemptuous term for Edvig's flawed abilities is "Protestant Freudianism." Edvig's Christian identity marks him as another thematic betrayer of Herzog's authentic (Jewish) self. Bellow presents this dismissal as yet another form of impotence. It allows Herzog to reject his therapy as inauthentic, leaving him an alienated island of stubborn Jewishness. Herzog is now betrayed on both sexual and psychoanalytic levels by both the Jewish-turned-Christian wife and the Christian-but-should-be-Jewish therapist. Even the conquest of an objectified Anglo-Christian fantasy sex object, Ramona, cannot purge Herzog's crisis of identity in the postwar era.

In 1988, in an article covering his long, lauded career, Bellow reflected on whether his work had any essentialist Jewish specificity. He described how he first learned about the inherent contradiction in being both a Jew and a Westerner.[13] As a Canadian-born Jewish child of Eastern European immigrants, the young Bellow became obsessed with reading about Benjamin Disraeli. Disraeli's theatrical performance and mimicry of the non-Jewish world fascinated the young boy. He described recognizing that even an enormously successful European statesman like Disraeli could only survive through the twin forces of what Bellow described as "study and artifice."[14] Like Disraeli, Bellow couched his Jewishness in universal codes. He described this tension, his efforts to "combine being a Jew with being an American and a writer," as the central theme of his work.[15] But Bellow emphatically rejected the notion that he had produced a universalized American assimilation myth. His work, as he saw it, was intrinsically and essentially Jewish.

Bellow's touchiness was a response to decades of criticism that he received from academics, such as Gershom Scholem, that he had intentionally obfuscated the specific Jewish themes that permeated his work. Bellow responded thusly:

> I did not wish to become part of the *Partisan Review* gang. Like many of its members I was, however, "an emancipated Jew who refused to deny his Jewishness," and I suppose I should have considered myself a "cosmopolitan" if I had been capable of thinking clearly in those days.[16]

In the 1920s, Scholem had slammed the scholars of the Frankfurt School as selling Jewish philosophy, rebranded as "dialectical materialism," to the Western (aka non-Jewish) world. Scholem had initially critiqued Jewish-born thinkers such as Walter Benjamin, Karl Marx, most of Freud's fin de siècle cohorts, Edmund Husserl, Theodor Adorno, and Max Horkheimer for hiding the Jewish specificity of their work.[17] By the 1950s, Scholem turned his focus on American writers such as Bellow, critiquing American Jewish authors for "de-Judaising" their work in an attempt to mitigate resistance by non-Jewish readers. Bellow resented this criticism. He claimed that his work remained distinctly Jewish and that Jewish specificity located through codings and metaphors responding to a distinct postwar crisis of identity in Diaspora Jewry.

Despite Scholem's indictment, Bellow perceived the crisis of the postwar American Jew in similar terms to Scholem's critique of European Jewish intellectuals in the 1920s. To both Bellow and Scholem, the Diasporic Jew had become untethered from an authentic identity. Jews began performing in ways meant to appease the Christian world. In Bellow's novels, this tension emerged in the debate over whether postwar Jews should aspire to an American universalism or remain true to their misanthropic impulses. Sexual desire for the non-Jew (the shiksa), usually depicted as an affair, externalized this crisis. But it also confirmed the specificity that Scholem believed lurked in the work of all Jewish modernists, from Benjamin to Kafka. Bellow's depiction of Jewish sexual carnality for the shiksa used negative stereotypes not as apologia but to invoke and embody postwar detachment after assimilation. It was a negation that, through the prism of fiction, also operated as an act of next-generation visualization for the emerging counterculture of the 1960s.[18]

Like Proust and Kafka before him, Bellow produced this subjectivity by hybridizing conflicting understandings and perspectives across a Christian-Jewish divide. As with Proust's Charles Swann and Kafka's many animal-humans, paradoxical modernism is represented through residual psychological trauma redirected into the sexual realm. The emancipated/alienated modern Jew embodies this tension. Yet, important distinctions emerge. Herzog (and David in *Call It Sleep*) is not constrained by the cultural barriers experienced in Proust's France and Kafka's Prague. The barriers of assimilation have been lifted, as confirmed by Madeleine's easy conversion/reinvention as a Christian. Still, Herzog remains unable to assimilate into the larger, non-Jewish, Western framework. He is stuck in a prewar understanding of Jewish masculinity triggered by repeated flashbacks to his immigrant father's life and experiences in the prewar era. The barriers are now internalized and psychoanalytic in nature. Herzog remains fixed in place by his own pathology as the queered, male Jew whom Daniel Boyarin describes as central to European imagination up to and through the nineteenth century.[19]

By focusing on the un-heroic, neurotic, Jewish intellectual as a new literary un-hero, *Herzog* reveals that émigré American and Canadian Jews such as Saul Bellow, even those who did not choose the path of Zionist reinvention, still found cause for battle. Only these battles were not located on the political, national, or cultural level. Instead, they operated as sexualized, eroticized metaphors of marriages, affairs, and redirected sexual desire. The modern postwar American Jew, like modernity itself, could only be produced through negative dialectics. This produced the Jewish Other as the defining alternative of Christonormative power. But the two subjectivities can never be fully bridged. Each requires the other for self-definition. Bellow's work had confirmed Gershom's philosophy, even as it appeared to negate it. It merely relocated the battle from the international sociopolitical level (Europe-Israel) to the internalized nuances and archetypes of the postwar American nuclear family.

MALAMUD'S MAGIC JEW

Like Bellow, Bernard Malamud was an acclaimed novelist and short story author of the 1950s and 1960s. Also like Bellow, Malamud repeatedly connected the postwar struggle of suburban alienation to the theme of Diaspora Jewish longing, frustration, and confusion. As the 1950s transitioned into the 1960s, Malamud recognized the same externalization and transference pattern that Bellow located in Herzog's desire for the Anglo-Christian fantasy as embodied by Ramona. The Jewish (alienated) desire to heal impossible postwar schisms, whether intergenerational or psychoanalytic, was expressed in depicting the taboo nature of Jewish sexual desire for the non-Jewish partner.[20]

Malamud's second novel, *The Assistant* (1957), was one of the first major works of literature in the postwar era to touch on this theme. The novel explored the rapidly disintegrating world of Jewish New York in the form of a failing grocery store owned by Morris Bober (a name perhaps echoing Martin Buber). Bober's secular Jewish daughter, Helen, and his Italian-American employee (and criminal), Frank Alpine, find that they are attracted to each other. Frank is depicted as a hot-headed, passionate, hyper-aggressive man. His kinetic aggressiveness is contrasted with the various Jewish men in the grocery store for whom Frank feels nothing but contempt. But his latent anti-Semitism is reserved only for Jewish men. When Frank spies on Helen in her bathroom and sees her naked for the first time, his act of voyeurism is depicted as alternately both romantic and violent:

> Her body was young, soft, lovely, the breasts like small birds in flight, her ass like a flower. Yet it was a lonely body in spite of its lovely form, lonelier. Bodies are lonely, he thought, but in bed she wouldn't be. She seemed realer to him now than she had been, revealed without clothes, personal, possible. He felt greedy as he gazed, all eyes at a banquet, hungry so long as he must look. But in looking he was forcing her out of reach, making her into a thing only of his seeing, her eyes reflecting his sins, rotten past, spoiled ideals, his passion poisoned by his shame.[21]

Malamud's lonely/lovely alliterative interplay, cast through the subjectivity of Italian-Catholic sexual shame, recalled the siren-like pull of the ghetto Jewess temptress of the 1910s and 1920s. Yet, where ghetto Jewesses drew Gentile men into displays of masculine bravery, Frank's longing for Helen leads him to commit a violent act against her father. He robs Morris's grocery while wearing a disguise, severely injuring Morris. Guilty over his actions, he returns to the grocery to work for Morris as an act of Catholic repentance. Frank struggles to confess his crime to Morris as well as to earn the love of Helen. But Frank's passions overwhelm him, and in the climax of the book, Frank coerces Helen into sex in what can plausibly be interpreted as only a semi-consensual act:

> Helen felt herself gently lifted and knew she was in his arms. She sobbed in relief. He kissed her eyes and lips and he kissed her half-naked breast. She held him tightly with both arms, weeping, laughing, murmuring she had come to tell him she loved him.[22]

Helen's submission to Frank operates as oedipal replacement. The cautious and passive Morris is unable to take actions to save either his daughter or his store. Helen finds relief by giving in to the more conventionally "masculine" aggressiveness that Frank represents. The story concludes with Morris's death, possibly a suicide, in which his defeat at the hands of an impossible American dream is reflected in his inability to prevent the encroaching forces of modernism taking hold of the Jewish world in which he lives. In a symbolic irony, Morris is replaced by Frank, who chooses to convert to Judaism and take over the store as his final act of Catholic penance. Helen replaces her father with Frank. But Frank also chooses to mimic Morris. Jewish masculinity, both passive and pacifist, abides through the non-Jew. Frank's conversion hybridized his efforts at a distinct form of Christian redemption with Morris's emphasis on Jewish piety.

This linking of sexuality, Jewishness, and postwar alienation emerges even more clearly in Malamud's most famous short story, "The Magic Barrel" (1958). Leo Finkle, a Yeshiva student in his late twenties, is studying to be a rabbi. He hires a matchmaker, Salzman, to find him an appropriate Jewish bride. Leo has spent so many years studying that he has no experience with women. Salzman informs Leo that he keeps those seeking a match on index cards and that he has so many index cards he's forced to store them not in a filing cabinet, but in a barrel. The titular "magic barrel," unseen by Leo, is an imaginative construct. It is the place in which carnality exists. It is where single Jewish women have filed cards seeking a male. After an unsuccessful date, Leo becomes obsessed with the one picture on an index card that Salzman won't identify. After pursuing her identity, Leo discovers that it is Stella, Salzman's own daughter. Salzman refuses to make the match, explaining that he has rejected his daughter for being, "a wild one—wild, without shame. . . . Like an animal. Like a dog. For her to be poor was a sin. This is why to me she is dead now."[23]

The animal metaphors of libidinal "Jewess" carnality once again represented a generational break. Leo insists on meeting Salzman's daughter. His anticipation is a combination of hopeful erotic fantasy and a sense of traumatic displacement and loss. Leo has chosen love over intellectually select-ing his partner. A strange haunting death hangs over his choice. The final line of the story makes this overt. As Leo and Stella meet, Malamud writes: "Around the corner, Salzman, leaning against a wall, chanted prayers for the dead."[24] "The Magic Barrel" was not a story of intermarriage. It osten-sibly featured the successful coupling of two Jewish characters. But Jewish carnality was a destructive action. Lust annihilated the last vestiges of post-war, immigrant Jewry. For Malamud, the awakening of Jewish sexuality was a signifier of next-generation Diaspora movement, just as it had been for the first wave of immigrants in the 1920s. But instead of the euphoric assimilation narrative of that period, spiritual crisis remained.[25]

PORTNOY'S SYNTHESIS

In 1967, *The Graduate* had integrated the aesthetic sensibilities and provocative sexual experimentations of European art cinema into the Hollywood mainstream by replacing the expected masculine hero (Rob-ert Redford) with an unlikely, nebbishy Jew (Dustin Hoffman). Philip Roth's *Portnoy's Complaint*, published in February 1969, did the same for the American novel. It distilled and accelerated the formal innovations of Bellow, Malamud, and other authors by linking extensive depictions of deviant, graphic sexuality to the neurotic compulsions of postwar Amer-ican Jewishness. Written as a first-person confession from thirty-three-year-old Alexander Portnoy to his psychotherapist, *Portnoy's Complaint* is an outrageous mix of sexual descriptions, neurotic self-hatred, and co-medic Jewish-mother-hatred all presented with unapologetic X-rated lan-guage.[26] The book's taboo-shattering approach to what was and was not permissible in mainstream American letters used the established literary framework of Jewish sexual deviancy as a launching pad for a new form of graphic literary art. Early in the novel, Portnoy's compulsive teenage mas-turbation experimentations are described in extensive detail, without apol-ogy or euphemism.[27] The sequences were so graphic in nature that liter-ary critic Bernard Avishai calls them a "great innovation" in the art of the novel.[28]

Jewishness was essential to the novel's comedic transgressions. Portnoy, like Hoffman-as-Benjamin in *The Graduate*, was an updated first-wave ar-chetype recalibrated for the new urban ethnic pride of the 1960s. Like Ben-jamin, Portnoy externalized the postwar generation's alienation, confusion, rage, and disaffection through transference into the sexual realm. His sex-ual anger was the product of two factors. The first was the emasculating role of Portnoy's suffocating Jewish mother stereotype. Roth's unapologetic embrace of psychoanalysis and the mother fixation as a distinctly Jewish phenomenon gave these sequences the comedic charge of politically incorrect satire. The second located in the institutional power of suburban, white, postwar Christian America that, at least throughout the 1950s, excluded Jewish masculinity from its normative codes. Like the jazz singers and ghetto Jewesses of the 1910s and 1920s, Portnoy's solution to cultural ghettoization was to seek out his opposite in the romantic/sexual realm: the blonde, Anglo-Saxon ideal that exemplified postwar America.

But the novel was keenly aware of its debt to first-wave archetypes. As in *Herzog*, immigrant assimilationist fantasies were reconfigured in the postwar era as psychoanalytic delusions. Whereas once the coupling of Jew and Christian offered an idealized progression narrative, Portnoy's erotic fascinations with the "Other" are instead deconstructed as the by-product of narcissism, sexual trauma, and the fractured psyche.

The young Portnoy becomes infatuated with Anglo-Saxon beauty through popular media archetypes introduced into his 1950s childhood by radio, movies, and magazines. He discovers, to his horror, that his loud, Jewish family is garishly at odds with the happy, genteel, white, Christian-American fantasy being sold to him through mass-market entertainment. This produces a fracture in the child's imagination. At first, Portnoy experiences loathing for himself and his Jewish mother. But with the onset of puberty, his neurosis shifts focus toward a carnal lust for an idealized blonde, small-nosed, Anglo-Christian female. Decades later, adult Portnoy's sexual compulsions continue to reference the 1950s-era media fantasies from his childhood. His various lovers, as described throughout the novel, are based on Hollywood movie iconography of the 1950s. Jane Powell, Elizabeth Taylor, and Debbie Reynolds are each referenced as ideal fantasies. Indeed, as Barry Gross observes, Reynolds becomes emblematic of Portnoy's obsession with finding the perfect "upturned" shiksa nose.[29]

As a young adult, Portnoy is finally able to attempt to soothe his feelings of self-hatred and inadequacy through sexual conquest. He experiences sex for the first time with his college girlfriend, an uptight Protestant named Kay Campbell. He meets her polite, Christian family at a Thanksgiving dinner and quickly becomes more infatuated with them than with Kay herself. This inspires the first of Portnoy's many nicknames for his women as Kay becomes "the Pumpkin." Portnoy's fixation on the Pumpkin's family locates in his fascination with how softly and respectfully they speak to each other.[30] They behave exactly as the Gentile families Portnoy fantasized about in the movies and on the radio during his childhood in the 1950s. But the Pumpkin's disappointing sexual skills are not enough to sus-

Karen Black and Richard Benjamin as Monkey and Alexander Portnoy in the film adaptation of Philip Roth's Portnoy's Complaint *(1972).*

tain Portnoy's interest. He moves on to Sarah Abbott Maulsby, a Republican WASP from New Canaan, Connecticut, whom he nicknames "the Pilgrim" due to her family's connection to the *Mayflower*. Although the Pilgrim is more sexually satisfying than the Pumpkin, Portnoy remains distraught as his compulsive X-rated fantasies about Christian women, once acted out, are still not enough to purge his self-loathing. Recognizing this, Portnoy laments to his therapist that "I don't seem to stick my dick up these girls, as much as I stick it up their backgrounds, as though through fucking, I will discover America."[31]

Portnoy's joyous discovery of the equally sexually compulsive Mary Jane Reid (Karen Black), whom he nicknames "the Monkey," appears to provide a solution.[32] The Monkey is minimally educated and equally self-hating about her poor white trash identity. She matches Portnoy's libidinal compulsions by fetishizing his Jewish intellectualism with the same fervor that he fetishizes her "Christian" body. In Portnoy's logic, this should mark the satisfactory pinnacle of his carnal quest. Yet, the Monkey is also not enough. Despite her willingness to participate in all sexual acts, including engaging in a threesome with Portnoy and an Italian prostitute named Lina, the Monkey's low level of intelligence eventually begins to repulse him.

The novel's Freudian satire culminates in Portnoy's final search to find a solution in the form of a Jewish female. He travels to Israel to find what the *New York Times* called his "bête noire," a "Jewish Pumpkin," a sexually adventurous Jewish-Israeli.[33] Naomi is the final externalization of Portnoy's Wandering Jew returning to the proverbial and relatively new Jewish homeland. But this solution also fails. Jewish Pumpkin reminds Portnoy of his mother, thereby rendering him impotent. He attempts to sexually punish her, but this also fails. Roth's satire of Freudian sublimation and transference is the final act that sends Portnoy into psychoanalysis. It is also the act that begins and justifies the innovative structure and X-rated language of the novel's form.

Roth's existential paradox is clear. Jewish-Christian coupling is ultimately an untenable solution to internalized trauma. But so is Jewish-Jewish coupling. Even Israel offers no haven from the fractured neurosis of the postwar Diaspora Jew. Freudian desire to use sex to negate the self is ultimately rendered as nothing more than an endless hall of mirrors. There is no solution. Portnoy's "complaint" is ultimately unknowable, locating beyond both word and image. It is neurosis and projection as sexual compulsion, a psychoanalytic joke in search of an impossible punch line told over hundreds of pages.

In presenting sexually compulsive Jewishness as a comedic but taboo literary monologue, Roth linked the introspective discontent of Bernard Malamud and Saul Bellow to the standup routines of boundary-pushing comedians such as Joan Rivers and Lenny Bruce. This confluence had been building for a decade. Roth's first notable work, *Goodbye, Columbus*, a novella published in 1959, hinted at the formula that Portnoy would ingratiate into the mass consciousness. Couching his social critique in a less politically charged 1950s-era love story, Roth presented sexual angst and cultural rebellion entirely within discourses of Jewish assimilation. The novel's protagonist is Neil Klugman, an urban, working-class Jewish male from New York. Neil becomes infatuated with Brenda Patimkin, a rich, upper-class, assimilated Jewish female from upstate New York. Neil and Brenda articulated the tension between ethnic Jewish alterity and universal assimilation taking place in the 1950s. Yet, Roth's critique, like Lenny Bruce's stand-up comedy, was focused not on the visible, urban Jew (Neil) but instead on the assimilated suburban banality embodied by Brenda. For Roth, assimilation was a fraud and a sellout. It was also the marker of bourgeois cowardice.

In the film adaptation of *Goodbye, Columbus* (1969), released the same year as the publication of *Portnoy's Complaint*, this schism becomes visible through both casting and performance. As Neil Klugman, actor Richard Benjamin embodies the visible, urban Jewishness of the Lower East Side. By contrast, Brenda Patimkin (Ali MacGraw) exemplifies the assimilated, barely Jewish Jews of upstate New York. MacGraw-as-Brenda is the non-Jewish-Jew able to pass by removing her Jewishness and fully integrating into suburban WASP culture.[34] Yet, her father, Ben Patimkin, played by Jewish actor Jack Klugman, offers a reminder of the previous generation's working-class New York roots.[35] As with David in *Call It Sleep* and Moses Herzog's ex-wife, Madeleine, in *Herzog*, Brenda is a problematic paradox of conflicting Christian and Jewish impulses. She becomes emancipated into postwar ecumenical Christian whiteness by virtue of her suburban, assimilated, tennis-playing life. Only the seductive Jewishness of Neil can hold her back.

The film's play with ethnic masquerade is highlighted in the first phone conversation between Neil and Brenda. Before they've even met, Neil calls Brenda up after finding her name in the phone book. They have the following flirtatious exchange:

> Brenda: What do you look like?
> Neil: I'm dark.
> Brenda: Are you a Negro?
> Neil: Sagittarius.[36]

When Neil discovers that she has had a nose job and is deeply embarrassed by her obviously Jewish father, Brenda's artifice begins to crumble. Their dynamic, similar to Hoffman and Ross in *The Graduate*, operates as an iconographic inversion of postwar assimilationist fantasy. Brenda, a manifestation of the assimilated Jew-as-Christian, represents the *Gentlemen's Agreement* universalization argument. Neil is the Jew-as-Jew, a thematic return of John Garfield. Brenda's failure to fully integrate and her attraction to Neil suggest the limits of Jewish self-erasure.

Portnoy's Complaint crystallized the tensions hinted at in *Goodbye, Columbus*. The novel is infamous for breaking numerous sexual and structural taboos in established American literature. It reveled in a rage-filled spasm of psychoanalytic neurosis that satirized the clichés and stereotypes of Jewish self-hatred. But Malamud, Bellow, and Bruce were not the novel's only influences. Roth also used Kafkaesque absurdism to amplify the nature of Jewish alienation. At one point in the novel, Portnoy compares his neurosis to the body crisis of Gregor Samsa.[37] The 1920s had seen Jewish bodies presented in code, as vessels for tragic, nightmarish corporeal crises of European transgression in the age of eugenics. Portnoy's sex acts with the "uncomplicated" shiksa, "the Monkey," revived Kafka's indictment in the realm of sexual transference.[38]

Roth aspired to be seen as a next-generation Kafka, not just another postwar Jewish author in the shadows of Malamud and Bellow. He once admiringly described Kafka as a Jewish "sit-down comic," an allusion that Sanford Pinsker argues was an act of self-inscription and Elaine B. Safer calls a distinct form of meta-fiction.[39] Roth's identification with Kafka was a deliberate entanglement between his Jewishness and his imagined transnational lineage. Kafka had presented the deviant Jewish body in modernist code. Roth updated Kafka's psychosexual body humor into postwar context through explicit sexuality and outrageous humor. Portnoy makes repeated references to his body as a "Jewish joke." He engages in fantasies of smothering women with his penis and expresses visceral hatred of his large, bulbous Jewish nose. This Kafka-esque body rage also extends outward. His idealized female is described as blonde, blue-eyed, with a petite "WASP" nose. Yet, Portnoy's stubborn corporeal Jewishness, replete with graphic sexual compulsion, also offers a distinct postwar cultural critique. It indicts decades of media-produced Anglo-Christian film, television, and magazine fantasy as equally complicit in his alienation.[40]

THE NEW LITERARY ICONOGRAPHY

Roth, Malamud, and Bellow were three of the many authors of the postwar era to use Jewishness—and Jewish sexuality more specifically—as the allegorical crisis point for generational break. Isaac Bashevis Singer, Chaim Potok, Norman Mailer, Joseph Heller, J. D. Salinger, and Arthur Miller were just some of the other Jewish-born writers who identified an explicit or minimally coded Jewish protagonist to express postwar suburban malaise.[41] Jewishness became such a central literary trope in postwar American literature that, as Cynthia Ozick observes, notable non-Jewish authors such as Gore Vidal, Katherine Anne Porter, Truman Capote, and Edward Hoagland collectively began complaining that the "Jewish Mafia" (Capote's term) in American letters had driven their work to the margins because it wasn't Jewish enough.[42]

In 1965, John Updike, noted chronicler of WASP gentility, made an awkward attempt to join the movement with his short stories about a single, Jewish, sexually adventurous antihero named Henry Bech. Updike's Jewish alter ego, a character who would recur in his work for two decades, allowed the writer the freedom to explore Bellow's Herzogian Jewish subjectivity.[43] Catholic-born author Joyce Carol Oates followed the same tactic. She won the 1967 O. Henry Prize for "In the Region of Ice," a short story about a classroom power struggle between Sister Irene, an emotionally repressed nun and teacher, and her brash and unstable Jewish student, Allen Weinstein.[44] Oates and Updike joined the Jewish literary movement by appropriating Jewish subjectivity as the means of exploring erotic transgression. No Kafkaesque jackal or ape metaphors were needed. Nor was the good Christian witness/protagonist of idealized Jewish nobility and virtue, as in Laura Z. Hobson's novel, *Gentlemen's Agreement* (1947). For Jewish and non-Jewish authors of the 1960s, the explicit "Jew" offered a disruptive agitation metaphor to critique the normative Anglo-Christian hierarchy that had defined, and repressed, so much of postwar American life.

Portnoy's Complaint was the culmination of this movement. It introduced a taboo-shattering, X-rated farce that overturned the genteel boundaries of postwar society. In combination with *The Graduate*, the novel moved a confrontational avant-garde form of urban, sexual, explicit Jewishness from the margins into the mainstream. It was at the center of a process that Matthew Frye Jacobson describes as relocating "the psychodrama of Jewishness and the multifold interpretation of its meanings . . . (to) the sexualized field of women's bodies."[45] Upon release, *Portnoy's Complaint* faced immediate public backlash from numerous moralists and op-ed writers accusing the text of obscenity and pornography.[46] Yet, Roth's credibility as an emerging American novelist and the veneration of the novel's boundary-pushing contents in *Esquire, New American Review, Partisan Review*, and the *New York Times* gave the book the literary cache it needed. Critical consensus won. Roth's depiction of Jewish sexual obsession with Christian beauty became, in 1969, the privileged representation to exemplify the end of the conservative mores of the postwar era.

THE COMEDY REVOLUTION

After the end of vaudeville in the 1930s, stand-up comedy first emerged as an extension of World War II GI-based entertainment. It was genteel, polite, and safe, trafficking in what can be understood as a broadcast approach to humor, politically inoffensive jokes that commented primarily on the everyday subject matter of suburban American married life. The structured setup/punch line delivery method provided a familiar, identifiable rhythm from early television to Vegas entertainment. The staccato comedy form allowed comedians such as Bob Hope to deliver broad bromides on popular subjects of the day exemplified by what Peter M. Robinson describes as inoffensive "barbs of straw."[47] This apolitical form of comedy was performed by Jewish and Gentile comedians alike. In addition to Hope, comedians such as Red Skelton, George Burns, Jackie Gleason, Jack Benny, and Joey Bishop mostly avoided politics, race, religion, and any other contentious issues of the day. Instead, they focused on domestic squabbles and the idiosyncrasies of self-deprecation. Live comedy, like postwar film and television, saw ethnic identity—whether Jewish, Italian, Irish, or otherwise—subsumed in a veneer of white, suburban fantasy.

But by the late 1950s, a pushback on this genteel form of humor began to emerge. Comedy studies scholar Gerald Nachman argues that this countermovement was steeped in acerbic social satire expressed through a highly ethnic and gendered lens. Black comedians such as Dick Gregory, Bill Cosby, and Godfrey Cambridge pushed the boundaries of racial discourses through performative innovations, albeit in very different political contexts. Phyllis Diller changed understandings of the contained domestic housewife through a radical performance of gender unruliness. Bob Newhart brought a conservative intellectualism into satire while Jonathan Winters created groundbreaking improvisations on early late-night television. Comedians began to push the boundaries of what could and could not be said through formal and stylistic innovations.

One of the dominant methodologies used by Jewish "rebel comedians" to express this challenge was the deployment of an overt, confrontational Jewishness at once both unapologetic and unafraid. Mort Sahl, Stan Freberg, Allan Sherman, Mike Nichols and Elaine May, Joan Rivers, Lenny Bruce, Jerry Stiller, Mel Brooks, and Woody Allen, among many others, began using the specificity of their Jewish identities as part of a new form of progressive politics and truth-telling. This visible Jewishness was a political response to both the anti-Semitism of HUAC investigations and the near-total absence of Jewish subject matter on mainstream film and television. It was deployed as a specific tool for critiquing postwar American conservatism.

Many of these performers emerged from the training grounds of the Catskills resorts in New York and the East Coast Borscht Belt comedy circuit and gradually began ascending into the American (Christian) mainstream. Collectively, these comedians produced three innovations in the art of stand-up. First, they began experimenting with formal structure, moving away from the setup/punch line Bob Hope tradition and toward monologues, sketches, confessionals, and improvisations. Second, they touched on previously taboo subject matter such as politics, sexuality, class, race, and religion, which had all been verboten in the culturally conservative discourses of mainstream postwar comedy. Third, they increased the emphasis and visibility of their Jewish backgrounds. Postwar comedy, like literature, discovered the potent vessel of Jewish figuration. In this work, the related issues of politics and sexuality merged. It became the taboo subject matter of a new form of edgy, urban address.

The erudite Mort Sahl was one of the first to break with postwar comedic form. Sahl dispensed with punch lines entirely, instead delivering extended political riffs and stream of consciousness monologues as early as 1953. This alteration of form in live comedy was accompanied by Sahl's fearlessness in self-identifying as an urbane Jewish intellectual. By the mid-1950s, Allan Sherman and Mickey Katz began producing Yiddish musical parodies of popular mainstream entertainment that recalled the Yiddish theater of the 1920s. Sherman's live performances of his 1956 *My Fair Lady* parody, *My Fairfax Lady*, used the crude associations of Jewish vulgarity to satirize the British class distinctions of Eliza Doolittle and Henry Higgins.[48] In Sherman's parody, Eliza spoke perfect English, thereby confusing the Yiddish-accented world of Fairfax Avenue in Los Angeles. By the early 1960s, a young Woody Allen performed neurotic self-criticism through extended monologues describing his unrequited lust for beautiful women. Joan Rivers mined the comedic potential of the lonely single Jewish girl trying to find a husband. Mike Nichols and Elaine May performed a sketch where Nichols played a Jewish NASA scientist being harassed at work by his overbearing mother (May).

Why was "Jewishness" such an important framework for postwar American comedy? In his influential essay published in 1951, Irving Howe argued that Jewish humor emerged primarily as the necessary by-product of turning tragedy into laughter as Jews left the shtetls and entered the modern world.[49] This progression narrative argued that emancipated Jews drew from the singular nature of their Diaspora experience and duplicitous insider/outsider status to offer unique insights into American culture.[50] Lawrence Epstein summarized this perspective, arguing that the American (Christian) public looked to the Jews, "the masters of handling history's troubles," as a model for coping with the anxieties of the fractured status of postwar modernity.[51] More recently, Vincent Brook, building on the seminal work of Sander Gilman, argues that it is the comic performance of self-hatred, one of the most visible identifiers of Jewish identity in the postwar era, that allowed Jewish comedy to flourish.[52] The act of making "Jewishness" visible produced an incongruity that inevitably led to comedic catharsis. Jewishness became an extension of the very incongruity that defined the modern comedic form.

Ruth Wisse, the author of *No Joke: Making Jewish Humor*, sees a political component emerging from the Jew's privileged position on the American stage. Wisse argues that Jewish humor focuses primarily on the transformation of the schlemiel into a modern "liberal humanist."[53] The shtetl schlemiel is society's loser. But, through the transformative power of modernist emancipation, the schlemiel becomes an unlikely winner. A comedic inversion takes place. In the postwar era, the link between Jewish identity and postmodern humor was understood, as Ruth D. Johnston has summarized, through shared slippages.[54] Postmodern theory focused on destabilizing the "holistic" efforts and goals of classical thinking. Similarly, the emancipated twentieth-century Jew was a wandering, liminal, complex construction, reminding the spectator of the repressions, absences, and fissures hidden under normative (Christian) culture.

To rethink the question, it is not so much whether postwar Jews were funny. It was what they represented in terms of critiquing the anti-humor origins of European Christendom. For more than a thousand years, European Christianity was defined by both its resistance to humor and, in a related fear, the uncontrollable body (sexual and otherwise).[55] Laughter was seen as the province of primitive human impulses, bestial savagery, and degraded culture. This cut across all denominations. From early monastic prohibitions on laughter to the ban on comedy enacted by the Puritans in seventeenth-century England, Christianity was overtly hostile toward humor.[56] Considered in this light, it is no surprise that Christian audiences turned so often to Jews to make them laugh. The chain of humor communication was transformed not only by the joke tellers but also by the shifting awareness of the spectator. This conceptual inversion visualized the Christian humor problematic by spotlighting the privileged (Christian) position of the spectator in the circulation of comedic meaning communicated between performer and audience.

Humor theorist John Morreall argues that comedy is primarily identified as a cognitive exchange between the joke-teller (performer) and the recipient (audience) in which both are participants in an active and generative cycle of meaning. Together, joke-teller and spectator produce a previously unseen boundary or taboo at which point a catharsis, usually in the form of laughter, occurs. In incongruity theory, the most popular humor theory model to examine this exchange, humor is located through the juxtaposition of contradictory barriers, paradoxes, or contradictions.[57] What the rebel Jewish comedians accomplished in the late 1950s and early 1960s was not simply an emancipation of Jewish humor from the postwar margins. It marked a discursive shift from "universal" humor into a distinct ethno-religious binary. This visualization critiqued the normalized, internalized cultural boundaries of postwar European-Christian-influenced American spectatorship. Incongruity moved from the text of the joke to the presumptive dissonance between Jewish performer and Christian audience. Jewish comedians were not funny simply because they were Jewish. They were funny because they were *not-European-Christians*.

Demarcation played a critical role within the emerging postwar cultural reevaluation taking place at the dawn of the civil rights movement, the women's rights movement, and the sexual revolution. The carnal, taboo-shattering Jew became the locus point for a new form of post-censorship rhetoric. Jewish comedy, at once both familiar and entirely new, operated as a Trojan horse. It provided the means by which counterculture politics were mainstreamed. But this discursive shift cannot be understood without also understanding the reconstructing of the postwar spectator. The joke was ultimately not on the stage Jew. It was on the Anglo-Christian audience that laughed at the exposure of their own predetermined biases and internalized privileges. Both totems were required to negotiate the most dangerous rupture of the era: the emergence of hard-core pornography and increasingly explicit language.[58]

One of the first comedy teams to demonstrate this emerging emphasis on Anglo-Christian-Jewish interplay was the real-life married couple, Jerry Stiller and Anne Meara. Stiller and Meara mocked themselves by riffing on stereotypes inspired by both their looks and ethnicity. She was tall. He was short. She was Irish. He was Jewish. They had met as struggling actors in New York in the 1950s and were married in 1954, with the Irish-Catholic Meara converting to Judaism to marry Stiller. Meara's conversion, however, remained entirely absent from their public personas and the comedy act, established in 1961. Trained in the nascent Second City improvisation style and inspired by the innovations of Nichols and May, Stiller and Meara performed sketches based on comedic premises that relied on their contrasts.

Within a year of performing together, the duo became a sensation, with breakthrough performances in New York nightclubs and on television.[59] The most famous of these sketches, performed numerous times on *The Ed Sullivan Show* and *The Tonight Show* in the early to mid-1960s, featured the ongoing love story of their most famous alter egos, Hershey Horowitz and Mary Elizabeth Doyle.[60] The first sketch to introduce the pair, called "Computer Dating," depicted Horowitz and Doyle meeting on a blind date after they were paired by an obviously flawed computer system. The subsequent dialogue played up the obvious contrast between the two ethnicities:

> Hershey Horowitz (Stiller): How do you do?
> Mary Elizabeth Doyle (Meara): How do you do?
> Hershey Horowitz: I'm Hershey Horowitz.
> Mary Elizabeth Doyle: I'm Mary Elizabeth Doyle.
> Hershey Horowitz: Doyle?
> Mary Elizabeth Doyle: Horowitz?
> Hershey Horowitz: Horowitz. H-O-R-O-W-I-T-Z. Hershey. My friends call me Hesh.

Mary Elizabeth Doyle: Doyle. D-O-Y-L-E. My friends call me Mary Elizabeth.

Hershey Horowitz: Is Doyle your real name?

Mary Elizabeth Doyle: Sure. Why wouldn't it be my real name?

Hershey Horowitz: I don't know. I mean, I was just hoping . . .

Mary Elizabeth Doyle: No, we're Doyles. We're Dempseys on my mother's side.

Hershey Horowitz: Dempsey.

Mary Elizabeth Doyle: Horowitz.

Hershey Horowitz: Shmulowitz on my mother's side. . . . These computers are wonderful things!

Mary Elizabeth Doyle: Oh, terrific!

Hershey Horowitz: I was reading all about it.

Mary Elizabeth Doyle: Takes all the guesswork out of meeting someone. It's electronic so you can't make any mistakes.

The premise had obvious roots in the Irish-Jewish screwball comedies of the 1920s. But by reviving an emphasis on ethnicity and playing up this conflict with the technologies of the modern world, Stiller and Meara used Catholic-Jewish contrast to visualize the changing sexual mores of the 1960s. As Stiller and Meara later explained in an interview, the premise "came out of the need to find another piece of ourselves. We were running out of tall woman-short guy (bits)."[61] The real-world marriage of the duo also gave their humor a certain gravitas. In appearances on shows such as *What's My Line?* in 1968, their banter played up both the broad comedy of married life and their physical contrast. But the humor was distinctly at odds with the genteel postwar comedy of the Bob Hope era. Unlike the gender-based, ethnic-free interplay between the Jewish George Burns and his Irish-Catholic wife and comedy partner, Gracie Allen, a generation earlier, Stiller embodied an obnoxious, loud, urban Jewish persona, representing a break from the suburbanism of the 1950s. Meara, like Elaine May, had equal agency in the production of the comedy. Stiller and Meara presented their public personas, both inside and outside of character, as an extension of their collaboration in building a successful career in entertainment.

By the early 1970s, Stiller and Meara saw their comedy career fade, perhaps replaced by the far more graphic next generation of Christian-Jewish interplay in Hollywood feature films. But their impact in performing the first visible template of Catholic-Jewish sketch comedy represented an important step between postwar vaudevillian stand-up and the New Comedy that would revolutionize Hollywood in the late 1960s. As Hershey Horowitz and Mary Elizabeth Doyle, they were both nostalgic and progressive. They invoked the screwball antics of the first wave while reviving this nostalgia in the new form of Second City sketch and character-based improvisation. The comedy team had torn down the techniques and performance practices of the postwar joke-teller, replacing it with an innovative performance style and a return of hip, urban ethnic visibility.

"ALL RIGHT SHEMEGAH, DROP THE YEAGAH!"

Lenny Bruce's influential contribution to the emerging, aggressive, boundary-pushing stand-up comedy scene of the late 1950s and early 1960s can be divided into two rhetorical innovations. The first located in his uninhibited, confessional performance style. Building on Mort Sahl's innovative political monologues, Bruce produced stream of consciousness riffs. He refused to temper his language or subject matter. This introduced the politics of performance itself as an ideological component of the New Comedy movement.[62] The second area located in Bruce's unapologetic linking of ribald sexuality, X-rated language, and the sensibilities of jazz music. "Offensive" language became a tool to deliver what he understood to be a patriotic blow against systemic tools of cultural control that had homogenized the culture of the postwar decades. Bruce continued to do this without fear of audience alienation or career recriminations, despite his subsequent arrests and prosecutions on obscenity charges.[63] As self-destructive as he was innovative, Bruce believed that breaking down the safety of spectatorship was a revolutionary act. He repositioned the audience as co-conspirators in his transgressions and thereby produced a collective act of political resistance.

Bruce made the connection among sex, politics, and taboo language clear in numerous jokes. One of his most frequently quoted lines—"Take away the right to say 'fuck' and you take away the right to say 'fuck the government!'"—makes this point.[64] This idea was also seen in Bruce's famous musical-comedy routine, "'To' Is a Preposition; 'Come' Is a Verb."[65] Occasionally performed with a backing jazz band, the routine denatured language deemed "offensive" into inoffensive subsections. Bruce chanted over and over: "Didja come? . . . Good! Didja come good? . . ." Using various pauses and emphasis changes, the repetition of this one single sentence was delivered as a jazz-beat rhythmic chanting, highlighting how inflection and sequence create meaning from otherwise "harmless" words like "did," "you," "come," and "good." His linguistic jazz-inspired cadences and bebop comedy riffs scrambled the signifiers of communication. It produced what Jacques Derrida called the spontaneous space of play that reveals *dif-*

férance, the fractures, reversals, and subjective contradictions infused in all systems of communication.[66]

As Bruce developed these performative techniques, one central element of his personal biography repeatedly emerged in his act: his Jewishness. Rather than appealing to the masses by tempering his humor, he performed an unapologetic, assaultive form of Jewish visibility that became, as David E. Kaufman points out, the central weapon of his intended discomfort.[67] By playing up his role as an urban, Jewish lothario driven by sexual compulsions, Bruce became the very monstrous Jewish id that had been driven to the margins and underground in the postwar years. The Anglo-Christian-Jewish erotic coupling, concurrently emerging in literature at the time, was produced through this technique in Bruce's comedy. He performed the role of the compulsively carnal Jewish seducer turned ideological truth-teller. The "Christian" was his presumably normative audience. But in linking the carnality of stereotypical Jewish Otherness to liberal urban politics, Bruce revised Anglo-Christian-Jewish intersubjectivity. By including his audience in his transgressiveness, Bruce offered vicarious "Jewishness" to Jewish and Gentile spectators alike. The Anglo-Christian outsider was now outside of the room. It was the establishment itself.

This dynamic reached critical mass in 1959. Bruce was already an established, if controversial, young comedian, but he had not yet fully developed his style. During an appearance on *The Steve Allen Show*, Bruce launched into a number of unrehearsed and overtly Jewish jokes, surprising Allen and shocking his audience.[68] Visible Jewishness, like the X-rated language that would soon come to define his career, was just another form of taboo, a sacred cow to be slain.

Bruce amplified this approach in his live act. He developed a routine describing a meeting between Adolf Hitler and a Jewish casting agent, a biting critique of anti-Semitic assumptions about amoral Jewish influence in Hollywood.[69] In another bit, Bruce played up his role as a Jewish pariah jester by apologizing for killing Christ, attributing it to a party that got out of control. In one of his most famous monologues from this period, he separated Jewish culture from biographical background and relocated it in the realm of an urban/rural divide. Items such as macaroons, bagels, fruit salad, and even Ray Charles were described as "Jewish." Lime Jell-O, Eddie Cantor, and even B'nai B'rith were called "goyishe."[70] This new form of hipster Jewishness was identified as outside institutional (Christian) control. Later that same year, Bruce became the face of the comedy movement that *Time* magazine labeled the "Sickniks."[71]

The cadences and rhythms of Yiddish also played a central role in Bruce's use of Jewishness as an agent of discomfort. Monologues such as "Religion,

Inc." and his character of "Father Flotsky" used Yiddish words to direct critiques at all areas of organized religion, including institutional Judaism.[72] He also frequently parodied famous phrases of the time by Yiddishizing key words.[73] One example was "All right shemegah, drop the yeagah!" This was a Yiddish parody of Humphrey Bogart's famous purported line (that Bogart never actually uttered), "All right, Louie, drop the gun!"

Bruce was certainly not the first postwar comedian to mine Yiddish for comedic value. Popular Jewish comedy records of the 1950s and 1960s had worked to soften and expand Jewishness as harmless ethnic comedy, both benign and universal. On LPs such as *You Don't Have to Be Jewish* and *Stories Our Jewish Mother Forgot to Tell Us*, comedians such as Phil Silvers, Milton Berle, and Myron Cohen sold a coded, nostalgic Catskills Jewishness that targeted both Jew and non-Jew alike.[74] In these recordings, Yiddishisms were deployed as funny-sounding immigrant language fragments that were nothing more than a part of a broader multi-ethnic American celebration.[75] But as Philip Roth would show a decade later in *Portnoy's Complaint*, Yiddish remained a stubborn reminder of the ethnic underpinnings of twentieth-century America that had been whitewashed in the 1950s.[76] Bruce's interspersed Yiddishisms may have echoed the linguistic slippages of familiar Yiddishkeit humor of that period. But, as Sanford Pinsker argues, Bruce's language actually represented a sharp break from the postwar comedy traditions that he appeared to be continuing.[77] His unapologetic scat-Yiddish became a marker of difference that framed the provocative sexuality that informed his stand-up persona. Bruce's Yiddish was assaultive rather than playful, a stubborn Jewishness lurking beneath his assimilated, handsome, white exterior. It became a truth claim that cleared the way for his taboo-challenging sexual subject matter. This presentation of Yiddish-as-exclusionary became a confrontational form of verbal Otherness. It celebrated unapologetic Jewishness as rebellion rather than assimilation, offering little connection to either the Yiddish theater of the 1920s or the Catskills comedy émigrés of the 1950s that it echoed.[78]

As David Kaufman observes, there was intentionality and artifice to this performance.[79] Bruce had grown up in a secular household, heard no Yiddish, and was entirely unfamiliar with even the most basic rituals of Jewish cultural life. His adoption of the Jewish moralist character came late to his comedy, nearly ten years into his career. As Albert Goldman argues in his seminal book, *Ladies and Gentlemen, Lenny Bruce!!*, it was a highly constructed performance taught to Bruce in the early 1950s by a fellow comedian and friend, Joe Ancis.[80] Jewishness offered Bruce an outsider identity, a performance cloak that allowed him to claim an urban, intellectual gravitas in the Mort Sahl tradition. It also placed him in an inherently adversarial position in relation to his presumably Christian audience. This dynamic created a visceral Anglo-Christian-Jewish boundary between (Jewish) performer and (Christian) audience that allowed Bruce's comedy to penetrate other cultural barriers, such as sex, gender, and race politics. Without first establishing this initial us/them binary, Bruce's subsequent humor would have failed to resonate with the same assaultive strength.

This Jewish/goyishe field of play also extended to Bruce's personal life. In 1951, he married a former burlesque entertainer by the name of Hot Honey Harlow (born Harriett Lloyd Jolliff in 1927). Harlow was a Catholic girl from a small town in Arkansas who rebelled through exhibitionism and bisexuality. The Bruce-Harlow marriage was replete with drugs, breakups, and problematic parenting skills.[81] But despite their mutual descent into addiction and alcoholism, her support legitimized Bruce's underground credentials as he built his comedy career in the 1950s. They appeared as actors together in low-budget exploitation films about the burlesque underworld such as *Dance Hall Racket* aka *Shame Shanty* (1953) and *Dream Follies* (1954). Both films were co-written and produced by Bruce and focused on his wife's good-girl-gone-bad sexuality. Jewish-Catholic intermarriage was still a rarity at the time. In the parlance of the times, Bruce not only discussed the urban jungle as a Talmudic Jewish pop culture critic, he also shtupped a shiksa stripper.

Despite an acrimonious divorce in 1957, Bruce followed Honey's lead in his subsequent construction of himself as a libertine Jewish playboy. His appearance on Hugh Hefner's syndicated *Playboy's Penthouse* on October 24, 1959, showed him romancing a variety of young women in the background as Hefner led the camera through the party. Bruce's extended riffs to the camera played up his controversy-courting inhibitions. The contrast between Hefner and Bruce, the two forms of American masculinity, was brought into greater relief: if Hugh Hefner was the superego of genteel, controlled, WASP 1950s American masculinity, Lenny Bruce was the raging, uncontained, primal Jewish id of the emerging 1960s.[82] The comfortable Bruce had earned his seat at the swinger's table.

THE BIG SCREEN LEAP

Lenny Bruce's performative and linguistic innovations came with a cost. Facing a broad political backlash, he was arrested and prosecuted for obscenity throughout the early 1960s.[83] His refusal to tone down his act and his highly publicized blacklisting, arrests, and jail time represented rebellious youth culture defiance. It was more in line with socialist Jewish radicals, such as Saul Alinsky, of the early to mid-twentieth century than with the soft Borscht Belt Jewish comedians selling hapless schlemiel comedy to the American public in the 1950s.[84] After years of legal troubles and a heroin addiction, Bruce died in 1966, just one year before Hoffman's act of shiksa liberation in *The Graduate* and three years before Philip Roth's Portnoy would make the outsider Jewish schlemiel an icon of the new sexual freedoms of the counterculture.[85]

It was not mere chance that the director of the first major studio film to explore notions of sexual taboo through incongruous Jewishness was Mike Nichols, another stand-up comedian from the late 1950s New Comedy movement. Nichols's selection of Dustin Hoffman as the (Jewish) face of "deviant" sexuality in *The Graduate* mainstreamed the unruly masculinity that Bruce's performances had developed in nightclubs just a few years earlier. Bruce did not live to see it, but his persona and his performance of Jewishness-as-rupture became one of the defining templates of the New Hollywood cinema and television to emerge in the late 1960s and 1970s.[86]

CHAPTER 6

Katie's Typewriter

HOLLYWOOD ROMANCE, HISTORICAL REWRITE,
AND THE SUBVERSIVE SEXUALITY OF
THE COUNTERCULTURE (1967–1980)

*All my life I wanted to be in a place like this, with a girl like you,
playing games like this!*

LENNY CANTROW (CHARLES GRODIN) TO KELLY CORCORAN
(CYBILL SHEPHERD), *THE HEARTBREAK KID* (1972)

*Mary (Kathryn Harrold): I don't think we should go together any-
more. This is too painful for me. I can't do this. It's over.
Robert (Albert Brooks): Marry me.*

MODERN ROMANCE (1981)

SECOND-WAVE COUPLINGS IN HOLLYWOOD FILM AND
television primarily emerged in two rhetorical forms. The first
offered a critical re-examination of Jewish absence during the nativist political crises of the 1930s and 1950s. Films such as *Fiddler on the Roof* (1971),
The Way We Were (1972), *The Apprenticeship of Duddy Kravitz* (1974), and
The Front (1976) used Christian-Jewish love stories as narrative frameworks
to provide empathetic historical correctives to Jewish-communist associations that had ruined so many careers and lives. The second focused on
the libertine sexual experimentations of the "free love" counterculture moment. In films such as *I Love You, Alice B. Toklas* (1968), *Bob & Carol & Ted
& Alice* (1969), *Getting Straight* (1970), *The Heartbreak Kid* (1972), *Portnoy's
Complaint* (1972), *Fritz the Cat* (1972), and *Annie Hall* (1977), among many
others, neurotic Jewish schlemiels pursuing Anglo-Catholic or Anglo-
Protestant partners exemplified the uncertainty of the sexual revolution.
Even in the far more sanitized subject matter of broadcast television, pro-

grams such as *He and She* (1967–1968), *All in the Family* (1971–1979), *Bridget Loves Bernie* (1972–1973), and *Rhoda* (1974–1978) used Christian-Jewish couplings as markers of the liberal politics and emancipated sensibilities of the emerging youth culture.

At the core of both groupings was the concept of historiography. Second-wave texts both echoed and complemented a massive political project undertaken by leading thinkers and intellectuals of the 1960s and 1970s. As Michel Foucault observed at the time, the singular, dominant narrative of "history" as a collection of events, upward progressions, and "great men" narratives had been successfully taken apart.[1] Foucault was celebrating decades of work by academics and intellectuals challenging the social, political, and structural dominance of entrenched, top-down historical progression narratives.[2] In 1976, Jacques Derrida founded the Greph Movement, which was intended to mobilize opposition to French governmental attempts to "rationalize" the educational system. Derrida argued that institutional approaches to the teaching of "history" invariably produced two oppositional constructions: the "national" and the "ethnic." Many Marxist critics and scholars agreed, challenging top-down models of history as obfuscating marginalized identities.[3] A decade after the rise of the American counterculture and the student uprisings in France in May 1968, the singular model of "history" had been successfully indicted as filled with erasures, absences, and hidden traumas.[4]

Paralleling and complementing Derrida and Foucault's radical critiques of history in Europe, feminist activists in the United States began critiquing essentialized understandings of gender and sexuality. The Summer of Love in 1967 brought with it images of political protest in the form of sexual exhibitions including public nudity and casual sex. Two years later, the famous phrase "the personal is political"—credited to a 1969 manifesto authored by Carol Hanisch, a leader of the radical feminist group the Redstockings—fueled second-wave feminists to further link the individual sex act to collective political resistance. Charlotte Kroløkke points out how two publications released in 1970, Juliet Mitchell's *The Subjugation of Women* and Shulamith Firestone's *The Dialectic of Sex: The Case for Feminist Revolution*, connected neo-Marxism with psychoanalysis to articulate the radical activist potential of the movement.[5] Discourses between present and past, visible and invisible, colonizer and colonized each began to find renegotiation through sexual experimentation and the provocations of previously taboo representations.

The increasing spending power of the youth culture created an opportunity in popular American media to visualize these new fantasies of transgression. The end of the censorship era in Hollywood in the mid-1960s and the influx of sexually graphic European art cinema opened the door. Popular screen culture responded by reviving a familiar coupling archetype to grapple with this representational shift. Following *The Graduate*, Jewish movie stars emerged, en masse, as the faces of a new form of youth culture movie star. Yet, despite their ascendant, visibly Jewish personas, this second wave was once again accompanied by the established caveat. In nearly every major performance involving a romantic or sexual pairing, these actors were coupled with their physical, emotional, and ideological opposites: the established, Christonormative, Anglo-Saxon love (or erotic) interest. The new Jewish visibility signified the rhetorical entrance of explicit sexuality. Their Anglo-Christian partners exemplified the normative codes they were violating, the privileged status of whiteness in the postwar decades.

As in the first wave, these couplings were able to produce a safe form of progressive, transgressive visualization. They allowed explicit sexuality and youth culture experimentation to enter the mainstream. But unlike the hopeful melting pot ambitions and forward-leaning assimilationist impulses of the first wave, this second wave also operated as a corrective to the screen absences of the 1950s. This produced a temporal ambiguity. Second-wave figurations were denied the happy endings and successful coupling-as-assimilation allegory that had been so prevalent in the more aspirational and utopian first wave. Emancipated sexual expression also brought with it the threat of myopia, narcissism, and emotional alienation. The "Me Generation" may have privileged the carnal Jew as the face of unruly youth culture. But that carnality brought with it the troubling association of an untethered society struggling with dissonance and fracture. It was a tension that would percolate through numerous film and television programs of the late 1960s and 1970s before eventually giving way to a nostalgic revival of postwar Anglo-Christian whiteness in the 1980s. But the second wave would leave its mark, privileging Anglo-Christian-Jewish couplings as the erotically charged figures of the counterculture generation for more than thirteen years.

STARS FOR AN UPTIGHT AGE

Paul Mazursky was one of the first studio filmmakers in the Hollywood New Wave to recognize the potency of visible Anglo-Christian-Jewish coupling. In both his script for *I Love You, Alice B. Toklas* (1968) and his directorial debut, *Bob & Carol & Ted & Alice* (1969), Mazursky linked the anxiety-provoking sexual freedoms of the counterculture to the neurotic stereotype of Jewish men attracted to proverbial shiksa beauties.[6] Harold

Repressed Jewish attorney Harold Fine (Peter Sellers) finds sexual liberation in the arms of a hippie love child (Leigh Taylor-Young) in the Paul Mazursky–scripted I Love You, Alice B. Toklas *(1968).*

Fine (Peter Sellers), the protagonist of *I Love You, Alice B. Toklas*, is a nerdy Jewish attorney trapped in a loveless engagement to a clichéd, sexless, meta-phorically castrating Jewish female, Joyce (Joyce Van Patten). The film the-matically links Joyce to Harold's equally clichéd, neurotic Jewish mother, Mrs. Fine (Jo Van Fleet). The meek Harold is caught in a Freudian tension state between (Jewish) mother and (Jewish) fiancée. Both directions are emasculating traps.

But before Harold can go through with the wedding, he locates an es-cape hatch from his increasingly rigid, claustrophobic, fully Jewish world. He falls in love/lust with a free-spirited, uncomplicated, non-Jewish hippie beauty, Nancy (Leigh Taylor-Young). Nancy's simple approach to sexual-ity and pleasure are explicitly at odds with the neuroticism and verbosity of both Joyce and Mrs. Fine. In choosing Nancy over Joyce, Harold acts out sexually as a form of rebellion against societal expectations. This operates in reverse symmetry to the journey of Benjamin Braddock in *The Graduate*. Rather than rescuing the fantasy shiksa from a Christian wedding, Harold rejects and disrupts his own Jewish wedding by fleeing the service.[7] In an act of comedic repetition, this disruption occurs not once, but twice, with Harold leaving Joyce standing at the altar. His solution to solve his bour-geois trap is to seek out the fantasy shiksa as an idealized figure of sexual liberation.

Following Benjamin Braddock, Harold was the next major Jewish screen protagonist to visualize psycho-sexual neurosis as an embodiment of generational rebellion. The idealized pixie beauty of Nancy, more a cipher than an actual character, produces idealized (Anglo-Christian) female beauty as the object of Freudian transference for Harold's internal conflicts. Her uncomplicated sexuality presents Harold with a way out from the repressive castration anxieties conflated by the Jewish mother/fiancé depictions. She is the avatar of hippie fantasy, a world of uncomplicated drugs, sex, and orgies without guilt or repercussion.[8] Yet, even after his successful entrance into the land of hippie orgies, Harold remains fraught with anxiety and confusion while trying to pretend he's capable of giving in to the fantasy of hedonism that the counterculture promises. But this commitment is undermined by his stubborn Jewish neuroticism, a fixed character trait that ultimately prevents him from achieving any form of lasting revolution.

Mazursky's screenplay offered a covert nod to the libertine sensibilities of the modernist artists, writers, and thinkers of pre–World War II Europe. The film's titular Alice B. Toklas, explained as a marijuana reference in the film, was also a reminder of the historical figure. Toklas was a famous poet, writer, art collector, and, along with her lover, Gertrude Stein (both Jewish), famous café society hosts at the center of avant-garde Left Bank France throughout the 1920s. Mazursky's playful invocation of one of the notable Jewish figures at the center of late modern art and literature introduced a complex through-line between the first and second waves. Similar to Mel Brooks's reuse of the name of James Joyce's Leopold Bloom (Gene Wilder) in *The Producers*, Harold's befuddled search for "Alice B. Toklas" was also a quest for a historical referent. He seeks a form of liberation in the youth culture reemergence of visible Jewishness of the late 1960s that actually traced back to the modernist thinking of the 1920s. Mazursky's subsequent directorial debut, *Bob & Carol & Ted & Alice* (1969), made this link between Jewish carnal desire for the shiksa and the counterculture even more explicit. While quite demure in its depictions of actual sex, the film was one of the first Hollywood releases to non-judgmentally celebrate the hippie "free love" movement as a potentially emancipatory force.

The opening sequence sends married couple Bob (Robert Culp) and Carol (Natalie Wood) Sanders to a weekend EST-like retreat in which they participate in a marathon group therapy session to try to become more honest with each other. This honesty begins to express itself sexually. After experimenting with an open marriage, they approach their married Jewish friends Ted (Elliott Gould) and Alice (Dyan Cannon) Henderson to join them in a partner-swapping experiment. Each couple struggles with infidelity to varying degrees and their friendship and their families begin to fray. The film concludes in Las Vegas, where the two couples plan to see a performance by Tony Bennett. They dress formally in postwar lounge style and drink martinis. The associations with the Rat Pack and Las Vegas suggest their dawning awareness that the framework of the 1950s and early 1960s is now stodgy and outdated. To solve their fears of antiquation, each couple dares the other to participate in an orgy without changing the tone of their marriages and the tenor of their friendships. Ted brings home the absurdity of this when he remarks, "First, we'll have an orgy. Then we'll go see Tony Bennett." Their subsequent awkward attempt at an orgy (ambiguously resolved) ends the film as more of an open-ended question than a resolved narrative. Mazursky's query asks the spectator to determine if the free love era can really be achieved without a moral and spiritual loss.

This premise performs a comedic inversion built around the notion of a generational breaking point. The real problems facing the Bob-Carol and Ted-Alice marriages are not the dangers of promiscuity or infidelity. The ultimate horror that both couples face is one of appearances. The more they attempt to stay current with youth culture trends, the more absurd they become. As the film's confused protagonists eventually realize, the new frontier for youth culture is no longer in social settings. It now locates in bed.[9]

In keeping with the insight of *The Graduate*, *Bob & Carol & Ted & Alice* self-reflexively locates Anglo-Christian-Jewish crossings at the heart of this counterculture indictment of the hypocrisies of the postwar nuclear family. The Anglo-Saxon Bob and Carol and the implied Jewish Ted and Alice begin as clearly demarcated types. Bob is a suave, masculine archetype. Carol is his doting, homemaker wife. By contrast, Ted and Alice are Jewish neurotics. Dyan Cannon, the child of a Jewish mother and Baptist father, played Alice as a neurotic but sexy female version of the Jewish schlemiel by way of the eroticized ghetto Jewess. As with Streisand (and, later, Bette Midler and Goldie Hawn), Cannon's character's sexual hang-ups, emotional immaturity, and neurotic judgment stand in stark contrast with the more genteel nature of the paragon of classic Hollywood beauty represented by Natalie Wood.[10] This is established comedically early in the film when Alice is discussing her son in therapy:

> Alice Henderson: He wanted to know why I had a tee-tee . . .
> Psychiatrist: Pardon me? I don't know what a tee-tee is.
> Alice Henderson: A vagina.
> Psychiatrist: Oh, it's a pet expression of yours.
> Alice Henderson: Yes, you know words: tee-tee, tinkle, po-po, wee-wee, kee-kee, poo-poo.
> Psychiatrist: I had never heard tee-tee before.

Alice Henderson: What expression do you use with your children?
Psychiatrist: Vagina.[11]

Alice's inability to pronounce "vagina," even to her therapist, is a joke meant to signify her role as the neurotic Jewish female stereotype. In an extended comedic sequence later in the film, Ted's attempts to seduce Alice play out as equally neurotic and comedically Jewish. After learning of Bob and Carol's newly open marriage arrangement, an aroused Ted tries to convince a still mortified Alice to have sex. She rejects him repeatedly and they begin to debate whether Ted would be okay if Alice didn't experience any pleasure. Ted's frustration and Alice's refusal to give in play out for nearly eight minutes as an extended vaudevillian riff. The bit concludes with an exasperated Ted giving in to Alice's suspicions about his primal urges:

Alice: Do you wanna do it just like that? With no feeling on my part?
Ted: Yeah!

Alice and Ted's comedic sexual hang-ups are contrasted throughout the film with Bob and Carol's semi-successful attempts to calmly transition into an open marriage free from neurosis and introspection. The somewhat fraudulent but genteel WASP repression of Bob and Carol and the hyper-verbal Jewish neuroticism of Ted and Alice form a conceptual meta-coupling as the film builds to their eventual attempt at an orgy. This coupling dichotomy draws from first-wave ghetto romances and ethnic screwball comedies even as it amplifies this tension for the group sex era.

Mazursky plays up this contrast by riffing on the established star personas of Robert Culp and Natalie Wood. Both were next-generation continuations of the Anglo-centric beauty standards of the postwar era. As an emerging television star, Culp personified the physicality and mannerisms of 1950s-era WASP masculinity. But, as a 2010 in-memoriam article in the *New York Times Magazine* pointed out, Culp's stardom was brief and only semi-successful. His looks and performance style made him more of a transitionary figure as American culture moved from the teen-idol male beauty of actors such as Troy Donahue, Tab Hunter, and Rock Hudson to the land of Elliott Gould and, as the *Times* put it, his "emotionally messy progeny."[12]

The film visualizes this handoff by repeatedly contrasting Culp with Gould. Culp's hyper-macho embodiment of the out-of-touch Bob satirized the aging postwar WASP male trying to adapt to a hippie subculture he failed to fully grasp. It was Gould's neurotic, overtly Jewish but also suave Ted who represented the new, alternative masculinity of the emerging counterculture.

After the breakout success of *Bob & Carol & Ted & Alice*, Gould quickly became a key figure in the transformation of Hollywood movie stars in the late 1960s.[13] In 1970, he was profiled by Jules Feiffer for a *Time* cover story. Feiffer historicized Gould's unlikely rise to stardom with the following description:

> There's been a shift in focus of movie heroes and movie stories. . . .
> Out of this shift came the possibility of careers for the likes of
> Gould, Alan Arkin and Dustin Hoffman. What really happened is
> that Hollywood is trying to update its mythology, and these are the
> stars of the new mythology.[14]

Feiffer linked the "new mythology" of New Hollywood through reference to three of the more notable Jewish actors of the era: Gould, Arkin, and Hoffman. Yet, despite being Jewish himself, Feiffer did not make any explicit mention of Gould's Jewishness. Instead, he used euphemisms. The popular cartoonist, playwright, and screenwriter of the Gould-starring black comedy, *Little Murders* (1970), Feiffer described Gould only as an "ethnic" type with an "urban" identity, writing that "(t)here has not been a film star of such distinctly urban identity since the days of John Garfield."[15] Gould, Hoffman, Arkin, and other Jewish movie stars signified to Feiffer a next-generation corrective. The "new mythology" of New Hollywood was as much about casting and (ethnic) looks as written text or performance style. The counterculture aesthetic was grounded in the kinky hair and Semitic faces of the unapologetic, carnal Jew.

Patricia Erens argues that Carl Reiner's *Enter Laughing* (1967) was actually the first film of the period to introduce libidinal "neurotic (Jewish) sons" chasing Anglo-Saxon women as the new archetype of youth culture dissatisfaction and alienation.[16] In Mel Brooks's *The Producers* (1968), Jewish desire for the shiksa was already understood as a slapstick punchline. Leopold Bloom (Gene Wilder) overcomes his childlike aversion to risk when his sexually deviant mentor, Max Bialystock (Zero Mostel), tempts him with the sexual lure of their belly-dancing Swedish secretary, the impossibly named Ulla Inga Hansen Benson Yansen Tallen Hallen Svaden Swanson (Lee Meredith).[17] In *Where's Poppa?* (1970), the Jewish matricide humor of *I Love You, Alice B. Toklas* is taken to its absurdist extreme. Jewish lawyer Gordon Hocheiser (George Segal) plots to kill his senile Jewish mother (Ruth Gordon) so that he'll finally be free to marry the shiksa woman of his dreams, Louise (Trish Van Devere).

By the early 1970s, the pattern was firmly established. In John Cassavetes's *Minnie and Moskowitz* (1971), Seymour Cassel starred as Seymour Moskowitz, a downwardly mobile Jewish hippie who becomes involved with a blonde shiksa beauty, Minnie Moore, played by Cassavetes's wife and creative partner, Gena Rowlands. Seymour's generational alienation takes place on a number of levels. He exhibits few signs of Jewish awareness or identity until his Jewish mother, Sheba (Katherine Cassavetes) arrives.[18] The appearance of the castrating Jewish mother stereotype—central to *I Love You, Alice B. Toklas* (1968), *Where's Poppa?* (1970), and *Next Stop, Greenwich Village* (1975), among many other films of the era—produced an intergenerational tension similar to *The Graduate* and, a generation earlier, *The Jazz Singer.* His loyalty to his Jewish mother and his sexual desire for the idealized shiksa externalized twin conflicts within Seymour. He is at once both an emancipated free-love hippie and a nice Jewish boy doting on his Yiddishe mama.

In casting both Jewish roles with non-Jewish actors, Cassavetes drew a distinction between his film and others of the period. The decision more closely associated with the universalist argument of postwar films such as *Gentlemen's Agreement* than with the Jew-as-Jew specificity of New Hollywood after *The Graduate.* The casting of Cassel as Moskowitz was even more unusual given that Cassavetes's frequent collaborator, Peter Falk, was exactly the type of Jewish character actor that might have fit this part. The reason for these choices are impossible to determine but may locate in the improvisational, universalist acting philosophy Cassavetes espoused. Seymour Moskowitz is a character alienated from his inner identity. As performed by a non-Jewish actor, Cassavetes's choice emphasized the performative nature of identity. This produced a very different mode of critiquing hippie alienation and identity crisis. It did not necessarily deny the counterculture's rejection of the Anglo-centric universalism of the 1950s. It merely extended it under a theatrical, rather than a casting, context.

Elaine May's *The Heartbreak Kid* (1972) perhaps most clearly codified the schlemiel-shiksa coupling as the privileged expression of counterculture alienation in the Hollywood New Wave. Jewish actor Charles Grodin was cast as Lenny Cantrow, the proverbial nice-Jewish-boy nebbish. Lenny simultaneously feels repulsion for a fully Jewish life and an emerging, neurotic, overwhelming shiksa lust. Just days after marrying a typical Jewish wife, Lila (played by the Jewish actress Jeanne Berlin, Elaine May's daughter), Lenny ends up leaving her to pursue his idealized Anglo-Christian

Kelly Corcoran (Cybill Shepherd), the idealized shiksa fantasy, first appears to Lenny Cantrow (Charles Grodin) as a vision in The Heartbreak Kid *(1972).*

muse, Kelly Corcoran (Cybill Shepherd). As with most shiksas in the Portnoy era, Kelly is introduced and framed as an idealized, angelic, blonde, blue-eyed, Anglo-Christian fantasy straight out of Lenny's presumed self-hating Jewish childhood.

Kelly's entrance in the film makes this dreamlike subjectivity clear. She is introduced through Lenny's point of view as she rises from the ocean waters, backlit by the sun. She approaches and stares directly into the camera, aligning the spectator with Lenny's gaze. Kelly is the shiksa-as-unicorn, a beautiful Christian interloper entering the fully Jewish vacation world of Miami Beach.[19] The newly married Lenny is positioned as a restless member of the youth culture of the 1970s. Once Kelly is introduced, Miami Beach quickly begins to signify the bourgeois prison of Jewish American life, as well as Lenny's potential lifelong estrangement from sexual fulfillment. Kelly Corcoran, the beatific but vacuous blonde from Minnesota, represents Lenny's way out of cultural imprisonment. But this rebellion is ultimately revealed to be an impulsive, destructive, and narcissistic act.

In each of these examples, New Hollywood had located and revived a familiar screen template. The unresolved juxtaposition of Jewish neurotic and Anglo-Christian object of desire provided screen culture with a forum for youth culture exploration. The New Screen Jew, at once both sexual and intellectual, id-driven and cerebral, became a privileged screen vessel to express the confusions, contradictions, and destabilizations of the "free love" era. Whether idealized muse or deconstructed object of satire, the Anglo-Christian partner reflected this intersubjective transition point. This coupling pattern not only navigated contemporary youth culture but also opened up an in-depth rhetorical framework to examine the traumas and absences of the previous decades. In addition to hippie and counterculture comedies, it emerged in one other popular film genre of the 1970s: the historical melodrama.

COUPLINGS AS CONTRAHISTORY

The enormous success of *Fiddler on the Roof* (1971) offers perhaps the most overt link between historical reappraisals and Anglo-Christian-Jewish erotic entanglement. The Broadway play, debuting in 1964, had been loosely based on *Tevye's Daughters*, a collection of 1890s short stories from Russian Jewish author Sholem Aleichem.[20] It debuted to immediate acclaim as part of an emerging revival of ethnic pride in the theater of the mid-1960s.[21]

While the play's setting was shtetl life in Russia in 1905, the text's nostalgia was focused firmly on established immigrant media genres of the 1910s and 1920s. The episodic structure and Jewish character humor recalled both New York's popular Yiddish theater and silent-era shtetl love stories such as *Judith of Bethulia* (1914) and *Surrender* (1927). The fourth wall-breaking audience address of Tevye the Milkman (Zero Mostel), both speaking and singing comically about his poverty-stricken lot in life, also recalled early sound-era ghetto comedies and comedic melodramas such as *The Cohens and Kellys* (1926), *The Jazz Singer* (1927), and *Abie's Irish Rose* (1928).[22]

But these allusions to early twentieth-century immigrant entertainment belied the play's distinct contemporary engagement. *Fiddler on the Roof* may have been ostensibly set in Russia in 1905. It may have nostalgically recalled the first wave of popular American immigrant media in the 1910s and 1920s. But its revisionist take on the tropes of patriarchy, gender roles, and sexual liberation offered a distinct commentary on the changing youth culture sensibilities of the mid- to late 1960s.

This covert counterculture allegory was expressed through the agency of Tevye's three single adult daughters, Tzeitel, Hodel, and Chava. Each daughter challenges the matchmaking traditions of shtetl life by expressing progressively transgressive romantic desires. At first, the challenges appear minor. Tzeitel falls in love with and wants to marry a poor Jewish tailor, Motel, rather than honoring her contractual obligation to marry the rich butcher, Lazar. After grappling with "tradition," Tevye agrees to Tzeitel's desire to marry for love. Hodel goes one step further, falling in love with the secular Jew, Perchik. He is a communist agitator, preaching political change and radical Marxist interpretations of the Torah. He eventually joins the Russian Revolution to bring communism to the masses.[23] The play's fearless connection between Jews and communism was just one of the signifiers that referenced a youth culture break from the anxieties and anti-Semitism of the 1950s HUAC blacklists.[24]

But it is Tevye's third daughter, Chava, who relocates the break between shtetl life and the modern world that spoke as much to 1964 as it did to 1905. Chava falls in love with the Russian non-Jew, Fyedka. When she asks for her father's blessing, Tevye refuses to acquiesce to Chava's desires. She informs Tevye that she will be marrying Fyedka anyway, with or without his blessing. Tevye's willingness to bend with tradition reaches its limits. He is unable to cross the divide of Jewish-Russian intermarriage. Yet, both the play and the film find a quasi-solution to this generational break. In both versions, at the moment Chava is about to leave, Tevye reaches an uneasy acceptance of her decision. In both versions, he quietly gives the couple his blessing.

Chava's act of marrying a Russian against her family's wishes marks the termination of Jewish "tradition" in the play. It is the exact moment that ushers in the end of shtetl life and signifies the entrance of Jews into the modern world. Tevye and his village are forced to flee to America to escape persecution. Chava's choice tempers this destruction by representing the hopeful melting pot ideology of American assimilation at the turn of the twentieth century. But the moment was not just historical commentary. Chava's selection of the non-Jew also signaled the rising awareness of second-wave feminist agency taking place. Just as Perchik operated as a thematic corrective to Jewish fears of HUAC, Chava's insistent self-empowerment corrected the invisibility of the postwar domestic female while simultaneously challenging the imposition of patriarchy on her life. In the mid-1960s, this thematic alignment with the women's rights movement was unambiguous.

But, as Rabbi Philip Graubart points out, the successful marriage of Chava and Fyedka was not, in fact, the original ending in the novel.[25] In Alecheim's version, Chava's marriage to Chvedka (later renamed "Fyedka" for the play and film) collapses tragically. Chvedka is revealed to be a violent alcoholic, unloving, and abusive. His brutishness validates Tevye's warnings that marrying a non-Jew can end only in destruction.[26] Chava eventually leaves Chvedka and returns to Tevye and her family. Aleichem's story was clear. Intermarriage was a bridge too far, even in modernity. Some traditions, such as the ban on Jewish/non-Jewish marriage, were worth preserving after all.

In the play and film, however, Chava and Fyedka are depicted as a warm, loving couple. Tevye's initial rejection of the marriage isolates him from his family and places him on the wrong side of history. When the Jewish village is attacked, Fyedka is identified as the Good Gentile. He renounces the violent pogrom and pledges his loyalty to Chava. They announce plans to flee to America, where they will be accepted. Tevye's final act of acquiescence to their decision is offered when he quietly blesses the couple ("God be with you") on their journey.

The rewriting of the Chava-Fyedka love story provides important insight into the relationship between second-wave Anglo-Christian-Jewish couplings and the renegotiation of history taking place in the popular media of the 1960s. *Fiddler on the Roof* was not intended to accurately depict historical events. It used history as a rhetorical trope to explore contemporary transitions and transformations. Jewish-Russian intermarriage was an untenable transgression for Aleichem in the 1890s. It didn't become a symbol of American cultural pluralism until the 1910s and 1920s. It was reintroduced in the 1960s as a nostalgic reminder of the emerging ethnic pride, sexual agency, and determinism of the postwar generation. But it was nostalgia as fantasy. Chava and Fyedka were not breaking from the "traditions" of shtetl life in the 1890s. Their relationship was a visible Jewish/non-Jewish love story, a rejection not of the absences and cultural conservatism the 1890s, but instead of the 1950s and early 1960s.

Two studio films, *The Way We Were* (1973) and *The Front* (1976), built on the Chava-Fyedka template to grapple with more recent historical traumas. Both films dealt with the cultural violence of the HUAC years, Joe McCarthy, the blacklist, and the 1953 executions of the Rosenbergs. These historical events provided context for mainstream studio films to rethink the ethnic visibility and cultural emergence of visible Jewishness as it was emerging in the 1970s. Barbra Streisand, Woody Allen, and Zero Mostel were Jewish actors playing Jewish characters who were facing reactionary politics based on anti-immigrant anti-Semitism of the 1940s and 1950s. But these performances also represented a clear break from the screen absences of the periods being depicted in the films. They were proud, visible Jews, playing Jews on screen, without fear of reprisal or recrimination. Their star turns not only rethought the anti-Semitism underpinning the political events of the 1950s. They also marked the end of that era simply by existing.

Despite this Jewish visibility, both films tempered their political critique through the reassuring framework of Anglo-Christian-Jewish Hollywood romance. This had two benefits. First, by locating a critical political historiography within a classic star-crossed romance structure, these films neutralized any presumed political threat contained in their liberal, pro-labor messages. Second, the privileging of the universality argument offered Anglo-Christian-Jewish couplings as a familiar signifier of its own form of nostalgic reassurance. Both films offered a critique of institutional anti-Semitism in the 1950s. But by preserving the familiar first-wave love story template, the formal aesthetics of each film contextualized this critique within the relative safety of familiar genre traditions.

The Way We Were signified its historical revisionism on two levels. First, the film is told in nonlinear flashbacks from the 1930s to the 1950s, an aesthetic reminder of New Hollywood's appropriation of the formal innovations of the European and other New Waves. The fractured chronology of the narrative operates as a discursive framework for the thematic idea of revisiting absent events from the dominant historical record. Second, the film's star-crossed romance between a rich WASP (Robert Redford) and a politically engaged socialist Jewish activist (Barbra Streisand) takes place against the backdrop of the HUAC and McCarthy investigations. The film's political critique is framed by the foregrounding of WASP/Jewish physiognomy while also inverting the normative gender roles. Hubbell Gardner (Robert Redford), a preppie "jock" infused with old money sensibilities, is the shiksa—or, in this case, the shagetz (Christian male). Redford was the established exemplar of Anglo-Christian male beauty and postwar American privilege. Katie Morosky (Streisand) is Gardner's opposite in both gender and physicality. Katie is a Jewish labor leader and political activist-agitator. She both displays active agency in her career and occupies the traditionally masculine role of sexual pursuer. By scrambling gender norms through WASP/Jewish inversion, *The Way We Were* links political disruption to representational hierarchies of beauty. As embodied by Barbra Streisand, the most visibly Jewish female movie star of the era, Katie drew an explicit connection among the labor movements of the 1930s, the prominent role of American Jews as leaders of those movements, and the absence of this fact from screen culture over the preceding three decades.

This inverted hierarchy of WASP/Jewish beauty uses the scrambling of gender norms to reflect the film's preoccupation with the politics of writing. Katie's typewriter is shown throughout the film as the object that gives her both personal and political agency. In contrast to the activist Katie, Hubbell Gardner is presented as an apolitical aristocrat turned unlikely Hollywood screenwriter. He begins as a beautiful body, easily passing through the gates of privilege without the work ethic that Katie demonstrates. Hubbell operates as an emblem of the top-down historical narrator of privilege that thinkers such as Foucault and Derrida were critiquing in the academy.

The Way We Were thematizes this philosophical clash between political activism and creative cowardice through the contrast of Redford's passive WASP beauty and Streisand's aggressive Jewishness. As Henry Bial points out, Katie is not fully attracted to Hubbell until she reads a short story he has written. It is then that Katie becomes drawn not just to Hubbell's Anglo beauty, but also to his potential as an active force for political change working within entrenched Anglo-Saxon power structures.[27] Over the course of the film, Katie repeatedly pushes Hubbell to write more challenging, politically engaged material. He resists, preferring to produce the easy genre fare that defined Hollywood in the 1940s and 1950s. Eventually, Katie's left-wing politics threaten Hubbell's career during the blacklist years, and the two eventually are unable to sustain their love affair.

In an interview, Streisand explained the film's critical link between postwar politics and Christian-Jewish cultural dichotomy, stating:

> Their breakup wasn't just about Hubbell (Robert Redford) shtupping another girl, it was about the political atmosphere of the times, the betrayals that occurred then, and the essential difference between the two characters.[28]

As Streisand notes, Hubbell and Katie were archetypes of sociopolitical conflict. Director Sydney Pollack used the template of their fractured, transcultural romance to thematize the painful history of leftist labor movements of the 1930s and the conservative pushback of the HUAC years in the 1940s and 1950s. This historicity was corporealized through the film's critique of archetypal gendered beauty standards. The predominant model of the second wave was nebbishy Jewish men pursuing shiksas, the Benjamin/Portnoy/Woody Allen model. But while the Christian/Jewish roles are gender-inverted in *The Way We Were*, this change is mostly cosmetic. Katie does not begin as the traditional postwar female-object recipient of the masculine gaze. She is instead identified as a quasi-male subject. It is Katie who first notices the classically beautiful Hubbell at a crowded bar. She approaches him, giving her the agency of seducer rather than seduced. As with Kelly in *The Heartbreak Kid*, Redford's desexualized, distant Hubbell embodies the blond-haired, blue-eyed object of attraction, acquisition, and objectification.

But this gender-inverted beauty binary is ultimately revealed to be a fraud. Despite physical looks, wealth, and privilege, Hubbell is ultimately an empty suit and a coward, an extension of Christian American complicity during the blacklist. This is expressed on the personal level in terms of his unwillingness to love Katie because of her proud Jewishness, unconventional looks, and unflinching political activism. But it also extends to his creative cowardice as a writer and screenwriter who is afraid to produce challenging material within the Hollywood studio system. Katie fails to convince Hubbell to use cinema as an agent for political change. The film is thus an indictment of blacklist cowardice. The corrective in 1973 locates not only in the visibility of a major Jewish Hollywood star in a starring role as a proud Jewish socialist, but also in the implicit acknowledgment that Hollywood cinema can and does operate as a persuasive tool of mass influence. Katie's willingness to bridge the WASP-Jewish cultural divide with Hubbell was a personal-is-political manifestation of the feminist activism that she advocated. But her failure to liberate Hubbell from his WASP-infused world produced an ambiguity at work within the film's historiography.

In the film's final scene, set in New York in the 1950s, many years after their breakup, the ambiguity at the center of second-wave couplings is made clear. Hubbell and Katie run into each other on the street in Manhattan. He reveals to her that he ended up as a writer on a television sitcom, a presumably hacky job that squandered whatever talent Hubbell had. Katie, meanwhile, has continued in her political activism. The two go their separate ways. The melodramatic sequence implies a culture-crossed love affair that could not transgress the anti-Semitic and class barriers of the 1940s and 1950s. But this melancholia was overruled by the triumphant star turn of unlikely movie icon Barbra Streisand.[29] Her role as a viable love interest for Robert Redford and the visibility of an unapologetic WASP-Jewish love story in a studio film represented New Hollywood's corrective to the reactionary, conservative forces of 1950s postwar Hollywood depicted in the film.[30]

Streisand's celebratory star turn also offered a corrective to the hidden Jewish backgrounds of so many leaders of the women's rights movements of the 1930s, 1940s, and 1950s. As Joyce Antler notes, feminists such as Betty Friedan, Phyllis Chesler, Letty Cottin Pogrebin, Vivian Gornick, and Bella Abzug were Jewish-born women who repeatedly refused to acknowledge or significantly downplayed the importance of their Jewish backgrounds.[31] Friedan, author of *The Feminine Mystique* (1963) and seminal second-wave feminist, studiously avoided all mentions of both her Jewishness and her role in labor movements of the 1930s and 1940s. Born Bettye Goldstein, she and her husband, Carl Friedman changed their name to Friedan shortly after their Jewish wedding in 1947. Friedan presented herself in public as nothing more than a typical suburban housewife.[32]

Yet, as Daniel Horowitz and Joyce Antler have argued, this was a conscious, strategic choice. Friedan feared that marking feminism as a by-

Publicity images of Robert Redford and Barbra Streisand in The Way We Were *(1973) and Kris Kristofferson and Streisand in* A Star Is Born *(1976).*

product of Jewish activism would dilute the reach of her work and define second-wave feminism as a specifically Jewish cause. *The Way We Were* addressed this historical gap. Katie's agency, both as a visible Jew and in her attraction and pursuit of Hubbell, mobilized the corrective of 1970s-era political historiography via alternative screen Jewishness. Katie/Streisand's value is confirmed via the erotic reciprocity of Robert Redford, an idealized Anglo-Saxon movie star.[33]

As with *The Way We Were*, Martin Ritt's *The Front* featured unapologetic Jewish visibility at the center of a historical corrective. The film tells the story of the blacklisted Jews of Hollywood in the 1950s by focusing on the intergenerational friendship between blacklisted Jewish comedian Hecky Brown (Zero Mostel, an actual victim of the blacklist) and the young, nebbishy, lunchroom cashier turned "front" for blacklisted screenwriters, Howard Prince (Woody Allen). Produced, written, and starring actors, writers, and directors who actually had been blacklisted in the 1950s, the film's unabashed connection between Jewishness and the HUAC/McCarthy investigations marked a symbolic response to the marginalization experienced by so many Jewish creatives in the 1950s. Hecky's persecution and hounding by HUAC investigators and his eventual suicide served as a reenactment of the experiences of people such as John Garfield and Philip Loeb, who had seen their lives destroyed by accusations of communism.[34] By allowing the people who had been damaged by HUAC to finally tell their story, the film offered revisionist historical catharsis.[35] But it was as much about celebrating the visibility of second-wave Jews in the 1970s as it was about correcting absence and persecution in the 1950s.

Woody Allen was one of the most visible comedic stars of the Jewish

New Wave, and his role in the film signified an intergenerational handoff. Allen's rare choice to appear in a film he didn't write or direct suggests his awareness of this historical debt to his career. Howard/Woody functions in the film as the observer-witness to the injustice and anti-Semitism of the McCarthy years. But Allen's Jewish star persona, well established by 1976, operated similarly to Streisand's fearless Jewishness in *The Way We Were*. Both confirmed a revisionist, vicarious victory over the institutional forces that destroyed the careers (and lives) of so many Jewish Catskills-era comedians of the 1950s.

The film's visual cartography also locates Anglo-Christian-Jewish romance as the key to its intergenerational corrective. The love story between Howard and the ambitious, idealistic, Connecticut-raised television producer, Florence Barrett (Andrea Marcovicci), is what pushes him to develop his identity beyond merely that of a shell for other writers. A dialogue exchange on one of their first dates illustrates the bringing together of Christian and Jewish culture:

> Howard: Where are you from?
> Florence: Connecticut.
> Howard: That's very ritzy.
> Florence: It's very proper anyway. I was very well bred—the kind of family where the biggest sin was to raise your voice.
> Howard: Oh yeah? In my family the biggest sin was to pay retail.[36]

Paralleling Redford's role as the Good WASP, Florence becomes outraged at the anti-Semitic persecution taking place under HUAC. Yet, unlike the Katie-Hubbell coupling, it is Florence who teaches Howard how to be more politically engaged. This translates into another personal-is-political choice. Her political resistance to HUAC is confirmed by her love of Howard. In both films, transgressive female sexual desire is tied to political action. Katie believes Hubbell is capable of being a great screenwriter, but she is ultimately let down by Hubbell's cowardice. Florence believes Howard is a screenwriting genius. She is also let down when she discovers that he has merely been acting as a front for other screenwriters.

Yet, *The Front* deviates from the ambiguity and breakup of *The Way We Were* by producing an ending rooted in fantasy wish fulfillment. In the film's final scene, political, generational, historical, and sexual renegotiations converge. After Brown's suicide, Howard is asked to testify to HUAC, led by an investigator identified only as Hennessey (Remak Ramsey). Hennessey asks Howard to give up Hecky's real (Jewish) name to confirm that he was a communist. This is presented merely as a formality so that they can officially close the investigation. This "naming" process requires Howard to confirm that Hecky was actually named Herschel Brownstein. Since Hecky is already dead, HUAC argues that it will not matter if Howard "names" him. The concept of retroactively "outing" Hecky's Jewishness, and thereby confirming his communist affiliation, makes HUAC's anti-Semitic undercurrent blatant.

As Howard considers their offer, he experiences an epiphany. He recognizes that the "naming" of the communist is the same as the "naming" of the Jew. In the film's ultimate embodiment of retroactive rewrite, Howard refuses to participate. Instead, he tells the HUAC accusers to "go fuck yourselves," gets up, and walks out the door.[37] Howard/Woody is no longer silenced, either within the world of the film's period-piece setting or in the undeniable visibility of Allen's Jewish pride. The sequence immediately cuts from Howard walking out of the HUAC committee to a close-up of Howard and Florence kissing. Howard lifts his hand to touch Florence's face, revealing that he is handcuffed. He is going to jail for refusing to name names. But, in so doing, he has won the affection of the Christian female.

The screen tragedy of Herschel Brownstein and the real-life career sufferings of Zero Mostel—and, by proxy, all Jews silenced by the blacklist in the 1950s—are retroactively resolved through the tropes of a Hollywood love story fantasy. Florence and Howard live "happily ever after." Katie and Hubbell break up. But both couples offered the same personal-is-political historical corrective. The process of confronting the legacy of historical injustice was embodied by the freedom to cross the personal divide between archetypal repressed Anglo-Christian and sexually unruly Jew.

JEWS IN SPACE

A number of studio period pieces of the 1970s expanded on the renegotiations established by the Chava-Fyedka, Katie-Hubbell, and Howard-Florence couplings. In *A Star Is Born* (1976) and *The Rose* (1979), Barbra Streisand and Bette Midler, respectively, each portrayed a talented Jewish singer on the verge of superstardom and caught up in a dysfunctional love affair with a hunky, masculine non-Jewish man.[38] In the former, Esther Hoffman (Streisand) is so focused on her enormous singing talent and career that she remains indifferent to her love affair with fellow performer John Norman Howard, played by an icon of hippie masculinity, Kris Kristofferson.[39] In *The Rose*, based on the life of Janis Joplin, Midler's star-making turn played on the notion of female Jewishness as "ugliness." Despite career success, Midler's character, Mary Rose Foster, struggles with low self-esteem, eventually tumbling into an affair with her limo driver, Huston Dyer (Frederic Forrest).

Despite numerous textual differences, both films lauded the "unconventional" physical looks of their female Jewish stars by confirming their sexual desirability in the eyes of the Anglo-Christian male. Both films also give their female protagonists rewards outside the erotic realm, problematizing the ultimate value of transgressive Anglo-Christian-Jewish couplings as a solution to historical absence.

Slapstick comedies also grappled with historical absences. Mel Brooks's *Blazing Saddles* and *Young Frankenstein* (both 1974), Woody Allen's *Love and Death* (1975), *Next Stop, Greenwich Village* (1975), and Brooks's *History of the World, Part 1* (1981) each re-examined and critiqued dominant genre narratives by interjecting Jewish visibility where previously there had been only codes and absence.[40]

The Apprenticeship of Duddy Kravitz (1974) was one of the films of this era to examine the political importance of marginalized postwar Jewish comedy. Based on the novel by Mordecai Richler, the film was set in 1950s Montreal and focuses on the ambitions of Duddy Kravitz, a poor Jewish eighteen-year-old dreamer with a plan to one day fund his own Catskills-like resort on a patch of empty land. Richler's satirical riff on youthful ambition and sexual confusion in the 1950s was a carefully constructed parody of postwar Zionism. Duddy's dream is to build his own Catskills. Resorts in the Catskills made it possible for Jewish entertainers to hang on to their careers even after being blacklisted. Diaspora Jews actually had their own "homelands" in the form of popular entertainment enclaves.[41]

Played by the emerging Jewish actor Richard Dreyfuss, Duddy was an amalgam of the land-settling, ambitious Ari Ben-Canaan in *Exodus* and the wandering, lost Benjamin Braddock in *The Graduate*. Duddy's delusional determination to fund his "homeland" satirized the confusion of the wandering Jewish Diaspora of North America. But this was not necessarily a critique. Duddy's confused, wandering schlemiel finds inspiration during a romantic picnic with his love interest, a beautiful French-Canadian hotel employee named Yvette (Micheline Lanctôt). After taking her to a lake, Duddy announces plans to buy the surrounding land and build his resort. His ambitions impress Yvette, amplifying her attraction to him. She, like Duddy's Catskills, is a fantasy figure. Following the pattern established by Paul Newman and Eva Marie Saint in *Exodus* (1960), Jewish masculinity (and land acquisition) is only confirmed by the erotic interest of the non-Jew. Both conquests are expressions of Duddy's ambitions and disassociation from his diasporic identity.

But, arguably, the peak of Anglo-Christian-Jewish coupling visibility in second-wave cinema was reached with the massive critical and popular success of two Woody Allen films in the late 1970s, *Annie Hall* (1977) and *Manhattan* (1979). Both films represented Allen's star persona transition from comedic, horny schlemiel to romantic leading man. In *Annie Hall*, the nonlinear structure and surreal flights of fantasy foregrounded New Hollywood's use of neurotic Jewish sexuality as a thematic companion to the mainstreaming of atemporal, avant-garde aesthetics.[42] The film features Allen in bed with different women, performing oral sex (off-camera), and makes references to underage sex, incest, and masturbation. The elevation of Allen's muse and former girlfriend, Diane Keaton, to the title role also confirmed the notion that the drive to impress and/or seduce the shiksa was the motivating force for Allen's artistic creation.[43] As Alvy Singer, a successful comedy writer and performer living in New York, Allen summarized the link among politics, Jewishness, sexuality, and deviancy with the following quip:

> Don't you see the rest of the country looks upon New York like we're left-wing, communist, Jewish, homosexual pornographers? I think of us that way sometimes and I live here.[44]

In *Manhattan*, Allen depicted a culturally taboo love affair between a forty-something writer, Isaac (Allen), and a seventeen-year-old high school student Tracy (Mariel Hemingway). Isaac's myopic, self-obsessed New York Jew suffers no qualms about his affair with a high school student, making only vague allusions to the fact that it troubles his analyst. Tracy is presented in the film as an old money, prep school, shiksa child of privilege. Her lack of complication, attributed to her youth, is also implied to be a result of her role as the idealized Christian-normative female fetishized by so many Jewish men of the second wave. The film tethers this transgressive erotic desire for the underage female to the creative process. The film begins with Allen's thwarted attempts to narrate a novel as a love letter to the island of Manhattan. The shiksa and the city are linked as related fantasies in the mind of the Jewish artist. They exist only in black-and-white and with a George Gershwin score.

Alvy's compulsive, myopic paranoia and Isaac's taboo sexuality were both by-products of Allen's triumph over the absences of screen culture in the previous generation. Riffing off Jewish stereotypes to embody the New Hollywood hero, Allen deployed "left-wing, communist, Jewish, homosexual pornographer" stereotypes as a means of trans-cultural reclamation. *Annie Hall* won the Academy Award for Best Picture (over *Star Wars*) in a rare triumph for a romantic comedy. The film, in tandem with *Man-*

hattan, confirmed the unapologetic return of Anglo-Christian-Jewish couplings to a Hollywood pinnacle not seen since *The Jazz Singer* (1927). That both peaks came at a time of ascendant social, political, and cultural permissiveness was not coincidental. Screen Jewishness and sociopolitical liberalism were once again indelibly linked in the form of romantic coupling.

BRIDGET LOVES BERNIE ON TELEVISION

Unlike New Hollywood, 1960s television dealt with counterculture politics primarily through allusion and metaphor. This took the form of a genre-coding process that Lynn Spigel and David Marc have described as fantastic voyages grounded in science fiction and monster archetypes.[45] Sitcoms such as *The Addams Family* (1964–1966), *Bewitched* (1964–1972), and *I Dream of Jeannie* (1965–1970), to name just a few, used magic and monsters to obliquely explore changing understandings of gender, race, and the politics of the Cold War. White, genteel, Anglo-Saxon characters dominated these programs. Visible Jewishness, as with most other nonwhite ethnicities, was almost entirely absent. There were, however, a few notable exceptions. Television sitcoms in particular represented one of the few genres to attempt to mirror New Hollywood's emerging iconography of Anglo-Christian-Jewish couplings as signifiers of youth culture.

The first major television show since *The George Burns and Gracie Allen Show* (1950–1958) that was built around an Anglo-Christian-Jewish couple was *He and She* (1967–1968). Created by Leonard Stern, the show dealt with the notion of religious intermarriage primarily in code. It ostensibly focused on the universal comedic foibles of a new marriage between two young, good-looking, urban dwellers. Richard Benjamin, in his first major screen role, played Dick Hollister, the husband of Paula Hollister (Paula Prentiss). Benjamin and Prentiss were married in real life, giving the show the veneer of safety and grounding it in the traditions of earlier sitcoms featuring other real couples such as *The George Burns and Gracie Allen Show* and *I Love Lucy* (1951–1960). Dick Hollister was never explicitly identified as Jewish on the show. However, Dick's physical appearance and performative style were both firmly in line with the emergent urban New York, Jewish nebbish concurrently exemplified by Dustin Hoffman in that year's *The Graduate*. Dick was a comic book artist with an urbane wit. He continued the hip Jewish archetype of stand-up comedians such as Mort Sahl, Lenny Bruce, Woody Allen, and Mike Nichols. Prentiss was the shiksa fantasy brought to life, the dream Anglo-Christian female for the generation of Portnoys that the show was thematically addressing. But the sexual dy-

namic between Benjamin and Prentiss made *He and She* a little too erotically charged for the white, homogenized slapstick of 1960s television (the
lead-in to *He and She* was *Green Acres*). The sophisticated wit and double
entendres of the show did not catch on, and *He and She* was canceled after
one season.[46]

The next major effort to bring the schlemiel-shiksa dynamic to prime
time was Norman Lear's breakout hit on CBS, *All in the Family* (1971–
1979). The marriage of Mike "Meathead" Stivic (Rob Reiner) and Gloria
Bunker (Sally Struthers) echoed the same coded dynamic introduced on
He and She. Similar to Dick Hollister, Meathead was not explicitly written as a Jewish character.[47] However, Reiner's outsized gesticulations, thick
New York accent, and unabashed liberal politics collectively suggested the
same hiding-in-plain-sight Jewish codes that Joseph Litvak identifies as urban "comicosmopolitanism."[48] Meathead is a bleeding-heart, liberal, anti-
war peacenik. He is loud and opinionated. He has a lazy work ethic and
is a perpetual academic. Yet, he is identified only as a second-generation
American child of Polish immigrants. Polishness as coded Jewishness was
presented in contrast with the show's lead character, curmudgeonly working-class bigot Archie Bunker (Carroll O'Connor). Mike Stivic's nebbishy,
college-educated, liberal hippie embraced Jewish stereotypes, yet Archie's
only racist epithet was to call Meathead a "Polack." The use of "Polack" as
coded anti-Semitism was further amplified whenever Jewish characters appeared on the show. Archie's anti-Semitism was directed toward them, not
Meathead. Mike Stivic's Jewishness remained cloaked. Despite his hippie
credentials and the Jewish actor playing him, he was a hybrid construction,
a continuation of the postwar tradition of coded Jewishness hidden inside a
counterculture veneer.

Bridget Loves Bernie (1972–1973) was the first show to bring the subtext
Jewishness of *He and She* and *All in the Family* directly into the text. The
CBS show, produced by Bernard Slade, was a loose adaptation of the 1920s
hit, *Abie's Irish Rose*. The show was also responding to the real-life intermarriage "crisis" taking place among American Jewry of the 1970s. Episodes explored the family tensions that emerge when a rich Irish school-
teacher, Bridget Fitzgerald (Meredith Baxter), marries a poor Jewish
cabdriver, Bernie Steinberg (David Birney). Bridget's repressed, upper-
class Catholic parents, Walter and Amy Fitzgerald (David Doyle and Au-
dra Lindley), and Bernie's delicatessen-owning parents, Sam and Sophie
Steinberg (Harold J. Stone and Bibi Osterwald), were brought into conflict through updated versions of the Irish-Jewish comedies of the 1920s.
Episodes such as "'Tis the Season" (December 16, 1972); "A Funny Thing
Happened on the Way to the Vatican" (September 23, 1972); "The In-Laws

Who Came to Dinner" (November 25, 1972); and "How to Be a Jewish Mother" (November 11, 1972) evoked classic *Cohens and Kellys* family collision comedy. But they did so within the framework of the ascendant schlemiel-shiksa love stories of New Hollywood.

The opening credit sequence montage in the pilot episode depicts the events of Bernie meeting and romancing Bridget. He picks her up as a passenger in his cab. He then waits for her all day outside the school where she works as a teacher. They go to Central Park and other scenic locations around New York. They're shown kissing in Bernie's cab. Then the title song, featuring the refrain "love is crazy," stops to allow the following exchange between Bridget and Bernie in a scenic shot by the East River:

> Bridget: You know this is crazy. I don't even know your full name.
> Bernie: Bernie . . . Steinberg. What's yours?
> Bridget: Bridget. Bridget . . . Theresa . . . Mary . . . Colleen . . . Fitzgerald.
> Bernie: I . . . uh . . .
> Bridget and Bernie (together): . . . think we have a problem.

Controversy over the show was immediate and intense. Airing directly after *All in the Family* on Saturday nights, the highly rated show (top five in the Nielsen ratings) was canceled after only one season due to an intense backlash. The cancellation was in part a response to anti-Semitic hate mail over the Christian-Jewish love story.[49] Protests also reportedly came from both Catholic and Jewish groups outraged at the program's cavalier attitude toward intermarriage. It remains one of the highest-rated shows ever to be cancelled.

The unusual cancellation of *Bridget Loves Bernie* suggests a clear demarcation between the mediums of film and television in the 1970s. While cinema began to self-identify through voluntary ratings systems as an exclusive medium of choice, television was still seen as universal, able to reach into the home and influence the unwilling or unwitting. Television was not able to mimic the success that mainstream cinema found in mining the youth culture appeal of Anglo-Christian-Jewish couplings. This difference in receptivity speaks to the specificities of the medium. By establishing a "love conquers all" romance facing the real-world tensions of generational break, *Bridget Loves Bernie* was hardly groundbreaking. The same basic material had achieved considerable success since the coded Jewishness of *The Graduate* and the explicit Jewishness of *I Love You, Alice B. Toklas*. In 1972, *The Heartbreak Kid*, based on largely the same premise, was a huge box-office success. But television was simply not able to engage this subject matter in the same direct way.[50]

In 1974, CBS tried again, spinning off the wisecracking Rhoda Morgenstern (Valerie Harper) from *The Mary Tyler Moore Show* into *Rhoda*. The first episode, "Joe" (September 9, 1974), follows Rhoda as she goes on a vacation to New York to see her younger sister, Brenda (future Woody Allen mainstay Julie Kavner). There Rhoda meets a handsome, non-Jewish, divorced man named Joe Gerard (David Groh). Playing with the hot topics of divorce and remarriage, Rhoda and Joe begin to date, causing her to give up returning to Minnesota to stay in New York to explore the romance. On *The Mary Tyler Moore Show*, Rhoda had been the sole Jewish character in the mostly Anglo-Saxon world of Minneapolis. *Rhoda* used the show's New York backdrop to build out Rhoda's Jewish world, with Joe stepping in as the Anglo-Saxon outsider. Her clichéd Jewish parents, Martin (Harold Gould) and Ida (Nancy Walker), are presented as marriage-obsessed, determined to see their daughter settle down, even if it ends up being with a non-Jew. Within the first seven episodes, Rhoda and Joe experience a whirlwind courtship, which leads to an engagement and, in the show's eighth episode, an hour-long special titled "Rhoda's Wedding" (October 28, 1974).

The massive cultural impact of Rhoda and Joe's television wedding offered the visible pinnacle of second-wave television couplings. The heavily publicized event drew more than fifty-two million viewers, becoming the second-highest-rated broadcast in television history to date. It was a record that would stand until *Roots* toppled it three years later.[51] The fictional wedding drew thousands of congratulatory cards to CBS Studios. It even inspired sportscaster Howard Cosell to interrupt his *Monday Night Football* broadcast on rival ABC and suggest to his viewers that they join him in changing the channel: "Let's go over to Rhoda's wedding quick. The chicken liver is getting rancid." Cosell's quip made clear not only the cultural impact of the episode, but also the centrality of Rhoda's Jewishness (and Joe's non-Jewishness) to its appeal. When contrasted with the struggles of *Bridget Loves Bernie* just a few years earlier, the shift in acceptable couplings on television was remarkable. Rhoda completed a next-generation Jewish update to the second-wave innovations introduced by the polite, genteel, WASP adventures of Mary Richards (Mary Tyler Moore) on *The Mary Tyler Moore Show*. The massive success of Rhoda's wedding exemplified the enormous cross-cultural appeal that visible Anglo-Christian-Jewish couplings had achieved by the mid-1970s.

Unlike Bridget and Bernie, Rhoda and Joe were able to achieve mainstream ratings success. Yet, both shows remained distinct from second-wave feature films through casting. While most viewers were likely unaware of the biographical backgrounds of each show's stars, neither Valerie Harper nor David Birney were Jewish. Likewise, the Jewish actress Bea Arthur, who played the liberal feminist Maude Findlay on *Maude* (1972–1978), watched as her culturally Jewish character (based on Jewish show creator Norman Lear's Jewish wife) was identified as an Anglo-Saxon. In a late career interview, Arthur explained the rationale behind this decision. She stated that Maude was intentionally not written as a Jewish character because "(i)f you made her Jewish . . . her courage in fighting bigotry would be personal instead of ideological."[52]

Arthur's quote reveals an understanding of the complex relationship among representation, gender politics, and political liberalism on television in the 1970s. The Jewish backgrounds of so many feminist leaders potentially undermined the universal message that second-wave feminists such as Arthur hoped to convey. Arthur and Lear feared that non-Jewish audiences would decode (and dismiss) an aggressive liberal, Jewish feminist. *Maude* therefore required a "universal" coding process. Streisand's visible and unapologetic representation of the role of Jews in labor movements in *The Way We Were* suffered from no such reservations. This suggests a clear demarcation in how the two mediums were viewed as cultural arbiters of the ideological issues of the time. Studio films were able to directly engage the rhetorical link between politics, history, and Jewish liberalism in ways that television still could not.

THE PORNOGRAPHIC SEMITE

Parody, as Judith Butler argues, is often used to expose the distinction between culturally constructed and naturalized configurations of gender and sexuality.[53] Freed from the conceptual ghettos of the postwar decades, Jewish schlemiels were transformed into conquering heroes, seducing idealized Anglo shiksas as beacons of the new sexual freedoms. As a hybrid construction between Jewish schlemiel and sexual dynamo, they produced what Butler describes as "subversive laughter," the visual recognition of what had previously remained unseen and taboo.[54]

They also parodied the historical anti-Semitic trope that David Biale describes as "Jewish rapists (who) threaten the purity of Christian women and, through them, Christian society."[55] Prior to the second wave, Jewish performers masked this subversive approach through what appeared to be de-eroticized slapstick or comedic takes on erotic longing.[56] But second-wave couplings offered cinema a safe intercultural bridge between the Anglo-Christian power of the 1950s and the uncertain multi-ethnic and second-wave feminist and sexual terrain of the 1970s.

Pornographic representations of screen Jewishness became a critical mitigating factor in the mainstreaming of graphic pornography in theatrical exhibition contexts. Parody was central to this normalizing process. Like their schlemiel counterparts in Hollywood, Jewish male porn stars of the 1970s played up their "Jewish" physiognomy to signify an erotic, deviant break from the Anglo-Saxon norms of the previous generation. The thick mustache and Semitic looks of Harry Reems as he seduced Linda Lovelace in *Deep Throat* (1972) offered a more explicit variation of Charles Grodin's pursuit of Cybill Shepherd that same year in *The Heartbreak Kid*. Jamie Gillis's comedic parody of Henry Higgins in *The Opening of Misty Beethoven* (1976) had more in common with Allan Sherman's 1956 *My Fair Lady* song parody, "My Fairfax Lady," than with the sanitized pornography of Hugh Hefner.

The humorous tone of many of these golden age explicit films played up the connection between pornography and mainstream cinema through neurotic Jewish masculinity. After the porn industry established its production and distribution models with the successful distribution of feature films in the 1970s, hard-core pornography began to reflect and parody the codes, conventions, and sensibilities of studio films. The graphic display of male Jewish schlemiels performing sex acts with Christian blonde women was both a critique and a continuation of the carnal, taboo-challenging subtext of the New Wave in Hollywood. *Screw* magazine publisher Al Goldstein and porn stars Harry Reems, Daniel Pacheco, Jamie Gillis, and Ron "The Hedgehog" Jeremy, with his Portnoy/Kafkaesque animetaphor nickname, each performed comedic takes on Jewish Borscht Belt humor in between graphic displays of sexual conquest. The vaudevillian joke of Jeremy's persona was that he was perfectly willing to embrace the "hedgehog" animality of Jewish stereotype if it meant that he was free to engage in carnal sex with numerous shiksa fantasies. But these visible, aroused Jewish males were also a political statement. Through pornographic evidence of sexual ability, Hebraic "studs" fulfilled Portnoy's neurotic compulsions and erased Woody Allen's nebbishy insecurities. They offered visible evidence of post-Israel masculine Jewish transformation from marginalized clowns to a conquering, counterculture, alternative masculinity. Successful conquest of the Anglo-Christian female confirmed this victory over the Victorian-era taboo.

The pleasures of pornography, as Linda Williams has observed, focus primarily on gendered discourses of power exchanges between oscillating and incongruous male and female perspectives.[57] The second-wave Jewish male, occupying a hybrid, transient state between comedic schlemieldom and newfound empowerment, expanded this oscillation from the obvious male/female binary to a complex Anglo-Christian-Jewish political interplay. From Lenny Bruce to Dustin Hoffman, the comedic male Jew was already an identifiable transom from the censorship to post-censorship eras. The successful pornographic seduction of the shiksa simply validated this. As Al Goldstein put it in a 1998 interview:

> The only reason that Jews are in pornography is that we think that Christ sucks. Catholicism sucks. We don't believe in authoritarianism. Pornography thus becomes a way of defining Christian culture and, as it penetrates to the very heart of the American mainstream (and is no doubt consumed by those very same WASPs), its subversive character becomes more charged.[58]

Goldstein's link between anarchic political rebellion and Jewish sexuality was hardly new to the 1970s. Nathan Abrams, building off Jay Gertzman's examination of Jewish business owners in the distribution of erotic literature in the 1930s, traces the taboo-pushing boundaries of 1970s hard core back to the history of early twentieth-century Jewish political radicalism. Abrams argues that Jewish sexual performers in hard core saw themselves as political culture warriors.[59] Successful seduction of the shiksa was an extension of the battle between conservative mores and an emancipated, libertine secular humanism. The scopophilic pleasures of watching Jewish men sexually satisfy Christian women offered a Portnoy-esque solution to the sublimations and repressions of the postwar decades. These films became, as Laura Kipnis describes it, "cultural alibis," safe spaces where transgressive and deviant impulses could be explored as liberating fantasies.[60] A similar point was made at the memorial of male porn star Jamie Gillis in 2010. Jewish comedian Gilbert Gottfried related Gillis's theory that all pornography was fueled by the erotic charge of watching Jewish men violate Catholic and Protestant women.[61]

Both the Gillis anecdote and the Goldstein quote locate an Anglo-Christian as both the targeted audience for their performances and the object of their sexual conquest. These conquering Jewish studs were self-aware that they were (at least primarily) not solely a Jewish fantasy intended for Jewish spectators. Their scrambling of masculine tropes offered multiple entrance points for men and women, Jewish and non-Jewish, to project deviant desires onto the iconography of the established counterculture Jewish Other.

Fritz the Cat (1972), the feature film adaptation of R. Crumb's *Fritz the Cat* underground comix, made this link between Jewish carnality and Christian spectatorship explicit. The film was one of a number of X-rated parody films to cross over to mainstream popularity in the wake of the massive success of *Deep Throat* (1972). It also offers one of the clearest examples of the link between representations of hard-core sexuality and the satirization of historical Jewish deviancy. In playing up the notion of the carnal Jewish animal as a visual representation of youth culture experimentation, it also became the first animated film to receive an X rating.

In the film, Fritz (voiced by Skip Hinnant) is introduced as a young, bourgeois Jewish college student who drops out of NYU to experience the "truth" of real life on the streets of New York. At first, Fritz tries to bring his middle-class Jewish girlfriend, Winston Schwartz (voiced by Judy Engles), along with him on his journey of sexual discovery. But her bourgeois impulses and desire to maintain Jewish exclusivity ultimately repel him:

> Fritz: You're a motherfucking bitch!
> Winston: I see the hard facts of life! I am realistic, something you're incapable of! You'd be better off with one of those stupid little morons like Charlene who you could just sleep with and throw away when you're done! You can't cope with a mature woman![62]

As with the Jewish love interests in *I Love You, Alice B. Toklas* and *The Heartbreak Kid*, Winston is identified as an extension of the castrating Jewish wife/mother. Her crack about "Charlene" suggests that Fritz seek out the sexually willing, uncomplicated shiksa rather than deal with the real-world (Jewish) relationship that she offers. Her self-identification as a "mature woman" offers Fritz a reminder of the bourgeois Jewish life that awaits him if he doesn't take rebellious action.

Fritz's subsequent breakup with Winston is the instigating act of the film. It sends him on his urban quest, unleashing him from his middle-class Jewish college world and pushing him to embark on his rebellious descent into hard-core drugs and sexual experimentation. The film's picaresque bildungsroman structure includes scenes of Fritz seducing women into group sex in a bathtub (and experiencing coitus interruptus when the police show up), smoking marijuana, experimenting with heroin, fleeing from the police, joining (and abandoning) leftist political rallies, and exploring homelessness with his new black hipster jazz friends (depicted as crows) in Harlem.

Yet, Jewishness haunts Fritz throughout the film. While fleeing the cops, he ends up hiding out in a synagogue. Fritz, like Seymour Moskowitz in *Minnie and Moskowitz*, is then forced to confront his subsumed Jewishness. He witnesses numerous orthodox Jewish dogs mumbling Hebrew prayers. Horrified, he manages to escape when the congregation decides to send more weapons to Israel, their collective rage causing a distraction that allows him to slip away. A subsequent newscast makes reference to the transnational circulation of Israeli politics and urban Jewry from which Fritz is fleeing:

> Newscaster: We interrupt the Israeli-Arab war for this special announcement! The President, after conferring with Israeli Prime Minister Golda Meir, has agreed to send more arms to Israel—based on the return of New York City and Los Angeles to the United States.[63]

The film's scattershot political satire, like the gonzo comix movement from which it drew, was intentionally diffuse. Hippies and conservatives were held up for equal ridicule. But the joke about Jewish control of New York and Los Angeles affirms Fritz's privileged status as a wayward, wandering Jew, playing "hippie" dress-up. His ongoing attraction to black culture—from his fascination with the sexual potency and seductive powers of the black male to his obsession with Harlem pool halls and jazz—satirized the long tradition of black-Jewish cultural interplay. Despite the satirical soup of signifiers through which Fritz moves, Jewishness becomes the only grounding metaphor left.

As originally conceived by R. Crumb, Fritz was described as a sexually bold amalgam of counterculture hipster life coded in a nostalgic recall for the cartoon imagery of the 1920s and 1930s.[64] He was not textually identified as Jewish. But Fritz's neurotic behavior and sexual obsessions thematically identified the character as a libidinal Jew, an amalgam of Portnoy and Lenny Bruce. Ralph Bakshi, the young Jewish-born animator who adapted *Fritz the Cat*, recalibrated these themes by making Fritz overtly Jewish. This decision created a significant rift between Crumb and Bakshi. According to Bakshi, his decision to make Fritz explicitly Jewish and to play with Jewish identity in the film enraged Crumb. In an interview, Bakshi stated:

> Crumb hates the picture because I slipped a couple of things in there that he despises, like the rabbis—the pure Jewish stuff. Fritz can't hold that kind of commentary . . . (The strip) was cute and well done, but there was nothing that had that much depth.[65]

Bakshi's insistence on Fritz's Jewish subtext reflects more than just the disagreement between the two artists. Crumb did not object to Jewish codes in Fritz so much as Bakshi's decision to make Fritz's Jewishness textual. Robert Crumb is not Jewish, but his work has long been read as crypto-Jewish in its depiction of neurosis, self-hatred, and sexual compulsion. His sexual obsession with Jewish women has permeated his work for decades. He was specifically focused on the exaggerated zaftig female Jewish body—not as critical or derogatory, but as a confessional extension of Crumb's deviant erotic fetishes. Crumb's marriage to the Jewish Aline Kominsky amplified this obsession, as Andrea Most shows, in Aline and Robert Crumb's collaboration in the mid-1990s, *Self-Loathing Comics #1*. The comic was based on Aline's self-hatred for her perceived Jewish ugliness.[66] Crumb's resistance to Bakshi's literalism can be read as an extension of the late modernist European avant-garde argument put forth by Kafka. Bakshi's next-generation response can be read as a variation of Philip Roth. Bakshi/Roth moved Crumb/Kafka's coded metaphors of animal-Jewish alienation and re-introduced them as both explicitly Jewish (and thus comedic) and anarchically sexual.

This carnality emerged in pop music as well. Jewish musical wunderkind and "bad boy" pop singer Serge Gainsbourg (born Lucien Ginsburg) famously began dating the preeminent icon of blonde French beauty, Brigitte Bardot, in Paris in 1967. This sparked intense controversy.[67] The romance subsequently informed Gainsbourg's controversial and massively successful pop song, "Je T'aime . . . Moi Non Plus" ("I Love You . . . Me Neither"). An alternating duet between a man and a woman punctuated with a female orgasm that builds over the course of the song, "Je T'aime . . . Moi Non Plus" caused an enormous scandal in France upon its release and made Gainsbourg an even more polarizing figure for "exploiting" the sexuality of Bardot. After breaking up with her, Gainsbourg re-recorded the female role with his next girlfriend, Jane Birkin. With lyrics such as "Je vais et je viens, entre tes reins" ("I go and I come, in between your loins"), Gainsbourg's subsequent hit "Les Sucettes" ("Lollipops") took these ideas even further, making double entendres about oral sex and implying pedophilia with the metaphor of the lollipop.[68] His public persona's unapologetic Jewishness and overt sexuality symbolized the generational break taking place in the late 1960s in line with the Left Bank Dreyfus tradition he revived.[69]

Concurrently, in New York, Lou Reed's "Nice Jewish Boy" journey through Andy Warhol's heroin-infused downtown offered another variation of both the urban "slumming" of Fritz the Cat and the carnal-musical lust of Gainsbourg. Reed, the lead singer of the Velvet Underground, became an ironic icon of the co-opting suburban Jewish hipster. It was an archetype that Norman Mailer had embraced a decade earlier in his famous

1957 essay for *Dissent*, "The White Negro: Superficial Reflections on the Hipster."[70] Mailer's article celebrated white urban youths who adopted the language and cultural affectations of African-Americans as the means of processing the atomic age. The article was not specifically focused on urban Jews. But, as Andrea Levine points out, Mailer's self-positioning was coded within a distinct Jewish rubric.[71] Just as Kafka's coded animals satirized anxieties of hidden identity, Mailer's beatnik hipsters were appropriators adopting other cultures as the means of coping with an increasingly untethered world.

Lou Reed updated Mailer's white-black interplay through an Aryan-Jewish lens. As the suburban nice Jewish boy turned downtown hipster, Reed sought validation not through emulating black culture but through seeking and acquiring the purest of Aryan white women. In this case, it was the German Warhol superstar, Nico (Christa Päffgen). Just as with Gainsbourg and Bardot in Paris, Nico became the Jewish Reed's ethereal muse, a Warholian pop art creation of idealized, superhuman Aryan beauty come to impossible life. The Reed-Nico coupling located at the center of the Velvet Underground's identification as a bohemian, avant-garde harbinger of a new form of music-art hybridity. Reed-Nico also furthered the iconography of the male Jewish hipster's sexual viability. Their visibility privileged Anglo-Christian-Jewish coupling at the vanguard of music, performance, image, and art.

THE REAGAN REVERSION

The eventual containment and dissolution of the second wave in the 1980s was brought about by a reactionary political movement similar to that of the 1930s. In both waves, Anglo-Christian-Jewish couplings had emerged as representative of an ascendant cultural and political liberalism. In the 1920s, these couplings signified the championing of immigrant culture and the libertine impulses of the Jazz Age. In the late 1960s and 1970s, they accompanied a period of historical revisionism, political activism, visible feminism, and experimental sexuality. Both movements subsequently declined in the face of a politically and culturally conservative backlash. The regression of the first wave in the 1930s was a response to panicked fears of communist infiltration, immigrant xenophobia, and the rise of homegrown anti-Semitism championed by media figures such as Father Coughlin, Charles Lindbergh, Dr. Francis Everett Townsend, and Reverend Gerald L. K. Smith and amplified by the economic downturn of the Great Depression.[72]

The end of the second wave was influenced by a nativist backlash rooted in reactionary Cold War paranoia. This pushback was exemplified by an effort to restore the traditional "family values" gender roles of the 1950s.[73] This masculine pushback eventually reached critical mass with the 1980 election of Ronald Reagan, an actual 1950s-era movie star "cowboy." With his macho visage, Reagan became the fulfillment of this conservative cultural longing for a return to retrograde, clearly defined gender roles and Anglo-Christian beauty values. His campaign promised a rejection of the Equal Rights Amendment and featured frequent criticism of the "moral relativism" of youth culture values. With Reagan's landslide defeat of the "wimpy" Jimmy Carter, the presidency reverted to an appeal to the traditional authority role of the conventional (non-Jewish) male.[74]

This reaction to the reaction can be observed emerging as early as the late 1960s. A nostalgia for the rugged individualism (and desexualized heroism) of the folkloric American cowboy emerged as a counterweight to the touchy-feely liberalism of the urban Jewish schlemiel. These cowboy figures offered up variations of laconic hyper-masculinity as nostalgia for postwar masculine power. Steve McQueen in *Bullitt* (1968), Gene Hackman in *The French Connection* (1971), Clint Eastwood in *Dirty Harry* (1971), Burt Reynolds in *Deliverance* (1972), Robert Redford in *Jeremiah Johnson* (1972), and Charles Bronson in *Death Wish* (1974), to list just a few examples, depicted quiet, macho men sent to the margins and eventually lashing out at the decaying, liberal, urban rot of a feminized culture that had abandoned them. These performances and characters were not necessarily conventionally heroic. The stars were physical rather than verbal, aggressive rather than passive. They offered a retrograde machismo delivering "Old West" vigilante justice as a response to the perceived permissiveness and moral relativity of the 1970s.

Films of the late 1970s and early 1980s such as *Kramer vs. Kramer* (1979), *Private Benjamin* (1980), and *Modern Romance* (1981) reflected this conceptual realignment. They deconstructed and ridiculed the increasingly exhausted trope of Anglo-Christian-Jewish couplings as an emancipatory extension of 1970s-era liberalism. The realist divorce narrative of *Kramer vs. Kramer* operated as a thematic bookend to the ambiguity of the Benjamin-Elaine elopement at the end of *The Graduate*. As Ted Kramer, a successful ad executive with a regressive understanding of marriage, Dustin Hoffman's established Jewish everyman persona moved to a place of frustrated dysfunction and emotional dissolution. Ted's breakdown is triggered by the abandonment by his wife, Joanne, played by the emerging star and icon of Anglophile beauty, Meryl Streep.[75] The Kramer divorce severed any hopeful future from Anglo-Christian-Jewish couplings. Hoffman's urban, Jewish masculinity was no longer the solution to generational angst. Streep's lost shiksa now appeared to be better off on her own.

Private Benjamin (1980), a screwball military farce, focused on the experiences of Judy Benjamin (Goldie Hawn), a pampered Jewish American Princess. Judy decides to join the army after her Jewish husband, Yale Goodman (Albert Brooks) dies while having sex with her on their wedding night.[76] As in 1970s films such as *I Love You, Alice B. Toklas* and *The Heartbreak Kid*, the opening of *Private Benjamin* depicts the disastrous fallout from a fully Jewish wedding. After Yale's death, Judy's subsequent experiences in the military force her to shed her stereotypical Jewish American Princess persona and gain a new form of feminist empowerment. This is confirmed via the familiar, if gender-inverted, coupling pattern. Judy has a brief affair with a dashing Frenchman, Henri Tremont (Armand Assante). But romance is not Judy's concern. Her agency is achieved by winning the respect of her skeptical training officer, Captain Lewis (Eileen Brennan).

Actor-director Albert Brooks directly satirized the exhaustion of second-wave progression narratives in *Modern Romance*. In the film, Brooks's Robert Cole is presented as a neurotic, loveless, dysfunctional Jewish narcissist living and working in Hollywood as a successful film editor. Robert is also carrying on a whiny, unromantic, on-again-off-again love affair with the appropriately Brahmin-named Mary Harvard (Kathryn Harrold). The near-plotless film intercuts between various scenes of Robert working on sound design for a mediocre B-picture and his cyclical boom-and-bust relationship with Mary. His obsessive-compulsive behavior toward her and his solipsistic narcissism play out as extended sequences leading to breakups, reunions, sex, fights, and more breakups. This devolution is linked to Robert's professional exhaustion with the possibilities of cinema. Narrative coherency, whether in Robert's ability to make logic out of the film he is editing or in his relationship with Mary, are simultaneously crumbling into a crisis of ennui and meaninglessness.

Brooks's metatextual satire offered a pessimistic coda for the second wave. The film's title, sarcastically emphasizing both modernism and love, operated as a titular oxymoron. It sarcastically rejected the potential of Anglo-Christian-Jewish couplings as a corrective to the repressions and absences of the postwar era. Despite Robert's compulsively Jewish verbosity and Mary's patient WASP acceptance, the two achieve no connection or intimacy. The rambling structure of the film furthers this indictment. Modern love has irreparably broken down. All that remains are lost individuals working on the bad genre films of the 1980s.

Part Three

THE THIRD WAVE: GLOBAL FOCKERS
AT THE MILLENNIUM (1993–2007)

*Is this not the most handsome young man you've ever seen in
your life? Used to call him a young Jewish Marlon Brando.
Can you believe I conceived him with one testicle? No really, it's true. I only have one because the other one never
dropped. It's called an undescending testicle. It's uh, not
uncommon. But look at him! Imagine what he would've
looked like if I had two!*

BERNIE FOCKER (DUSTIN HOFFMAN), *MEET THE
FOCKERS* (2004)

HE 1980 ELECTION OF RONALD REAGAN
marked the delayed fulfillment of Nixon's "silent
majority" pushback on the perception of counterculture radicalism and insurrection throughout the 1970s. Reagan's early career
as a B-picture movie star of the 1950s and his "Morning in America" presidential campaign had emphasized a thematic cultural revisionism. The election of a postwar Anglo-American movie star
hero marked a convergence of screen iconography and postwar
culture clash. This new Americanism was built around a revival of
the postwar Anglo-Saxon hero.

Scholars such as Yvonne Tasker and Martin Flanagan have described this period as the age of "musculinity," a period where displays of spectacular gendered bodies served as evidence of a restored
national pride.[1] Screen iconography quickly followed Reagan's
nostalgic reestablishment of postwar tropes. Emerging male movie
stars such as Tom Cruise, Kevin Costner, Chuck Norris, Richard

Gere, and Patrick Swayze joined holdovers Clint Eastwood, Robert Redford, Nick Nolte, and Sylvester Stallone, among others, as exemplars of noble, virtuous, laconic physicality.[2] Conversely, female movie stars such as Kim Basinger, Bo Derek, Meg Ryan, Sharon Stone, Jessica Lange, Darryl Hannah, Meryl Streep, and Michelle Pfeiffer resurrected the Anglo-centric beauty standards of postwar performers such as Doris Day, Grace Kelly, and Eva Marie Saint. These stars collectively formed what Susan Jeffords calls the "Reagan Heroes," hyper-masculine and hyper-feminine gendered-body archetypes that exemplified a retrograde reconstruction of an idyllic (white, Anglo-Saxon) America as embodied by previously established postwar screen fantasies.[3]

This retro-nostalgic, Anglo-Christian screen body also operated as a historical corrective. It wiped out the troubling gender and sexual politics of the 1970s by replacing unruly screen Jews of the second wave with a reinforced Anglo-centric movie star hierarchy. Second-wave stars such as Bette Midler and Richard Dreyfuss moved into supporting character roles, no longer playing viable romantic leads in mainstream studio fare.[4] Elliott Gould, George Segal, and Richard Benjamin saw their careers as leading men dissipate.[5] Barbra Streisand and Dustin Hoffman remained movie stars, but their identities as unruly substitutes for the Anglo-Christian traditions of the 1950s reached full gender inversion. Hoffman appeared in drag in *Tootsie* (1982) even as his character pursued a romance with his WASP beauty *objet du jour*, played by Jessica Lange. Streisand's directorial debut, *Yentl* (1983), a ten-year dream project, brought her gender-bending unruliness back to its Eastern European origins. Her starring role as an orthodox Jewish woman who poses as a Yeshiva boy so that she could study the Torah was a financial disappointment. It was ridiculed by critics as a too-Jewish vanity project, out of step with the escapist Hollywood entertainment of the era.[6] Both *Tootsie* and *Yentl* continued Hoffman and Streisand's roles as unruly Jewish movie stars, probing the boundaries of gender and sexual normativity through incongruity. But this continuation of second-wave exploration was increasingly rare in the 1980s.

Jewish absence was even more striking on television. As Joyce Antler notes, not a single television program in Nielsen's top twenty shows featured an identifiably Jewish character between 1983 and 1987.[7] While the display of newly hyper-masculine and

Anglo-feminine bodies brought with it its own sets of discursive meanings and problematic signifiers, the second wave, the era of the comedic-erotic Jewish schlemiel coupled with the Anglo-Christian partner, was effectively over.[8]

At this same moment, images of anthropomorphized robots and cyborg bodies began to take hold. The Aryan-esque post-human cyborgs Roy Batty (Rutger Hauer) and Pris (Darryl Hannah) in Ridley Scott's *Blade Runner* (1982) both exemplified and satirized the notion of blond hair and blue eyes as ideal proto-human archetypes.[9] The cyborgs depicted by Arnold Schwarzenegger in *The Terminator* (1984) and Robert Patrick in *Terminator 2* (1991) located the white, European, Anglo-Germanic body at the center of this new screen fantasy body type.[10] These powerful hyper-masculine and hyper-feminine stars reset screen culture to the pre-*The Graduate*, pre-Dustin Hoffman era. Following Reagan's lead as a sunny, optimistic president/cowboy, they tempered this reversion by infusing it with technology and visual spectacles informed by an increasing emphasis on the technological body as aspirational ideal.

But by the early 1990s, visible Jews and visible Anglo-Christian-Jewish couplings returned en masse. Reagan-era Cold War anxieties had given way to the Clinton-era revival of multicultural identity politics. These third-wave couplings revived the familiar, safe, mostly comedic form of transgressive cultural and gender interplay as a pushback to the pushback, a next-generation corrective to Reagan-era absences.

In a surprising reversal of the second wave, third-wave couplings emerged not in cinema but in the seemingly innocuous form of the prime-time television sitcom. *Chicken Soup* (1989), *Anything But Love* (1989–1992), *Roseanne* (1988–1997), *Seinfeld* (1989–1998), *Mad About You* (1992–1999), *The Nanny* (1993–1999), *Dharma & Greg* (1997–2002), *Will and Grace* (1998–2006), and *Curb Your Enthusiasm* (1999–) each featured third-wave Anglo-Characters such as Paul Buchman (Paul Reiser) on *Mad about You* and Dharma Finkelstein (Jenna Elfman) on *Dharma & Greg* directly explored the legacy of 1960s-era liberal Jewishness by performing as confused next-generation offspring. Unruly "Jewesses" such as Roseanne Barr's Roseanne Connor character on *Roseanne*, Fran Drescher as Fran Fine on *The Nanny*, and Debra Messing as Grace Adler on *Will and Grace* celebrated female Jewish visibility on a level not seen since the ghetto love stories of the 1920s. Their return navigated the shift from the New Conservatism of the Reagan era toward an increasingly globalized, multi-cultural post–Cold War landscape.

By the mid-1990s, Broadway shows such as *Angels in America* (1993), *Rent* (1996), *Parade* (1998), and *Hedwig and the Angry Inch* (1998) and, in the early 2000s, *The Last Five Years* (2000), adapted these televisual Anglo-Christian-Jewish coupling patterns as the means to explore the entanglement of history, memory, and sexuality on the stage. Hollywood cinema of the late 1990s and early 2000s soon followed. A new generation of Jewish or Jewish-identified movie stars chased Anglo-Christian females in broad sex comedies and romantic farces. Third-wave Jewish or Jewish-coded schlemiels such as Adam Sandler, Ben Stiller, Jason Biggs, Seth Rogen, and Jason Segel began once again to haplessly chase the proverbial shiksa in films such as *There's Something About Mary* (1998), *The Wedding Singer* (1998), *American Pie* (1999), *Meet the Parents* (2000), *Saving Silverman* (2001), *Knocked Up* (2007), and *Forgetting Sarah Marshall* (2008).

Collectively, these familiar-yet-reworked couplings offered a recognizable product that was at once both nostalgic and a response to the absences of the 1980s. They fit the emerging concept of "glocalism," global media product malleable enough for myriad local and regional marketplaces around the world. Second-wave cultural-political unruliness was replaced with either psychological neuroses or chronological disruptions. This offered a means for engaging a global rather than a national spectatorship. Established archetypes and familiar intercultural binaries from earlier eras became prepackaged templates for an increasingly polyglot distribution methodology. The stage and screen "Anglo-Christian" became an easily understood figure of institutionalized Western hegemony. The stage and screen "Jew," however, became reconfigured from its specific national context into a wandering signifier of depoliticized, multiethnic "foreignness." She was familiar enough from the earlier waves to maintain consistency across a wide range of American entertainment product. But by drawing upon the traditions of the ahistorical, wandering Jewish archetype, she remained malleable enough to adapt to any number of cross-cultural reception points.[11]

This watering down of Jewish difference became, as Sander Gilman observes, the privileged metaphor for the new frontier of economic multiculturalism.[12] Throughout the third wave, it was this form of individuation, rather than any broader sociopolitical context, that defined the movement. It produced easily adaptable product for any number of global marketplaces and increasingly fluid networks of distribution. It allowed these texts to visualize what Roland Robertson calls the tension state between the global and the local at the heart of the post–Cold War 1990s media industries economies.[13]

CHAPTER 7

Spiegelman's Frog

CODED JEWISH METAMORPH AND CHRISTIAN WITNESSING (1978–1992)

The Holocaust trumps art. . . . We (the Jews) are here to carry on the traditions of the Marx Brothers and Harvey Kurtzman, as far as I'm concerned.

ART SPIEGELMAN, INTERVIEW, *TABLET*, 2013

*I*N THE 1980S, EXPLICIT SEXUALITY (AND EXPLICIT Jews) on screen retrenched from the mainstream to the margins. Pornography, aided by the rise of home video, shifted from the rhetoric of counterculture revolution to the rhetoric of technological innovation. In 1985, Donna Haraway's highly influential article, "A Cyborg Manifesto: Science, Technology, and Socialist Feminism in the Late Twentieth Century," posited a link between fantasies of the cyborg as a rupturing agent and the legacy of feminist and gendered discourses of the 1970s.[1] A decade later, Vivian Sobchack, Marsha Kinder, and Bruce Clark, among others, described how screen bodies of the 1980s increasingly visualized transitions between human and post-human states to express the increasing entanglement between technology and society.[2] This concept of a taboo, machine-like rupturing screen body was identified by scholars through the concept of the "metamorph."[3] Metamorphs exemplified the new technologies of special effects in the 1980s by visualizing the spectacular body through innovative techno-transformation.[4] But they also opened up a new rhetorical model for gender and sexuality to be negotiated through incongruous physicality.

These techno-incongruous morphing bodies had a conceptual counterpoint. As Anglo-Christian bodies moved to the center of American screens, their proto-robotic metamorphs were also reflected and counterpointed by a newly metamorphic Jewishness. Visible screen Jewishness, closely tied to the emergence of the radical counterculture politics of the 1960s and 1970s, was already established as a taboo violating incongruity. In the 1980s, instead of robots and cyborgs, this fractured Jewishness circulated through the codes of animality and body dysmorphia. This functioned as a thematic recall of Jewish codings in the 1950s. Jewishness was still recognizable through identifiable codes such as vocal cadence, urban neuroticism, and other cultural reference points. But whereas 1950s-era Jewish codes focused on the depoliticized "comicosmopolitan" that Litvak and Bial, among others, have studied, this denatured Jewishness operated as a residual signifier of the newly subsumed discourses of historical memory in the Reagan era.[5]

Disparate genre examples of this technique include *The Fly* (1986), *An American Tail* (1986), *Dirty Dancing* (1987), *The Princess Bride* (1987), and *When Harry Met Sally* (1989), each using coded Anglo-Christian-Jewish interplay while removing Jewishness from the text. These films are linked by their collective rejection of the second-wave progression narrative. Instead of celebrating the transgressive coupling as a sign of generational rebellion, these texts sought to sublimate Jewishness under the veneer of the approving gaze of the Christian witness. This witnessing no longer confirmed the successful bridging of intercultural obstacles and barriers. These texts instead held Jewishness in a state of tense metamorph and without resolution. This stasis produced 1980s-era Jewishness as ephemera. It was understood as a vestigial relic of the 1970s counterculture, a form unable to remain distinct in the hazy transformations of Reagan-era screen fantasies. It was a structuring absence that would last more than a decade before the emergence of the third wave on 1990s television finally obliterated new conservatism's fantasies of whiteness and gentility once and for all.

However, there was one previously verboten subject that allowed visible screen Jewishness to flourish, un-coded, throughout the 1980s: the Holocaust. Examples of this include the NBC miniseries, *Holocaust* (1978); films such as *Zelig* (1982), *Sophie's Choice* (1982), and *Enemies: A Love Story* (1989); and Art Spiegelman's acclaimed graphic novel, *Maus: A Survivor's Tale* (1986/1992).[6] These texts relied on a familiar technique to ease this mainstreaming of previously transgressive imagery and subject matter. In nearly every example of the period, German, Polish, or British-Anglo protagonists were coupled with the Jewish survivor/victim in erotic, romantic, or sado-masochistic relationships.[7] So long as the veneer of melodrama framed the re-creation, historical concerns over representation were safely mollified.

This operated as irony. The one area of mass culture fantasy where Jews were safely able to appear as Jews in the 1980s was the one subject left unaddressed during the second wave of Jewish visibility and historical renegotiation in the 1970s. Yet, even in this delayed grappling with the central inchoate horror experienced by global Jewry in World War II, the Anglo-Jewish-Christian coupling remained firmly in place. It provided safe reassurance. The once impossible-to-re-create subject matter of the Holocaust was normalized by the familiar pattern. It also became the final respite for the screen Jew in the age of Reagan.

THE ANIMORPH AND THE METAMORPH

In her exploration of the rhetorical and affective links between Holocaust media and incest trauma, Janet Walker describes a paradox that locates at the intersection of history, memory, and screen media.[8] Traumatic experience induces memory to alter, damage, or invent fictions as a central method of coping. Media dedicated to ferreting out "the real" from the witness can thus commit a form of retroactive violence. In seeking the One True Truth of historical events, artistic re-creation overlooks and, in some cases, does damage to the ambiguities that memory can produce.

Art Spiegelman's acclaimed graphic novel, *Maus* (1986/1992), was one of the first pieces of mainstream popular entertainment to directly address the crisis of representation in grappling with the Holocaust. It also drew the same rhetorical connection that Walker notes between the slippages within personal narratives of sexual trauma and the incomprehensibility of a collective event as monumental as the Holocaust. *Maus* began in the early 1970s in San Francisco as an experimental form of visual autobiography meant to purge Spiegelman's personal demons. He began his career in the 1970s as an editor on popular underground comics, including *Arcade* and *Raw*, both inspired by the counterculture sensibilities made famous by R. Crumb and his comix series, *Zap*, in the 1960s. The first volume, *Maus I: A Survivor's Tale: My Father Bleeds History* (1986), was completed and released a decade later. It emerged directly in the middle of a fifteen-year period that Yosefa Loshitzky describes as "the Americanization of the Holocaust."[9] A twenty-year project, *Maus* spanned the rebellious 1960s-era counterculture sensibilities of the second wave to the universalizing Jewishness that would define the post–Cold War third wave in the 1990s. It was also one of the first major texts to directly broach an implicit prohibition on Holocaust re-creation in art.

This corrective took decades to manifest. In 1946, Theodor Adorno had written that to write poetry after Auschwitz would be barbaric.[10] Hannah Arendt, one of the most visible public intellectuals trying to make sense of the Shoah, observed similarly that "history has no more difficult story to tell."[11] In the wake of the full revelation of Holocaust atrocities, Adorno and Arendt perceived the potential for cultural violence in trying to summarize such incomprehensibility. An event as monumental, complex, and beyond understanding as the Shoah could not, and perhaps should not, be reduced to the often manipulative techniques of any artistic medium.[12] To depict the Holocaust, no matter how noble the intention, had an element of the profane. To do so was potentially an act of historical violence.[13]

Maus broached this prohibition through the unlikely distancing effect of the cartoon. Spiegelman's childlike illustrations removed any sense of the uncanny, thereby mitigating any fears of conflating the real event with its fictionalized depiction. It was the very un-seriousness of the medium that allowed Spiegelman to engage an impossible historical event and broach Adorno and Arendt's warnings. It also featured another mitigating technique: Spiegelman explored the crisis of trauma representation by personalizing it through the familiar second-wave binary of Anglo-Christian-Jewish romantic entanglement.

Volume one examines the events experienced by Art's father, Vladek, during his life in Germany under the rise of the Third Reich in the late 1930s. Spiegelman himself also appears in his work, struggling with and unable to resolve his problematic relationship with his father. In this bifurcated narrative, *Maus* simultaneously addresses both the events of the Holocaust (as experienced by Vladek) as well as its residual effect on the next generation. This tension between past and present causes the novel itself to split into two concurrent narratives. In the past, Vladek's Holocaust journey is depicted by fully drawn animals as human stand-ins. In Spiegelman's present, humans wear animal masks. The animal-metaphor past and the contemporary human-animal hybrid visualize the distinction between artistic interpretation and the flaws of memory. In Vladek's retelling, his memory conveys a cohesive series of events. Art dutifully and accurately records them. But this claim to "represent" the Holocaust is undercut by the silly nature of Art's childlike illustrations. The process of converting the historical into the creative is indicted by the form itself. Even in the present day, Art can only wear the mask of a mouse. He cannot fully metamorph. He remains trapped between past and present, real and imagined. This is visualized by the tension between Art's human and animal worlds.

Volume two, *Maus II: A Survivor's Tale: And Here My Troubles Began* (1992), expands on Art's struggles with interpretation by musing on the identity of his French Catholic wife, Françoise. The first page of volume two demonstrates Spiegelman's recognition of this important second-wave trope. The descriptive header on the first page establishes the self-reflexive tone of volume two: "Summer vacation. Françoise and I were staying with

Art Mouse contemplates how to depict his French wife, Francoise, after her conversion to Judaism, in Art Spiegelman's Maus II: A Survivor's Tale: And Here My Troubles Began *(1992).*

friends in Vermont. . ." Spiegelman's mouse alter ego sits under a tree, staring at a blank page as he prepares to begin drawing volume two. He is joined by his wife, also drawn as a mouse-human. Their dialogue establishes Spiegelman's discomfort with representation:

> Françoise: What are you doing?
> Art: Trying to figure out how to draw you . . .
> Françoise: Want me to pose?
> Art: I mean, in my book. What kind of an animal should I make you?
> Françoise: Huh? A mouse, of course!
> Art: But you're French!
> Françoise: Well . . . how about the bunny rabbit?
> Art: Nah, too sweet and gentle. I mean the French in general. Let's not forget the centuries of anti-Semitism . . .
> Françoise: Hmmph.
> Art: I mean, how about the Dreyfus Affair? The Nazi collaborators! The—
> Françoise: Okay! But if you're a mouse, I ought to be a mouse, too. I converted, didn't I?
> Art: I've got it! . . . Panel one: My father is on his exercycle . . . I tell him I just married a frog . . . Panel two: He falls off his cycle in shock. So you and I go to a mouse rabbi. He says a few magic words and zap! . . . By the end of the page, the frog has turned into a beautiful mouse!
> Françoise: Hmmph. I only converted to make Vladek happy.
> Art: Yeah, but nothing can make him happy.
> Françoise: You know, you should have married what's-her-name? The girl you were seeing when we first met? . . .
> Art: Sandra?
> Françoise: Yes. Then you could just draw mice. No problem.
> Art: C'mon. I just dated Sandra to get over my prejudice against middle-class New York Jewish women. They remind me too much of my relatives to be erotic . . . [14]

Art-Mouse's casual reference to the un-erotic nature of Jewish women suggests Jewish-Jewish couplings operate as a form of conceptual incest. Like Philip Roth and Woody Allen before him, Spiegelman's erotic desire for the Christian (in life and in art) seeks to resolve this neurotic stereotype in the familiar, established way. But resolution is not possible. Oscillating

Françoise-Mouse/Frog provides neither comfort nor solution. Art-Mouse's desire to perceive Françoise-Mouse as fully mouse (Jewish) can only take place when she is safely rendered as a non-Jewish frog.

In starting volume two in this way, Spiegelman uses erotic transference to visualize the crisis of representation. Art's struggle to depict Vladek's memories was the core problematic of volume one. Françoise-Mouse's metamorph visualizes the same impossibility. Her oscillation expresses Art's frustrated search for an externalized referent for an incomprehensible event. Her unstable identity as Jew-Mouse and French-Frog links Vladek's sublimated traumatic memory to his son's externalized sexual compulsions. As both the author and a character within his own work, Art-Mouse can do nothing to resolve this paradox. All he can do is recognize the impossibility of resolution by conflating both conflicting states in his art.[15]

Maus does this by using an artistic and philosophical technique that Akira Lippit calls the "animetaphor."[16] Lippit describes how human perception of the uncanny nature of the animal in media creates an intermediary phantom caught between human and animal states. In volume one, Spiegelman's cartoon animals had satirized the eugenics stereotypes of the Third Reich. If Jews are mice, as the Nazis argued, then Germans must be cats, Poles are pigs, and so on. Various other ethnics appear in differing animal masks, denoting the cultural construction of their biological distinctions.[17] In volume two, Spiegelman complicates this critique by extending it. In the wake of Art-Mouse's inability to do artistic justice to his father's memories, he transfers this tension onto the identity of his wife, Françoise. His refusal to resolve the problematic nature of re-creating traumatic Jewish history positions the female Christian witness as a vital but contested externalization of this tension.

Spiegelman was not the first to adapt second-wave Anglo-Christian-Jewish coupling archetypes to grapple with the unrepresentable nature of the Holocaust. Predating the official publication of *Maus* by seven years, the acclaimed 1978 miniseries, *Holocaust,* was the first major piece of mainstream entertainment to breach Adorno's prohibition.[18] Following the critical and commercial success of the taboo-shattering slavery saga *Roots* (1977), the miniseries was designed to be a provocative piece of mainstream entertainment. Airing on four consecutive nights, April 16 to 19, 1978, the event-programming stunt was wildly successful. It was viewed by more than 120 million Americans and approximately 200 million around the world after its rebroadcast in 1979 (including its controversial airing in West Germany).[19]

With a large cast and high production values, the soon-to-be-Emmy-winning melodrama sparked an enormous revival in Holocaust interest.[20] This came despite vehement criticism by Holocaust survivor and renowned author Elie Wiesel that the miniseries trivialized and insulted the memory of the Shoah.[21] The landscape of mainstream representation was altered.[22] Within months of its airing, President Jimmy Carter established the President's Commission on the Holocaust and unveiled plans to open the Holocaust Memorial Museum in Washington, DC.[23] The Holocaust was suddenly safe for mainstream engagement.[24]

Tracing the story of two families, one German (Dorf) and one Jewish (Weiss), *Holocaust* broad-stroked the major events of World War II through familiar soap opera structure. The central dramatic tension of the miniseries focused on the intermarriage between the Jewish Karl Weiss (James Woods) and Polish Inga Helms (Meryl Streep) and the subsequent fallout of Holocaust events on Karl, Inga, and their families. Karl's arrest and eventual death in Auschwitz is depicted as an example of the arbitrary nature of collective targeting induced by the Nazis. His camp experiences are counterpointed by Inga's determined but futile efforts to find and save him. Despite Karl's tragic death in Auschwitz, the conclusion of the miniseries offered a form of next-generation hope. Karl's death is tempered by Inga's pregnancy and the eventual birth of their child. Her child mitigates Karl's death and, by extension, the scope of the tragedy. Within the text, it confirms the ideological potency of visualizing successful German-Jewish coupling as the solution to Nazi eugenics.

But this figural mediation also solved one of the central prohibitions on depicting the Shoah's unknowability. The future-child offered an identifiable iconography of philosophical transcendence over the troubling abstraction of how to depict collective trauma. As *Holocaust* demonstrated, a single representative screen birth could assuage anxieties over the residual violence of appropriating the historical Holocaust through the tropes of genre-based entertainment.[25]

Four years later, the Academy Award–winning *Sophie's Choice* (1982) solidified this mediation technique in mainstream Hollywood cinema.[26] It was also the first film to depict, at length, the imagery of the camps. Meryl Streep again starred as the aggrieved Polish-Catholic witness and victim at the center of the narrative. In the infamous titular "choice," Zofia "Sophie" Zawistowski (Streep) approaches a Nazi prison guard and pleads for her life and the life of her family. The dialogue that follows reframes the historical Holocaust in both eroticized and Christianized contexts:

> SS officer: You're so beautiful. I'd like to get you in bed. Are you a Polack? You! Are you also one of those filthy communists?

Sophie: I am a Pole! I was born in Cracow! I am not a Jew. Neither are my children! They're not Jews. They are racially pure. I am a Christian. I am a devout Christian.

SS officer: You are not a communist? You are a believer?

Sophie: Yes sir, I believe in Christ.

SS officer: You believe in Christ the redeemer?

Sophie: Yes.

SS officer: Did He not say . . . "Suffer the children, come unto me?" (pause) You may keep one of your children.

Sophie: I beg your pardon?

SS officer: You may keep one of your children. The other must go away.

Sophie: You mean, I have to choose?

SS officer: You are a Polack, not a Yid. That gives you a privilege, a choice.[27]

Sophie's function at the center of the drama operates as a thematic and conceptual metamorph. As with Inga and Karl's child, she is both Jew and not-Jew. Her "choice" is an impossible one, a paradoxical rubric that renders only victimhood in its wake. Yet, her crisis emerges from the very idea that her Polish-Christian identity might give her increased value in the eyes of a Nazi soldier. Her belief in the Polish-Catholic distinction from the Jews renders the Holocaust a universal trauma. Yet, her subsequent impossible choice becomes universally accessible by the very nature of revealing the illogic of genetic distinction. With little time to comprehend the enormity of the moment, Sophie chooses to give up her daughter to save her son and herself. Her proposal of genetic hierarchy is redirected into a gendered choice.

Sophie's Choice expanded Holocaust trauma through the tropes of accessible melodrama. As portrayed by Meryl Streep, famous for her long blonde hair and aquiline nose, the character of Sophie, an extension of Streep's career-making role as Inga in *Holocaust*, moved the Aryan/German/Polish-Catholic co-victim to the center of Holocaust trauma.[28] Both characters functioned as universalizing avatars. The titular moment in *Sophie's Choice* expanded on the Jewish specificity of Holocaust trauma by focusing on Sophie's oscillating identity. As with Spiegelman's mouse-frog dilemma, Sophie becomes a liminal construction in the eyes of the Nazi guard. Her burden becomes the spectator's burden. It offers a mimetic entry point for Jewish and non-Jewish spectator alike.

The link between Shoah trauma and postmemory is also reflected in the film's depiction of Sophie's postwar cruel, violent relationship with the equally troubled Jewish survivor, Nathan Landau (Kevin Kline). Together, Nathan and Sophie express a loveless form of eroticized, ritualized, internalized violence. They are not romantic, nor does this Anglo-Christian-Jewish coupling lead to any form of catharsis. Their collective inability to survive the memories of the camps leads only to their suicide. It made explicit the link between eroticized sublimation/transference and the historical event from which it drew. Sophie's impossible choice and her loveless cohabitation with the Jewish Nathan confirmed the defining paradigmatic entry point for Holocaust cinema of the 1980s.[29] Psychosexual transference between Jew and Christian opened a rhetorical framework for Holocaust visualization to take place.

By the late 1980s, media critics began to push back against this form of historiography. In 1989, Frank Sanello of the *Chicago Tribune* penned "Is TV Trivializing the Holocaust?," wondering if prime-time television mini-series such as *Twist of Fate* (NBC), *Murderers Among Us: The Simon Wiesenthal Story* (HBO), and *War and Remembrance* (ABC) were inappropriately exploiting the Holocaust to produce big-budget "event" melodramas.[30] But these critical concerns were increasingly brushed aside. The profitability of historical re-creation had been established. It would continue well into the late 1980s and 1990s with films such as *Au Revoir Les Enfants* (1987), *Europa Europa* (1991), *Schindler's List* (1993), and *Life Is Beautiful* (1998), each presenting German-Jewish coupling as homosocial, erotic, or sadomasochistic variations on a theme.[31] But Spiegelman's mouse-frog problematic remained in each of these texts. The Jewish specificity of historical events had become subsumed. Jewishness had metamorphed into animality, dysmorphic bodies, or, as with Meryl Streep, the Anglo-Christian herself. Representation in art had been achieved. But at what cost?

This problematic notion of linking Anglo-Christian-Jewish couplings to historical revisionism was expanded beyond Holocaust subject matter in the 1981 Best Picture Academy Award winner, *Chariots of Fire* (1981). The film was an unlikely success story. The slowly paced period piece, an independent British production, told the story of two British athletes preparing for the 1924 Olympics. It featured languid aesthetics and dreamlike experimental music. The central narrative focuses on the unlikely friendship that develops between Jewish sprinter Harold Abrahams (Ben Cross) and his chief competition for the Olympic team, devout Christian Scotsman, Eric Liddell (Ian Charleson). Over the course of the film, Harold and Eric discover that, despite religious and cultural differences, both are motivated by similar desires and emotions. However, their respective religious identities affect each runner differently. While a student athlete at University of Cambridge, Harold struggles with anti-Semitism. But it is Eric's sacrifice that becomes the major crisis in the film's third act. Although he is favored to win, Eric refuses to participate in the 100-meter race because the event is on a Sunday, the Christian Sabbath. His dedication to Christianity supersedes his loyalty to Great Britain. Harold's Jewishness provides no such conflict. Harold races and wins the gold medal. Eric participates in a different race and also wins gold. As the film's final coda makes clear, Harold returns to England and is hailed as a British hero. Eric travels to China to begin Christian missionary work. Harold's journey from Jewish outsider to British hero is counterpointed by Eric's rededication to his Christianity and ultimate estrangement from an increasingly secular, modern British life.

Through the Eric/Harold binary, *Chariots of Fire* offers a historical fantasy of British Empire. The dreamlike imagery, extended use of slow-motion tracking shots, and New Age soundtrack by Vangelis confirmed the film's break from any claim to re-creating historical accuracy. This notion of cinematic expressiveness as historical reimagining solidified in how the film inverted the Jewish/Christian power dynamic. It is Eric, not Harold, who struggles with religious isolation and dual loyalty to his religion and his nation. Their friendship, depicted as intensely homosocial, was also a taboo update on British masculinity.[32] As Steve Neale observed when reviewing the film in 1982, the aesthetic fetishization of male bodies in slow motion and Eric's struggle with his religious commitments combined to communicate the hidden nature of Anglo-Christian homosexual desire.[33] Harold is identified as the Jewish object by which Eric's turmoil can externalize itself. This pairing established one of the rare same-gendered Christian/Jewish couplings of the period. But in locating Eric, not Harold, at the center of the conflicts, the film inverted second-wave couplings while depoliticizing the Jewish specificity of Harold's struggles.

One year later, using a mockumentary format and digital manipulation of historical footage, Woody Allen's *Zelig* riffed on the religious-historical Anglo-Christian-Jewish coupling binary found in *Chariots of Fire*. As a thematic companion piece to that film's avant-garde aesthetic breaks from period-piece cohesiveness, *Zelig* similarly obfuscated distinctions between the real and the fictive through documentary-fiction interplay. Ostensibly a documentary about Leonard Zelig (Allen), a supposedly real figure from the 1920s, the film purports to be a search for historical truth. It consists of assemblages of current-day interviews with intellectuals (both real and fictionalized) and archival clips (both real and fictionalized) with Allen seamlessly integrated into both worlds as the mysterious subject of the "documentary." This creates an uncertain tableau and operates as a metatextual critique of cinema itself. The film's rhetorical and genre slippages are then reflected in the unusual morphing body of Leonard Zelig himself. Zelig is identified as an American Jewish nebbish born to immigrant parents. His father is identified as a Yiddish theater actor. Biographical Jewishness and theatrical family origins are cited as reasons for Zelig's corporeal desire to fit into his surroundings. He is also supernatural, displaying an impossible physical ability to transform his body to match any cultural context. When surrounded by African-Americans, Zelig becomes black. When surrounded by Nazis, he becomes a Nazi.

As with Art Spiegelman's Mouse/Frog in *Maus*, Allen's historical meta-joke is clear. Fat, thin, male, female, or ape-like, Zelig's "hidden" Jewishness as foregrounded spectacle exemplified Vivian Sobchack's understanding of the meta-morph as a transgressive, intertextual rhetorical device. Instead of producing a coherent piece of historical fantasy, as in *Chariots of Fire*, *Zelig* destabilizes, and therefore foregrounds, the inherent untrustworthy nature of the medium. In *Chariots of Fire*, Harold wins a gold medal, refuting eugenics-era theories of Jewish physical inferiority. He becomes fully British. Zelig's supernatural skills at assimilating lead only to the ironic inversion of becoming a Nazi before finally successfully fleeing into the obscurity he always craved.

As with Art-Mouse/Françoise-Frog, Inga/Karl, Sophie/Nathan, and Eric/Harold, *Zelig* locates the mainstreaming of Jewishness through the centering of the Anglo-Christian witness. In *Zelig*, this witness figure is literally a psychoanalyst, Dr. Eudora Fletcher (Mia Farrow).[34] She films Zelig, attempting to use rationality, science, and media to explain the inexplicable nature of his malleability. The eventual love between Eudora and Zelig leads him to give up his metamorphic abilities, a conceptual shedding of Jewish distinction, before their breakup sends Zelig on his path toward Nazi assimilation. In Allen's historical satire, no solution is possible. Jewish anxieties were either rendered impotent under the normalizing gaze of Eudora's WASP psychoanalytic gaze or fully inverted into Nazi transformation.

WHEN BABY MET JOHNNY

Despite the abundance of Holocaust media, visible Jewishness in the 1980s was increasingly subsumed in a blanket of Reagan-era, Anglo-Saxon whiteness. Three box office successes of the mid-1980s, *An American Tail* (1986), *Dirty Dancing* (1987), and *When Harry Met Sally* (1989), demonstrate how pervasive this textual absence had become. All three films appeared to maintain the relationship between historical renegotiation and Anglo-Christian-Jewish couplings established in the second wave. The Jewish Fievel Mousekewitz's (voiced by Phillip Glasser) immigrant adventures with an Irish mouse, Bridget (voiced by Cathianne Blore), in *An American Tail*; Baby (Jennifer Grey) and Johnny's (Patrick Swayze) romance in *Dirty Dancing*; and Harry (Billy Crystal) and Sally's (Meg Ryan) extended friendship/courtship in *When Harry Met Sally* each offered nostalgia for first- and second-wave pairings.

Yet, these romantic progression narratives actually produced cultural erasure. Despite clear Jewish subject matter, characters, and texts, none of these films directly addressed the Jewish identities of their Jewish protagonists, preferring codes and other nuanced signifiers of ethno-religious identity. They revived the ambiguities of earlier immigrant Catholic-Jewish and Protestant-Jewish love stories as a nostalgic return to the pre-counterculture, postwar era of the 1950s, when Jews existed only as alternative Christians.

The Steven Spielberg-produced and Don Bluth–animated *An American Tail* is perhaps the most remarkable of these examples. It used *Maus*-like animetaphors to revive the ethnic specificity of the first-wave immigrant journey in no uncertain terms. The wholesome family film also re-created a pastiche of the familiar Irish-Jewish pairings of the first wave in the 1910s and 1920s. Fievel Mousekewitz, a young male mouse, lives with his large mouse family under the home of a human (Jewish) family named Moskowitz. The house is located in Russia at some point in the late nineteenth century. When the Moskowitz home is set ablaze in a violent Russian pogrom, the Mousekewitzes flee on an adventure to America. Young Fievel is soon separated from his family. Alone on the streets of immigrant-era New York, he is befriended by two other mice, Toni Toponi (voiced by Pat Musick), an Italian mouse, and the young Irish mouse, Bridget. Bridget and Toni teach Fievel how to avoid the various gangs of vicious cats that prey on immigrant mice on the streets of New York.

Yet, this immigrant adventure tale contains a remarkable structuring absence. In stark contrast to its thematic progenitor, *Fiddler on the Roof* (1971), *An American Tail* contains no mentions of Jewish identity anywhere in the film. This is true despite clear allusions to Fievel's Jewishness during his numerous adventures. Film critic Roger Ebert noted as much in his two-star review of the film:

> One of the central curiosities of *An American Tail* is that it tells a specifically Jewish experience but does not attempt to inform its young viewers that the characters are Jewish or that the house burning was anti-Semitic. I suppose that would be a downer for the little tykes in the theater, but what do they think while watching the present version? That houses are likely to be burned down at ran-

dom? This bleak view of a cold and heartless universe is enforced on-board the ship to America, where little Fievel amuses himself by staring at barrels full of pickled herring with much the same delight that a modern mouse child might tune in Pee-Wee Herman's Saturday morning show.[35]

Despite Ebert's criticism, Fievel's textual Jewish absence but thematic Jewish presence gave the film a universal appeal in keeping with other Jewish metamorphs of the 1980s. *An American Tail* went on to gross more than $80 million dollars on an $8-million-dollar budget, becoming the highest grossing non-Disney animated film to that point.[36]

A year later, in 1987, an independently financed box office success, *Dirty Dancing*, offered a similar process of obfuscation. The film at first appears to be following the historical renegotiations of second-wave period-piece films such as *The Way We Were* (1973) and *The Front* (1976). It reconsiders the cultural identity politics of the early 1960s through both a star-crossed Catholic-Jewish romance and an inverted power dynamic. The young Jewish American Princess at the center of the film, Frances "Baby" Houseman (Jennifer Grey), is an ambitious teenager constrained by postwar patriarchy. As her name implies, she has been "babied" by her overprotective but loving Jewish doctor father (Jerry Orbach). But her ambition and intelligence communicate that she is not of this metaphorical suburban New York shtetl. Her love interest, a masculine, stoic, working-class Catholic, Johnny Castle (Patrick Swayze), offers her a way out of her enclosed Jewish world.

As with Anglo-Christian-Jewish couplings in *The Jazz Singer* (1927) and *Fiddler on the Roof* (1971), the union of Baby and Johnny is tinged with melancholia for the lost world it ultimately supersedes. But it is also identified as an inevitable element of progress. Johnny allows Baby to break with tradition and gain entrance into the modern world. But *Dirty Dancing* was distinct from the second wave in one critical way. Given that the film is clearly about a Jewish world, set in a visible Jewish location, and stars Jewish actors playing Jewish characters, *Dirty Dancing* is notable for how it mutes all textual references to Jewish identity. The words "Jew" or "Jewish" do not appear in the screenplay and are never spoken in the film. Jewish identity is performed in code even as it remains obvious in Jewish jokes about the prices of shoes, old Catskills guests complaining about the heat, and the nebbishy cadences and dialogue of the various Catskills guests.

Another break from unruly Jewishness of the second wave located in the film's political agenda. Despite an apparently emancipatory historiography, *Dirty Dancing* was directly at odds with the political agendas of period-piece second-wave couplings in the 1970s. The postwar Jewish world of the

Catskills offered an inverted landscape. Jews held both economic and cultural power. Christian America is identified on the margins as the resort's servants and waitstaff. This inversion is echoed by the film's gender politics. Unlike the outsider status of the blacklisted Jewish writers in *The Front* or of the leftist labor agitator Katie in *The Way We Were*, the hyper-masculine Johnny is the disenfranchised outsider. He is a quasi-gigolo, hired ostensibly to teach dance to aging, sexually frustrated Jewish women. But his real source of income is private "dance lessons," offering the masculine attention and, in some cases, implied sexual satisfaction that their Jewish husbands cannot apparently provide. In this Reagan-era, Borscht Belt rewrite, subversive Jewish sexuality moves from emancipatory to exploitative. When various young Jewish men flirt with Baby, they are represented as sleazy and shallow, primarily focused on money and class snobbery. In contrast to Baby, her sister, Lisa (Jane Brucker), is presented as the stereotypical Jewish American Princess. These negative Jewish stereotypes are positioned in stark contrast to both the alienated Baby and the laconic, undereducated, but virtuous and noble Johnny. The film's codes longed not for the transgressive emancipation of the counterculture but for the *Gentlemen's Agreement* universality of the late 1940s.

This removal of Jewish specificity brought with it another form of melancholia. The film's triumphant final dance sequence, when Baby runs to Johnny and he successfully lifts her over his head, is textually depicted as a triumphant moment of love conquering cultural divisions. But it is also the moment that inspires the owner of the resort, Max Kellerman (Jack Weston), to observe that business in the Catskills is coming to an end, soon to be replaced by television. Kellerman's resigned loss is presented as an inevitable multicultural gain for a more inclusive America. But the Baby/Johnny coupling was distinct from the assimilationist fantasies of both earlier waves. *Dirty Dancing* longed for the end of the politically loaded Anglo-Christian-Jewish love stories of the second wave and a return to the postwar gender roles of its 1950s setting.[37] The politics and identity scrambling of the second wave had been replaced by a conventionally masculine leading man lifting a purportedly emancipated woman literally off her feet.[38]

When Harry Met Sally was perhaps the clearest heir in the 1980s to second-wave Anglo-Christian-Jewish coupling comedies. Yet, as discussed in the introduction to this book, the film also contained a startling textual erasure. Directed by Rob Reiner, television's 1970s-era prototype coded Jew from *All in the Family*, the film appears to offer a nostalgic revival of archetypes. Harry is the familiar neurotic, hyper-verbal, and hyper-sexual second-wave Jewish male. He compulsively sleeps with women, lashes out at those he disagrees with, and prides himself on confrontation and obnoxiousness. Sally is the demure, uptight, Anglo-Saxon shiksa fantasy. The Harry-Sally dynamic appears to be a direct continuation of the interplay between Lenny Cantrow (Charles Grodin) and Kelly Corcoran (Cybill Shepherd) in *The Heartbreak Kid* (1972).

But despite its allusions to second-wave sex comedies, the film is coded as inherently nostalgic for an even earlier era. Second-wave coupling comedies looked forward, albeit uncertainly, to the impact of the new sexual freedoms of the counterculture. *When Harry Met Sally* is instead an exercise in nostalgia for the postwar-era, pre-counterculture, rom-com fantasies that the second wave had explicitly rejected. This locates in the film's aesthetic framing devices. The soundtrack is devoid of era-appropriate pop music. Instead, it features retro–Big Band torch songs performed by Harry Connick Jr., such as "It Had to Be You," "Love Is Here to Stay," and "Let's Call the Whole Thing Off." These songs give the film an anachronistic context. The recurring holiday of Christmas is also the film's main structuring motif. In the first Christmas montage, Harry is seen helping Sally carry a Christmas tree up to her apartment. In their final expression of love, set on New Year's Eve, the setting is adorned with Christmas trees. The notion of a Christmas love story aligned the film closer to fantasy romances of the 1950s, such as *White Christmas* (1954) and *An Affair to Remember* (1957), than to the second-wave romances of Dustin Hoffman, Barbra Streisand, and Elliott Gould.

Reiner's previous film, *The Princess Bride* (1987), had riffed on the notion of symbolic Judaism and metamorph as a self-reflexive in-joke. The film begins with a Yiddish-inflected, Jewish-coded grandfather, played by Jewish actor Peter Falk, taking out the titular book to read to his sick six-year-old grandson (Fred Savage). In the world within the book, various ethnic characters such as the Sicilian Vizzini (Wallace Shawn), the Spaniard Inigo Montoya (Mandy Patinkin), and the nebbishy gnomes Miracle Max (Billy Crystal) and Valerie (Carol Kane) were played by Jewish actors performing campy ethnic masquerades straight out of vaudeville traditions. Yet, all of this barely coded symbolic Jewishness circulated around an idealized love story between two blond, blue-eyed Anglo ideals, Westley (Cary Elwes) and Buttercup (Robin Wright). The film's satire of white, Christian beauty types was an essential element of its subversive parody. Westley and Buttercup were now located at the center of the beauty standards of 1980s cinema. But lurking in the margins of the "true love" purity of their coupling were their opposites. These subversive, hidden, metamorphic Jews were necessary to create the context for this fantasy of European whiteness.

When Harry Met Sally appeared to respond to the fairy tale Anglo-Christian coupling of *The Princess Bride* by restoring second-wave couplings to the fore. Yet, even in this practically overt Christian-Jewish love story, the film relied on codes. One distinction between the shooting script and the produced film reveals the film's anxiety toward visible Jewishness. After their first sexual experience causes Harry to panic and flee, he subsequently calls Sally and leaves a message on her answering machine. In the film, Harry offers only to do the "traditional Christmas grovel" as his mea culpa for his actions. Yet, the same line of dialogue from Castle Rock's final shooting draft (August 3, 1988) shows a very different Harry: "It's the holiday season, this doesn't happen to be my holiday, but I thought I might remind you that this is a season of forgiveness and charity . . ."[39]

In Nora Ephron's screenplay, Harry is clearly identified as a Jewish character struggling to relate to, and manipulate, Sally's emotional attachment to Christmas. In the finished film, this line, and Harry's subsequent manipulation, were both removed. Despite Billy Crystal's Jewish persona, Harry's Jewishness remains performance-based, but also textually irrelevant. He is a full participant in Christmas. The sequence allows Harry a comedic outsider voice. But it blurs the insider/outsider distinction by refusing to emphasize Jewish specificity.

Fievel/Bridget, Johnny/Baby, Harry/Sally, and the comedic masquerades in *The Princess Bride* each operated as thematic reminders and continuations of second-wave Anglo-Christian-Jewish coupling patterns. But these texts also offered a distinct break from the textual Jewish visibility and politically charged historical revisionism taking place in the 1970s. Their collective removal of textual Jewishness was an act of universalization and de-politicization. Harry, Fievel, and Baby's ethno-cultural identities performed what Herbert Gans calls "symbolic Judaism."[40] Each text remains clearly identifiable as Jewish through cultural codes and performative markers. But by not emphasizing Jewish specificity, thematic Jewishness became symbolic, a floating signifier of multi-ethnicity and cultural Otherness identifiable and applicable to numerous non-Jewish spectatorships.[41] These films exemplified Spiegelman's mouse-frog dilemma. Jewishness was now both visible and invisible, caught in a relational state between the residual transgressive impulses of the second wave and the conservative Anglo-return exemplified by popular media during the Reagan years.

BRUNDLEFLY'S SYNTHESIS

The use of Jewish metamorph and the increasing centrality of the Christian witness in popular media of the 1980s can perhaps most clearly be seen in David Cronenberg's 1986 horror film, *The Fly*. The remake of the

1958 Vincent Price B-movie offers a deceptively complex horror text. Science, memory, and the sublimated residual traumas of eugenics converge in the character of Seth Brundle (Jeff Goldblum), a thirty-something, brilliant eccentric working on a revolutionary teleportation device. The importance of the Anglo-Christian witness to Seth's unwitting descent into a Jewish metamorphic nightmare is essential to Cronenberg's update. Seth's story is introduced through the perspective of an ambitious young journalist, Veronica "Ronnie" Quaife (Geena Davis). Ronnie meets Seth at a party, where he awkwardly flirts with her, eventually convincing her to come back to his home laboratory to see his latest invention. Ronnie assumes this is nothing more than a bad pickup line. But when she arrives at Seth's home loft-laboratory, he demonstrates his device by transporting one of her stockings between two large, somewhat ominous telepods. His subsequent successful wooing of Ronnie is powered by his incredible intellectual achievement, not his physical acumen or seductive charms.

Cronenberg's conflation between sexual seduction and technology frames this developing romance at the center of the narrative. The early stages of the film structure the refinement of Seth's scientific breakthrough as an extension of both his personal and professional relationship with Ronnie. Before she gives in to his advances, Ronnie demands that Seth must agree that she can write the exclusive story on his device. The two then enter into both a romantic and a professional working relationship predicated on Ronnie's role as the documentarian/witness. She videotapes Seth's work as he continues to make progress solving the final problem, successfully teleporting a living creature.

At first, despite a number of technical setbacks, Seth's successful seduction of Ronnie fuels his refinement of the teleportation process. But after Ronnie fails to show up for a date, an emotionally insecure and drunk Seth decides to recklessly test the updated device by transporting himself. He makes a mistake, letting a housefly into the telepod at the moment of teleportation. Without realizing it, Seth becomes genetically fused with the housefly's DNA. As Bruce Clarke notes, Cronenberg produces a post-human metamorph exemplified by delay and postponement.[42] Seth emerges from the telepod and at first appears fine. But he gradually begins to transform. He becomes increasingly violent and sexually aggressive. He gains fly-like characteristics such as the ability to climb walls and vomit digestive enzymes on his food. This descent into a mutant human-fly hybrid takes place while he becomes progressively aware of his fate, a process that he self-mockingly refers to as "Brundlefly."

Brundlefly's transformation from Einstein-level genius to monstrous bug man is alluded to throughout the film by various Kafka-esque references

Ronnie (Geena Davis) grapples with the synthesis of technology and pregnancy while contemplating the metamorphing body of scientist Seth Brundle (Jeff Goldblum) in David Cronenberg's The Fly *(1986).*

to the waking dream state. Early in his transformation, Seth describes the telepod experience as an "awakening." He believes he has become the best version of himself, a proto-eugenics argument for genetic cleansing. He is subsequently consumed with both a voracious sexual appetite and a hunger for sugar. When Ronnie grows tired of his compulsive carnality, an angry Seth rejects her. In search of a partner able to keep up with his sexual proclivities, he enters a bar and quickly targets a young woman, Tawny (Joy Boushel). In a display of alpha-male conflict, Seth proves his worth to Tawny by challenging her male suitor to an arm-wrestling contest in which Seth breaks the other man's wrist. The display of power is so overwhelming (and graphic) that Tawny immediately agrees to Seth's aggressive sexual advances. The emphasis on Seth's tensions between intense physicality and intellectual ability are made in the following exchange:

> Tawny: Are you a body builder, or something?
> Seth: Yeah, I build bodies. I take them apart, and put them back together again.[43]

Even though Tawny is able to keep up with Seth sexually, she is still not enough. He demands that she also enter the telepod to be genetically cleansed and therefore an adequate partner. When his efforts are interrupted by Ronnie, Seth becomes enraged:

> Seth (to Ronnie): You're afraid to dive into the plasma pool, aren't you? You're afraid to be destroyed and re-created, aren't you? I'll bet you think that you woke me up about the flesh, don't you? But you only know society's straight line about the flesh. You can't penetrate beyond society's sick, gray, fear of the flesh. Drink deep, or taste not, the plasma spring! You see what I'm saying? And I'm not just talking about sex and penetration. I'm talking about penetration beyond the veil of the flesh! A deep penetrating dive into the plasma pool![44]

Brundlefly insists that sexuality and technology are corporeally linked. This amplifies the (Jewish) destabilization, and threat, that he represents. The notion of teleportation as a cleansing ritual is also referenced by Brundlefly as movement from a dream to waking state. This revelation is delivered to the mediating apparatus of Ronnie's video camera when Seth states to her (and us):

> I'm an insect who dreamt he was a man and loved it. But now the dream is over . . . and the insect is awake.[45]

Cronenberg's human-animal-insect presented as a waking dream uses Freudian themes of subconscious horror to explore an amalgam of anti-Semitic discourses. For centuries, the Jewish body had been marked as a hybridized paradox of conflicting forces. As early as the thirteenth century, depictions of Jews as horned goats defined Jewish monstrosity as an animal incapable of controlling his sexual impulses.[46] By the nineteenth century, as Sander Gilman has shown, animality merged with technology to present Jewish difference as the corporeal manifestation of the reckless dangers of the new sciences.[47] Seth is increasingly aware of the irony of his impending fulfillment of Gothic horror's long-standing anti-Semitic nightmare. His early insistence that he has been "cleansed" and "baptized" by the telepods satirizes the notion of Jewish conversion. When Seth realizes that the telepod hybridized his DNA with a housefly, his ironic musings begin to echo the self-aware animal-human hybrids of Kafka. Like Red Peter, Josephine Mouse, the jackals, and Gregor Samsa, Seth retains awareness about the limitations of his animal state. He remarks to Ronnie, his witness and the eventual narrator of his tragic fate, that he will ultimately be controlled by these basest insect/animal impulses.

Little scholarship on *The Fly* has remarked on the film's metamorphic Jewish subtext.[48] Yet, Seth's coded Jewishness is a critical aspect of Cronenberg's critique of postmemory and the residual traumas of the technology age. It can be located through a number of codes and allusions. Actor Jeff Goldblum's Jewish looks, name, verbal cadences, and performance style were at sharp odds with the dominant Anglo-Christian stars of the 1980s. Seth's role as a genius scientist also conveys notions of Jewish eccentricity. His nervousness, social anxiety, and compulsive sexual drive all locate Seth firmly within the hyper-carnal second-wave schlemiels of the 1970s. Yet, Jewishness is not a textual element of Seth's character. He is never explicitly identified as Jewish, nor does he make any comments or use any words that infer a Jewish cultural or religious background.

Despite its depiction of Seth's intellectual Jewish schlemiel wooing the adoring Ronnie, *The Fly* is not a second-wave coupling narrative. It instead follows *Zelig*, *Maus*, and *Sophie's Choice* in portraying Jewish trauma visibility as both a crisis state and an impossible articulation. Ronnie's role has shifted. She is no longer the externalized object of Seth's transformation from Jewish schlemiel to conquering hero. Instead, she represents the normative (Christian) witness to Brundlefly's eventual descent into corporeal decay, irrational violence, and Jewish de-coherence. As Seth begins his metamorph into Brundlefly, Ronnie resumes her role as journalist, videotaping and recording his physical changes. Similar to Inga in *Holocaust* and Dr. Eudora Fletcher in *Zelig*, she serves as the Anglo-Christian witness to Brundlefly's increasing fragmentation between his morphing insect-human flesh and his decaying, rational mind.

This transformation embodies the Gothic perversions that Judith Halberstam describes as central to the anti-Semitic underpinnings of nineteenth-century horror literature.[49] Like the witnesses/narrators in *Dracula* and *Frankenstein*, the normative (Christian) witness narrates and observes the spectacle of the coded-Jewish deviant consumed and transformed by the crisis of the new sciences. Yet, Cronenberg complicates this Gothic and Kafkaesque subject/witness binary with the revelation of Ronnie's pregnancy. Brundlefly and Ronnie's unborn child is a product of a transgressive Christian-Jewish coupling metamorphed by Brundlefly's scientific work. The fetus operates as an inversion of Disraeli's "blank page" cast through the reactionary framework of Nazi eugenics theory. Ronnie's stakes—her future baby—create a reproductive entanglement. It manifests an implicit next-generation horror of Christian-Jewish cohabitation distinctly at odds with second-wave progression narratives.[50] The imagined future-horror is ultimately revealed in the scene in *The Fly* when Ronnie gives painful birth to a horrific twitching grub.[51] The sequence is revealed to be a dream, Ronnie's nightmare. Cronenberg's use of a dream to depict the unimaginable is critical to framing the context of future-horror as cinematic projection.

In his 1917 essay, "Mourning and Melancholia," Freud describes how the dream state helps patients re-create their imagined past by transforming it into an imagined tableaux.[52] Ronnie's nightmare manifests the Anglo-Christian-Jewish hybrid as a monstrous animetaphor lurking in the subconscious of the 1980s. Her decision to seek out an abortion operates as an inverted correlative of the aspirational futurism signified by Brundle's telepods. The desired removal of her fetus-fly is a thematic de-coupling, a technological negation. *The Fly* imagines late modern secular Jewish science as both seductive and destructive. Abortion offers Ronnie the ability to remove the nightmare of (Jewish) deviancy increasingly embodied in her womb.

Brundlefly's insect-like drive to stop this abortion and preserve his offspring leads to yet another tragic synthesis. Brundlefly violently interrupts the abortion, kidnaps the still-pregnant Ronnie, and brings her back to his laboratory. With slurring remnants of speech, he explains his plan to force Ronnie into the pod with him, genetically fusing them together as a solution to both his impending demise and her fears of childbirth. The experiment goes wrong and Ronnie escapes, leading to Brundlefly fusing/splicing with the telepod technology itself. The final form that emerges from the telepod is that of a creature that is equal parts insect, man, and machine. Cronenberg's tri-metamorph brings together the paradoxical ends of anti-Semitism into one single impossible form. Jews were seen as emblems of both machine-like futurism and savage primitivity. In Brundlefly-telepod's final form, this impossibility is visualized. In raising her shotgun and firing the bullet that ends Brundlefly-telepod's life, Ronnie transforms from tragic (Christian) witness of (Jewish) modernist deviancy to benevolent executioner.

THE LAST JEW/CINEMA IN THE WORLD

Cronenberg's career-long fascination with animal-human-machine hybridity can be seen in everything from the VHS-human hybrids of *Videodrome* (1983) to the mutant hallucinations of *Naked Lunch* (1991) and the car-human sex fetish violence of *Crash* (1996). Academics have examined this work from a number of perspectives. Barbara Creed describes his films as extensions of surrealist art celebrating sexual taboo without apology or shame.[53] Ernest Mathijs has explored metaphors of AIDS in *Shivers* (1975) and *Rabid* (1977), while Murray Forman summarizes Cronenberg's central focus as an exploration of masculinity "mediated by modern technology."[54]

Yet, the subject of Jewishness has been almost entirely left out of discussions of Cronenberg's work. This is true despite the fact that Cronenberg himself is Jewish and was raised in a suburban Jewish household outside Toronto in the 1950s. When asked by Nathan Abrams in 2014 whether his Jewish identity influenced his filmmaking, Cronenberg responded:

> Undoubtedly it has because it's influenced the formation of my sensibility and my life. My parents weren't fanatical about it, I never was in a synagogue, I was never bar mitzvahed. My mother did speak some Yiddish to me, but that's not a religious thing, that's a cultural thing and I still have an affection for Yiddishness as a result. It would be easy to say that Jews always feel like outsiders in any society because of the diaspora and there are a lot of philosophical and interesting cultural things you could say, but I don't know that in my case that was particularly true. I always felt very much a Canadian and embedded in Canada, so I would mix the Jewishness with the Canadian-ness. I don't think you can separate these components of a life.[55]

Cronenberg's self-described entanglement between his "Jewishness" and his "Canadian" identities informs the hybrid metaphors in his work. This became fully clear in a short film he directed in 2007. He was one of thirty-four directors commissioned to write and direct a short film for the sixtieth anniversary of the Cannes Film Festival, a collection eventually called *Chacun Son Cinéma* (*To Each His Own Cinema*). He wrote, directed, and starred in a single-take, four-minute short film, shot on video, called *At the Suicide of the Last Jew in the World in the Last Cinema in the World.* The film's single uninterrupted image is a live video stream close-up of Cronenberg himself, facing the camera, sitting in a bathroom stall. Two off-camera news reporters flippantly and bemusedly give context to the image as if it is taking place in a live feed television format. Cronenberg is not identified by name, but only as the "last Jew left on earth," identifying the diegesis as a presumably dystopian future world.

The disembodied voices of the off-screen hosts serve as an example of sound theorist Michel Chion's concept of the *Acousemêtre*.[56] Their lack of embodiment further emphasizes the "Last Jew" as a body and, even more specifically, as a Jewish body. The news hosts are the normative (Christian) witnesses to this impending tragedy. They explain to the spectator that the Last Jew has locked himself in a run-down bathroom in what is announced as the last movie theater in existence. The theater had been set for demolition. The Last Jew has decided to take his own life, on camera, on live television, as a form of protest. The hosts seem unconcerned, treating the impending suicide as mildly amusing entertainment. They identify the Last Jew as a filmmaker of some renown, making it clear that Cronenberg is either representing himself or a close facsimile.

The short film culminates as the Last Jew/Cronenberg raises his gun to his temple. The moment of the Last Jew/Cronenberg's suicide is also the moment the live feed ends. The film's conflation is clear: without cinema, there is no cinematic Jew, and without the cinematic Jew, there is no cinema. Anxieties of surveillance culture, the crisis of auteur filmmaking, and the visibility of overt Jewishness in screen media are simultaneously negated by the removal of the body from the screen. As with Kafka's Red Peter, this modernist crisis plays out on a thematic stage. The crisis of Jewishness becomes entertainment for the normative Christian spectator.

At the Suicide of the Last Jew in the World in the Last Cinema in the World resolves the previously coded function of Jewish metamorph in *The Fly*. Cronenberg visualizes synthesis between body and apparatus by expanding on the already-existing coded-Jewish mind/body tensions of Gothic horror traditions. In 1986, Ronnie's video camera records Brundlefly's mutation from Jewish mind (Brundle) to deviant body (fly) through the crisis of corporeal decay. In 2007, the reality television camera trains its unblinking eye on Cronenberg himself. His shift from Jewish body to un-body signifies the end of the medium in which he works. Both examples speak to the monstrous legacy of eugenics theory. The Jewish scientist-fly and the Jewish filmmaking auteur are each suspected of using new technology to distort, corrupt, and infect normative (Anglo-Christian) values, ideas, and bodies. In 1986, Jewish metamorph is thematic and implicit. In 2007, Cronenberg's self-identification/self-indictment is rendered both literal and ironic.[57] In both examples, like Kafka's parables, the tenuous, unstable role of animal-human-technological hybridity cannot resolve. The Jewish metamorph could only be repeated as theatrical tragedy.

THE CHRISTIAN WITNESS

Whether in Holocaust narratives, monster films, fantasies, or romantic comedies, second-wave Anglo-Christian-Jewish couplings came apart in the 1980s through a scrambled recoding infused by fragmentation and absence. In a politically conservative era in which home video pornography compartmentalized previously mainstream explicit screen imagery, the second-wave carnal Jew became untethered and decorporealized. Jewish metamorph and Christian witnessing responded to this as a conceptual de-coupling. The sexual politics and political liberalism of the previous era were reversed. History, as reframed by Reagan-era nostalgia for the 1950s, was now once again visualized through reassurance narratives and universal accessibility. This was done by visualizing the mutating Jewish body not as emancipation allegory, but as a metamorphic impossibility.

CHAPTER 8

Seinfeld's Mailman

GLOBAL TELEVISION AND THE
WANDERING SITCOM (1993–2000)

Will (Eric McCormack): You're about as Jewish as Melanie Griffith in A Stranger Among Us.
Grace (Debra Messing): Well, you're about as gay as Tom Selleck in In and Out.

WILL AND GRACE (1999)

O N DECEMBER 9, 1993, THE TENTH EPISODE OF THE fifth season of *Seinfeld* aired on NBC. "The Cigar Store Indian" explored the comedic fallout after Jerry (Jerry Seinfeld) purchases what he considers a kitschy wooden cigar store Indian. Jerry's exuberant, childlike enjoyment of the statue brings unintended consequences from a politically correct world that views the Indian as a racist relic of a bygone era. Jerry finds himself accused by his new Native American girlfriend, Winona (Kimberly Norris), of harboring hidden racist biases. Jerry attempts to assuage these concerns as the two walk down a New York street:

> Jerry: I think if you spent any time with me at all, you'd see I'm very sensitive to these matters as well. You wouldn't be hungry by any chance, would ya?
> Winona: I guess I could go for a bite.
> Jerry: You like Chinese food? 'Cause I once went to a great Szechwan restaurant in this neighborhood. I don't remember the exact address . . .
> Jerry spots a mailman crouched emptying a mailbox.
> Jerry: Uh, excuse me, you must know where the Chinese restaurant is around here. . . .

215

The mailman stands and is revealed to be Asian. He takes offense.
Mailman (Benjamin Lum): Why must I know? Because I'm Chinese? You think I know where all the Chinese restaurants are?
(adopts hackneyed Chinese accent) Oh, ask honolable Chinaman for rocation of lestaulant.
Jerry: I asked because you were the mailman. You would know the neighborhood.
Mailman: Oh, hello American Joe. Which way to hamburger, hot-dog stand?
The mailman storms away.
Jerry: I didn't know that . . .
Winona: You know, it's late. I should probably just go home.
Jerry: I, I had no idea.[1]

Winona was one of the rare identifiably non-white, non-Anglo-Christian girlfriends who circulated through the show as Jerry's various love interests. Her visible ethnicity amplified his panic about his own ethnic disassociations and embedded biases. The comedic riff on political correctness worked into the show's familiar technique of creating social and cultural roadblocks that inevitably prevent Jerry from any long-term, successful romantic partnership. But it also served as important insight into the show's creative growth and simultaneous explosive popularity.

Jerry's Jewish unmasking is made fully clear later in the episode when he explains the incident to his best friend, George Costanza (Jason Alexander). Jerry decides to stake his own claim to the ethnic awakening taking place around him:

> Jerry: Ya know, I don't get it. I'm not allowed to ask a Chinese person where a Chinese restaurant is? I mean, aren't we all getting a little too sensitive? I mean, somebody asks me which way is Israel, I don't fly off the handle.[2]

The moment appeared to be nothing more than a comedic payoff, an over-reactive defensive response to undeserved criticism that Jerry is a bigot. Jerry responds to his apparent racial insensitivity by offering his own dubious claim of ethno-cultural victimization. But the "Israel" reference remains a remarkable moment of clarity for an American Jewish performer on a top-rated, prime-time American television sitcom. Despite his genial, culturally detached character, Jerry Seinfeld was no longer operating in code or ambiguity. He was clearly, overtly Jewish.

Seinfeld is now understood by scholars and fans alike as one of the most visible Jewish sitcoms in television history. But the show's overt Jewishness was a gradual development. The pilot, "The Seinfeld Chronicles," had initially been rejected in 1989 by NBC's Jewish network president, Brandon Tartikoff, with an infamous memo that criticized the show as "too New York, too Jewish."[3] Early seasons engaged Jewish subject matter only obliquely through character archetypes and the occasional Yiddishism. Despite culturally Jewish behavior and affect, the characters of Elaine (Julia Louis-Dreyfus), George (Jason Alexander), and Kramer (Michael Richards) were each explicitly identified as non-Jewish. Jerry made occasional references to his Jewish identity in passing, but the program's humor in its early seasons focused primarily on character-specific minutia and everyday life subject matter.

As the show gained in ratings, however, it gradually began to tie its acerbic, emotionally detached comedic tone to the specific world of New York Jewish identity. Episodes were structured around the hiring of a mohel to perform a bris ("The Bris," Season 5, Episode 5, October 14, 1993); the black-and-white cookies and babka bread purchasing rituals in a Jewish deli ("The Dinner Party," Season 5, Episode 13, February 3, 1994); and the two-part scandal over Jerry and his girlfriend making out during a screening of *Schindler's List* ("The Raincoats," Season 5, Episodes 18 and 19, April 28, 1994), to give just a few examples. Subsequent seasons focused on Jewish story lines with Seinfeld and his thematically (if not textually) Jewish friends going to bar mitzvahs ("The Serenity Now," Season 9, Episode 3, October 9, 1997) and engaging other elements of a distinct Jewish cultural life.[4]

This contextual unmasking coincided with the show's massive ratings ascent. By Season 4, *Seinfeld* was consistently making the Nielsen Top Ten.[5] Season 5 (1993–1994) saw the show become the highest-rated program on television. Its unapologetic integration of urban New York Jewish life, cultural rituals, and characters was increasingly identified as a central element of its success. It was a shift in both tone and subject matter that would have been impossible in the stand-up climate Jerry Seinfeld and co-creator Larry David had worked in just a few years earlier in the 1980s. It also marked a clear tonal break.[6] *Seinfeld* was understood as an "anti-sitcom," an acerbic backlash against the genteel (white, Anglo-Saxon) humor of the sitcoms of the 1980s.[7]

The four major networks quickly grasped this economic potential. They began tapping into the personas of other Jewish stand-ups, leading to a slew of copycat "Jewish" programming.[8] Vincent Brook describes this period as the moment when a small number of prominent Jewish stars on sitcoms began "outing" themselves, either explicitly or through obvious code.[9] Concurrent with Jerry Seinfeld, Jackie Mason and Richard Lewis adapted to this new Jewish visibility on *Chicken Soup* (1989) and *Anything But Love* (1989–1992), respectively. In the next eight years, Joel Fleischman (Rob Morrow) on *Northern Exposure* (1990–1995), Jonathan Eliot (Jonathan Silverman) on *The Single Guy* (1995–1997), Stacey Colbert (Debra Messing) on *Ned and Stacey* (1995–1997), Fran Fine (Fran Drescher) on *The Nanny* (1993–1999), Dharma Finkelstein (Jenna Elfman) on *Dharma & Greg* (1997–2002), and Grace Adler (Debra Messing) on *Will and Grace* (1998–2006) were each identified and publicized as visibly Jewish actors playing visibly Jewish characters.[10] Other shows operated in thinly veiled code, as seen in obvious Jewish characters such as Paul Buchman (Paul Reiser) on *Mad About You* (1992–1999) and Ross Geller (David Schwimmer) on *Friends* (1994–2004).[11]

Each of these shows was also tempered by the now-familiar, established coupling caveat. The Jewish protagonist was married to, romancing, or lusting after Anglo-Christian partners. This longing could be literal, as with Fran Fine's love for her boss, the repressed British aristocrat Maxwell Sheffield (Charles Shaughnessy) on *The Nanny*. Or, it could be thematic, as with Grace Adler, who, despite marrying the proverbial nice Jewish doctor, Dr. Marvin "Leo" Marcus (Harry Connick Jr.), in Season 4 of *Will and Grace*, remained a conceptual couple with her non-Jewish, gay best friend, Will Truman (Erik McCormack). Or, it could be ephemeral, as with the various Anglo-Christian women-of-the-week pursued by Jerry Seinfeld on *Seinfeld* or by Jonathan Eliot on *The Single Guy*.[12]

Like their screen forebears in the late 1960s and the 1970s, these shows were built around the star personas of an emerging group of Jewish performers. However, these entertainers came of age under very different historical and cultural parameters. In the 1970s, Bridget and Bernie on *Bridget Loves Bernie* and Mike and Gloria on *All in the Family* had struggled with overcoming societal and parental objections to their marriages. Sitcom couples in the 1990s faced no such barriers. Paul Buchman's neurotic quibbles with Jamie (Helen Hunt) on *Mad About You* and Fran's at-first unrequited pursuit of Maxwell Sheffield on *The Nanny*, to pick two examples, depict sitcom Jewish-Anglo-Christian couples struggling not with societal resistance but with internal confusion and relationship angst. The only elements preventing Jews and Anglo-Christians from getting together were the emotional shortcomings of the characters themselves.

Devoid of both generational and cultural critiques, third-wave sitcoms offered an easily adaptable forum of denatured, gender-based relationship conflict. Their inward focus on psychology, rather than politics, allowed these shows to become a valuable global media product. They carried the form, if not the content, of established entertainment over the previous three decades. This familiarity easily translated American cultural specificity to international markets on increasingly lucrative global distribution pipelines. The entrenched coupling binary offered a valuable framework to explore archetypal transgression. The third-wave "Jew" was just different enough to embody a universal Otherness. The third-wave "Christian" was a benign but familiar embodiment of entrenched norms. Together, on nearly a dozen sitcoms totaling more than a thousand hours of syndicated entertainment, this coupling conflict model was perfectly positioned. It provided the means to distribute and adapt domestic television product for numerous international regions and cultures. In just a few short years, third-wave Anglo-Christian-Jewish couplings had become a foundational building block of the increasingly global mass media industries.

FROM STAND-UP TO SITCOM

Since the earliest days of broadcasting, the situation comedy has served as the most robust genre for engaging topicality and political controversy.[13] Sitcoms of the 1950s such as *The Goldbergs* (1949–1956), *The Amos 'n' Andy Show* (1951–1953), *The Beulah Show* (1950–1952), and *Mama* (1949–1957) each provoked national discussions on immigrant, race, gender, and working-class issues. *Mary Tyler Moore* (1970–1977) and various shows developed and produced by Norman Lear's Tandem Productions—such as *All in the Family* (1971–1979), *Maude* (1972–1978), *Good Times* (1974–1979), and *The Jeffersons* (1975–1985)—used a mix of humor and pathos to provide a national forum for discussions of race and gender throughout the 1970s. In the late 1970s, the innovative serialization of *Soap* provided what Jason Mittell describes as the earliest seeds of the complex, nuanced television product that would come to dominate discussions of quality programming in the 2000s and 2010s.[14]

Third-wave Anglo-Christian-Jewish sitcoms tapped into this tradition by updating the genre's familiar topicality. This was as much an economic as a creative development. Studio films of the 1980s increasingly shied away from controversy to focus on blockbuster-driven sensation and fantasy star vehicles, opening the door for television to revive the second-wave template as a familiar mediation binary.[15] Like the second wave in cinema, these programs deployed Jewishness as the means to explore various ethno-cultural taboos. Debates over delayed marriage, sexual promiscuity, gay rights, and other topical issues could be safely explored within the episodic confines of humorous relationship banter. Yes, as Brett Mills summarizes, these sitcoms primarily featured fantasies of reassurance. They produced an Americanized, generic comedy performance style that was disconnected from any specific Jewish-ethnic, cultural, and religious roots.[16] They carried the formal properties of second-wave sociopolitical conflict. But they mined these transgressive roots for humor and narrative possibilities rather than the controversial and disruptive explorations of the second wave.

The first prototypes for these third-wave couplings emerged in the star personas of two self-titled shows of the late 1980s: Garry Shandling on *It's Garry Shandling's Show* (1986–1990) and Roseanne Barr on *Roseanne* (1988–1997). While neither show made more than the briefest of passing mentions of their titular characters' Jewish identity, both shows self-consciously satirized their star personas as Jewish stereotypes. Shandling's neurotic, narcissistic schlemiel was the first hint of a return of the 1970s-era Jewish protagonist on television.[17] Roseanne's configuration was new. She performed as the previously rarely seen, but often alluded to, loud and intentionally offensive Jewish American Princess housewife.[18] Both of these shows also tempered the visible Jewishness of their titular stars through romantic union. Roseanne's television husband, Dan Connor (John Goodman), was a classic working-class Polish Catholic.[19] Shandling's love interest, and eventual wife on the show, was the non-Jewish Phoebe Bass (Jessica Harper).[20] These partnerships served as neutralizing agents, tempering the acerbic nature and radical impulses of Shandling and Barr's screen personas.

Jackie Mason's *Chicken Soup* (1989) and Richard Lewis's *Anything But Love* (1989–1992) followed Shandling and Barr in bringing more overt Jewish schlemiel-dom back to prime time. Jackie Mason, an ordained rabbi-turned-comedian, and Richard Lewis, an intense free-form comic who treated the stage as an extension of his therapy, both made frequent references to their Jewish backgrounds in their stand-up comedy routines of the 1980s. Perhaps as a result, they were also two of the first comedians to produce openly Jewish sitcoms in the early years of the third wave. Both played Jewish characters in the second-wave tradition. Both also mitigated this through romantic pairing with the non-Jew.

Chicken Soup aired after *Roseanne* and featured the Yiddish-inflected comedian Mason finding love in middle age with an Irish woman, Maddie Peerce (Lynn Redgrave). The *Cohens and Kellys* framework was both familiar and unusual, given the de-emphasis on Jewish specificity at the time. *Anything But Love* was less overt. But it still marked a break from the whitebread, genteel sitcoms of the previous decade. It featured Richard Lewis as Marty Gold, a clearly identified Jewish yuppie falling for his non-Jewish co-worker, Hannah Miller (Jamie Lee Curtis).[21] By the second season, references to Marty's Jewish identity became more overt. This culminated in an episode titled "The Days of Whine And Haroses" (Season 2, Episode 21, March 21, 1990), in which Marty introduces Hannah to his Jewish family by taking her to their Passover seder. The extended seder sequence draws humor by contrasting the prayers and rituals with Hannah's confusion as she clumsily tries to participate. It concludes with a trick played on Hannah by Marty's jealous ex-fiancée. She convinces Hannah that throwing a piece of matzo against the wall is a time-honored Jewish tradition, causing Hannah to engage in broad, disruptive slapstick during the ceremony.

Mason and Lewis's early third-wave experimentations with visible Jewishness were a direct result of the stand-up comedy boom of the 1980s. In the 1970s, the confessional style and unapologetic racial subject matter of Richard Pryor and the X-rated language and politics of George Carlin had established live comedy as a boundary-pushing performance space and star-making vehicle. Locations such as Mitzi Shore's Comedy Store in Los Angeles became breeding grounds for new television and feature film personalities. Experimental comedians such as Robin Williams, Steve Martin, and David Letterman moved almost immediately from the stage into mainstream television or feature film success. Within just a few years, more than four hundred comedy clubs had opened around the country.[22] Comics such as Eddie Murphy, Sam Kinison, and Bill Hicks took on the personas of rock stars. They peppered their routines with X-rated words and made politically incorrect jokes about race, gender, and sexuality. These performers began collectively pushing the form, approach, and content of stand-up comedy performance in ways not seen since the "Sicknik" experimentations of Lenny Bruce, Mort Sahl, and Nichols and May in the early 1960s, as discussed in chapter 5. By 1980, this comedian-to-television pipeline was one of the most lucrative development areas in Hollywood.

Yet, while provocative race, sex, and gender humor dominated the 1980s comedy boom, Jewish subject matter remained strikingly absent. Jewish-born comedians such as Paul Reubens, Andrew "Dice" Clay, Carol Leifer, Roseanne Barr, Richard Belzer, Howie Mandel, Bob Saget, Yakov Smirnoff, Paul Reiser, Brad Garrett, Rita Rudner, and Jerry Seinfeld had acts that were nearly completely devoid of references to either their Jewish backgrounds or Jewish culture more generally.[23] Even the obviously Jewish Rodney Dangerfield, one of the most successful multiplatform comedians of the 1980s, avoided Jewish specificity.[24] Jewishness was instead communicated through code. Dangerfield's self-deprecating schlemiel catchphrase, "I don't get no respect," and Rita Rudner's subversively materialist Jewish American Princess persona were both clearly presented as character riffs on Jewish stereotypes. But actual references to Jewish identity or culture remained absent from their routines and jokes. This was even more remarkable given how the humor of the period trafficked in confrontation and shock. Comedians such as Sam Kinison and Bill Hicks assaulted sacred cows through politically incorrect, X-rated language, and intentionally provocative, offensive terminology. Black comedians such as Eddie Murphy and Paul Mooney performed confrontational race comedy. Yet, outside of Richard Lewis and Jackie Mason, Jewishness remained almost entirely removed from stand-up comedic discourse in the 1980s.

Two examples of televised young comedian showcases hosted by Dangerfield in his New York comedy club offer examples of this absence. In both *Rodney Dangerfield's Ninth Annual Young Comedians Special* (HBO, 1985) and *Rodney Dangerfield's Young Comedians Special* (HBO, 1987), not one of the Jewish-born comedians appearing on the programs made a Jewish reference in their routines. These performers included Rita Rudner, Bob Saget, Roseanne Barr, Robert Schimmel, Yakov Smirnoff, Richard Belzer, and Jerry Seinfeld. Their comedy focused instead on what *New York Times* critic Stephen Holden described at the time as "a style of humor born out of fatigue and disappointment. The collective feelings that it reassuringly addresses are a sense of mediocrity and meanness of life."[25] Rudner offered one explanation for avoiding Jewish subject matter throughout her career in an interview in 2011: "I don't do Jewish stuff because I don't want people to be left out. If I mention the Torah in Alabama, it's not going to go down that well."[26]

Rudner's fear of alienating non-Jewish audiences was a reflection of the dominant understanding for Jewish performers in the 1980s comedy scene. They were not necessarily hiding their backgrounds. Their language, verbal cadences, looks, and neurotic self-deprecation all firmly located in the identifiable traditions of postwar American Jewish stand-up comedy. But they refused to address their backgrounds with any specificity, referring instead to urban life, neuroticism, and other familiar tropes of cultural Jewishness.

Many of these performers continued to code and obscure Jewishness in their subsequent sitcom personas. Roseanne referenced that she was "part Jewish" on *Roseanne* but made no real efforts to integrate that identity into plot points or narrative events. Paul Buchman on *Mad about You* remained unidentified. Ross and Rachel Geller on *Friends* were rarely addressed as Jewish despite clearly Jewish families, looks, and performance styles.[27] But neither were they identified as Christian. They existed in an intentionally ambiguous state. They performed obvious Jewish tropes without clarifying their actual backgrounds.

When the transition from coded to explicit Jewishness began to emerge on the American television sitcom, it was the result of changing cultural and political sensibilities. The fall of the Soviet Union and the election of Clinton in 1992 opened the door for a renewed interest in ethno-centric liberal subject matter.[28] This shift away from Reagan's nostalgic postwar gender reversions and toward Clinton-era multiculturalism was a central part of the subsequent popularity of third-wave love stories.

Television's increasingly global economic power also influenced this shift. The 1993 repeal of the Financial Interest and Syndication Rules (Fin-Syn) and the market ownership deregulation introduced by the 1996 Telecommunications Act sparked a period of controversial and massive megacorporate mergers. These included Disney-ABC (1996), Viacom's purchase of CBS (1999), AOL Time-Warner (2000), and Comcast's acquisition of NBC Universal (2009). These acquisitions, as Jennifer Holt has shown, proceeded at a reckless, breakneck pace with often disastrous economic results.[29] The need for large volumes of identifiable product and familiar character conflicts was immediate and urgent.

Reviving second-wave coupling templates became an obvious solution to this need. With the election of Bill Clinton, the identity politics of the late 1960s had been recast in a nostalgic, safe glow. Popular media were no longer negotiating national-cultural fault lines. The overt sitcom Jew partnered with either a single or multiple Anglo-Christian love interests was the perfect blend of nostalgia and safety for this changing economic climate. It offered a means-tested form of gendered interplay perfectly suited for transnational shift.

Even more striking, these sitcoms congealed around an emerging new proto-"Jewess" persona: the sexualized, proudly female, proudly Jewish sitcom star. It was a construction that drew directly from both the ghetto love stories of the 1920s and the legacy of radical feminism in the 1970s. This new sitcom "Jewess" arrived as a breakthrough television persona. She was at once familiar to American audiences and also perfectly positioned to negotiate the new gender politics of the 1990s.

RETURN OF THE RADICAL JEWESS

Roseanne was the first major sitcom of the third wave to recognize this link between first-wave, working-class ghetto love stories and second-wave radical feminism. Television of the late 1960s and 1970s had been slow to adapt to the visible Jewishness taking place in popular cinema. In terms of female representations, Barbra Streisand, Joan Rivers, Bette Midler, Madeline Kahn, and Carol Kane, among others, collectively updated the "unkosher comedienne" personas of the 1910s and 1920s (Sophie Tucker,

Belle Barth, Totie Fields) into the feminist context of the 1960s and 1970s.[30] Yet, outside of *Rhoda* and perhaps *Maude*, television mostly avoided exploring the Jewish female's comedic unruliness.

Roseanne does not, at first, to appear to have any significant Jewish identity. The show is primarily understood as a critique of American working-class life and the problematic nature of ascribed gender roles within the family unit. In her seminal book on unruly women in popular media, Kathleen Rowe argues that Roseanne Barr's fearless display of her overweight body was at the center of both critiques. Roseanne's disruptive physique assaulted established gender, beauty, and income standards.[31] Rowe locates this rebellious presentation of disruptive femininity as part of a continuation of unruly women from Mae West to Lucille Ball.[32] In this reading, Roseanne's Jewishness, whether in the codes of her character or her established stand-up persona, is not an important factor in the show's radical politics.

This is understandable. Jewishness (and religion more generally) was rarely a major subject on the show. In the episode "I Pray the Lord My Stove to Keep" (Season 5, Episode 22, May 3, 1994), the show addressed the religious background of the Connor family. At first believing their son, D. J. (Michael Fishman), is skipping school, Roseanne and Dan (John Goodman) discover that D. J. has instead begun going to church. When the two confront their son about his sudden interest in religion, he turns the tables by asking them about their background. Roseanne reveals that she had a Jewish father and Lutheran mother:

> D. J.: I just had some questions about God and stuff.
> Roseanne: Well, why didn't you come to us if you had questions? There are no two better people to answer your questions than me and your dad.
> D. J.: OK . . . what religion are we?
> Roseanne: I have no idea . . . Dan?
> Dan: Well . . . my mom's mom was Pentecostal and Baptist on the side of my dad. Your mom's mom was Lutheran and her dad was Jewish.
> D. J.: So what do we believe?
> Roseanne: Well, we believe in . . . being good. So basically we're good people.
> Dan: Yeah, but we're not practicing.[33]

Roseanne's apparent lack of interest in her religious background demonstrates how the aggressive gender and class politics of the show were explicitly disconnected from any specific ethno-religious rhetoric. She even leaves it to her husband to identify her Jewish parentage, giving the revelation no emphasis or importance.

But this textual near-absence does not dismiss the relationship between Roseanne's Jewish persona and the show's provocative engagement with questions of queerness, patriarchy, gender roles, and other aspects of identity. Jewishness and queerness often overlap through related rhetorical discourses, a concept that Janet Jakobsen calls "twinning."[34] Both have an ability to "pass" within society as white/heterosexual (Christonormative) without being seen or identified. This rhetorical link between subversive gender politics and Jewishness conflated Jewishness and queerness as equally dangerous sociopolitical phenomena. It was a sociopolitical twinning that eventually produced what Helene Myers describes as an inevitable political alliance.[35]

Roseanne Connor's unruly, coded Jewishness can be understood as an extension of this alliance. The show did not shy away from presenting Roseanne as a queered figure undermining the tropes of televisual suburban domesticity. In the 1990 episode "Trick or Treat" (Season 3, Episode 7, October 30, 1990), Roseanne cross-dresses as a man in support of her son's desire to dress up as a witch for Halloween. In "Don't Ask, Don't Tell" (Season 6, Episode 18, March 1, 1994), she shares a controversial on-screen kiss with a gay character played by Mariel Hemingway. The show contained numerous other examples of Roseanne challenging societal taboos and overturning gender norms. Yet, despite years of provocation on issues of gender, sexuality, and body politics, the character's thematic Jewishness remained unexamined and overlooked. This queer-Jewish interplay was foregrounded through familiar second-wave twinning codes in which feminist activism required Jewish erasure. The polysemy of Roseanne-the-comedian and Roseanne-the-character, frequently conflated in the popular media of the time, also influenced public reception to the gender and class politics put forth by the show. Roseanne's confrontational nature, controversial statements, and very public Jewish wedding to costar Tom Arnold, on January 20, 1990, further established her identity as a politically active and openly Jewish feminist.

Another lens to read Roseanne's Jewishness locates in her on-screen pairing with actor John Goodman. Her titular character's transgressive persona was presented in tandem with Dan Connor, a loving, mostly deferential, Anglo-Catholic husband. The Dan-Roseanne coupling was one of the first visible Christian-Jewish partnerships of the third wave. It revived and updated the class politics of second-wave feminism through the lens of second wave Anglo-Christian-Jewish iconography. In tapping into this template,

Roseanne remained thematically Jewish in the same way Maude Findlay (Bea Arthur) was thematically Jewish but textually non-Jewish on *Maude* a generation earlier. Both performed radical gender politics through Jewish code rather than text. This conflation is even more visible when *Roseanne* is understood as part of a collection of third-wave Anglo-Christian-Jewish texts in which Jewishness was central to their critique of 1980s-era gender norms and marginalizations.[36]

FLASHY GIRLS FROM FLUSHING

After *Roseanne*, the next major sitcom to follow this updated second-wave gender politics pattern was *The Nanny* (1993–1999). The brightly colored, animated opening title sequence directly parodied two sitcoms of the 1960s, *Bewitched* (1964–1972) and *I Dream of Jeannie* (1965–1970).[37] In the animated opening narrative, Fran Fine is rescued from her drab job as a makeup saleswoman living in suburban Queens (and its fully Jewish world) by the aristocratic, wealthy, but repressed WASP British theater producer, Maxwell Sheffield. The notion of discovery/rescue echoed Captain Nelson's discovery of Jeannie's bottle during the opening credits of *I Dream of Jeannie*. The self-reflexive revival of this magical female trope in *The Nanny* humorously identified Fran Fine as an updated version of supernatural WASP housewives Jeannie (Barbara Eden) and Samantha (Elizabeth Montgomery). Similar to her magical housewife progenitors, Fran spends the first few seasons perpetually trying, and failing, to gain the undivided (and sexual) attention of her "master."

Yet, while the rhetoric of gendered containment with Jeannie and Samantha focused on their supernatural superiority, Fran's "power" locates in her Jewishness. Maxwell is presented as financially successful but emotionally stunted and repressed. In seeking out a Jewish nanny for his children, Maxwell implicitly acknowledges the value of Fran's emotional exhibitionism. This is counterpointed by her inability to find love with a "nice Jewish boy" as demanded by her overbearing Jewish mother, Sylvia Fine (Renée Taylor), and grandmother, Yetta Rosenberg (Ann Morgan Guilbert). The emphasis on Jewish matriarchy contrasts with the patrician tendencies of Maxwell and his sarcastic British butler, Niles (Daniel Davis).

For the show's first few seasons, Fran's Jewishness is depicted at odds with Maxwell's WASP world. Their mutual attraction remains unstated, as Fran makes numerous attempts at dating Jewish men. These inevitably fail due to obstacles beyond her control. In one of the more overt examples, "Kissing Cousins" (Season 4, Episode 13, January 15, 1997), Fran falls in love with a successful Jewish doctor, Bob (Jon Stewart), only to discover that they are cousins. The notion of Fran's desired Jewish-Jewish coupling as "inbreeding" is played for laughs in the episode's denouement. This familiar trope of both the first and second waves kept in place the one implicit caveat for Jewish screen visibility: taboo coupling with another Jew.

In "The Wedding" (Season 5, Episodes 22 and 23, May 13, 1998), Fran and Maxwell finally get married, despite objections from both of their families. The subsequent culture clash between the families directly invoked classic *The Cohens and Kellys* banter while solidifying the notion of Maxwell as the liberating agent for Fran's princess fantasies.

By the late 1990s, the third-wave pattern, developed by *Seinfeld*, *The Garry Shandling Show*, *Chicken Soup*, *Anything But Love*, *Roseanne*, and *The Nanny*, had reached critical mass. Nostalgia for the radical freedoms of the 1960s was central to a number of these next-generation texts. *Dharma & Greg* (1997–2002) merged the liberation identity politics of *The Nanny* with the implicit connection between next-generation Jewishness and the residue of second-wave feminism in *Roseanne*. As with *The Nanny*, the title sequence defines Dharma Finkelstein (Jenna Elfman). A magical, sexually unruly genie/Jeannie-type, she is a 1960s-era flower child of anti-establishment Jews-turned-Buddhists-turned-Hindus. Their radical teachings have left her confused and disinterested in adapting to the more conservative climate of the 1990s. Even Dharma's name uses incongruity to make a humorous point. Her first name, "Dharma," suggests the meditative by-product of spiritual truth seekers. Yet, with a last name like Finkelstein, she cannot ultimately abandon her Jewishness.

As with the second-wave Anglo-Christian-Jewish couplings she evokes, Dharma is a comedic hybrid caught between two worlds.[38] This becomes a metaphor for the tension of domestic containment with her husband, Greg (Thomas Gibson). Weekly episodes were built around the various struggles experienced by Dharma's inability to resolve her hippie outsider impulses with her marriage to a culturally conservative partner. Like Lucy and Roseanne before her, Dharma's unruly presence is linked to her disruption of traditional gender roles. But her marriage to Greg ultimately operates within the familiar containment of sitcom tradition.

The romantic evolution of Charlotte York (Kristin Davis) on HBO's *Sex and the City* (1998–2004), and in the films, *Sex and the City* (2008) and *Sex and the City 2* (2010), offers a reverse case study of erotic Jewishness as emotional liberation. In the show's first few seasons, Charlotte is established as an Anglo-WASP cliché, a chaste, blushing, sexually modest Episcopalian, who was raised in a rich, conservative, Connecticut household. Each of the three other female characters of the ensemble, Carrie (Sarah Jessica Parker), Samantha (Kim Cattrall), and Miranda (Cynthia Nixon) are presented as sexually adventurous. All three experiment with and discusses sex in graphic terminology. Charlotte, however, remains mostly demure. In an early episode, "Secret Sex" (Season 1, Episode 6, July 12, 1998), she reveals that one of her rare sexual affairs was with a Hasidic Jewish artist named Shmuel (Glenn Fleshler). Yet, despite occasionally giving in to erotic temptation, Charlotte insists that she dreams of an idealized, romantic (Christian) white wedding. This wish eventually comes true in Season 3 (2002) when she meets and marries the rich, white, Anglo-Saxon Trey MacDougal (Kyle MacLachlan). The show subverts Charlotte's fantasy through comedic incongruity. The marriage is revealed to be a sham, both loveless and sexless, as the repressed, mostly asexual Trey disappoints her sexually and otherwise. After an extended inability to conceive, the couple divorce ("All that Glitters," Season 4, Episode 14, January 13, 2002). The breakup offers a critique of Charlotte's idealized Anglo-Christian white wedding fantasy as nothing more than a childish cartoon.

In the show's sixth and final season (2004), *Sex and the City* located a solution for its "Episcopalian Princess." Charlotte is startled to discover that she has fallen in love with a man who at first utterly repulses her physically, her divorce lawyer, Harry Goldenblatt (Evan Handler). Harry is introduced in "The Big Journey" (Season 5, Episode 7, September 1, 2002) as the prototypical sweaty, loud Jewish lawyer. He is brash, obnoxious, bald but with excessive body hair, and funny. This at first offends Charlotte's sensibilities. Harry is the corporeal antithesis of Trey, but he is eventually identified as a real version of Charlotte's Prince Charming fantasy.

This maturation process for Charlotte used the comedic irony of the bestial Jewish lawyer replacing the upper-class WASP ideal. It also solidified the Anglo-Christian-Jewish coupling as a form of third-wave truth claim. Charlotte decides that converting to Judaism is important to demonstrate her love to Harry ("Great Sexpectations," Season 6, Episode 2, June 29, 2003). The series finale, "An American Girl in Paris: Part Deux" (Season 6, Episode 20, February 22, 2004), reveals that, despite conception problems, Charlotte and Harry are happily married and in the process of adopting a child from China.[39] The coda is clear. Charlotte's real-world family ends up nothing like the Anglo-Christian fantasy she had been taught to covet as a child. As with the prime-time sitcoms it emulated, *Sex and the City* signified the maturation of the Anglo-Christian female through her erotic epiphany regarding the potent alt-value of the comedic Jewish schlemiel.

But perhaps the most distilled version of third-wave sitcom Jew-ish unheroism presented in tandem with Anglo-Christian partnership oc-curred on *Curb Your Enthusiasm* (2000–). Created by Larry David, the co-creator of *Seinfeld*, *Curb* self-identified as a metatextual experimentation of form. The show removed the familiar laugh track and studio settings of the network sitcom, replacing it with a blurred, free-form improv style. In so doing, the soft-peddled connection among Jewishness, neurotic solip-sism, and sexual compulsion at the heart of the comedy in *Seinfeld* was am-plified. *Seinfeld* had self-identified as a conscious rejection of 1980s positive-message family sitcoms such as *The Cosby Show* (1984–1992) and *Family Ties* (1982–1989). It accomplished this by fracturing the families of domes-tic sitcoms into the pseudo-family alienation of four actively dating singles, George, Elaine, Jerry, and Kramer.

Curb Your Enthusiasm continued this break from established sitcom form by fracturing the very form of the sitcom itself. Episodes of *Curb* took place within the same Seinfeldian existential paralysis of character. Good deeds are misinterpreted. Noble efforts at benevolence are punished. All the major characters are depicted as miserable no matter how much money or success they acquire. But the show's formal breaks from convention up-dated the willingness of *Seinfeld* to at least aesthetically adhere to sitcom tradition. David's comedy of discomfort refused to resolve any number of formal, textual, or thematic tensions. The show was shot improvisation style, on location, and without a detailed script. This made *Curb Your En-thusiasm* one of the first experimental sitcoms to completely break away from the traditional three-camera setup.

HBO, the premium cable network, played an important role in allow-ing these aesthetic innovations. But these formal deviations were accompa-nied by a thematic one. *Curb Your Enthusiasm* was the first major program to emphasize explicit Jewishness among the majority of characters on the show without fear of alienating a potentially uncomprehending studio au-dience. As the creator, lead writer, and star of *Curb Your Enthusiasm*, David repeatedly and unapologetically focused on his own Jewish specificity. This had already located at the center of *Seinfeld*'s rejection of Anglo-centric, 1980s-era sitcom gentility. But in the Woody Allen-esque blurring of Art and Life in David's improvisational "real" world, Jewishness was now ines-capable as a formal and thematic rupturing agent.

Larry maintains his outsider status not simply by being a Jew in a Chris-tian world, but also by being an outsider Jew in a *Jewish* world.[40] This

Larry David (Larry David) and Cheryl David (Cheryl Hines) struggle to understand each other on Curb Your Enthusiasm *(1999).*

second-level alienation is also established by the fact that Larry's circle is made up nearly entirely of Jewish friends and coworkers. These include Jeff Greene (Jeff Garlin), Richard Lewis playing a version of himself, Marty Funkhouser (Bob Einstein), and Larry's primary foil, Jeff Greene's wife, Susie Greene (Susie Essman).[41] In tense and painful interactions with his "friends," Larry struggles as much with fitting into the Jewish world as the Christian world. He is a hybrid misanthrope, caught between worlds, unable to resolve either his external conflicts or his internal identity.

The counterpoint to Larry's neurosis, tension, and fractured sense of self is the familiar one, his perpetually patient, blonde, blue-eyed shiksa wife, Cheryl (Cheryl Hines).[42] But whereas other third-wave, Anglo-Christian-Jewish coupling sitcoms maintained some form of romantic possibility, the Larry-Cheryl dynamic denies even this modicum of relief. The program implies little actual love between the two, going so far as to feature their divorce as simply another set of events in Larry's list of complaints ("The Divorce," Season 8, Episode 1, July 10, 2011). Unlike other shows of the third wave such as *Mad About You, The Nanny, Dharma & Greg,* and *Will and Grace, Curb Your Enthusiasm* is not very concerned with the relationship dynamics between Larry and Cheryl. Instead, it is a starring vehicle about a rich, wildly successful Jewish misanthrope. In this break with sitcom tradition, Larry's ultimate foe is internal rather than external. Extending the comedic paradox of what Benjamin Wright calls David's un-Jewish Jewishness, the character is so neurotically divided that he ends up occupying *both* sides of the Anglo-Christian-Jewish coupling dynamic.

Whether accidentally eating crèche cookies and then gagging on a pubic hair after interrupting a nativity scene tableau ("Mary, Joseph, and Larry," Season 3, Episode 9, November 10, 2002) or having a splash of his urine land on a portrait of Jesus in a bathroom ("The Bare Midriff," Season 7, Episode 6, October 25, 2009), Larry's inadvertent yet offensive assault on Christian norms is what gives his character an outsider identity. Yet, his disruptive misanthropy equally targets Jewish culture. Whether pretending to be orthodox to convince a Jewish doctor to help Richard Lewis ("The Ski Lift," Season 5, Episode 8, November 20, 2005) or insulting a Holocaust survivor by equating his experience to the television show *Survivor* ("The Survivor," Season 4, Episode 9, March 7, 2004), Larry is equally curmudgeonly and offensive.

The show also introduced a rare example of a Jewish-Jewish coupling to counterpoint the Larry-Cheryl dynamic. David's manager, Jeff, and his Jewish wife, Susie, offer familiar Jewish archetypes in rare partnership. This is amplified by Cheryl and Susie as a gendered WASP-Jewish contrast. Susie's loud, castrating Jewish American Princess loathes Larry. Cheryl exhibits seemingly unending (if unamused) patience with his many neurotic shortcomings. Yet, both are equally exasperated by Larry's social failings and lack of interpersonal skills.

Cheryl and Susie, as two female cultural archetypes, play a critical role in the existential trap of Larry's experiences. They allow Larry to oscillate between offensive polarities and parallel cultural alienations without resolving either one. In this post-Jewish televisual deconstruction, the stereotypes of loud Jewish American Princess and reserved shiksa are united in their mutual contempt for a completely alienated loner.[43]

THE NANNY: A CASE STUDY

Why were so many visible Anglo-Christian-Jewish couplings recurring on American situation comedies of the 1990s and early 2000s? Certainly, reviving familiar second-wave banter offered sitcoms an easy, recognizable formula to counter the Anglo-WASP representational hegemony of the 1980s. But another answer locates in the medium's rapidly changing economic models of distribution. The global expansion of ABC, CBS, NBC, and FOX in the late 1990s and early 2000s required malleable product for increasingly complex international markets.[44] Newly formed multimedia mega-corporations quickly discovered that the seemingly domestic-centric sitcoms produced in the United States had lucrative economic viability. This value came through syndication, with original episodes dubbed into regional and national languages. But it also emerged in adaptation licensing deals in which the program's original scripts were reproduced, and altered, by a regional cast and production company able to steer this product for individual markets.

Anglo-Christian-Jewish sitcom couplings proved remarkably robust, adaptable, and lucrative for this changing economic climate. At the center of each major network's expanding distribution pattern was a sitcom featuring either textual or thematic Jewish characters in relationships or marriage with Anglo-Christian partners. ABC's flagship comedy was *Roseanne*, with *Dharma & Greg* following in the late 1990s. NBC found lucrative global distribution for *Seinfeld, Mad About You,* and *Will and Grace.* CBS distributed *The Nanny.* This relationship between emerging third-wave sitcoms and media globalization at first appears to be coincidental. Whatever domestic programming the networks held in the 1990s inevitably became part of their global distribution pattern. But what is also clear in these examples is how easily the well-established Anglo-Christian-Jewish coupling pattern worked in markets around the world. Many of these markets remained entirely unfamiliar with the sociopolitical specifics from which these shows were drawing as part of their comedic coupling dynamics.

The remarkable global economic success of *The Nanny* offers one case study that demonstrates the value of malleable Anglo-Christian-Jewish couplings. The regional-specific tensions between Fran Fine's loud, obnoxious, Queens Jewish American Princess persona and Maxwell Sheffield's uptight British gentility would appear to limit the program's transnational value. Fran's numerous references to her Jewish background, including jokes about her family's seats in the synagogue, her search for a "nice Jewish boy," and the garish stereotypes of Queens Jewishness depicted by her family were entirely specific to the show's cityscape milieu. But the show's success in emerging international markets suggests robust and distinct global/local (glocal) adaptability. "Jewishness" originally emerged in screen media as a privileged signifier of late modern transformation. In the third wave, it demonstrated this mutability once again. On the glocal market, the "Jew" was no longer Jewish, but simply a recognizable and adaptable avatar of a universal trope: the cultural minority.

The Nanny found massive global success in both direct syndication and format reproduction. In the decade after the show ended its six-year run in 1999, syndication rights sold to more than ninety countries. This included distribution to numerous regional and cultural contexts lacking any familiarity with the references to American Jewish culture. The program also had worth as an adaptable format in a diverse array of national and regional broadcast contexts. The show saw successful direct adaptations in countries including Russia, Argentina, Turkey, Chile, Ecuador, Greece, Mexico, and Poland.

But there was a caveat. In each of these adaptations, Fran's Jewish identity was altered to fit the ethnic or cultural equivalent of a recognizable "outsider" identity. The Russian version, *My Fair Nanny*, which debuted in 2004 to wide acclaim (with more than 173 episodes produced), identified the nanny as "Vika," a Ukrainian woman who moves to Moscow to pursue her dreams. Poland's *Niania* (134 episodes produced) set the show in Warsaw and removed all references to the ethnic background of "Frania" entirely. In *La Niñera*, Fran became "Florencia," a young Argentinean woman from Lanús who moves to the big city of Buenos Aires. In the Mexican version, also titled *La Niñera*, "Francisca" moves from Roma to Mexico City, suggesting her possible Gypsy origins. Judaism, a culture long identified as a rootless, wandering diaspora, had become a valuable totem for global distribution. While problematic in actual geopolitics, the wandering screen "Jew" proved to be an enormously malleable concept in global media industries. It became a wandering signifier of Otherness, a key for visualizing intercultural barriers through the industrial mechanisms of the newly triumphant glocal adaptability of television franchises.

The show's enormous global success for the newly formed Viacom-CBS came about despite the fact that the show never once cracked the top ten in domestic ratings in the United States. The ratings were initially so mediocre that *The Nanny* was nearly cancelled after its first season. Laura Turner Garrison credits this surprising global success primarily to the relatable class struggle embedded in the text.[45] But this does not explain the show's similar success with syndication. Dubbing dialog certainly mitigated some of the Jewish specificity of the program. The Italian version of the original program, renamed *La Tata*, used dubbing and rewrites to omit all references to Fran's Jewish background. This was done primarily through name changes and line alterations. Fran became "Francesca Cacace" from the rural province of Frosinone. The dubbed version led to what Chiara Francisca Ferrari, in *Since When is Fran Drescher Jewish?*, describes as the stubborn residue of "Otherness" that could not be removed by intercultural audiovisual adaptation alone.[46] For some, like Ferrari, Fran's Jewishness was entirely replaced by the codes of a different form of cultural alienation. For others, visible Jewishness of the original program remained. It located not only in the performances of the principal characters but also in numerous episodes set in delis, synagogues, and weddings in which Jewishness remained attached to the floating Otherness that distribution attempted to hide.

Whether the success of *The Nanny* translated as visibly Jewish or simply as an intercultural class conflict template for broad romantic situation comedy, it revealed how well worn the template of the third wave had become. Even denatured of its original form, this Jewish-without-Jewishness still offered the modernist codes of transgressive desire that defined the ideological push of Americanism in all three waves discussed in this book. It simply relocated the national context of earlier Christian-Jewish couplings to the transnational market. This offered both the figural and narrative pleasures of disruptive romantic interplay in a prepackaged, familiar, and ready-to-adapt form. The new mega-corporations craved familiar, translatable material for their increasingly lucrative global markets. In the familiar, nostalgic tone of the couplings of the third wave, they found it. These sitcoms offered a translatable template in which specificity of subject matter converged with the necessary adaptability for intercultural recontextualization around the world.

The Nanny was hardly alone. In 2013, *Forbes* reported that *Seinfeld* had generated nearly three billion dollars in global syndication profits after going off the air in 1998.[47] In late 2014, *Deadline Hollywood* announced that Sony Pictures, China's CCTV6's HuaCheng Pictures, and Croton Media closed a deal for a direct adaptation of *Mad About You* to be produced in China in 2015.[48] This is just one example of the versatility of adapting third-wave texts. Revived Jewish-Christian pairings exemplified a specific cultural memory in the American domestic context. But they also offered a tested comedic template that spoke to an increasingly global, polyglot transnational audience. This alignment with America's globalizing media industries in the late 1990s and 2000s was a by-product of second-wave nostalgia. But with second-wave domestic politics replaced by the emphasis on myopia and extended youth, they were also perfectly calibrated templates to become global products in America's post–Cold War ideological mass media expansion.

CHAPTER 9

Gaylord's Tulip

FLUID AND FLUIDITY AT
THE MILLENNIUM (1993–2008)

Prior Walter: Are you a ghost, Lou?
Louis Ironson: No. Just spectral. Lost to myself. Sitting all day on cold
park benches wishing I could be with you. Dance with me, babe.

ANGELS IN AMERICA (1993)

When we're in public, let's just tone down the Jewish thing, OK?

FAWN MOSCATO (ZOE LISTER-JONES), NEW GIRL (2015)

*T*HE GLOBAL SUCCESS OF THIRD-WAVE ANGLO-
Christian-Jewish sitcoms in the early 1990s was quickly followed by the reintroduction of similar coupling patterns in two other mediums. On Broadway, a new wave of experimental playwrights began to
explore the power and potency of resurrecting the familiar coupling iconography in new theatrical contexts. The first major example was seen in the
groundbreaking reception to Tony Kushner's 1993 Pulitzer Prize–winning
two-part play, *Angels in America, A Gay Fantasia on National Themes.* The
play premiered to enormous critical and popular acclaim just six months
before Jerry Seinfeld would "out" himself as a Jew on "The Cigar Store Indian" episode of *Seinfeld.*

Although the play and the *Seinfeld* episode at first appear to have little in
common, both understood how visible Jewishness was emerging as a con-
ceptual break with the codings and absences of popular media in the 1980s.
Set in 1985, but also examining the legacy of anti-Semitism from the 1950s,
Angels in America focused on residual "too Jewish" fears that had driven
Jewishness into hiding. In offering this corrective, the play's visible Jew-

ishness ushered in the new sexual frankness of the post–Cold War Clinton years. It also embraced and reclaimed the age-old anti-Semitic canard that Jewishness and queerness were indelibly linked.

Angels in America was followed by *Rent* (1996), *Ragtime* (1998), *Hedwig and the Angry Inch* (1998), *Parade* (1998), and *The Last Five Years* (2000). Each play presented provocative subject matter and expressive formal experimentations intended to engage the problematic relationship among identity, sexuality, and historical memory. Collectively, these plays self-identified as being explicitly at odds with escapist, depoliticized 1980s-era Broadway fare such as *Cats* (1982–2000), *Phantom of the Opera* (1988–), and *The Lion King* (1997–). This demarcation was solidified in how each play foregrounded the transgressive boundaries of Anglo-Christian-Jewish couplings as a way to experiment with chronological time, whether stage-time or historical timelines.

The second area of third-wave emergence began in a new subgenre of the sex comedy, the fluid comedy. R-rated studio films such as *There's Something About Mary* (1998), *American Pie* (1999), *Meet the Parents* (2000), and *Knocked Up* (2007) began to explore the link between visible Jewishness and sexual taboo. This was done by using graphic imagery of semen, feces, menstrual blood, and urine as provocative comedic set pieces for hapless Jewish movie stars. This taboo imagery drew inspiration, as Geoff King notes, from the upheaval of normative themes and codes first introduced in counterculture cinema, pornography, and the underground comix of the late 1960s and 1970s.[1]

Fluid comedies wedded this graphic imagery to the concurrent, emergent third-wave Jewishness. This graphic visual excess also operated as a depoliticized corrective to and revival of the sexual transgressions performed and embodied by the second wave. Explicit imagery in the late 1960s and 1970s was a sociopolitical reaction to and rejection of postwar values. In the third wave, this became recalibrated as a new form of stabilization. The assaultive nature of taboo images hid a fantasy of reassurance and stability. Anglo-Christian-Jewish couplings no longer challenged external sociopolitical and cultural barriers. Instead, they looked backward, using the radical shock factor of screen taboo as an intergenerational rhetoric of reassurance and continuance at a time of global dominance for the American media industries.

THE GAY FANTASIA

Angels in America, A Gay Fantasia on National Themes, Part One: Millennium Approaches was immediately hailed as the first major work of theater to emerge on Broadway in the early 1990s. The play's bold, unapologetic political engagement with the AIDS crisis of the 1980s drew a direct connection between historical re-creation and subculture marginalization. It did so by reviving the figural centerpiece of both earlier waves of political liberalism in popular media, the Anglo-Christian-Jewish coupling. Part One of the nearly eight-hour drama premiered on May 4, 1993, at the Mark Taper Forum in Los Angeles to rapturous critical and commercial acclaim. Playwright Tony Kushner authored a tapestry of everyday life in which love, identity, and sexual desire within individuals became reflections of cultural histories and historical crises during a period of political and sexual closeting. Six months later, Part Two premiered, with both parts playing in repertory.[2] The politically charged subject matter—the exploration of gay life, both out and closeted—challenged audiences accustomed to lighter fare. The unabashed liberal politics also put forth a potent critique of Reagan-era indifference to AIDS in the 1980s. It was theater as sociopolitical critique, and it had a transformative impact on subsequent Broadway theater of the mid-1990s.

Set in New York in 1985, the sweeping multi-character, multi-plotted drama was the first major theatrical experience since Larry Kramer's *The Normal Heart* (1985) to examine the political and cultural context of the AIDS crisis during the Reagan years. Echoing the play's provocative subject matter was a second layer of representational critique: the play is blatantly Jewish.[3] Jewishness, as a religion, a philosophy, and a cultural identity, moves though nearly all the play's numerous plotlines, framing a pastiche of both gay and straight lives grappling with generational fallouts and emotional crises. The 1980s-era Jewishness had moved into metamorph and code to allow for Reagan's sunny fantasies of Anglo-Christian restoration to ascend to the center of American popular culture. Kushner's response followed the template of the second wave in the late 1960s: the privileging of sexually and culturally unapologetic Jewishness as liberal political critique.

Kushner integrates one historical event at the center of the many narratives, the decline and death of Roy Cohn (Ron Liebman) from AIDS. Cohn, the Jewish lawyer who had famously prosecuted the Rosenbergs in 1951 and then went to work for Senator Joseph McCarthy in his crusade against communism, is presented as a closeted gay man for whom self-hatred and Jewishness are extensions of the same postwar disassociations. When Cohn is first diagnosed in the play, he denies to his doctor both that he is gay and that he has AIDS. Instead, Cohn insists that he is merely a lifelong bachelor and has liver cancer. Kushner's indictment of closeting as a form of conservative fiction therefore linked the persecution of the Mc-

Carthy years in the 1950s to the AIDS crisis in the 1980s. As Cohn slowly gets sick, he refuses to acquiesce to his reality even as he suffers hallucinations. Even when the ghost of Ethel Rosenberg confronts him over his actions, Cohn remains defiant. He dies, unrepentant, an indictment of Jewish self-denial as complicit in numerous intersecting postwar traumas.

The real Cohn had been known as McCarthy's "Jewish Pit Bull," the Semitic face meant to give cover to McCarthy to inure him from charges of anti-Semitism.[4] In Kushner's interpretation of Cohn as a tragic Shakespearean (or perhaps Dickensian) figure, Rosenberg's ghost emerges, Hamlet-style, as a haunting reminder of repressed Jewishness operating as its own form of closeting. She haunts Cohn as a reminder of the unresolved legacy of this sublimation as it carried forward into the Reagan years.[5] This link between queerness and Jewishness—from Otto Weininger to Adolf Hitler, and from Joseph McCarthy to Ronald Reagan—locates Cohn's struggle within the Benjaminian "Last Angel" framework of the play's title. The blacklist of the 1950s and the AIDS crisis of the 1980s reveal the same cultural processes of erasure and subsumed memory in Cohn's dual Jewish and queer closeting.

Counterpointing Cohn's denial is the romantic pairing of two young, urbane, gay New Yorkers, the Anglo-Saxon Prior Walter (Stephen Spinella) and his lover, an uptight Jewish lawyer named Louis Ironson (Joe Mantello). Prior and Louis represent both physical and personality contrasts. Prior is a good-looking young, white, Anglo-Saxon Protestant of inherited wealth and cultural privilege. He is also HIV-positive. The panicked, nervous Louis begins as the second-wave Jewish cliché: highly verbal, neurotic, and self-centered. Despite taking numerous sexual risks over the course of the play, Louis remains HIV-negative. In intercutting these stories, Kushner draws a thematic link between Cohn's impending death and Ironson's denial. Both characters are products of subsumed Jewish trauma. Ironson's narcissism and self-denial are next-generation extensions of the same internal struggles of Roy Cohn.

As the parallel stories of Louis and Cohn play out, Kushner creates an intergenerational pastiche of what Alisa Solomon and James Fisher describe as the metaphorical Jew of history.[6] Cohn is the hidden, displaced, self-hating, postwar Jew who tried to ingratiate himself into Anglo-Saxon American conservatism. Louis is the liberal, neurotic, self-destructive Jew of the 1980s. Both seek approval from the Anglo-Saxon power structure. Kushner's depiction of American Jewishness is one of alternating longing and repulsion for a world that can never fully accept them.

Both the play and the miniseries open on a funeral for Louis's grandmother, a survivor of pogroms who immigrated to the United States

Prior Walter (Justin Kirk) and Louis Ironson (Ben Shenkman) break up under the stress of the conservative social climate and AIDS crisis of the mid-1980s in Mike Nichols's 2003 HBO adaptation of Tony Kushner's Angels in America: A Gay Fantasia on National Themes *(1993).*

through Ellis Island. In this opening scene, Louis listens to the rabbi explain the struggle of her Ellis Island journey and efforts at assimilation. Starting with this grand progression narrative at a moment of death, Kushner traces the origins of intergenerational Jewish postmemory back to the first generation of immigrant Jews of the 1910s and 1920s. Louis's feelings of inadequacy regarding his own life are the inciting incident of the play. His subsequent confusion, self-hatred, and ritual compulsion to seek sexual validation through the non-Jewish partner are each linked to his inability to feel worthy of her sacrifices.

After returning from the funeral, a panic-stricken Louis struggles to confront the fact that his lover, Prior, has HIV. As Prior grows sicker, Louis flees, unable to cope. He begins an affair with a closeted, married Mormon lawyer, Joe Pitt (David Marshall Grant). Louis's sublimated and redirected death panic, a dual reaction to his grandmother's and his lover's declining health, eventually seeks out the blond-haired, blue-eyed embodiment of his opposite in the form of a Mormon. This compulsive sexual selection is driven by the desire for self-negation. As with Cohn's prosecution and the eventual execution of Ethel Rosenberg a generation earlier, Louis seeks to both purge and deny his Jewishness. Yet, both lawyers fail to do so. Cohn remains haunted by the memory of Ethel, a Yiddishe mama archetype whose ghost continues to taunt him over the course of the play as he dies from AIDS. Louis likewise finds no relief. His desire for the WASP or the Mormon lover are ultimately false efforts to cure the alienation that he has internalized.

At first, the Prior/Louis coupling appears to be yet another use of Anglo-Christian-Jewish entanglement to explore themes of political and cultural displacement. But *Angels in America* was not merely a continuation of the political-personal historiography seen in the 1970s. The play's eventual disinterest in both couples and Louis's descent into self-pity and isolation identified its intervention not as a historical corrective but as a dissonant, decoherent critique. This de-coherence is also expressed in the play's fractured breaks from its diegetic world. Characters easily step in and out of fantasy sequences. The multi-character, sweeping yet episodic narrative refuses easy answers and structured closure. The blurring of the real and stage Roy Cohn furthers this obfuscation between the real and the fictive. This experimentation with form thematizes the play's exploration of the AIDS crisis as incomprehensible fracture, rather than restorative cohesion.

Kushner's titular reference to Walter Benjamin's famous "Last Angel of History" served as a self-reflexive reminder of the play's awareness of how sweeping historical events are actually produced through the minutia of everyday life. In 1937, on the cusp of witnessing the full specter of the emerging Holocaust in his native Germany, forty-eight-year-old German-Jewish cultural theorist Walter Benjamin penned his famous "Theses on the Philosophy of History." Inspired by *Angelus Novus*, a drawing by Paul Klee, Benjamin proposed obliterating the notion of history as a causal chain of events. He argued that history must be understood as a single, extended, traumatic displacement between the seen and the unseen, playing out over and over, generationally, for centuries.

As with the mouse-mountains to which Benjamin aspired while experimenting with hashish (see chapter 1), this concept of a witnessing Angel was rooted in the link among fragmentation, modernism, and Jewish mysticism. Anglo-Saxon privilege, in the form of Walter, locates at the core of American progression narratives. Louis's (and Cohn's) Jewishness operates as its alienated counterweight. Witnessing the tragedy of the gay plague is the Last Angel, a female siren who appears to Prior during his illness after Louis leaves him. The Last Angel identifies the AIDS crisis as both an extension of European-American immigrant Jewish displacement as well as an extension of modernist modes of alienation. The real Roy Cohn's failing health was a modern Shakespearean tragedy. His actions in the 1950s and his twin self-hatred as both a Jew and gay made him a villain. But this closeting was its own form of residual historical debris. The romantic entanglement of American Christian aristocracy (Prior Walter) and Jewish immigration (Louis Ironson) reflected Cohn's postwar crisis of identity by recalling second-wave visibility. But when Louis abandons Prior in his time of need, another tragedy takes place. By reducing the historical to tales of coupling and death, Kushner deploys Benjamin's Last Angel as the connective tissue between the personal and the political. Benjamin's angel argued that trauma and sublimation lurked as haunting specters within the grand narratives of history. In Kushner's update, narrative causality itself is another form of false reassurance. History can only exist in art as tangential affect. Its fractured legacies located not in grand narratives but in the margins, in transgressive desire.

Ten years later, the 2003 HBO version of *Angels in America* amplified the play's renegotiation of second-wave historiography tropes. This began in the choice of director Mike Nichols to adapt the play into a miniseries. In 1967, Nichols had upended normative masculine identifiers by casting Dustin Hoffman rather than Robert Redford in *The Graduate*, as discussed in chapter 4. In 2003, Nichols performed another thematic casting substitution. He cast Al Pacino, one of the most famous Italian-American actors of the New Hollywood movement, as Roy Cohn. Pacino-as-Cohn produced a similar inversion affect. The actual Cohn's Jewish and gay identities were sublimated and consumed by postwar conformity in the McCarthy era. Pacino-as-Cohn offered a haunting reminder of historical trauma by foregrounding this displacement through inversion. The character was a second-level ironic revision. It introduced a casting counterpoint that problematized the very concept of visible screen Jewishness in the late 1960s and 1970s as a response to the political and cultural absences brought about by HUAC and Joe McCarthy. In Nichols's meta-joke, if Benjamin Braddock could be played by Dustin Hoffman, Roy Cohn could be Al Pacino.

Nichols amplified this notion of displaced historical Jewishness by also casting one of the most famous shiksa actors of her generation, Meryl Streep, in not one, but two Jewish roles. Streep appears as both the ghost of Ethel Rosenberg and in Hasidic drag as the wizened (fictional) sage, Rabbi Chemelwetz. This pastiche, featuring the star of *Holocaust* and *Sophie's Choice*, represents the ironic completion of Roy Cohn's assimilationist, denatured Jewish dream. In Nichols's take on Kushner's gay fantasia, both Al Pacino and Meryl Streep can be Jewish. On Broadway, this absence was indicted as residual traumas of the conservative era that had exacerbated the AIDS crisis. On HBO, it marked a break from the wholesome Anglo-Christian nuclear families of the prime-time network sitcom era. But both versions were about transforming and updating the mediums in which they appeared for the new identity politics of the 1990s.

Three years after the Broadway success of *Angels in America*, Jonathan Larson's Pulitzer Prize–winning musical, *Rent* (1996), confirmed the pairing of Christian and Jewish men as a template for exploring memory, subjectivity, screen media, and the traumas of AIDS. The central story within the large ensemble cast is the friendship of musician Roger Davis (Adam Pascal) and documentary filmmaker Mark Cohen (Anthony Rapp), two young, unemployed artists living in poverty in the East Village of New York in 1989 at the peak of the AIDS crisis. While not explicitly romantic or sexual, the pairing of Roger and Mark thematically continued the Prior/Louis dynamic in *Angels in America*. Like Prior, the laconic, Anglo-Christian Roger has AIDS. Like Louis, the neurotic, verbose Mark does not. Louis and Mark operate as twin witnesses to the impending illness of their partners. Mark remains both inside and outside the text, the Jewish filmmaker witness recording a period of cataclysmic change brought on by the AIDS crisis. The more cowardly Louis refuses to participate, attempting to hide and isolate himself from his partner's inevitable death.

Roger's love affair with the equally AIDS-afflicted Mimi (Daphne Rubin-Vega) is presented as a tragic star-crossed fairy tale, echoing the *La Boheme* source material. In contrast, Mark's rejection by his bisexual girlfriend, Maureen (Idina Menzel), is familiar schlemiel comedy. When it is revealed that Maureen has left Mark for a lesbian relationship with Joanne (Fredi Walker-Browne), an Ivy League–educated lawyer, Mark's masculine lack becomes central to the comedic voice of the play. In contrast, Roger is the authorial straight man, narrating and explaining the events as the ensemble struggles with death, poverty, and creative ambitions.

The enormous critical and economic successes of both *Angels in America* and *Rent* in the mid-1990s proved a turning point. Mainstream Broadway theater could now directly engage with marginalized ethno-cultural identity and alternative sexuality in ways that film and television of the time could not. Three period-piece musicals—*Parade* (1998), *Ragtime* (1998), and *Hedwig and the Angry Inch* (1998)—soon followed this approach. Each explored the intersection of history, politics, media, and memory by focusing on transgressive, taboo Anglo-Christian-Jewish couplings. *Parade* focused on the events surrounding the lynching of Jewish shop owner Leo Frank (Brent Carver) over false accusations that he'd raped and murdered one of his employees, a thirteen-year-old Catholic girl named Mary Phagan (Christy Carlson Romano) in Georgia in 1913. With music and lyrics by Jason Robert Brown, *Parade* did not shy away from direct discussions of Frank's assimilated Jewish identity. Even as the forces of historical anti-Semitism marshal against him, he remains clueless, a displaced Jew only able to recognize his displacement at the moment of his death. This is revealed in the play when Frank chooses to sing the *Sh'ma*, the holiest Hebrew prayer, at the moment of his lynching. His epiphany is to reveal himself as a Jew. The revelation was as much a commentary on visible Jewishness in the Broadway theater of the 1990s as it was on the play's ostensible period subject matter. The depiction of an alienated, emancipated Jew struggling to comprehend the legacy of American anti-Semitism directly spoke to the revisionist historicity taking place.

Similar to *Parade*, *Ragtime* (1998) revisits the immigrant experience of the first few years of the twentieth century. The narrative follows three intersecting stories of Jewish, black, and Anglo-Saxon families. Each family eventually overlaps and blurs into the other as they become increasingly assimilated. In the Jewish story, Tateh (Peter Friedman), a Yiddish-inflected artist, emigrates from Latvia with his young daughter and struggles to make ends meet in the ghettos of New York. Tateh's assimilation follows a familiar path. He eventually marries the character of Mother (Marin Mazzie), the matriarch of an aristocratic, Brahmin family living in New Rochelle, New York. Mother's husband, Father (Mark Jacoby), has died violently in World War I. The play's naming conventions establish the basic theme of Anglo-Saxon power coming apart in the twentieth century. The breakup of the national-historical model of marriage, Mother and Father, allows Tateh full entrance into American society through the familiar path of intermarriage.

Hedwig and the Angry Inch (1998) uses very different formal and thematic styles while offering a similar assimilation narrative, albeit ostensibly outside of the United States. Written by and starring John Cameron Mitchell, *Hedwig* maps the political crisis of German identity during reunification in the late 1980s through a gender-queered glam-rock band led by a German transsexual and her drag queen husband. East German rock star Hedwig (Mitchell) presents an amalgam of 1970s-era glam rock steeped in the political crises of the late 1980s. Hedwig, formerly Hansel, struggles with a failed sex change operation that leaves her in a hybrid state. Her scrambled gender signifiers comment on the confusion of Europe at the critical moment of the end of the Cold War. This is reflected by Hedwig's troubled relationship with her husband, Yitzak, a Croatian Jewish drag queen.[7] The abusive Yitzak heckles Hedwig, operating as both foil and support system as Hedwig tells her life story. Through winning the love of Yitzak, Hedwig's eventual transformation from Hansel Schmidt to Hedwig Robison acts as a next-generation take on *The Jazz Singer*. Cross-dressing has replaced blackface and the Anglo-German has taken center stage while the Jew has moved to the wings. But the Anglo-Christian-Jewish coupling of Yitzak and Hedwig validates these transformations just as it did for Jack and Mary in 1927.

From *The Melting Pot* (1909) to *Fiddler on the Roof* in the 1960s, the transgressive yet progressive nature of the Jewish-Christian coupling was an established trope of the American stage. When it reemerged in the 1990s, it used familiar iconography and period-piece settings to rethink and revisit how history and memory are preserved through artistic re-creation. Prior/Louis, Mark/Roger, Leo/Mary, Tateh/Mother, and Hedwig/Yitzak each foregrounded and subverted variations of anti-Semitic historical stereotypes. Leo, Louis, and Mark are neurotic, verbose nebbishes. Yitzak is the wandering Israeli hyper-masculine male in full gender masquerade. But each character produces Jewishness as a manifestation of the stereotypes and marginalized cultures lurking within the grand sweeping events of history.

The uniting element within each of these plays is the critique of the constructed nature of historical chronology. The entrance of transgressive Jewish deviancy, real or imagined, into each of these landscapes creates an immediate temporal dissonance. The Jew is a timeline disruptor. Part One of *Angels in America* is titled *Millennium Approaches*. The entrance of the Last Angel of History signifies a transcendent break between the real and the spirit worlds even as Ethel Rosenberg haunts the 1980s as a specter of anti-Semitic violence in the 1950s. Songs in *Rent* such as "Seasons of Love" (lyric: "525,600 minutes") and "What You Own" (lyric: "when you're living in America at the end of the millennium") make repeated references to the passage of time and crossing from the twentieth century to the twenty-first century. "The Origin of Love" from *Hedwig and the Angry Inch* offers a pastiche of historical constructions of erotic taboo from ancient Greece to today. This occurs as Hedwig's gendered body paradox operates as a metaphor for the impossibility of postwar German reunification. "New Music" from *Ragtime* thematizes the miscegenation between European immigrant melodies and American ragtime through melodic crossings that scramble any easy progression narrative. Each of these plays indicted the inherently linear, chronological form of live theater as the means to critique the embedded biases of historical progression narratives.

This anxiety of temporal crossing was distilled to its most basic binary in Jason Robert Brown's off-Broadway love story musical, *The Last Five Years* (2000). Composer/lyricist Brown's follow-up to *Parade* featured only two characters, the Catholic Cathy Hiatt (Lauren Kennedy/Sherie Rene Scott) and the Jewish Jamie Wellerstein (Norbert Leo Butz). The minimalist set and unusual narrative structure linked temporal discontinuity to the isometric opposition of an Anglo-Christian-Jewish love story told in two parts. The story focuses on Cathy and Jamie's discordant five-year-long romance, marriage, and divorce. The play is structured in contradictory timelines. The hopeful, idealistic Jamie sings about the major events of his courtship of Cathy from their first meeting to their final breakup, five years later. The mournful Cathy experiences these same events, but in reverse chronological order, beginning with the divorce and ending with meeting Jamie for the first time. Both storylines are performed simultaneously. This creates a dissonance in which each character is experiencing a different event in the timeline. By the midpoint of the musical, the spectator is forced to recall earlier events as they play out a second time, told through the perspective of the opposite character.

This timeline scrambling creates a bifurcated theatrical experience. Jamie and Cathy are prevented from occupying and experiencing the same event at the same time. The themes of subjective, chronological dissonance become a metaphor for their relationship dissolution. This plays out on both gender and ethno-cultural fault lines. Jamie's first song, "Shiksa Goddess," establishes the familiar Portnoy/schlemiel purging of self-hatred through acquisition of the Anglo female. As Jamie moves forward and Cathy works backward, they meet in the middle to sing only one song, "The Next Ten Minutes." This temporal and spatial union at their wedding is short-lived. When the song ends, Jamie continues forward into the marriage while Cathy continues in reverse, tracing back to the origins of the relationship.

Through temporal fracture, the coming together and breakup of Anglo-Christian-Jewish couplings in these plays offered a revival of the socio-political potency of the second wave. In this third-wave indictment, time-lines are revealed to be an extension of Anglo-Christian fantasy, a form of enforced, ideologically polarized storytelling that obscures the marginalized and ignores the traumatized. As with Holocaust media in the 1970s and 1980s (discussed in chapter 7), the rupturing and scrambling of stage-time by "Jewishness" offered a reminder of the impossibility of reducing real historical events to a cohesive (Christian) form.

In each of these examples, "Jewishness" on stage operated as rupturing manifestations of Benjamin's Last Angel, a reminder of this impossible relationship between historical event and artistic recreation. Louis Ironson, Roy Cohn, Mark Cohen, Leo Frank, Yitzhak, and Jamie Wellerstein collectively embody (and satirize) stereotypes of Jewish men as queered, flawed, alienated, marginalized, and disassociated observers of the Christonormative world. But, through achronological and temporal disconnect, they reclaim a semblance of lost and marginalized memory. In this third-wave iteration, the specific pairing of Anglo-Christian and Jew was no longer just a topic for narrative exploration. It had become an allegorical tool meant to offer a collective indictment of any historical truth claim within the populist tropes of mass culture fantasy.

Experimental time chronologies on Broadway used the established tropes of Anglo-Christian-Jewish couplings to critique and scramble dominant modes of telling history. Graphic fluid comedies of late 1990s Hollywood appeared to have nothing in common with this approach. This raunchy film movement used displays of semen, urine, vomit, menstrual blood, birthing vaginas, and exposed penises as apparently nothing more than comedic shock props building on sex comedy genre traditions.[8] This emerging taboo-challenging subgenre also hinted at the metamorphic body mutations of the 1980s. The graphic display of fluids quickly became framed by a familiar allegory.[9] The screen body that most often ushered in this transformation was, perhaps unsurprisingly, the comedic, neurotic Jew. The witness and object of these explosive secretions was, once again, the Anglo-Christian. The graphic display of bodily fluids may have been new to mainstream popular cinema. But the comedic tension released by this imagery was not.

The wave built slowly. The first third-wave movie star to proudly and unapologetically revive Jewish/shiksa humor was actor-director Ben Stiller.[10] Stiller, the child of second-wave Catholic-Jewish comedy team Jerry Stiller and Anne Meara, was a natural to inherit the generational pattern. His directorial debut, *Reality Bites* (1994), established his emerging role as a next-generation, self-aware schlemiel. Early in the film, Stiller's character, Michael Grates, "outs" himself as Jewish to both his romantic interest, Lelaina (Winona Ryder), and to the audience, confessing to Lelaina that he is a "non-practicing Jew." Her humorous response, "Well, I'm a non-practicing virgin!," played off the second-wave tradition of Jewish outing as a form of sexual confession.[11]

Later that year, *Saturday Night Live* (1975–) star Adam Sandler performed the soon to be enormously popular "The Hanukah Song" during a "Weekend Update" segment (Season 20, Episode 7, December 3, 1994). The bouncy sing-along, delivered directly to the camera, was introduced as a corrective to the feeling of Jewish alienation during the Christmas season. The song consisted of "outing" a list of various Jewish celebrities and entertainers who had previously not been widely known to be Jewish. Sandler's unapologetic third-wave identity operated as a historical corrective to the codings, marginalization, and obscurity of visible Jewishness in the 1980s.

Together, Stiller and Sandler marked a near-simultaneous breakthrough in returning male Jewish visibility to the center of mainstream cinema.[12] Sandler's infantile man-child persona on *Saturday Night Live* easily translated to slapstick feature comedies such as *Billy Madison* (1995), *Happy Gilmore* (1996), and *The Wedding Singer* (1998).[13] But it was Ben Stiller's performance in the massively successful *There's Something About Mary* (1998) that solidified the transition of sitcom patterns, and the emergence of fluid comedy, into mainstream studio success.

Stiller's performance as Ted, a former high school geek with a stalker-like obsession with Mary (Cameron Diaz), reintroduced the libidinal, carnally disruptive Jew into the mainstream rom-com. But there was an update to the familiar pattern. The first major comic set piece features the high-school-aged Ted accidentally getting his genitalia caught in his zipper on prom night. Mary, along with her parents, enters the bathroom and witnesses the accident. Ted's humiliation is compounded when the medical team arrives and he is wheeled out on a gurney for the world to see. From an obvious Freudian perspective, the scene can be read as a comedic take on castration anxiety. But it also contains an allusion to Jewish circumcision as a hidden marker of difference. The thwarted attempts of the Jewish schlemiel to acquire the blonde dream girl contextualize the film in a late-1960s, post-Portnoy configuration. But the display of Ted's genitalia caught in his zipper offered a new graphic boldness. Stereotypical male Jewishness, at once both compulsively sexual and utterly inept, was embodied by visceral imagery and graphic subject matter. The tactility of Ben Stiller's injured Jewish body on physical display was a new form of meta-morph. It introduced an updated version of second-wave schlemiel through a new visual trope: the comedic display of the Jewish penis.

A later comic sequence builds to produce the iconic imagery that was essential to the film's advertising strategy. In a hotel room in Miami, Ted decides to masturbate before his date with Mary. The film shows Ted masturbating through a lingering close-up on his facial reaction. His contorted face is intercut with Mary arriving at the exact moment of Ted's orgasm. As he quickly attempts to gather himself, he realizes he's lost track of his heretofore unseen semen. When Ted opens the door for Mary, the semen is revealed to be clinging to his ear. The delayed reveal, just as with Ted's zipper-stuck genitalia, pays off as a graphic punch line. The audience does not see the reveal until Mary does. She is the shiksa witness to Ted's psychosexual trauma.

Semen and injured genitals mark repeated humiliations for Ted in front of Mary. But they also perform Jewish return as an eventual triumph over the obstacles of stereotypical Jewishness. Ted eventually succeeds in wooing Mary away from a number of other suitors (the last of whom is, in a final joke on contrasting masculine archetypes, hyper-masculine football player Brett Favre). The tried-and-true humor of the hapless Jewish schle-miel's pursuit of the shiksa found itself updated by graphic imagery as a new form of comedic outrageousness.

The massively successful high school sex comedy *American Pie* (1999) confirmed the same Jewish-fluid body connection. Similar to the first ver-sion of Ted in *There's Something About Mary*, Jim Levenstein (Jason Biggs), the film's protagonist, is a horny, virginal high school nerd.[14] Jim's role as a young, compulsively libidinal Jewish schlemiel is tempered by the film's self-aware, next-generation reminder of the Jewish origins of this humor. This is presented in the character of Jim's Dad, Noah Levenstein (Eugene Levy). Jim's Dad is an equally hyper-sexual, even more perverted elder schlemiel, a satire of the taboo carnal Jews of the second wave. Through-out the film, Jim's attempts at sex are repeatedly thwarted by either his well-meaning father or various other external obstacles. But, in a comedic twist, Jim's father responds to Jim's sexual experimentations not with outrage but with encouragement. He buys Jim a number of graphic porn magazines. He makes frequent, awkward attempts to discuss sex with Jim. This in-version of the typical parental obstacles in the sex comedy offered a re-minder of the previous generation's own experimentations with sexual ad-ventures. As the title implies, it locates Jim's sexual impulses not as a danger to the nation, but as a supportive element of a new, sexually liberal but pro-American sensibility.

American Pie contains numerous examples of fluid humor. In one se-quence, the character of Kevin (Thomas Ian Nicholas) relieves his sexual tension by masturbating into a cup at a party. Shortly thereafter, Jim's luck-less, horny friend, Stifler (Seann William Scott) accidentally drinks from the semen-tainted drink, nearly causing him to vomit. In the film's titu-lar sequence, the horny Jim, having been told that a vagina feels like "warm apple pie," decides to at first finger and then mount an apple pie his mother has recently baked. The frustrated (Jewish) virgin mounting an icon of American nationalism brought to the fore competing discourses of sexual taboo and national preservation that defined the genre it was reviving. Jim was the inheritor of the legacy of the subversive post-Portnoy second wave.

Jim's sexual haplessness reaches its comedic nadir in the film's parody of a pornographic fantasy sequence. Jim convinces Nadia (Shannon Eliza-beth), a sexually cartoonish Czechoslovakian exchange student, to accom-pany him back to his house to study. Jim and Nadia enter his room, caus-ing Jim to experience a sexual panic attack. He leaves the room and then returns to discover that Nadia has located the porn magazines his father purchased for him. Assuming this is the inevitable humiliation and antici-pating her disgust, Jim profusely apologizes. But the normative gender roles

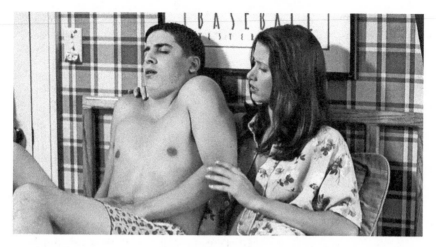

Nerdy Jim Levenstein (Jason Biggs) finds his attempts to seduce Czechoslovakian for-
eign exchange student Nadia (Shannon Elizabeth) ruined by performance anxiety, the
distractions of graphic pornography, and the emerging threat of the Internet in American Pie *(1999)*.

quickly invert. Aroused by the magazines, Nadia becomes the empowered figure, taking over the traditional masculine role. She begins to masturbate to the magazines, while demanding that Jim dance in front of her and perform a slow strip tease. Jim is both feminized and objectified. At first, he is humiliated by the dance, only reluctantly participating to satisfy Nadia's request. But Jim gradually discovers he enjoys the dance, getting more and more into it and losing focus on Nadia. The two are interrupted when Jim discovers that he's left his web camera active and is accidentally broadcasting the entire experience on the Internet to his friends and family. The performance space in which hapless Jewish sexuality is inherently comedic had been updated for the emerging virtual space of new media. But the joke followed the same premise. Jim was the ineffectual Jewish schlemiel tripped up into chaos by his compulsive carnal desires for the non-Jewish female.

The final reward for Jim's survival of numerous humiliations is the successful conquest of the shiksa. At first, this is presumed to be Nadia. But in the finale of the film, Jim discovers that his nerdy, flute-playing, band-camp-obsessed classmate, Michelle Flaherty (Alyson Hannigan), is the real partner for his sexual maturation. Michelle reveals this by perverting her own stereotype as the innocent, sexless female virgin. She announces to Jim that she repeatedly used her flute at band camp to masturbate. Her awkward revelation is the cue that Jim has finally located a viable sex partner. The scene concludes with yet another inversion. Michelle climbs on top of

Jim, smacks him in the face, and demands that he answer the question, "What's my name, bitch?" Jim is once again on the bottom, feminized, and transformed into a "bitch." But this confirmation of Jewish stereotype still represents a triumph. The Jewish schlemiel had succeeded.

In these early examples, semen, vomit, visible erections, and injured penises became to the third wave what graphic language, adultery, and unbridled displays of lust had been to the second. Jim, like Ted in *There's Something About Mary*, is the specter of second-wave carnality returned as safe context for the emerging popularity of comedic, graphic transgressions.

SECOND-WAVE SPECTERS

One of the first studio pictures to mainstream second-wave/third-wave tension was the massively successful romantic comedy, *Meet the Parents* (2000). It offered a nostalgic recall of Anglo-Christian-Jewish family screwball comedies from *The Cohens and Kellys* (1926) to *The Heartbreak Kid* (1972). Yet, an important distinction codified around the film's third-wave Jewish protagonist, Greg "Gaylord" Focker (Ben Stiller). In both the first and second waves, male and female Jews were keenly aware of the cultural and generational barriers attempting to block their coupling with Anglo-Christian partners. Greg lacks this awareness. An assimilated Jew who remains completely unaware of anti-Semitism as a viable structural force, he is unprepared for the resistance he experiences when he meets Harry Byrnes (Robert De Niro), the vaguely anti-Semitic Protestant father of his girlfriend, Pam Byrnes (Teri Polo). Harry is identified as a politically conservative, clueless product of the silent majority of the 1960s, longing for the time before drugs, sex, and rock and roll ruined everything. Greg fails to recognize how his Jewishness marks him as a continuation of counterculture sensibilities in the eyes of Harry.

This post-"Jewish" cluelessness offered both a cultural indictment of alienated Generation-X Jews and a satire of generational privilege among Jews and non-Jews alike. It also satirized the hidden legacy of second-wave barriers still at play in the 1990s and 2000s. The film's submerged cultural fault lines remained imperceptible to Greg and, by proxy, his generation of assimilated Jews.

One sequence highlighted this lack of awareness. Greg presents a gift to Jack shortly after meeting. Jack opens the present to reveal nothing more than a large pot of dirt. Greg explains that the dirt contains the seed of a Jerusalem tulip, a flower so rare that it takes months to bloom. The absent flower immediately forms a visual joke. By not being present and yet being identified as from Jerusalem, the relationship between Jewishness and the absence that locates at the center of twentieth-century anti-Semitism is made clear to the audience, if not yet to Greg himself. To Jack, the unflower and Greg are both negative, flawed constructions of incomplete identity.[15]

Through a continuing series of unfortunate events, Greg's Jewishness continues to emerge as the central cultural dividing factor. His job as a nurse is mocked by two members of the extended Byrnes family, Dr. Larry Banks (James Rebhorn) and his son, Dr. Bob Banks (Thomas McCarthy). When asked to say grace by Jack before dinner, Greg ends up improvising lyrics from "Day By Day," a song from the 1960s musical, *Godspell*. When Greg's lost suitcase arrives from the airlines, Jack picks the lock and discovers ladies underwear. The suitcase was not Greg's, but the confusion furthers Jack's notion that Greg is secretly gay/queer, an amoral, Jewish pervert.

The film moves closest to the graphic techniques of fluid comedy in a sequence when Greg is forced to wear a tight Speedo bathing suit during a pool party. The various Anglo-Christian men in the extended Byrnes family take turns pointing and laughing at Greg's crotch, a direct allusion to the notion of Jewish men containing circumcised and therefore inadequate genitalia.[16] This feminizing/queering of Greg as a Jewish interloper in a Protestant world is also affirmed through physiognomic contrast with his rival for Pam's affections, the hyper-confident, Anglo-Saxon Wall Street millionaire Kevin Rawley (Owen Wilson). As Jack's fantasy son-in-law candidate, Kevin is presented as the Anglophilic ideal taken to a cartoonish extreme. He is a religiously Christian, wealthy, polite, sexually confident stockbroker who was once engaged to Pam. As the classic blonde shiksa object of desire, Pam becomes the contested object over which Greg and Kevin spar.

The cliché of Kevin as a privileged, hyper-masculine Christian is made clear in the sequence when Jack takes Greg to Kevin's house. Kevin reveals that he's carved a wedding altar for Pam's sister's wedding out of a single block of driftwood. Kevin's impressive woodworking skills delight Jack as confirmation of Kevin's superior masculinity. This also provokes insecurity in Greg, as shown in the following exchange:

> Greg (to Kevin): What made you decide to become a woodworker?
> Kevin: I guess I would have to say Jesus. He was a carpenter, and I just figured if you're going to follow in someone's footsteps, who better than Christ?
> Greg: Hmm.

Jack: Greg's Jewish.

Kevin: Are you?

Greg: Yeah.

Kevin: Well, so was J. C.! Wow. You're in good company.[17]

Kevin's apparently benevolent condescension highlights the comedic intercultural conflict taking place. Greg enters the film unaware of his Jewishness as an important factor in his identity. Through contrast with Kevin's exaggerated Christianness, massive economic success, woodshop skills, and blondness, Greg becomes increasingly aware of the cultural signification of his background. This third-wave revival of second-wave contrast becomes its own form of intergenerational conflict, akin to the Jewish-Irish screwball comedies of the 1920s.

In the sequel, *Meet the Fockers* (2004), the comedic revival of second-wave coupling nostalgia is made even more literally. Dustin Hoffman and Barbra Streisand are introduced as Greg's parents, Bernie and Rozalin Focker. The film's use of the two most famous archetypes of unruly counterculture sexuality in the 1960s operates as a metatextual casting joke. They emerge as the id-like manifestation of Jack's subconscious anxieties about the true depth of Greg's hidden, counterculture-infused Jewish perversions.[18] Jack's worst nightmare about his future son-in-law has been confirmed. The two most famous sexualized Jewish schlemiels of the late 1960s have emerged to confirm it.[19]

The Hoffman/Streisand pairing also operated as a second-wave corrective. In the second wave, the lack of Jewish-Jewish couplings was a notable structuring absence. It remained for decades as the central non-negotiable caveat for Jewish visibility. So long as the screen Jew pursued the Christian partner, the screen Jew could perform unapologetic Jewishness while also remaining accessible to the non-Jewish spectator.[20] *Meet the Fockers* thus violated the one implicit taboo still in place after decades. Hoffman and Streisand, previously never paired together on screen, are finally free to celebrate their unbridled Jewishness.[21]

Yet, their purpose within the narrative is also to champion, encourage, and unabashedly celebrate Greg's marriage to the Anglo-Saxon Pam. This codified the handoff from second wave to third wave. The unbridled carnality of Hoffman and Streisand, exaggerated to comedic effect throughout the film, is negated by their advancing ages. Their hermeneutic Jewish world is tempered by the next generation. In order for the delayed Streisand/Hoffman coupling to take place, Stiller has to pursue his own Anglo-Saxon object of conquest and assimilation.

Meet the Parents and *Meet the Fockers* used contrasting Christian and

Suspicious father Jack Byrnes (Robert De Niro) administers a lie detector test to potential son-in-law Greg "Gaylord" Focker (Ben Stiller) in the most successful of the third-wave screwball coupling comedies, Meet the Parents *(2000).*

Jewish archetypes to visualize the legacy of culture conflicts of the 1960s and 1970s. Their enormous box-office success also confirmed the lucrative viability of returning Anglo-Christian-Jewish couplings to mainstream American cinema in the 2000s. They were two of the more notable of a wave of independent and studio films that began to grapple with similar second-wave specters.

Barry Levinson's semi-autobiographical *Liberty Heights* (1999) is another example. The film focused on nostalgia for the pre-counterculture suburbia. Set in Baltimore in the 1950s, the film centers on two Jewish brothers, played by Adrien Brody and Ben Foster, who explicitly date non-Jewish women, a blonde WASP (Carolyn Murphy) and an African-American (Rebekah Johnson). It also addressed the still mostly verboten subject of racial miscegenation, an issue nearly completely ignored in the second wave.

Keeping the Faith (2000) features a religious love triangle so steeped in Jewish-Catholic screen coupling traditions that Lawrence Baron describes it as a "multicultural *Jazz Singer*."[22] Ben Stiller's role as Jake, a reform rabbi, is contrasted with Edward Norton as Father Brian, Jake's best friend from childhood, now a Catholic priest. Jake and Brian are both obsessed with Anna (Jenna Elfman), their childhood friend turned mutual love interest. The barriers preventing Rabbi Jake and Father Brian from coupling with Anna are presented as cultural. Jake cannot marry outside his faith. Brian is celibate. The resolution to this coupling ends when Anna agrees to convert to Judaism to marry Jake, a decision that Brian accepts and embraces.[23]

The Jason Biggs vehicle, *Saving Silverman* (2001), provided an even more overt example of the virginal Catholic female fantasy. Recalling both *I Love You, Alice B. Toklas* and *The Heartbreak Kid*, *Saving Silverman* created a crisis of identity for the Jewish schlemiel through triangulation between a castrating, implied-Jewish fiancé, Judith (Amanda Peet), and an idealized, Christian female love interest, Sandy (Amanda Detmer). Jason Biggs's archetypal schlemiel, the passive, nerdy, Darren Silverman, becomes overwhelmed when he gets engaged to the beautiful but domineering Judith. Darren's best friends, J. D. (Jack Black) and Wayne (Steve Zahn), attempt to "save" Silverman by breaking up the impending nuptials. The pun on conversion/resurrection of the ineffectual Jewish male is made clear when Silverman's friends reintroduce him to his true love from high school, Sandy, a Catholic who is about to take her vows as a nun. "Saving" Silverman requires an erotic conversion. He must leave the Jewish American Princess and marry the blonde, blue-eyed embodiment of Catholic religious purity.[24] Only then will Silverman survive.

Kissing Jessica Stein (2001), an independent film co-written and starring the Jewish Jennifer Westfeldt in the titular role, relocated this notion of Jewish sexual transgression into gay subject matter. Jessica's Jewishness is foregrounded not only by her last name but also through numerous interactions with her Grandma Esther (Esther Wurmfeld), her rabbi (Hillel Friedman), and a scene set at Stein's family seder. As with *Liberty Heights*, the transgressive barrier locates by shifting the Anglo-Christian-Jewish barrier into a new area of transgression. Jessica begins a relationship with the non-Jewish Helen Cooper (Heather Juergensen), a transgression identified as both ethno-religiously cultural and gendered. Jessica's female schlemieldom is belied by her "conventional" attractiveness as the object of pursuit. She ultimately determines that she's not gay, however, and in the film's conclusion, another, far subtler, transgression is suggested. Jessica Stein's Jewish coworker, Josh Meyers (Scott Cohen), asks her out. The film concludes by hinting that the two will eventually fall in love and be together. Even in a tale of lesbian experimentation, it is the rare Jewish-Jewish coupling that remains beyond the film's reach.

Gay subject matter was not the only area being explored through transgressive Anglo-Christian-Jewish couplings. In 2003, the broad hip-hop-parodying romantic comedy *Marci X* was one of the first major studio releases of the third wave to focus on the female Jewish protagonist and to cross the racial divide. Directed by 1960s schlemiel icon and screen Portnoy, Richard Benjamin, and written by Jewish playwright Paul Rudnick, *Marci X* features Lisa Kudrow as Jewish American Princess stereotype Marci Feld. Marci is the reluctant inheritor of a struggling hip-hop record label founded by her father. Her clueless, forced entrance into engaging urban, black popular culture allows the film to play comedy across a broad range of racial and ethnic stereotypes. The plot leads Marci into a love story with African-American rapper Dr. S (Damon Wayans). The title's "X" riffs on 1960s-era black power removal of last names as a protest against slavery. But in assigning the "X" to Marci, the relational Jewishness/blackness demonstrated how third-wave relational couplings scrambled the identity politics of the 1960s.[25]

Garden State (2004) centralized ethno-religious identity as a form of denaturing. The film's meditative musings on twenty-something angst focus on the romantic relationship between writer-director-star Zach Braff's Jewish character of Andrew Largeman and his Christian love interest, Sam (Natalie Portman). Yet, the film complicates this familiar coupling binary by scrambling each family's ethno-religious stereotype. Sam's family is coded as stereotypically Jewish. They are neurotic, quirky, loud, and obnoxious, own numerous pets, and have an adopted African exchange student, Titembay (Ato Essandoh). In contrast, Andrew's purportedly Jewish father (Ian Holm) lives in a state of intense repression, isolation, and emotional dysfunction. This inversion is furthered by casting. Ian Holm's repressed WASP patriarch is textually "Jewish" but conceptually Anglo-Christian. The culturally Christian Sam is conceptually Jewish in performance and as identified by the Jewish actress Natalie Portman.

Until her directorial debut, *A Tale of Love and Darkness* (2016), in which she starred as a troubled Holocaust survivor, Portman had never played an explicitly Jewish character on screen. This was true despite the fact that Portman was well known in the popular press not only as openly Jewish but also because she was born in Israel and can speak fluent Hebrew. In a 2010 interview, Portman stated: "I've always tried to stay away from playing Jews. . . . I get like twenty Holocaust scripts a month, but I hate the genre."[26] Rachel Weisz, another Jewish-born actress who rarely plays Jewish characters, offered a similar perspective: "(W)e're Jewish, but we can get away with just being exotic. We're kind of Jews in disguise. Those cultural stereotypes about the Jew with the big hooky nose and the fleshy face rub off on you. In some way acting is prostitution, and Hollywood Jews don't want their own women to participate. Also, there's an element of *Portnoy's Complaint*—they all fancy Aryan blondes."[27]

Both Weisz and Portman's reticence to tackle female Jewishness on screen was a response to lingering shiksa idealization. This absence operated as its own form of second-wave specter. Weisz's reference to *Portnoy's Complaint* recalled the Hoffman/Streisand handoff in *Meet the Fockers*. Portman's reluctance to "out" herself was far closer to the career of Judy

Holliday than to that of Barbra Streisand. Their effort to disentangle Jewish women from second-wave iconography suggested a double standard at work. Jewish men still found their status both culturally celebrated and validated through the eyes of the Anglo-Christian love interest. Even with third-wave visibility on television sitcoms, female Jewish performers in cinema remained coded in an abstract, "exotic" status.

ROMANTIC FLUIDITY AND THE (JEWISH) BROMANCE

In the late 2000s, the films of Judd Apatow began to bridge the rom-com with the fluid com around the tropes of Anglo-Christian-Jewish pairings. Apatow's body of work, informally referred to as "bromance" romances, contested the traditional heterosexual love story by presenting groups of friends living lives of delayed maturity. Jewish masculinity played a critical role in Apatow's comedic technique. *Knocked Up* (2007) is probably Apatow's clearest example of this approach. The film hybridized the comedic techniques of the fluid comedy with an inverted coupling narrative structure.[28] The central conceit of the film located familiar second-wave schlemiel-shiksa contrast and romance. Posters and ad campaigns for the film featured the Jewish face of little-known actor Seth Rogen with the tagline, "What if this guy got you pregnant?" After an unlikely one-night stand with Ben Stone (Rogen), a lazy, unemployed, pot-smoking Jewish loser, Alison Scott (Katherine Heigl), an idealized, ambitious, talented blonde beauty, discovers that she is pregnant. To play up the contrast between the two, *Knocked Up* makes repeated references to Ben's Jewishness. When Ben and Alison first meet, she comments on his thick, curly hair in the following exchange:

> Alison: I love your curly hair! It's great . . . do you use product or anything?
> Ben Stone: No . . . I use, uh, "Jew," it's called.[29]

Much of the comedic tension between Ben and Alison emerges from their Jewish-WASP contrast. When Alison goes into labor, Ben is unable to locate her doctor, who is out of town, attending a bar mitzvah. Ben is forced to explain what a bar mitzvah is to the uncomprehending Alison. His housemates (Jason Segel, Martin Starr, Jonah Hill, and Jay Baruchel) also make repeated references to Jewishness, establishing Ben as living in a fully Jewish but infantilized world, much like that of Judy Benjamin in *Private Benjamin* (1980). His unexpected seductive success with Alison and her subsequent pregnancy are the calls to action that force Ben out of his Jewish group and into the larger world.

Unlike the second wave, no external barriers prevent Alison and Ben from coming together. To locate comedic tension, the film shifts its focus toward the internal struggle between the polite, ambitious Alison and the lazy man-child Ben.[30] The second-wave struggle for the schlemiel to seduce the shiksa is also removed. Ben's masculine flaws do not play out through his inability to seduce Alison. They instead emerge in his subsequent inability to cope with the maturation process that dealing with pregnancy requires.

The relationship between Ben and Alison also plays off the humor of unequal value. Ben's Jewish schlemiel is repeatedly identified as genetically inferior to Alison, the idealized blonde, blue-eyed object of beauty, by Alison's sister, Debbie (Leslie Mann). This is amplified by the fact that Leslie is also married to an implied-Jewish schlemiel, Pete (played by Jewish actor Paul Rudd). Ben and Alison's subsequent decision to have the child and attempt a relationship confirmed that the barriers of second-wave coupling had fallen. But the comedy located new problems within the couple's inability to feel validated by their choices.

Knocked Up continued the connection between taboo Jewishness and fluid comedy in the form of Alison's pregnant body. A shock-joke image of the live birth at the end of the film operates as a comedic violation of these established norms. At the moment Alison is about to give birth, Jay (Jay Baruchel) wanders into the birthing room to offer help. Jay (and the audience) experiences a direct image of Alison's pubic-hair-free genitals in mid-birth. The graphic image of Alison's vagina, a delayed reveal similar to Ted's injured scrotum in *There's Something About Mary*, pays off as a comedic violation. The breaching of cinematic taboo uses normative rupture as punch line. Yet, this violation is rendered safe and familiar though the comedic Jewish sexual panic it inspires in Jay.

Two additional films produced by Apatow in the late 2000s used similar graphic fluid comedy around archetypal Anglo-Christian-Jewish couplings. In the opening scene of *Forgetting Sarah Marshall* (2008), the sad crypto-Jewish protagonist, Peter Bretter (Jason Segel), is dumped by his dream girl, the blonde shiksa fantasy figure, Sarah Marshall (Kristen Bell). Stepping out of the shower, Peter is standing fully naked in front of Sarah when she breaks up with him. The shock-comedy moment uses a delayed reveal, eventually cutting to a close-up full frontal shot of Peter's naked penis. The imagery operates as a satire of (Jewish) castration anxiety, even as the film subsequently transitions into a far more conventional rom-com.[31] In *Superbad* (2007), a high school buddy virgin sex comedy written by Jewish writers Seth Rogen and Evan Goldberg, the anxieties of co-leads Seth (Jonah Hill) and Evan (Michael Cera) are visualized as sexual panic. Seth's disgust at discovering he has menstrual blood on his pants after dancing with a young woman and Evan graphically vomiting on his romantic interest right before he experiences intercourse for the first time are two of the more notable examples of the film's fluid comedy.

Apatow's creative ensemble of writers, actors, and directors, a group made up almost entirely of Jewish men, bridged the gap between the third-wave subgenres. In each of his films, vomit, urine, semen, and menstrual blood combine to identify graphic, taboo fluid comedy as the replacement for the antiquated sociopolitical barriers of the second wave. But these films also emphasized the idealized romantic/nostalgic aspirations of the traditional screwball pairing. Delayed maturity, rather than social or political issues, became the new comedic entanglements between screen Jews and their shiksa fantasies. But these conflicts were eventually surmountable. Romantic idealism, rather than cynicism or ambiguity, became the predominant message of these popular third-wave examples.

EXPANSION AND EXHAUSTION

By the late 2000s, the third wave was reaching both pinnacle and exhaustion. Couplings expanded in a number of new directions with a particular focus on the children of intermarriage.[32] The prime-time comedic soap *The O.C.* (2003–2007), focused on Seth Cohen (Adam Brody), the only child of a Jewish father, Sandy Cohen (Peter Gallagher), and Christian mother, Kirsten Cohen (Kelly Rowan).[33] *The Big Bang Theory* (2007–) and *New Girl* (2011–) both engage established tropes of the sexualized Jewish schlemiel within larger group contexts. On *The Big Bang Theory*, Howard Wolowitz (Simon Helberg), a nerdy Jewish aerospace engineer, offers a next-wave take on the second-wave schlemiel. Despite living at home with his dominating Jewish mother, Mrs. Wolowitz (Carol Ann Susi), Howard eventually gets engaged to an attractive Polish-Catholic woman, Bernadette Rostenkowski (Melissa Rauch). This familiar triangle set off an ongoing battle for control of Howard between Bernadette and Mrs. Wolowitz. Yet, in a comedic spin, Howard's mother is never seen on the show, except briefly from behind. She exists only as a disembodied, off-screen voice. Relieved of her corpus, Mrs. Wolowitz operates as an ephemeral Jewish joke. She becomes a satirical representation of the spectral (Jewish) Freudian phantoms haunting Howard's many neurotic impulses.[34]

A similar dynamic was produced around the Jewish yuppie Schmidt

(Max Greenfield) on *New Girl*. Schmidt offers a blend of familiar nebbishy traits (cooking, emotional outbursts) with a sexual proclivity to rival the carnal pursuits of second-wave Jews in the *Portnoy* era. In Season 1, Schmidt eventually begins dating Cecelia Parekh (Hannah Simone), a model of Indian descent. In an episode called "Kids" (Episode 21, April 17, 2012), Cece believes she has accidentally become pregnant with Schmidt's baby. Upon hearing the news, a joyous Schmidt remarks, "An Indian-Jewish baby? Who wouldn't want that? Think about the bone structure!" Schmidt then follows this up by listing a number of increasingly Jewish potential baby names while talking to the presumed fetus inside Cece's belly: "If you are a boy, I'm gonna name you Mordecai. Or Avra-cham . . . Menachem Mendel Schneerson . . ." Schmidt's indifference to Cece's Indian background is part of the joke of his narcissistic personality disorder. But the humor of his Jewish names suggests his subconscious connection to his ethno-cultural identity. Both Schmidt and Howard Wolowitz recall the 1970s tropes of schlemiel narcissism and neurotic indifference. Their respective engagements to the Catholic Bernadette and Indian Cecelia further cement these couplings as a form of nostalgic recall.[35]

Independent cinema also continued to use third-wave templates to explore marginalized identities. The coupling of actors Bryan Greenberg and Uma Thurman in *Prime* (2005) used Anglo-Christian-Jewish culture clash to explore the taboo notion of a much older woman with a younger man. *Nick and Norah's Infinite Playlist* (2008) and *Obvious Child* (2014) explore the sexual longings of the neurotic, young Jewish females attracted to non-Jewish men.[36] *Celeste and Jesse Forever* (2012) and *The Five-Year Engagement* (2012) examine delayed maturity and the crisis of marriage through coupling tensions brought about by secular Jewish characters who are surprised to discover connections to their repressed ethno-religious past.

By the early 2010s, these examples were increasingly moving to the margins. In studio films, Ben Stiller and Adam Sandler continued to star in romantic comedies. But Jewishness was an increasingly less relevant part of their on-screen characters.[37] On television, *Will and Grace, Mad About You, The Nanny,* and *Dharma & Greg* had all gone off the air. Sitcoms began replacing coupling comedy by emphasizing the interplay of multicultural groups and collectives engaging various social and class hierarchies to produce their narrative tensions. Shows such as *Two and a Half Men* (2003–2015), *How I Met Your Mother* (2005–2014), *Two Broke Girls* (2011–), *The Office* (2005–2013), *It's Always Sunny in Philadelphia* (2005–), and *Parks and Recreation* (2009–2015) focused on single life, friendship groups, and workplace. The raunchy feminist comedy of Jewish comedians, including Amy Schumer on *Inside Amy Schumer* (2012–) and the *Broad City* (2013–) comedy team of Abby Jacobson and Ilana Glazer, has continued to identify boundary-pushing sexuality as the province of taboo-violating Jewish unruliness. But scripted entertainment began to look elsewhere for visualizing societal fracture.

Perhaps the clearest coda to the third wave was seen in the sixth season of *Curb Your Enthusiasm* when Cheryl (Cheryl Hines) finally decides to divorce Larry (Larry David). By finally breaking up the Larry/Cheryl marriage, the neurotic Jewish shiksa lust and misanthropic alienation that had defined Anglo-Christian-Jewish couplings in the *Seinfeld* cycle had reached a thematic end point.[38]

Plato's Retweet

> *Ali (Gaby Hoffmann): You are telling me I didn't have a Bat Mitz-*
> *vah because Dad wanted to go out in the woods and dress up like a*
> *woman?*
> *Shelly (Judith Light): That, and you were a spoiled brat.*
>
> TRANSPARENT (2015)

*T*HE SECOND SEASON OF AMAZON STUDIO'S EMMY-
winning show about transgender and transsexual identity,
Transparent (2014–), begins with a gay wedding. Freed of societal prohibitions on gay marriage, Sarah Pfefferman (Amy Landecker) prepares to
marry her fiancée, Tammy Cashman (Melora Hardin). Sarah, the eldest
daughter of the Jewish Pfefferman family at the center of the show, is recently divorced and coming to terms with her lesbian identity. Her emergence is occurring at the same moment that her father, Mort Pfefferman
(Jeffrey Tambor), has begun to live openly as Maura, a transgender woman.
Yet, despite noble efforts to live authentic lives, Sarah, Maura, and the rest
of the Pfefferman clan struggle with generationally inflicted narcissism and
dysfunctional confusion rooted in their identities as Jews. Sarah's fiancée,
Tammy, a WASP Episcopalian, struggles with none of these issues. She is
the familiar screen Anglo-Saxon, a loving, Christonormative ideal. Despite
this open path to apparent happiness, Sarah self-sabotages the wedding.
She collapses in the bathroom in a state of neurotic confusion. Her reason,
expressed to her dysfunctional Jewish family members, is a familiar one:
Sarah is convinced that the incompatible WASP-Jewish dynamic of the two
families will ultimately prevent the union from succeeding.[1]

The collapse of the Sarah-Tammy wedding riffed on the recurring historical-cultural fault line analyzed in this book. From its debut in late 2014, *Transparent* has offered a groundbreaking exploration of transgender and transsexual identities, pushing the boundaries of what was and was not seen in mainstream entertainment. Yet, even in this world of enlightened visibility, embedded intergenerational schisms between Anglo-Saxon and Jewish archetypes remain. The lesbian nature of the Sarah-Tammy union was new to mainstream entertainment. But the embattled and collapsing Christian-Jewish wedding comedy drew from 1920s films such as *The Cohens and Kellys* and *Abie's Irish Rose*, Benjamin Braddock's cross-swinging liberator in *The Graduate*, and the wedding antics in *The Nanny, Meet the Fockers*, and *Knocked Up* in the 1990s and 2000s.[2]

In the introduction I proposed the concepts of "Christonormativity" and "coupling theory" as guiding theoretical frameworks for my research. Christonormativity is the process of sublimation of pre-Christian and non-Christian morality through the establishment of normative codes and iconography. It was an act of erasure developed over centuries of European art, politics, philosophy, and literature. Coupling theory provides a framework to unpack this interplay between absence and presence. The rhetoric of chronology, both individual (through reproduction) and national-historical, circulates between holistic and fragmented frameworks using the obvious totems of gendered, sexual, and other culturally recognizable figurations.

In the myriad examples provided in this book, from Benjamin and Mary Anne Disraeli to the Sarah-Tammy wedding in *Transparent*, Anglo-Christian-Jewish couples have negotiated the tensions of the mass media age. Couplings can embody Christonormativity and (Jewish) taboo, old world and new, desire and transcendence, chronology and disruption, cohesion and dissonance. Within this interplay, the uneasy relationship among ethnonationalism, identity, spectatorship, and technology is explored. As the entrenched power of European nation-states gave way to the dominance of the United States, the "Jew" manifested these tensions as an extension of Christonormative bifurcation. But, as coupling theory argues, both were part of the same generative process.

At the center of this entanglement is the contested notion of love. Plato's *The Symposium*, 2,500 years ago, argued that love was the search for an idealized state, what Lydia Amir describes as "the supreme object of desire."[3] When expressed as homosexual love, this desire located in creating one's self in the gendered other. When expressed heterosexually, love refracted into the imagined futurity of potential children. But, according to Plato, all cases of love—romantic, platonic, familial, and/or sexual—are an expression of a desire to immortalize the self through the other.[4]

When Constantine the Great legitimized the small but dedicated Christian sect as the official religion of the Roman Empire in 312, homosexuality, prostitution, and other libertine understandings of sexuality were subsequently repressed. Images were central to this containment. After Constantine, the European Christonormative landscape used the imagery of Jesus, the Virgin Mary, and the redemption of Mary Magdalene to redirect the meaning of "love" away from the sexual/carnal/corporeal and toward the idealized, abstract, and divine. This redefinition—what is now understood as platonic love—removed sexuality in favor of an idealized state of sexlessness and self-sacrificing devotion. This brought with it the production of a negative dialectic. The residue of pre-Christian sexuality remained.

This carnality was transferred into the most visible form of pre-Christian identity, the "Jew." This constructed Jewishness remained as a requisite, essentialized rejoinder to any claims of attainment of Jesus-like perfection. In this self/other binary, the "Jew" was the manifestation of the sexual while Christianity claimed the ephemeral, transformative, and transcendent aspects of "love" for itself.

Constructed Jewishness-as-deviance was not limited to medieval Christian fantasies. In his 2001 study of the eruption of anti-Semitism among the Muslim underclass of Indonesia, James T. Siegel describes a phenomenon he terms "the Jewish uncanny."[5] Playing off the old joke that if they didn't have Jews then they would have to invent them, Siegel describes a nationalist self-image that relied on the dread of an abstract globalized menace. Even in a country with almost no actual Jews, "Jewishness" was a productive and valued construction of Otherness. It allowed Indonesian culture a totem to visualize the boundaries of their nation under transnational assault. But this constructed Jewish threat cannot be considered merely a haunting specter of historical political events. There is no record of Jewish influence or cultural presence in Indonesia. Instead, Jewishness had become, as Siegel puts it, "the threat of specters to come."[6]

Why Harry Met Sally argues that this haunting specter, this ephemeral "Jewishness," came about as a requisite extension of the processes of an increasingly cosmopolitan, globally interconnected world. The "Jew" circulates across global media as a duplicitous, incongruous reflection of the legacy of European Christian power. The "Jew" is both white and non-white, assimilated but not quite Christian, sexually emancipated and also neurotically self-destructive. In its idealized state, denatured Jewishness manifests as utopian platonic love. This occurs as the Jew is transformed into a symbol of modern Christian transcendence through coupling. In reactionary forms, it manifests as carnal corruption and deviant animality, with the

"Jew" provoking the fear and hatred of nativist hysteria and backlash. In this reading, the "Jew" operates as a threat to the purity of the nation-state and a corporeal barrier to the post-Constantine platonic ideals of sexless (Christian) transcendent love.

It is my hope that coupling theory will not be limited to Anglo-Christian-Jewish focus. The production of Otherness, whether locating in bodies, robots, cyborgs, aliens, or other metaphors for diaspora cultures and subculture identities, can be analyzed through similar coupling theory models. Human-alien love stories in films and television shows such as the mini-series *V* (1983), *Enemy Mine* (1985), and *Alien Nation* (film, 1989; series, 1989-1990), for example, offer but one potential area for coupling theory analysis. The exotic "native" as an expression of primitive desire can be reconsidered through any number of ethnonational, transnational, and postcolonial coupling frameworks in everything from the BBC's *Doctor Who* (1963–) to James Cameron's *Avatar* (2009). The coupling of human and robot in films as diverse as *Metropolis* (1927), *Blade Runner* (1982), *Her* (2013), and *Ex Machina* (2015) offer a wealth of additional material to consider how couplings mediate the crisis of post-human identity.

Numerous works of scholarship have, of course, already considered these texts and their reception as repositories for gendered, sexual, ethnic, technological, and psychological debates. But the traditions of textual analysis almost always privilege the single representation. Coupling theory argues for a rethinking of this process by reconfiguring the "couple" as a singular construction in which both figures are entangled reflections of a single dialectical conversation. How a culture decides what is, and is not, acceptable in the coupling fantasies it produces and consumes remains an important, under-theorized area for scholarly investigation. Couplings are visceral binaries at the intersection of gender, race, sexuality, class, and other rhetorics of representation. But to stop at representational analysis is to miss the larger negotiation taking place. Every recurrence at least obliquely engages the binary at work within Plato's originary theory of love. But it does so through the lens of centuries of post-Christian demarcation.

Coupling theory proposes reading these couplings as figural "re-tweets" of the ongoing tension between Plato and his Christianized platonic ideals. As Philip Rieff argues, the divorcing of pleasure from procreation and its inherent rejection of individual sexual expression has remained the "consensual matrix of Christian culture."[7] With the invention of moving screen media, couplings embodied this tension between Christian containment and sexual emancipation brought about by the visual stimulation of the mass media age. Each coupling echoes the same discursive pattern repeating itself under updated cultural and political contexts. Casting choices, stereotypes, performance styles, and other codes of narrative language negotiate the normative and the deviant, the powerful and the subaltern, whether under a Christonormative-Jewish framework or in any other geographic, theoretical, or cultural context. It is a mode of inquiry that I hope will inspire other scholars of media and culture in the years to come.

Notes

INTRODUCTION. SALLY'S ORGASM

1. For a summary of these references, see Drew Mackie, "'I'll Have What She's Having!' See *When Harry Met Sally*'s Deli Scene through Pop Culture History," *People*, July 11, 2014, www.people.com/article/when-harry-meet-sally-deli-scene-ill-have-what-shes-having.

2. Megan Gibson, "Here's How Rob Reiner Taught Meg Ryan to Fake an Orgasm for *When Harry Met Sally*," *Time*, July 11, 2014, http://time.com/2976152/meg-ryan-rob-reiner-when-harry-met-sally.

3. The sketch was part of director Jason Bell's *British Invasion*, an assemblage of famous British movie stars re-creating iconic moments in film history. See Allison Takeda, "Keira Knightley Re-Enacts Meg Ryan's Famous Orgasm Scene from *When Harry Met Sally*: Watch!" *Us Weekly*, February 4, 2015, www.usmagazine.com/entertainment/news/keira-knightley-re-enacts-when-harry-met-sally-orgasm-scene-video-201542#ixzz3idOCoY68.

4. The line is ranked thirty-third on the American Film Institute list of the most famous lines in film history. See "AFI's 100 Years . . . 100 Movie Quotes," www.afi.com/100years/quotes.aspx.

5. Introduced and refined in Depression-era comedies such as *It Happened One Night* (1934) and *The Awful Truth* (1937), screwball comedies locate erotic tension (and comedy) through the sublimated desire of the protagonists, which is turned into hostile banter. See Dana Polan, "The Light Side of Genius: Hitchcock's *Mr. and Mrs. Smith* in the Screwball Tradition," in *Comedy/Cinema/Theory*, ed. Andrew Horton (Berkeley: University of California Press, 1991), 136.

6. In 1989, Caryn James's somewhat critical review of the film for the *New York Times* described director Rob Reiner's film as a clumsy attempt to mime the Jewish humor and urban milieu of Woody Allen. See Caryn James, "It's Harry [Loves] Sally in a Romance Of New Yorkers and Neuroses," *New York Times*, July 12, 1989.

7. Nathan Abrams, "Jewish-Christian Relations on Film: *When Harry*

Met Sally (1989)," *Jewish/Non-Jewish Relations: Between Exclusion and Embrace*, http://jnjr.div.ed.ac.uk/primary-sources/contemporary/jewish-christian-relations -on-film-when-harry-met-sally-1989.

8. Walker Connor was one of a number of political science scholars in the 1980s and 1990s to argue that the link between nationalism and ethnicity was critically underexplored in understanding the often irrational motivations of many public policies. For more, see Walker Conner, *Ethnonationalism: The Quest for Understanding* (New Jersey: Princeton University Press, 1993).

9. Connor builds off Karl Deutsch's work in the 1960s to note that the assumption that ethnic affiliations would decline as modernization progressed turned out to be significantly incorrect. The link between ethnicity and modernization was therefore counterintuitive yet undeniable. Ibid., 31–35.

10. Jacques Lacan, *The Four Fundamental Concepts of Psychoanalysis: The Seminar of Jacques Lacan, Book XI* (New York: W. W. Norton, 1981), 194. Barbara Creed, "Film and Psychoanalysis," in *The Oxford Guide to Film Studies*, ed. John Hill and Pamela Church Gibson (Oxford: Oxford University Press, 1998), 151.

11. Lilie Chouliaraki and Norman Fairclough describe this tension as between interpretive and structuralist approaches that alternate between collective and individual identities. See Lilie Chouliaraki and Norman Fairclough, *Discourse in Late Modernity: Rethinking Critical Discourse Analysis* (Edinburgh: Edinburgh University Press, 2001), 1–4.

12. Gerard Delanty, building on Jürgen Habermas's social theory of modernity, argues that this emergent mass media cosmopolitanism was less an ethos grounded in universal connection than a de-emphasis on space, territory, and tribalism. Gerard Delanty, "The Cosmopolitan Imagination: Critical Cosmopolitanism and Social Theory," *British Journal of Sociology* 57, no. 1 (2006): 27–28.

13. In Lacanian terms, the unresolved rhetorical coupling can be understood as visualizing the "lack," what Lacan calls the "*objet petit a.*" This becomes a screen media extension of both Freud's mirror stage and the sado-erotic tensions of what Barbara Creed describes as the link between the screen body and the apparatus that produces it. It is a concept we can perhaps whimsically think of as the *objet petit oy.* See Lacan, *The Four Fundamental Concepts of Psychoanalysis*, 194, and Creed, "Film and Psychoanalysis," 4–6.

14. Joshua Louis Moss, "'Woody the Gentile': Christian-Jewish Interplay in Allen's Films from *What's New, Pussycat?* to *Midnight in Paris*," in *Woody on Rye: Jewishness in the Films and Plays of Woody Allen*, ed. Vincent Brook and Marat Grinberg (Waltham, MA: Brandeis University Press, 2013), 100. Jean-Luc Nancy, *Dis-Enclosure: The Deconstruction of Christianity* (New York: Fordham University Press, 2008), 38.

15. Susanna Drake, *Slandering the Jew: Sexuality and Difference in Early Christian Texts* (Philadelphia: University of Pennsylvania Press: 2013), 6–7.

16. Richard Dyer, *White* (New York: Routledge, 1997), 53.

17. Ibid., 17–28.

18. Dyer argues that the process of "gentilizing" images of Jesus and Mary—

a Nordic whitening of skin tone, blue eyes, and blond hair—was subsequently reinforced through centuries of medieval and Renaissance art. This was done to draw a visual distinction between Christianity and the Jewish/North-African Orientalist origins of Jesus's historical past. Ibid.

19. Otto Weininger, *Sex and Character: An Investigation of Fundamental Principles* (New York: G. P. Putnam and Sons, 1906).

20. Omer Bartov, *The "Jew" in Cinema: From* The Golem *to* Don't Touch My Holocaust (Bloomington: Indiana University Press, 2005), 16.

21. The scientific argument that biological racial mixing would lead to societal breakdown predated Adolf Hitler by nearly fifty years. It was developed in the 1860s and 1870s by Arthur de Gobineau and Francis Galton before moving to Germany through the published work of eugenicist Alfred Ploetz in 1895.

22. For a critical deconstruction of the flaws in Benjamin's reading of Baudelaire and his subsequent linking of mobility, spectatorship, and modernity, see Martina Lauster, "Walter Benjamin's Myth of the 'Flâneur,'" *Modern Language Review* 102, no. 1 (Jan. 2007): 139–156.

23. Anne Friedberg, *Window Shopping: Cinema and the Postmodern* (Berkeley: University of California Press, 1994), 23–27.

24. Suture, a concept at work in film theory since the 1960s, argues that cinema stitches together gaps in perception and meaning to create the illusion of cohesion. See Christian Metz, "Imaginary Signifier," in *Film and Theory: An Anthology*, ed. Robert Stam and Toby Miller (Oxford: Blackwell, 2000), 403–435. See also Stephen Heath, "From Narrative Space," in *Contemporary Film Theory*, ed. Anthony Easthope (New York: Longman, 1993), 68–94.

25. Nathan Abrams, *The New Jew in Film: Exploring Jewishness and Judaism in Contemporary Cinema* (New Brunswick, NJ: Rutgers University Press, 2012), 16–17.

26. See Sander Gilman, *The Jew's Body* (New York: Routledge, 1991), and *Making the Body Beautiful* (Princeton, NJ: Princeton University Press, 1999).

27. Henry Bial, *Acting Jewish: Negotiating Ethnicity on the American Stage and Screen* (Ann Arbor: Michigan University Press, 2005), 16.

28. Joseph Litvak, *The Un-Americans: Jews, the Blacklist, and Stoolpigeon Culture* (Durham, NC: Duke University Press, 2009), 30–31.

29. Daniel Boyarin, *Unheroic Conduct: The Rise of Heterosexuality and the Invention of the Jewish Man* (Berkeley: University of California Press, 1997), xxiii.

30. Erin Graff Zivin, *The Wandering Signifier: Rhetoric of Jewishness in the Latin American Imaginary* (Durham, NC: Duke University Press, 2008), 176.

31. Vincent Brook, *You Should See Yourself: Jewish Identity in Postmodern American Culture* (New Brunswick, NJ: Rutgers University Press, 2006), 4–6.

32. Ella Shohat, "Ethnicities-In-Relation: Toward a Multicultural Reading of American Cinema," in *Unspeakable Images: Ethnicity and the American Cinema*, ed. Lester D. Friedman (Champaign: University of Illinois Press, 1991), 216. See also Karen Brodkin, *How Jews Became White Folks & What That Says About Race in America* (New Brunswick, NJ: Rutgers University Press, 1998); David R. Roediger,

The Wages of Whiteness: Race and the Making of the American Working Class (New York: Verso, 1991); and Hasia Diner, *In the Almost Promised Land: American Jews and Blacks, 1915–1935* (Baltimore: Johns Hopkins University Press, 1977).

33. Aamir Mufti, *Enlightenment in the Colony: The Jewish Question and the Crisis of Postcolonial Culture* (Princeton, NJ: Princeton University Press, 2007).

34. Zadie Smith, "F. Kafka, Everyman," *New York Review of Books*, July 17, 2008.

35. Ruth Ellen Gruber, *Virtually Jewish: Reinventing Jewish Culture in Europe* (Berkeley: University of California Press, 2002).

36. Yuri Slezkine, *The Jewish Century* (Princeton, NJ: Princeton University Press, 2004), 1–3.

37. Ibid., 2–3.

38. David Nirenberg, *Anti-Judaism: The Western Tradition* (New York: W. W. Norton, 2013).

39. Karl Marx, "On the Jewish Question," in *The Marx-Engels Reader*, 2nd ed. (New York: W. W. Norton, 1972), 32.

40. Jean-Paul Sartre, *Anti-Semite and Jew: An Exploration of the Etiology of Hate* (New York: Schocken Books, 1948).

41. Fanon observed the relational roles that "Negro" and "Jew" played in threatening the colonial Western hegemony, writing, "The Negro symbolizes the biological danger; the Jew, the intellectual danger." Fanon's concept of a relationship among anti-Semitism, racism, and colonialism has been integrated in areas as diverse as critical race theory, postcolonial theory, and queer theory. See Frantz Fanon, *Black Skin, White Masks* (New York: Grove Press, 1967), 165.

42. Gilles Deleuze and Félix Guattari, *A Thousand Plateaus: Capitalism and Schizophrenia* (Minneapolis: University of Minnesota Press, 1987), 290–291.

43. For example, I argue that certain texts that explicitly identify a character as non-Jewish, such as "Ratso" Rizzo in *Midnight Cowboy*, can be reconfigured by the public identity and persona of the performer.

44. Kirk and Michael Douglas both went public with their revived sense of Jewish pride in the 2000s. But since neither actor was visible about their Jewish identities at the peak of their careers, I have excluded their texts from analysis. This is not to say that their texts and performances should not also be given reconsideration under the Christian-Jewish coupling framework proposed in this book. In particular, Michael Douglas's masculinity-in-crisis films in the late 1980s and early 1990s—including *Fatal Attraction* (1987), *Wall Street* (1987), *Basic Instinct* (1992), and *Disclosure* (1994)—offer a particularly engaging set of texts.

45. Literature examples in this book do not contain visual figuration. Anglo-Christianness is located in both European and American literature as an assumptive norm. A character is presumed to be white, European Christian unless otherwise identified through textual identifiers such as last names and character descriptions.

46. The purification of the body was at the center of this dichotomy. Baptism, the washing away of the "original sin," was used to purify Christian infants. By the time of St. Thomas Aquinas, the Church had developed a litany of sexual prohibi-

tions, including prohibiting sex during Lent and on Sundays and complete bans on masturbation, oral sex, and sex outside of procreative intent.

47. George L. Mosse, *Nationalism and Sexuality: Middle-Class Morality and Sexual Norms in Modern Europe* (Madison: University of Wisconsin Press, 1985), 16–17.

48. Dyer, *White*, 27.

49. See Moss, "'Woody the Gentile,'" 102–104.

50. Ibid., 102–106.

51. See Joyce Antler, *The Journey Home: How Jewish Women Shaped Modern America* (New York: Schocken Books, 1997); Judith Plaskow, *The Coming of Lilith: Essays on Feminism, Judaism, and Sexual Ethics, 1972–2003* (Boston: Beacon Press, 2005); Hasia Diner, Shira Kohn, and Rachel Kranson, eds., *A Jewish Feminine Mystique? Jewish Women in Postwar America* (New Brunswick, NJ: Rutgers University Press, 2010); Judith R. Baskin, ed., *Jewish Women in Historical Perspective* (Detroit, MI: Wayne State University Press, 1998).

52. For an excellent collection of academic essays on this topic, see Daniel Boyarin, Daniel Itzkovitz, and Ann Pellegrini, eds., *Queer Theory and the Jewish Question* (New York: Columbia University Press, 2003).

PART ONE. THE FIRST WAVE

1. Walter Benjamin, *On Hashish* (Cambridge, MA: Harvard University Press, 2006), 73.

2. Benjamin's highly influential 1936 essay, "The Work of Art in the Age of Mechanical Reproduction," remains one of the foundational texts examining how mass media alters our perceptions of the real, the indexical, and the simulation.

3. Adam Kirsch describes Benjamin's search for epiphanies in drug-induced states of intoxication as the natural extension of his work in cultural, literary, and Marxist political analysis. See Adam Kirsch, "The Philosopher Stoned: What Drugs Taught Walter Benjamin," *New Yorker*, August 21, 2006, www.newyorker.com/magazine/2006/08/21/the-philosopher-stoned.

4. Philip Brey, "Theorizing Technology and Modernity," in *Modernity and Technology*, ed. Thomas Misa, Philip Brey, and Andrew Feenberg (Cambridge, MA: MIT Press, 2003), 33.

5. Benjamin's mouse-mountain invoked the same dialectical approach that had inspired Hegel's master/slave dialectic, and then Marx and Engels's corrective, dialectical materialism sought to critique the concept of singular knowledge through the collision of opposites. This discursive method of contrast became the foundations for the field of phenomenology. For more, see Georg W. F. Hegel, *The Phenomenology of Spirit (The Phenomenology of Mind)* (London: Oxford University Press, 1976).

6. In his case study of early twentieth-century German Jews, Bauman traced how Jewish assimilation produced cultural estrangement as an entirely new form

of alienation separate and distinct from the markings of ethnicity, religion, or race. See Zygmunt Bauman, *Modernity and Ambivalence* (Malden, MA: Polity Press 1991), 118–123.

7. For more on Scholem's analysis of Benjamin's connection to Jewish spiritual philosophy, see Gershom Scholem, *Walter Benjamin: The Story of a Friendship* (New York: New York Review of Books Classics, 2003).

8. For Adolf Hitler, appointed chancellor in 1933, just two years after Benjamin's mouse-mountain journal entry, no such coding was needed. His goal was to reverse the transgressions of the modern age through rigid hierarchies, clear classifications, and demarcated social controls. In establishing clear racial classifications, Nazis offered anxiety-stricken Germans a bulwark against the transnational impulses of the modernist ethos that Benjamin championed.

9. In 1897, Max Nordau warned the first Zionist Congress that efforts at assimilated Jewishness were doomed, writing that "racial anti-Semitism denies the power of change by baptism, and this mode of salvation does not seem to have much prospect." For more, see Max Nordau, "Address at the First Zionist Conference" (speech, Zionist Congress, Basel, Switzerland, August 29, 1897), www.mideastweb.org/nordau1897.htm.

10. Friedrich A. Kittler, *Gramophone, Film, Typewriter* (Redwood City, CA: Stanford University Press, 1999), 70–71.

CHAPTER 1. DISRAELI'S PAGE

1. Adam Kirsch, *Benjamin Disraeli* (New York: Schocken Books, 2008), 22–23.

2. Geoffrey Wheatcroft, "What Disraeli Can Teach Us," *New York Review of Books*, December 4, 2008, 27–28.

3. R. W. Davis, "Disraeli, the Rothschilds, and Anti-Semitism," *Jewish History* 10, no. 2 (1996): 9–10.

4. Disraeli's baptism was understood as a formality. Many Jews sought conversions to get around laws and prohibitions on Jewish activity in England. Despite his public appearances in church, few in Britain would have assumed Disraeli treated his conversion as anything more than an act of cultural acquiescence.

5. Andrea Gogröf-Vorhees argues that postmodernism was defined by an oscillating, self-reflective, ironic identity that embodied the sensibilities of the new freedoms of a cosmopolitan Europe. See Andrea Gogröf-Vorhees, *Defining Modernism: Baudelaire and Nietzsche on Romanticism, Modernity, Decadence, and Wagner* (New York: Peter Lang Publishing, 1999), 22–23.

6. Christopher Hibbert, *Disraeli: The Victorian Dandy Who Became Prime Minister* (New York: Palgrave Macmillan, 2006), 48.

7. Helen Rappaport, *Queen Victoria, A Biographical Companion* (Santa Barbara, CA: ABC-CLIO, 2003).

8. Ibid., 127–128.

9. Kirsch, *Benjamin Disraeli*, 103.

10. Disraeli was converted by his father in a small religious ceremony sim-ply meant to make his life easier. Lionel de Rothschild, the first British Jew to be elected to the House of Commons, ran into the barrier that Disraeli's father had cleared for Disraeli. Despite his enormous economic power, Rothschild had to wait until anti-Jewish laws were rescinded in 1858 before serving in office.

11. Daisy Hay, *Mr. and Mrs. Disraeli: A Strange Romance* (New York: Farrar, Straus and Giroux, 2015).

12. Robert P. O'Kell, *Disraeli: The Romance of Politics* (Toronto: University of Toronto Press, 2013), 240.

13. Sarah Bradford, *Disraeli* (London: Weidenfeld and Nicolson, 1982).

14. Stanley Weintraub, *Disraeli: A Biography* (New York: Truman Talley Books/Dutton, 1993), 293–294.

15. Ibid., 277.

16. Ibid., 336.

17. Benjamin Disraeli, *Benjamin Disraeli Letters, 1860–1864* (Toronto: University of Toronto Press, 2010), xii. Via Robert P. O'Kell, book review, *Victorian Studies* 52, no. 4 (2010): 679.

18. Disraeli, *Benjamin Disraeli Letters, 1860–1864*, 220–230.

19. The friendship appeared to be genuine. Even after his political career ended in 1880, Disraeli and Queen Victoria maintained close ties. Many saw the aging former prime minister as a Jewish outsider unworthy of respect. But the queen's af-fection remained unwavering. Victoria stayed in close contact with Disraeli right up to his death in 1884. Christopher Hibbert, *Queen Victoria in Her Letters and Journals: A Selection* (London: John Murray Publishers, 1984), 90. Via Rappaport, *Queen Victoria*, 128–131.

20. O'Kell, *Disraeli*, 403.

21. Albert D. Pionke, *Plots of Opportunity: Representing Conspiracy in Victorian England* (Columbus: Ohio State University, 2004), 120–121.

22. George A. Kennedy, "Reading Disraeli with Stendhal" in *Narrative Ironies*, ed. A. Prier and Gerald Gillespie (Amsterdam: Rodopi, 1997), 254.

23. Pionke, *Plots of Opportunity*, 121.

24. As Neil Davison points out, James Joyce makes reference to the novel in one of his letters. Despite his lack of respect for Disraeli's talents as an author, Joyce was likely influenced by Disraeli's themes in his construction of Leopold Bloom in *Ulysses*. See Neil R. Davison, *James Joyce, Ulysses, and the Construction of Jewish Identity: Culture, Biography, and the "Jew" in Modernist Europe* (Cambridge: Cambridge University Press, 1998), 32.

25. For more on the analysis of the political themes in Disraeli's novels, see Michael Flavin, *Benjamin Disraeli: The Novel as Political Discourse* (Brighton, UK: Sussex Academic Press, 2005), 1, and O'Kell, *Disraeli*, 216–217.

26. David Cesarani, *Disraeli: The Novel Politician* (New Haven, CT: Yale University Press, 2016), 96–99.

27. O'Kell, *Disraeli*, 216–217.

28. Ibid., 227.

29. Ibid., 263–266.

30. Philip Rieff argues that Disraeli applied the emerging concept of Zionism, the transnational "New Israel," as an origin story for the emancipated Jews of England. Philip Rieff, *The Jew of Culture: Freud, Moses, and Modernity* (Charlottesville: University of Virginia Press, 2008), 22–23.

31. Ibid., 15.

32. Kirsch, *Benjamin Disraeli*, 17–19.

33. Sollors links this shift from "descent" ethnicity, defined by biography, to a consent or choice model as defining how American culture differentiated itself from Europe. See Werner Sollors, *Beyond Ethnicity: Consent and Descent in American Culture* (New York: Oxford University Press, 1987).

34. Kirsch, *Benjamin Disraeli*, 22–23.

35. Ibid., 17–19.

36. The rise of the dandy in the urban milieu of the mid- to late nineteenth century has been a source of great scholarly interest. Baudelaire's seminal definition, written in 1863, described dandyism as a reactive body, a performance of "opposition and revolt" that served as a complex signifier of global transformation. The dandy uses clothes, style, and mannerisms to demonstrate how taste culture could be used to challenge gender, class, and national distinctions. The dandy thus both embraced, but also satirized, modernity's contradictions. For more, see Charles Baudelaire, *The Painter of Modern Life and Other Essays*, trans. Jonathan Mayne (New York: Phaidon Press, 1970), 27–28.

37. Biographer Stanley Weintraub credits Disraeli's widespread appeal to his larger-than-life identity as a mythic adventurer whose fifty-year political climb to become the "right hand" of Queen Victoria was a result of tenacity, pugnaciousness, and a highly motivating sense of alienation. But in focusing on Disraeli's persona, the important role of Mrs. Dizzy in his public life often gets overlooked. Weintraub, *Disraeli*, xii–xiv.

38. Scholarly works on Disraeli's life, as Geoffrey Wheatcroft notes, are a diverse and eclectic collection. Biographies have focused on everything from the themes of Disraeli's novels to the ambiguities of his sex life. These include works such as W. F. Monypenny and G. E. Buckle's seminal *The Life of Benjamin Disraeli, Earl of Beaconsfield* (1920); Robert Blake's 1966 biography, *Disraeli*; Jane Ridley's 1995 *Young Disraeli*; and, in 2008, Adam Kirsch's *Benjamin Disraeli*.

39. Venita Datta, "The Dreyfus Affair as National Theater," in *Revising Dreyfus*, ed. Maya Balakirsky Katz (Boston: Brill, 2013), 30–33.

40. Suleiman cites Voltaire's intervention in the Calas Affair a century earlier—what Suleiman calls a "proto-Dreyfus" scandal with a Protestant victim—as one example comparable to the active role that public intellectuals played in defending Dreyfus. See Susan Rubin Suleiman, "The Literary Significance of the Dreyfus Affair," in *The Dreyfus Affair: Art, Truth, and Justice*, ed. Norman L. Kleeblatt (Berkeley: University of California Press, 1987), 120–121.

41. Christopher E. Forth, *The Dreyfus Affair and the Crisis of French Manhood* (Baltimore: Johns Hopkins University Press, 2004), 2.

42. Norman L. Kleeblatt, ed., *The Dreyfus Affair: Art, Truth, and Justice* (Berkeley: University of California Press, 1987), 160–161.

43. The image appeared on the cover of V. Lenepveu's *Musee des Horreurs* political parody poster. Animality was central to numerous anti-Semitic critiques of Dreyfus. Ibid., 244.

44. "The Dreyfus Case," *Harvard Law Review* 13, no. 3 (1899): 214.

45. This reach extended beyond France. Numerous fairgrounds and cafés across Europe screened footage of the Dreyfus retrial in 1899 by ordering prints directly from Georges Méliès's *Star-Film Catalogue*. This included both location shooting from the actual trial in Rennes and the eleven-part fictionalized pro-Dreyfus re-creation directed in 1899 by Méliès himself.

46. Sander Gilman, *Franz Kafka, the Jewish Patient* (London: Routledge, 1995), 71.

47. Gilman notes how Freud couched his terminology in language meant to obfuscate any associations to Jewishness in the field of psychoanalysis to explicitly respond to these sorts of anxieties. See Sander Gilman, *The Case of Sigmund Freud: Medicine and Identity at the Fin De Siècle* (Baltimore: Johns Hopkins University Press, 1993), 106–108.

48. Piers Paul Read, *The Dreyfus Affair: The Scandal that Tore France in Two* (New York: Bloomsbury Press, 2012), 78–79.

49. Ibid., 79.

50. Louis Begley, *Why the Dreyfus Affair Matters* (New Haven, CT: Yale University Press, 2009), 64.

51. Read, *The Dreyfus Affair*, 79–80.

52. Begley, *Why The Dreyfus Affair Matters*, 226.

53. Leslie Derfler, *The Dreyfus Affair* (Westport, CT: Greenwood Press, 2002), 66–68.

54. Zola was unusual. Most La Belle Époque artists refused to address the Dreyfus affair for fear of reprisal, with the notable exception of Henri de Toulouse-Lautrec. Indeed, most of these artists were apolitical; even the reportedly anti-Semitic Edgar Degas did not produce any work or quotes addressing the events of the trial. See Linda Nochlin, "Degas and the Dreyfus Affair: A Portrait of the Artist as an Anti-Semite," in *The Dreyfus Affair: Art, Truth, and Justice*, ed. Norman L. Kleeblatt (Berkeley: University of California Press, 1987).

55. Zola soon found himself under the same suspicions of disloyalty. He was forced to flee to London a year later while facing his own charges of treason. See Emile Zola, "J'accuse! . . ." *L'Aurore*, January 13, 1898, 1.

56. Early cinema pioneers such as Société Française de Mutoscope et Biographe, the French chapter of Biograph, and the Lumière Company's Francis Doublier shot numerous shorts of the events of the trial. Some were re-creations while others featured documentary captures of the various personalities of the trial entering and exiting the courthouse at Rennes. Lucie appears in a number of these one-reelers. See "Lives in Film No. 1—Alfred Dreyfus Part 2" at http://thebioscope .net/2010/03/11/lives-in-film-no-1-alfred-dreyfus-part-2.

57. Jean-Denis Bredin, *The Affair: The Case of Alfred Dreyfus* (New York: George Braziller Inc., 1986), 168–169.

58. Ruth Harris, "Letters to Lucie: Spirituality, Friendship, and Politics During the Dreyfus Affair," *French Historical Studies* 28, no. 4 (2005): 603.

59. Forth, *The Dreyfus Affair and the Crisis of French Manhood*, 66–70. Harris, "Letters to Lucie," 609.

60. Sander Gilman observes how the political issues of Dreyfus frequently crossed over into a physiologic debate about whether the Jewish body could ever be truly French. See Sander Gilman, *Franz Kafka*, 71.

61. Bredin, *The Affair*, 3–7.

62. This recasting of Lucie as silent, heroic sufferer may have echoed the extremely popular nineteenth-century opera of the time, *La Juive*, which told the story of a martyred Jewish lover, Rachel, who refused to convert despite her love for a Christian nobleman. As noted by Harris, "Letters to Lucie," 609.

63. Baudelairean theatricality was not simply located in Benjamin Disraeli. Andrea Gogröf-Vorhees, building off Foucault, locates modernity as the pivotal moment at which modern society began to perform personas as a social rather than a cultural construction. See Gogröf-Vorhees, *Defining Modernism*.

64. The problematic, liminal status of Jewish masculinity—what Christopher E. Forth describes as a "dialectic between visibility and invisibility"—meant that neither version could ultimately assuage suspicions of Dreyfus's betrayal. If Dreyfus was presented as conventionally (Christian) masculine, he was accused of performing a deviant act of masquerade. If his Jewishness was foregrounded, it confirmed that he was not fully French. See Forth, *The Dreyfus Affair and the Crisis of French Manhood*, 38–39.

65. Nordau described the crisis of the post-ghetto Jew as one of "mimicry," citing Dreyfus as his example. Dreyfus had believed that if he could successfully mime traditional French masculinity, he would be accepted. But this attempt, according to Nordau, was doomed to failure. In the end, the Jew was destined to remain ostracized from European Christian culture. The only solution was emigration to Palestine to found a Jewish state. Nordau, "Address at the First Zionist Conference."

66. Derfler, *The Dreyfus Affair*, 62.

67. Richard L. Rubenstein and John J. Roth, *Approaches to Auschwitz: The Holocaust and Its Legacy* (Louisville, KY: Westminster John Knox Press, 2003), 95.

68. As Michael Marrus argues, Arendt, a cosmopolitan Jewish intellectual, believed "(t)he modern Jewish experience . . . was at the very center of the Dreyfus crisis, just as it was at the center of Nazism." Michael R. Marrus, "Hannah Arendt and the Dreyfus Affair," *New German Critique*, no. 66 (1995): 161.

69. Hannah Arendt, *The Origins of Totalitarianism* (New York: Meridian, 1958), 45, 93. Marrus, "Hannah Arendt," 153.

70. Sartre, *Anti-Semite and Jew*.

71. Ibid., 130–131.

72. Sartre's analogy served as a foundational metaphor throughout the latter

half of the twentieth century, influencing philosophers, writers, artists, and politicians in a variety of fields and debates.

73. Hasia Diner suggests that much of the tension of American Jewish identity stemmed from the fact that European Jews were primarily rural while American Jews reinvented themselves as urban dwellers. Hasia Diner, *The Jews of the United States: 1654–2000* (Berkeley: University of California Press, 2004), 74–75.

74. As Jonathan Sarna notes, American Jews also experienced a schism by splitting into competing secular and religious formations. See Jonathan Sarna, *American Judaism: A History* (New Haven, CT: Yale University Press, 2004), 128–129.

CHAPTER 2. KAFKA'S APE

1. Maurice S. Friedman, *Martin Buber: The Life of Dialogue* (New York: Routledge, 2002), 215.

2. Walter Sokel describes the centrality of animal-human hybridity in Kafka's work as an extension of Kafka's own duality as both an alienated Jew and a secular modernist thinker. See Walter Sokel, *The Myth of Power and the Self: Essays on Franz Kafka* (Detroit: Wayne State University Press, 2002), 69, 281.

3. The Haskalah, the Jewish Renaissance, was a hundred-year movement that began in the late eighteenth century and was led by German-Jewish philosopher Moses Mendelssohn. Jewish intellectuals sought to modernize Jewish thinking by moving away from religious dogma and toward science and critical thinking methodologies. Many European Christians accused the movement of mimicking, or "aping," the Age of Enlightenment that served as Mendelssohn's inspiration.

4. Sander Gilman argues that Kafka's link between animality and biological Jewish stereotypes was a response to eugenics theory. Gilman reads Kafka's critique in observing that "a Jewish *fin de siècle* writer's modernity is inseparable from his allegedly diseased nature." See Sander L. Gilman, *Jewish Frontiers: Essays on Bodies, Histories, and Identities* (New York: Palgrave Macmillan, 2004), 12.

5. Ibid., 283.

6. This impossibility of Jewish transformation through assimilation became the comedic premise explored by the transforming body of Leonard Zelig (Woody Allen) in Woody Allen's *Zelig* (1982). See chapter 7.

7. Gilman, *Jewish Frontiers*, 60.

8. Buber's analysis of word doublings and fractured language had enormous cross-disciplinary influence, informing, among many fields of study, the semiotics and structuralist theories of linguists Charles Sanders Peirce and Claude Levi-Strauss, the culture industry interrogations of Frankfurt School founders Walter Benjamin, Theodor Adorno, and Max Horkheimer, and the deconstructionism of Jacques Derrida and Noam Chomsky.

9. Martin Buber, *I and Thou* (New York: Simon & Schuster, 1970), 53.

10. The Jewish specificity of Buber's work must be located as a structuring absence. Buber frequently mentions Buddha and the Gospels and makes numerous

other references to non-Jewish religions. But he never once explicitly mentions the Jewish religion. Like Marx, Buber manifestly avoided any mention of his Jewish background in his intellectual work. Yet, the codes of Jewish thinking permeate the work. See Walter Kaufman, introduction to *I and Thou* by Martin Buber (New York: Simon & Schuster, 1970), 32.

11. For more, see Friedman, *Martin Buber*, 84–85.

12. The notion of the Jew-as-rodent reached its nadir a decade later in the Nazi propaganda of the 1930s and 1940s.

13. Gilman, *Franz Kafka, the Jewish Patient*, 30–32.

14. Akira Mizuta Lippit describes this link between animality and modernism as the "animetaphor." See Akira Mizuta Lippit, *Electric Animal: Toward a Rhetoric of Wildlife* (Minneapolis: University of Minnesota Press, 2000), 55.

15. Ibid., 57.

16. Vanessa Lemm argues that the concept of animality was central to Nietzsche's critique of culture, noting how he embraced, rather than denied, the animal impulses of the human as part of the process of becoming human and, eventually, over-human (the *übermensch*). See Vanessa Lemm, *Nietzsche's Animal Philosophy: Culture, Politics, and the Animality of the Human Being* (New York: Fordham University Press, 2009), 4–8.

17. Critics of Heidegger have sought to locate actual evidence of anti-Semitism in his work, but the search has remained elusive. However, the long-delayed 2014 publication of Heidegger's *Black Notebooks* diaries, written from 1931 to 1943, gave new ammunition to those who saw Heidegger's commitment to National Socialism as running far deeper than he had previously revealed. Heidegger's subsequent involvement with the Nazi Party should not automatically dismiss the breadth and significance of his intellectual contributions. But neither can it be overlooked, as the *Black Notebooks* diaries reveal. For more on this discussion, see Jennifer Schuessler, "Heidegger's Notebooks Renew Focus on Anti-Semitism," *New York Times*, March 30, 2014.

18. Sander Gilman shows how centuries of anxiety in Western Christendom focused on the power of language, both written and spoken, as possessing mystical Jewish power. Christian fears of Jews using hidden or double language spoke to anxieties of Jewish infiltration into Christian society. The Jew, as Gilman summarizes, was seen as "possessing all languages or no language of his or her own." See Gilman, *The Jew's Body*, 12.

19. Dreyfus's military identity possibly also triggered a personal response in the young author. Despite ill health and asthma, Proust had enlisted in the French army in 1889 at the age of seventeen. His undistinguished career lasted barely a year.

20. Edward J. Hughes, *Proust, Class, and Nation* (New York: Oxford University Press, 2011), 266.

21. Edmund White, *Marcel Proust: A Life* (New York: Penguin Books, 1999), 9–10.

22. The literary output of Proust and Disraeli share little formal or thematic re-

semblance beyond this notion of protean Jewishness highlighted here. Proust's innovations of form and meditations on memory were a revolution of form, quite distinct from the fanciful but creatively unremarkable output of Disraeli. Easy conclusions should be avoided when comparing such disparate works from different countries written nearly half a century apart. However, both authors located an entanglement between Jewish Otherness and entrenched Christian power within erotic and romantic couplings.

23. Cynthia Gamble notes that Proust's link between coded homosexuality and suppressed Jewishness recurs numerous times, including the comparison of homosexuality to the suffering of the nation of Israel in *Cahier 6* and the celebrated linkage in *Sodome et Gomorrhe 1*. See Cynthia Gamble, "From *Belle Epoque* to First World War" in *The Cambridge Companion to Proust*, ed. Richard Bales (New York: Cambridge University Press, 2001), 62–63.

24. Sheila Stern observes that Proust spent 1896 to 1902 working on *Jean Santeuil*, an ambitious political novel that centered on the events of Dreyfus, before eventually abandoning it. Proust reconfigured the political and historical events depicted in this aborted work into the memories of numerous characters in *In Search of Lost Time*. See Sheila Stern, *Proust: Swann's Way* (New York: Cambridge University Press, 1989), 13–14.

25. Marcel Proust, *Remembrance of Things Past, Vol. 1: Swann's Way*, trans. C. K. Scott Moncrieff (Hertfordshire, UK: Wordsworth Editions Limited, 2006).

26. Proust's use of Swann to embody the crisis of emancipated Jewish identity was similar to the expressed anxieties that troubled Herzl and Nordau in the First Zionist Conference in 1897. Could the emancipated Jew fully integrate into non-Jewish Europe in the age of eugenics and after the scandal of Dreyfus?

27. Hughes, *Proust, Class, and Nation*, 6.

28. Ibid., 89.

29. For more on Proust's linguistic fractures, see Daniel Karlin, *Proust's English* (London: Oxford University Press, 2005), 3–5.

30. Marcel Proust, *Sodom and Gomorrah*, trans. John Sturrock (New York: Viking Press, 2004).

31. Lynn R. Wilkenson, "The Art of Distinction: Proust and the Dreyfus Affair," in "Comparative Literature," special issue, *MLN* 107, no. 5 (1992): 980, 982.

32. Ibid., 992.

33. Proust scholar Edward J. Hughes describes this as a "collective ideological formation" that builds in Proust's narrator through a mixture of Jewish race and Christian atavism. See Hughes, *Proust, Class, and Nation*, 153.

34. Richard Griffiths, "'The Clash of Races' and 'The Jewish Intelligence': A Specifically French Form of Social Anti-Semitism," *Patterns of Prejudice* 37, no. 1 (2003): 51–53.

35. Paul LaFarge notes that the relationship between the Catholic boy and the Jewish boy is Svengali-like and that Silbermann's intelligence and charisma are unmistakably Jewish in nature. See Paul LaFarge, "School Ties," *Tablet*, November 4, 2005, www.tabletmag.com/jewish-arts-and-culture/books/837/school-ties.

36. Ibid., 1.

37. Benjamin Ivry, "Finding Rabbis and Wandering Jews: French Jewish Symbolists Rediscovered," *Forward*, May 7, 2010, www.forward.com/articles/127592.

38. This also had parallels to *The Odyssey*. Odysseus traced his lineage to both mortals and Gods but was, in the end, mortal.

39. The schlemiel was an established archetype from popular Jewish-Yiddish theater—the young male Jewish loser, usually cowardly, miserly, and insecure.

40. Neil R. Davison, *James Joyce, Ulysses, and the Construction of Jewish Identity: Culture, Biography, and "the Jew" in Modernist Europe* (New York: Cambridge University Press, 1998), 91–94.

41. Ibid., 186–188.

42. Ibid., 100.

43. Ibid., 17.

44. Ibid., 62, 106–107.

45. Dan Chiasson observes that a real event in 1904, the year Joyce began work on the book, also likely influenced Bloom's construction. Joyce recovered from a bar fight with the assistance of a Jewish Dubliner named Alfred Hunter. See Dan Chiasson, "'Ulysses' and the Moral Right to Pleasure," *New Yorker*, June 16, 2014, www.newyorker.com/books/page-turner/ulysses-and-the-moral-right-to-pleasure.

46. Asahel Grant, *The Nestorians: Or, the Lost Tribes* (London: William Clowes and Sons, 1843), 162.

47. Joyce's explicit sexuality was a source of constant battles with the Catholic Church over his entire career. He actively rejected what was known as the "social purity" movement, a church-led religious effort to purge what was seen as corrupting depictions of premarital sexuality from literature. For more, see Katherine Mullin, *James Joyce, Sexuality, and Social Purity* (New York: Cambridge University Press, 2003).

48. Joseph Allen Boone, "A New Approach to Bloom as 'Womanly Man': The Mixed Middling's Progress in *Ulysses*," *James Joyce Quarterly* 20, no. 1 (1982): 67–68.

49. At 4,391 words, one of Molly's sentences became the longest in English literature at the time.

50. Leopold Bloom's resilience in the face of this betrayal also recalibrates masculinity under a distinctly Jewish rubric. See Paul Schwaber, "The Enigmatic Jewishness of Leopold Bloom," in *Psychoanalysis and Culture at the Millennium*, ed. Nancy Ginsberg (New Haven, CT: Yale University Press, 1999), 151.

51. Daniel Boyarin describes how Diaspora Jews at the turn of the twentieth century exemplified numerous examples of alternative masculinity in direct opposition to an Anglocentric warrior/hero model. See Boyarin, *Unheroic Conduct*.

52. Bloom produced a Jewish archetype that, David Biale argues, quickly became dominant in European literature of the period. See David Biale, *Eros and the Jews: From Biblical Israel to Contemporary America* (Berkeley: University of California Press, 1997), 7.

53. Leon Edel, *Bloomsbury: A House of Lions* (New York: J. B. Lippincott Company, 1979), 172.

54. Ibid., 197–199.

55. Victoria Glendinning, foreword to *The Wise Virgins* by Leonard Woolf (New Haven, CT: Yale University Press, 2007), vi–x.

56. Victoria Glendinning, *Leonard Woolf: A Biography* (New York: Simon and Schuster, 2006), 194.

57. In 1922, Hogarth Press published what is widely considered one of the most important modernist poems of the twentieth century, T. S. Eliot's *The Waste Land*. Eliot's poem suggests religious identity is irrelevant to life and death in section IV, titled "Death by Water":

> Entering the whirlpool
> Gentile or Jew
> O you who turn the wheel and look to windward,
> Consider Phlebas, who was once handsome and tall as you.

See T. S. Eliot, *The Waste Land* (New York: W. W. Norton and Company, 2000), x.

58. Barnes has been rendered impotent by an injury sustained in war, forcing him to vicariously experience sexuality through the actions of his Jewish friend. Hemingway's positioning of the carnal Jewish subject perceived through the sexually constrained Christian observer/narrator evokes Kafka's animetaphor and Buber's I/Thou intersubjectivity.

59. Sander Gilman, *Smart Jews: The Construction of the Image of Jewish Superior Intelligence* (Lincoln: University of Nebraska Press, 1997), 175–176.

60. The character was based on Hollywood wunderkind Irving G. Thalberg.

61. Historian Steven Beller notes that assimilated Viennese Jews were increasingly prominent in self-identifying as voluntary heirs to the rich history of German intellectual life. For more, see Steven Beller, *Vienna and the Jews: 1867–1938: A Cultural History* (New York: Cambridge University Press, 1989), 149–152.

62. Otto Weininger, *Sex and Character: An Investigation of Fundamental Principles* (New York: G. P. Putnam and Sons, 1906), 16–19.

63. Daniel Pick, "Svengali and the *Fin-de-Siècle*," in *Modernity, Culture and "the Jew*," ed. Bryan Cheyette and Laura Marcus (Stanford: Stanford University Press, 1998), 107.

64. Gavin Schaffer, "Perverts and Purists: The Idea of Jewish Sexual Difference in Britain, 1900–1945," in *Jews and Sex*, ed. Nathan Abrams (Nottingham, UK: Five Leaves Publications, 2008), 107–108.

65. In the years 1905 and 1906, the pattern of Christian-Jewish intersubjectivity emerged as the template of negotiation for both modernists and nativists. In those years, *The Protocols of Zion* grew in popularity, Dreyfus was exonerated, and Marcel Proust's beloved mother died, and he first began formulating *Swann's Way*. Also, Vanessa and Virginia Stephen began the first Bloomsbury seminars in England. A year later, Joyce began work on *Ulysses*.

66. In the introduction to *The Plot*, his graphic novel adaptation of the real history of the *Protocols of Zion*, artist Will Eisner cites the work of Russian historian

Mikhail Lepekhine in unearthing Golovinski's role in the forgery. See Will Eisner, *The Plot: The Secret Story of* The Protocols of The Elders of Zion (New York: W. W. Norton and Company, 2005), 2.

67. Michael Hagemeister, "*The Protocols of the Elders of Zion*: Between History and Fiction," in "Dark Powers: Conspiracies and Conspiracy Theory in History and Literature," ed. Eva Horn, special issue, *New German Critique*, no. 103 (2008): 83–95.

68. Adolf Hitler, *Mein Kampf* (New York: Houghton Mifflin Company, 1998), 422.

69. When, at the age of eighty-two, Freud was forced to leave Vienna for London in the 1930s, the Vienna Nazi Party justified its actions by criticizing the entire field of psychoanalysis as a "pornographic Jewish specialty." See "Freud Leaves Vienna for London Refuge, Declaring He Plans to Come Here Later," Associated Press, June 5, 1938, www.freerepublic.com/focus/f-chat/2026386/posts.

70. Via Michael Slade Shull, *Radicalism in American Silent Films, 1909–1929* (Jefferson, NC: McFarland & Company, Inc., 2000), 87–90.

71. Ibid., 132.

72. Erin Graff Zivin, *The Wandering Signifier: Rhetoric of Jewishness in the Latin American Imaginary* (Durham, NC: Duke University Press, 2008), 74–75.

73. Ibid., 124.

74. Jacobo Timerman, *Prisoner Without a Name, Cell Without a Number* (Madison: University of Wisconsin Press, 1981), 130.

75. Christopher Hitchens, "The 2,000–Year-Old Panic," *Atlantic*, March 2008.

76. Rebecca West, *Black Lamb and Grey Falcon: A Journey Through Yugoslavia* (London: Penguin Books, 2007), xxxvi. Via Hitchens, "The 2,000–Year-Old Panic."

77. Albert Einstein, *London Times*, November 28, 1919. Via *The New Quotable Einstein*, ed. Alice Calaprice (Princeton, NJ: Princeton University Press, 2005).

78. Building off Sander Gilman's work on the historical Jewish body, Matthew Frye Jacobson notes the irony in that late modern Jewish cosmopolitanism became indicted by the very scientific philosophies that it had championed as emancipatory and progressive. See Matthew Frye Jacobson, *Roots Too: White Ethnic Revival in Post-Civil Rights America* (Cambridge, MA: Harvard University Press, 2006), 171.

79. Judith Halberstam, *Skin Shows: Gothic Horror and the Technology of Monsters* (Durham, NC: Duke University Press, 1995), 18.

80. Ibid., 88.

81. See David A. H. Hirsch, "Dickens's Queer 'Jew' and Anglo-Christian Identity Politics: The Contradictions of Victorian Family Values," in *Queer Theory and the Jewish Question*, ed. Daniel Boyarin, Daniel Itzkovitz, and Ann Pellegrini (New York: Columbia University Press, 2003), 319.

82. Pick, "Svengali and the *Fin-de-Siècle*," 107.

83. Boyarin, *Unheroic Conduct*, 262.

84. Hitler, *Mein Kampf*, 680.

85. Jürgen Habermas describes this critical tension point in Hitler's fascism as locating in the segmented nature of rationality itself, as an extension of time in the modern age. Habermas highlights how Walter Benjamin appropriated concepts from Jewish mysticism to introduce the notion of "now-time" as a way to rethink the complex relationship between the present and the past. See Jürgen Habermas, *The Philosophical Discourse of Modernity: Twelve Lectures* (Cambridge, MA: MIT Press, 1990), 11, 18–19.

86. Hitler, *Mein Kampf,* 254.

CHAPTER 3. ABIE'S IRISH ROSE

1. Michael Alexander notes how Jewish cultural acceptance and assimilation in the late 1920s occurred in tandem with the success of entertainers such as Al Jolson in Hollywood. See Michael Alexander, *Jazz Age Jews* (Princeton, NJ: Princeton University Press, 2001), 144–148.

2. Jews were just one element of a significant wave of ethnic visibility throughout screen culture of the 1920s. Rudolph Valentino, dubbed the "Latin Lover" despite having no Hispanic background, showed the box-office power of portraying exotic, foreign masculinity in films such as *The Four Horsemen of the Apocalypse* (1921), *The Sheik* (1921), and *Son of the Sheik* (1926) before his untimely death in 1926. Valentino's famous shirtless torture scenes in *The Sheik* produced an explicit link between sadomasochistic voyeurism and the perception of non-white ethnicity. The African-American Paul Robeson, the Chinese-American Anna Mae Wong, and the Japanese Sessue Hayakawa were other famous ethnic stars of the era.

3. Patricia Erens, *The Jew in American Cinema* (Bloomington: Indiana University Press, 1984), 30–34.

4. Tom Gunning, "Crazy Machines in the Garden of Forking Paths: Mischief Gags and the Origins of American Film Comedy," in *Classical Hollywood Comedy*, ed. Kristine Brunovska Karnick and Henry Jenkins (New York: Routledge, 1995), 99–100.

5. "Early American Silents: The Cohen Films," National Center for Jewish Film, www.jewishfilm.org/Catalogue/cohenseries.htm.

6. J. Hoberman and Jeffrey Shandler, *Entertaining America: Jews, Movies, and Broadcasting* (Princeton, NJ: Princeton University Press, 2003), 32.

7. Douglas Gomery, *Shared Pleasures: A History of Movie Presentation in the United States* (Madison: University of Wisconsin Press, 1992), 21.

8. While many of the filmmakers (Thomas Edison, Georges Méliès, George Albert Smith, Edwin Porter) in the first decade of popular cinema were developing the potential of the medium, character depictions and/or performance beyond a simple "type" remained less developed. Ethnicity, gender, class, and race were communicated through clear, easily identifiable visual codes such as dress, facial hair, body type, and casting. The body, and not performance or narrative, was the primary dictate of cinematic representation in this period. See numerous essays in

André Gaudreault, Nicolas Dulac, and Santiago Hidalgo, eds., *A Companion to Early Cinema* (Hoboken, NJ: Wiley-Blackwell, 2012).

9. Iconography of the helpless, innocent white female also made good dramatic sense and could be found in film as early as Edward Porter's groundbreaking *The Great Train Robbery* in 1903.

10. Lary May, *Screening Out the Past: The Birth of Mass Culture and the Motion Picture Industry* (Chicago: University of Chicago Press, 1980), 213.

11. Louis Harap, *The Image of the Jew in American Literature: From Early Republic to Mass Immigration* (Syracuse, NY: Syracuse University Press, 2003), 335.

12. Interestingly, it was the Scotch-Irish actress Irene Wallace who became the first breakout star of the ghetto Jewess love story genre. J. Hoberman theorizes that her non-Jewish background may have been the reason. It allowed her to both express her sexuality in character while assuaging audience concerns that the depiction of Jewish jezebel eroticism was not a negative stereotype. See J. Hoberman, *Bridge of Light: Yiddish Film Between Two Worlds* (Lebanon, NH: Dartmouth College Press, 2010), 30–31.

13. The seductive potency of the Jewess was not confined to ghetto roles and was perhaps best exemplified by the French-born Jewish theater actress, Sarah Bernhardt. Frequently billed as "the most famous actress the world has ever known," Bernhardt became an enormously successful star, one of the most famous celebrities to move from the stages of La Belle Époque to star in some of the earliest and most successful American silent cinema shorts. Bernhardt's bold display of unapologetic female sexuality aligned her with the Jewess persona even as she avoided this specificity in her roles.

14. Modifications to this requirement reoccurred in numerous Yiddish cinema films in which Jewesses directed their erotic gaze at secular Jews rather than at Christians, a transgression still contained within the broader American Jewish community. Examples can be seen in *East and West* (1923), *Kosher Kitty Kelly* (1926), and *The Cantor's Son* (1937). The secular Jew figure internalized the same binary by positioning secularism as an extension of modernism and therefore in direct contrast to the shtetl traditions of immigrant Jewish life. See Hoberman, *Bridge of Light*, 68–70.

15. Joyce Antler, *Talking Back: Images of Jewish Women in Popular Culture* (Hanover, NH: Brandeis University Press, 1998), 32.

16. Hoberman, *Bridge of Light*, 30–31.

17. Edward Wagenknecht, *The Movies in the Age of Innocence* (New York: Ballentine Books, 1962), 84.

18. Miriam Hansen, *Babel & Babylon: Spectatorship in the American Silent Film* (Cambridge, MA: Harvard University Press, 1991), 229.

19. Karen Brodkin notes that the raunchy, highly sexed-up Jewess was a staple of Yiddish theater throughout the 1910s and into the 1920s. Celebrated stars such as Fannie Brice, Frances Marion, Vera Gordon, Molly Picon, and Sophie Tucker operated as Jewish parallels to the iconography of what Brodkin calls the "African American mothers of the blues." Brodkin positions the sexualized Jewess as

a coded signifier invoking and subverting the tropes of the stereotypical African-American female. This aligns the Jewess stereotype with the Al Jolson and George Jessel minstrel act and places Griffith's *Judith of Bethulia* and *Birth of a Nation* in an even more interesting racial and gender counterpoint. See Brodkin, *How Jews Became White Folks & What That Says About Race in America*, 126.

20. This seduction sequence occurs directly after another Christian-Jewish miscegenation scene when the Jewish Golem tenderly picks up a young, blond Aryan child in the playgrounds of Prague. Bartov concludes, "(s)ex and the Jews, the threat posed by Jewish women and men to the natural order of things and the transformation that sexual intercourse with gentiles entails, are at the center of cinematic imagination from its very cradle." See Bartov, *The "Jew" in Cinema*, 6.

21. Amelia S. Holberg, "Betty Boop: Yiddish Film Star," *American Jewish History* 87, no. 4 (1999): 291–312.

22. Jonathan D. Sarna, "Intermarriage in America: The Jewish Experience in Historical Context," in *Ambivalent Jew: Intermarriage in America*, ed. Stuart Cohen and Bernard Susser (New York: Jewish Theological Seminary, 2007), 130.

23. Erens, *The Jew in American Cinema*, 30–34, 39.

24. Eric L. Goldstein, *The Price of Whiteness: Jews, Race, and American Identity* (Princeton, NJ: Princeton University Press, 2006), 128.

25. Although no print of *Private Izzy Murphy* survives, the plot can be surmised from archival reviews and publicity stills. For a synopsis, see *Private Izzy Murphy*, www.imdb.com/title/tt0017290/plotsummary?ref_=tt_ov_pl.

26. Michael Rogin, *Blackface, White Noise: Jewish Immigrants in the Hollywood Melting Pot* (Berkeley: University of California Press, 1998).

27. Rogin, *Blackface, White Noise*, 82, and Vincent Brook, "The Four Jazz Singers: Mapping the Jewish Assimilation Narrative," *Journal of Modern Jewish Studies* 10, no. 3 (2011): 401–420.

28. Cathy Schlund-Vials, "Fathers, Sons, and Symbolic Ethnicity: Considering Two Generations of *The Jazz Singer*," *Americana: The Journal of American Popular Culture* (March 2004), www.americanpopularculture.com/archive/film/neil_diamond.htm.

29. One of the expansions of cinematic language that sound introduced was the ability to produce what theorist Michael Chion describes as "doubles and ghosts" that locate between picture and image. Jack Robin's aural presence at the moment of ethnic doubling via blackface suggests the trauma of European Jewry in refusing to stay silent. See Michael Chion, *The Voice in Cinema* (New York: Columbia University Press, 1999), 136.

30. Rogin, *Blackface, White Noise*, 82–83.

31. Matthew Frye Jacobson, *Whiteness of a Different Color: European Immigrants and the Alchemy of Race* (Cambridge, MA: Harvard University Press, 1998), 121.

32. Rogin, *Blackface, White Noise*, 8, 116.

33. Erens, *The Jew in American Cinema*, 105.

34. Ibid., 98.

35. J. Hoberman points out that while the genre remained popular, production had shifted from Hollywood to Yiddish cinema by the late 1910s. See Hoberman, *Bridge of Light*, 34–36.

36. Max Davidson, a German-born Jewish actor, found great success performing as a nebbishy Jewish schlemiel with a heart of gold in a series of two-reel comedies produced by Hal Roach's studio. These included *Jewish Prudence* (1927), *Pass the Gravy* (1928), and *The Boy Friend* (1928). Davidson was so successful that his movies were promoted as "Max Davidson comedies" and featured numerous references to kosher food and Yiddish, along with some of the less complimentary stereotypes like cheapness and greediness. See Donald W. McCaffrey and Christopher P. Jacobs, *Guide to the Silent Years of American Cinema* (Westport, CT: Greenwood Press, 1999), 102.

37. Ibid., 106.

38. Erens, *The Jew in American Cinema*, 106.

39. It was a common anti-Semitic trope that had informed both Shakespeare's Shylock and Dickens's Fagin. Ronald Florence has written on one such example, an incident in Damascus in 1840 in which the Jewish community fell under attack after accusations that they'd sacrificed a priest as part of secret religious rituals. See Ronald Florence, *Blood Libel: The Damascus Affair of 1840* (Madison: University of Wisconsin Press, 2004).

40. May, *Screening Out The Past*, 43–44.

41. *The Melting Pot* was one of the first mainstream successes to define what Vincent Brook describes as the pop culture template for an emerging ideology of multi-ethnic assimilation. See Vincent Brook, *Something Ain't Kosher Here: The Rise of the "Jewish" Sitcom* (New Brunswick, NJ: Rutgers University Press, 2003), 22.

42. David Biale, "The Melting Pot and Beyond: Jews and the Politics of Cultural Identity," in *Insider/Outsider: American Jews and Multiculturalism*, ed. David Biale, Michael Galchinsky, and Susannah Heschel (Berkeley: University of California Press, 1998), 23–25.

43. Jay Gertzman, *Bookleggers and Smuthounds: The Trade in Erotica 1920–1940* (Philadelphia: University of Pennsylvania Press, 2002), 105–107.

44. Ibid., 105–114.

45. Ibid., 206–207.

46. Gertzman argues that there was a direct line from the prosecutions of Jewish bookstore owners of the 1920s and 1930s and the rebellious anti-establishment censorship that challenged positions of counterculture publishers of the 1960s and 1970s. He contends that traces of anxiety toward Jewish sexuality can be seen in the criminal prosecutions of such disparate work as Harvey Kurtzman's *Mad Magazine* and Lenny Bruce's stand-up comedy in the 1950s and early 1960s, as well as in *Screw Magazine* founder Al Goldstein's legal troubles in 1968. Ibid., 287.

47. For more, see Steven Carr, *Hollywood & Anti-Semitism: A Cultural History up to World War II* (New York: Cambridge University Press, 2001), 68–71.

48. Daniel J. Kevles, *In the Name of Eugenics: Genetics and the Uses of Human Heredity* (Cambridge, MA: Harvard University Press, 1995), 44–45.

49. Charles Benedict Davenport, *Heredity in Relation to Eugenics* (New York: Holt, 1911). Via Kevles *In the Name of Eugenics*, 47.

50. Elof Axel Carlson, "The Hoosier Connection: Compulsory Sterilization as Moral Hygiene," in *A Century of Eugenics in America: From the Indiana Experiment to the Human Genome Era*, ed. Paul A. Lombardo (Bloomington: Indiana University Press, 2011), 18–19.

51. The Galton Society was founded in 1918 in New York and named after the pioneering London eugenicist Sir Francis Galton. It consisted of hundreds of scientists and academics insisting that the Nordic race was superior to all others and proposing various ways to preserve that genetic superiority. These included legal prohibitions and sterilization. The organization thrived into the late 1930s.

52. Carlson, "The Hoosier Connection," 75.

53. Unlike their European counterparts, Chinese, Japanese, and Korean immigrants had been barred for some time, dating back to the Chinese Exclusion Act of 1881.

54. Jacobson, *Whiteness of a Different Color*, 84.

55. The connection in the Leopold and Loeb case between Jewish and Queer anxieties was so pronounced that their names were changed to the far more Christian-sounding "Shaw" and "Morgan" for *Rope*, Alfred Hitchcock's 1948 adaptation of the events.

56. Hal Higdon, *Leopold and Loeb: The Crime of the Century* (Champaign: University of Illinois Press, 1999), 147, 214–215.

57. Neal Gabler, *An Empire of their Own: How the Jews Invented Hollywood* (New York: First Anchor Books, 1988), 129.

58. David Desser and Lester D. Friedman, *American Jewish Filmmakers*, 2nd ed. (Champaign: University of Illinois Press, 1993), 1–2.

59. Historian Steve Ross has shown how, despite accusations of liberalism, Hollywood conservatives, led by Louis B. Mayer, actively pushed back against the liberal politics of so many Hollywood power players in the 1920s. Steve Ross, *Hollywood Left and Right: How Movie Stars Shaped American Politics* (New York: Oxford University Press, 2011), 82–83.

60. *The Volcano* (1919) featured such overtly anti-Semitic casting that complaints forced the studio to belatedly change the surname of the hero of the film from "Garland" to "Levison." The titles were also revised to change the Bolshevik character's name from "Minsky" to "Minskiovich," a belated concession to the American Jewish lobby. See Shull, *Radicalism in American Silent Films, 1909–1929*, 91.

61. Paul Buhle, *From the Lower East Side to Hollywood: Jews in American Popular Culture* (London: Verso, 2004), 67–68.

62. Brodkin, *How Jews Became White Folks & What That Says About Race in America*, 175–180.

63. The de-Judaizing and de-Semitizing of US film in the 1930s was not as complete as conventional wisdom has it: twenty-four films featuring Jews were released between 1934 and 1939 compared to sixty-three in the prior six years. See Erens, *The Jew in American Cinema*, 428–433.

64. Thomas Doherty's in-depth study of the tensions in Hollywood during the rise of Nazism is an invaluable resource in understanding how the studio moguls grappled with representation throughout the 1930s. See Thomas Doherty, *Hollywood and Hitler: 1933–1939* (New York: Columbia University Press, 2015).

65. Erens, *The Jew in American Cinema*, 96.

66. Horace Kallen, *Judaism at Bay: Essays Toward the Adjustment of Judaism to Modernity* (New York: Arno Press, 1972), 197–199.

67. Blonde women represented a sign of immigrant ascension in the emerging gangster genre of the early 1930s. Jewish actors, such as Paul Muni and Edward G. Robinson, played Italians who acquired beautiful, white, non-Italian "molls" as a sign of their rise up the economic ladder. James's Irish gangster in *Public Enemy* (1931) demonstrated that this formula was not limited to Jews or Italians.

68. The casting of non-Jewish British thespian George Arliss also worked to denature the film of Jewish specificity. And in both an ironic and tragic coda to this film, footage of the Rothschilds lending money through their bank was stripped of all context and ended up as "evidence" of Jewish corruption in Joseph Goebbels's notorious piece of Nazi propaganda, *Der Ewige Jude* (*The Eternal Jew*) in 1940. See Joan Clinefelter, "A Cinematic Construction of Nazi Anti-Semitism: The Documentary *Der Ewige Jude*" in *Cultural History Through a National Socialist Lens: Essays on the Cinema of the Third Reich*, ed. Robert Reimer (New York: Camden House, 2000), 142.

69. That same year in France, Jean Renoir's *La Grande Illusion* offered a similar use of Christian-Jewish homosocial interplay. The friendship between the implied-Jewish Rosenthal (Marcel Dalio) and the Catholic Maréchal (Jean Gabin) became the subject of much debate over Renoir's use of Jewish stereotypes. Maurice Samuels notes that explicit references to Rosenthal's Jewish identity are not made in the film. Instead, the film identifies Rosenthal through codes associated with Jewish stereotypes. Given Proust's struggles a generation earlier in the wake of Dreyfus, Renoir's reasons for wanting to include a Jewish soldier among the prisoners of World War I were likely noble. But the motivations for not explicitly mentioning Rosenthal as a Jew were also a reminder of how problematic overt Jewishness had become in screen culture of the 1930s. See Maurice Samuels, "Renoir's *La Grande Illusion* and the 'Jewish Question'" in *The Modern Jewish Experience in World Cinema*, ed. Lawrence Baron (Waltham, MA: Brandeis University Press, 2012), 41.

70. Nico Carpenter, "Representing the Past and Present in *The Life of Emile Zola*," in *The Modern Jewish Experience in World Cinema*, ed. Lawrence Baron (Waltham, MA: Brandeis University Press, 2012), 33–34.

71. Playwright Tony Kushner argues that this was Hollywood's reaction to rising anti-Semitism in Europe. Studio executives simply removed all textual Jewish references. See Tony Kushner, "One of Us? Contesting Disraeli's Jewishness and Englishness in the Twentieth Century," in *The Modern Jewish Experience in World Cinema*, ed. Lawrence Baron (Waltham, MA: Brandeis University Press, 2012), 233–235.

72. This took place despite the fact that some of the most famous politically engaged European Jewish authors were then immigrating to the United States to flee Hitler and Mussolini. By the late 1930s, Thomas Mann, Aldous Huxley, Bertolt Brecht, Theodor Adorno, and Arnold Schoenberg were just a few of the notable writers who sought refuge, and paychecks, in the sunny confines of Southern California. See Lisa Colletta, *British Novelists in Hollywood, 1935–1965: Travelers, Exiles, and Expats* (New York: Palgrave MacMillan, 2013), 16–18.

73. Elizabeth Kendall, *The Runaway Bride: Hollywood Romantic Comedy of the 1930s* (New York: Cooper Square Press, 2002), xiv–xv.

74. In a notable exception, Edward G. Robinson's opposition to Nazism in the 1930s and his commitment to leftist labor issues in the 1940s made him a target for the House Un-American Activities Committee and unleashed an avalanche of anti-Semitic hate mail. For more, see Ross, *Hollywood Left and Right*, 114–115.

75. Paul Franklin, "Jew Boys, Queer Boys," in *Queer Theory and the Jewish Question*, ed. Daniel Boyarin, Daniel Itzkovitz, and Ann Pellegrini (New York: Columbia University Press, 2003), 135–158.

76. Yiddish cinema and Yiddish theater both continued to thrive throughout the 1930s, playing mostly in clustered urban centers such as New York's Lower East Side. Many of the films offered counter-narratives to the assimilationist message of films such as *The Jazz Singer*. In countless Yiddish films, the young Jewish protagonist invariably fell back in love with a Jewish love interest after being tempted by the allure of the Anglo-Christian partner. Numerous examples exist, including *The Cantor's Son* (1937) and *Overture to Glory* (1940). For more on the thriving Yiddish cinema of the 1930s, see Eric A. Goldman, *The American Jewish Story Through Cinema* (Austin: University of Texas Press, 2013), 42–44.

77. Jeffrey Shandler, *Jews, God, and Videotape: Religion and Media in America* (New York: New York University Press, 2009), 56–60.

78. Jacobson, *Roots Too*, 2–3.

PART TWO. THE SECOND WAVE

1. Will Herberg, "Who Are the Hippies?" *National Review*, August 8, 1967, www.nationalreview.com/article/414343/who-are-hippies-will-herberg.

2. Lester Friedman defines the Hollywood New Wave as the moment American cinema congealed as a distinct art form, before the advent of home video in the early 1980s broke down the barriers between film and television and, eventually, new media. Lester Friedman, *American Cinema of the 1970s: Themes and Variations* (New Brunswick, NJ: Rutgers University Press, 2007), 3.

3. Kristen Thompson and David Bordwell, *Film History: An Introduction*, 3rd ed. (New York: McGraw-Hill, 2010), 478–479.

4. Peter Biskind marks this period as beginning with the impact of *Bonnie and Clyde* (1967), *The Graduate* (1967), and *Easy Rider* (1969) and ending, thirteen years

later, in the financial debacle of Michael Cimino's *Heaven's Gate* (1980). Peter Biskind, *Easy Riders, Raging Bulls: How the Sex-Drugs-and-Rock 'N' Roll Generation Saved Hollywood* (New York: Simon & Schuster, 1998), 16–17.

5. As Steven Bayme notes, until the mid-1960s, Jews were intermarrying at one of the lowest rates of any ethnic or culturally distinct group in the United States. Between the mid-1960s and the mid-1970s, that intermarriage rate went from under 10 percent to nearly 35 percent, triggering a crisis among religious American Jews hoping to preserve their culture. See Steven Bayme, *Jewish Arguments and Counterarguments: Essays and Addresses* (Hoboken, NJ: Ktav Publishing House, 2002), 195.

6. Hoberman and Shandler, eds., *Entertaining America*, 220. Bial, *Acting Jewish*, 86–87.

7. Matthew Frye Jacobson describes this revival of ethnic pride as a nostalgic desire to "look back to the East Side immigrant ghetto." Jacobson, *Roots Too*, 131.

8. The late 1960s revival of the unruly Jewess character, while less frequent, was most notably embodied by Barbra Streisand in her star turn as Fanny Brice in *Funny Girl* (1968). Other female Jewish performers of the period, such as Carol Kane, Madeline Kahn, Bette Midler, and Goldie Hawn, followed closer to the Judy Holliday model of duplicitous masquerade for comedic effect.

9. This visibility became, as Eric A. Goldman notes, a paradoxical state between integration and assimilation. The more visible Jews assimilated, the more they were free to be at once both loudly and proudly sexual and loudly and proudly Jewish. But this visible assimilation required confirmation, via the sexual realm, of the idealized beauty standards of Anglo-Christian-American postwar traditions. See Goldman, *The American Jewish Story through Cinema*, 9.

CHAPTER 4. BENJAMIN'S CROSS

1. Many Palestinians prefer the name *an-Naksah* (The Setback) for the war.

2. Yoram Meitel, "Six Days of War: June 1967 and the Making of the Modern Middle East," *Shofar: An Interdisciplinary Journal of Jewish Studies* 22, no. 4 (2004): 179–181.

3. Judith Thurman, "Nowhere Woman: Yasmina Reza Returns to Broadway," *New Yorker*, March 16, 2009.

4. Ibid.

5. Nurith Gertz, "Holocaust Survivor's Point of View," in *Divergent Jewish Cultures: Israel and America*, ed. Deborah Dash Moore and S. Ilan Troen (New Haven, CT: Yale University Press, 2001), 221.

6. Homi K. Bhabha, *The Location of Culture* (London: Routledge, 1994), 122.

7. Lawrence Grossman, "Transformation Through Crisis: The American Jewish Committee and the Six-Day War," *American Jewish History* 86, no. 1 (1998): 27–54.

8. Gavin Smith, "Of Metaphors and Purpose: Mike Nichols Interview," *Film Comment*, May 1999.

9. Sam Kashner, "Here's to You, Mr. Nichols: The Making of *The Graduate*," *Vanity Fair*, February 28, 2008, www.vanityfair.com/culture/features/2008/03/graduate200803.

10. Ibid.

11. Ibid.

12. A famous exception was Scotch-Irish actress Irene Wallace, who often starred as the "Jewess" in the ghetto love stories of the 1910s.

13. Thomas Doherty, *Pre-Code Hollywood: Sex, Immorality, and Insurrection in American Cinema, 1930–1954* (New York: Columbia University Press, 1999), 339. Rogin, *Blackface, White Noise*, 78.

14. An exception occurred in a small number of studio films—such as *Gentlemen's Agreement* (1947)—produced in the wake of World War II in the late 1940s.

15. Steve Cohan, *Masked Men: Masculinity and the Movies in the Fifties* (Bloomington: Indiana University Press, 1997).

16. Litvak, *The Un-Americans*, 30.

17. Norman Cohn, *Warrant For Genocide: The Myth of the Jewish World Conspiracy and* The Protocols of the Elders of Zion (London: Serif, 1996), 226.

18. Bial, *Acting Jewish*, 33.

19. Ibid.

20. Interestingly, the subject of anti-Semitism was a late addition to the film. The novel on which the film was based, Richard Brooks's 1945 *The Brick Foxhole*, was about homophobia, but anti-Semitism was seen as a less taboo subject at the time. The script change also confirmed the topicality of Jewish issues of identity in the late 1940s.

21. Dialogue via the Internet Movie Database, www.imdb.com/title/tt0039416/quotes.

22. Judith E. Doneson, *The Holocaust in American Film* (Syracuse, NY: Syracuse University Press, 2002), 51–54.

23. Bial, *Acting Jewish*, 33–35.

24. This representational shift can perhaps be traced to Charlie Chaplin's star turn in *The Great Dictator* (1940). In a variation of his Little Tramp character, Chaplin played an unnamed Jewish barber living in a Nazi-like country, Tomania. The barber is persecuted, chased, and eventually ends up in disguise, being mistaken for the Hitler-like dictator himself, "Hynkel" (also played by Charlie Chaplin in a dual-role performance). In linking Jewish identity to non-Jewish performance, *The Great Dictator* was one of the first films to argue universal Jewishness as a progressive political response to Nazi eugenics.

25. June Havoc, like Peck, was not Jewish in real life. This furthered the notion of performative Jewishness through casting, even if most viewers were likely not aware of Havoc's biographical background.

26. Garfield, born Jacob Julius Garfinkle, was reportedly not happy when Jack Warner requested he change his name to something less Jewish. As the first major movie star to perform the "method" acting style, Garfield called for authenticity, and his Jewish identity became central to both his choice of characters and his act-

ing style. See Thom Andersen, "Un-American," in *Hollywood: Politics and Film in the Blacklist Era*, ed. Frank Krutnik, Steve Neale, Brian Neve, and Peter Stanfield (New Brunswick, NJ: Rutgers University Press, 2007), 258–259.

27. Garfield's ethnic carnality set the stage for Marlon Brando's subsequent breakthrough as the sexually explosive Stanley Kowalski in *A Streetcar Named Desire* (1951), a stage role originally intended for Garfield himself.

28. Samuel J. Rosenthal, "John Garfield: Golden 'Boychick,'" in *Entertaining America: Jews, Movies, and Broadcasting*, ed. J. Hoberman and Jeffrey Shandler (Princeton, NJ: Princeton University Press, 2004), 174.

29. Victor S. Navasky, *Naming Names* (New York: Hill and Wang, 2003), 368–369.

30. Jacobson, *Whiteness of a Different Color*, 130–131.

31. Bial, *Acting Jewish*, 33–35.

32. Robert Nott, *He Ran All the Way: The Life of John Garfield* (New York: Limelight Editions, 2003), 261.

33. Gabler, *An Empire of Their Own*, 369.

34. Carr, *Hollywood and Anti-Semitism*, 155–157.

35. Via Sally Denton, *The Pink Lady: The Many Lives of Helen Gahagan Douglas* (New York: Bloomsbury Press, 2009), 107–108.

36. Janet R. Jakobson, "Queers are Like Jews, Aren't They? Analogy and Alliance Politics," in *Queer Theory and the Jewish Question*, ed. Daniel Boyarin, Daniel Itzkovitz, Ann Pelligrini (New York: Columbia University Press, 2003), 76.

37. Mel Brooks described the panic in the writers' room of *Your Show of Shows* over an impending HUAC visit: "We didn't know if they were after Communists, Jews, or just short people." Mel Brooks and Carl Reiner, interviewed by Larry Karaszewski at the Egyptian Theater, Los Angeles, July 23, 2010.

38. With origins in many classic Biblical Jewish/non-Jewish romantic adventures, the film was a big-budget historical melodrama centered on the Jewish king, David, and his lust for the non-Jewish Bathsheba (Susan Hayward). The erotic charge of Jewish-Christian coupling is rendered explicit in the film's dialogue when Bathsheba seductively tells the brooding David, "If the law of Moses is to be broken, let us break it with full understanding of what we want from each other." See Joel Samberg, *Reel Jewish* (New York: Jonathan David Publishers, 2000), 44–45.

39. The only Jewish actor given one of the Jewish roles was Edward G. Robinson, cast as Dathan, the Hebrew Judas figure who betrays Moses to the pharaoh. The Jew-as-Jew could only be visible in a negative context as Judas, the betrayer of the Anglo-Saxon Charlton Heston as Moses. See Cohan, *Masked Men*, 133.

40. As Eric A. Goldman notes in his comprehensive study of Jewish cinema, 1958 was a transformative year for Jewish representations in the postwar era. See Goldman, *The American Jewish Story through Cinema*, 6.

41. One notable exception was Kirk Douglas's role as a Holocaust survivor in the low-budget Stanley Kramer-produced film, *The Juggler* (1953). In the film, directed by former HUAC blacklist victim Edward Dmytryk, Douglas plays a

German-Jewish Holocaust survivor and renowned vaudevillian juggler struggling with post-traumatic stress after relocating to Israel. The film functioned as much as a promotion vehicle for the nascent Israel as it did a narrative about the Holocaust, a subject that was downplayed in the film. In another exception, Jewish convert Elizabeth Taylor played the crypto-Jewish character of Rebecca in *Ivanhoe* (1963), but this is a debatable counter-example.

42. Vincent Brook describes this casting decision as offering a distilled reflection of the entire period of Jewish absence in the 1950s. See Vincent Brook, "The Four Jazz Singers: Mapping the Jewish Assimilation Narrative," *Journal of Modern Jewish Studies* 10, no. 3 (2011): 401–420.

43. For more on Gertrude Berg's influence on radio and in early television, see Michele Hilmes, *The Nation's Voice: Radio in the Shaping of American Culture* (Minneapolis: University of Minnesota Press, 1997).

44. Thomas Doherty, *Cold War, Cool Medium: Television, McCarthyism, and American Culture* (New York: Columbia University Press, 2003), 41.

45. Ibid., 46.

46. The real-life event would be re-created by actor and fellow blacklist victim Zero Mostel in *The Front* (1976).

47. Vincent Brook, *Something Ain't Kosher Here: The Rise of the "Jewish" Sitcom* (New Brunswick, NJ: Rutgers University Press, 2003), 22.

48. Gabler, Rich, and Antler, *Television's Changing Image of American Jews*, 15.

49. George Lipsitz, "The Meaning of Memory: Family, Class, and Ethnicity in Early Network Television," *Cultural Anthropology* 1, no. 4 (1986): 386–387.

50. Donald Weber, "The Jewish-American World of Gertrude Berg: *The Goldbergs* on Radio and Television, 1930–1950," in *Talking Back: Images of Jewish Women in American Popular Culture*, ed. Joyce Antler (Hanover, NH: Brandeis University Press, 1998), 97–100.

51. The anxiety was not only directed at Jews. The intermarriage framework of *I Love Lucy* featured a playful satire of domestic bliss in the arguments and battle-of-the-sexes comedy of the Cuban Ricky Ricardo (Desi Arnaz) and Lucy McGillicuddy Ricardo (Lucille Ball). *I Love Lucy* became the first breakout sitcom of the 1950s to transform the ethnic Other into a proto-white American. Desi Arnaz inspired just as much attention from HUAC as had Philip Loeb. He and Lucille Ball faced repeated accusations of un-American activities, and they countered this, as best they could, by presenting Ricky Ricardo as just another variation on the Anglo-Christian father figure. See Doherty, *Cold War, Cool Medium*, 52–55.

52. Gabler, Rich, and Antler, *Television's Changing Image of American Jews*, 32–34. David Marc, *Comic Visions: Television Comedy and American Culture* (Boston: Unwin Hyman, 1989), xiii.

53. Marc, *Comic Visions*, 75

54. Litvak describes Loeb as a member of the "comicosmopolitan" group of Jewish actors who responded to HUAC by struggling to couch their ethnicity in broader rubrics of comedy and performance. Litvak, *The Un-Americans*, 156–158.

55. David Zurawik, *The Jews of Prime Time* (Hanover, NH: Brandeis University Press, 2000), 50–51.

56. Neal Gabler, Frank Rich, and Joyce Antler, *Television's Changing Image of American Jews* (Los Angeles: Norman Lear Center, 2000), 12.

57. Ibid., 10–17.

58. In 1994, Robert Redford's *Quiz Show* revisited anxieties over Jewish visibility on television in the 1950s, exploring the true story of the 1956 scandal over rigged questions on the NBC game show *Twenty-One*. Motivated by discomfort with their long-term winner's unapologetic Jewishness, the Jewish producers of *Twenty-One* (Hank Azaria and David Paymer) replace the nebbishy, intellectual Herbie Stempel (John Turturro) with a conventionally handsome, erudite WASP intellectual, Charles Van Doren (Ralph Fiennes). Redford, the preeminent masculine, blond movie star of the 1960s, was perhaps also commenting on his own role as an idealized Anglo-Saxon alternative to the "funny-looking" Jewish movie stars who emerged during the second wave of the late 1960s and 1970s.

59. Joel Samberg, *Reel Jewish* (New York: Jonathan David Publishers, 2000), 58.

60. Zivin, *The Wandering Signifier*, 74–75.

61. Mosse, *Nationalism and Sexuality*, 134.

62. Boyarin, *Unheroic Conduct*, 246.

63. Deborah Dash Moore and S. Ilan Troen, *Divergent Jewish Cultures: Israel and America* (New Haven, CT: Yale University Press, 2001), 217–218.

64. Boyarin, *Unheroic Conduct*, 248.

65. Biale, *Eros and the Jews*, 176–177.

66. Yosefa Loshitzky, *Identity Politics on the Israeli Screen* (Austin: University of Texas Press, 2001), 6.

67. Loshitzky makes this point by noting that Ben-Canaan has no character arc or epiphany; his goals are clear and linear the entire time. Ibid., 7.

68. *Exodus* does feature a Jewish love story between teenage Holocaust survivor Karen Hansen (Jill Haworth) and the radical Zionist Dov Landau (Sal Mineo). However, Karen's Danish-Jewish identity, blonde hair, blue eyes, and tiny nose are so Teutonic in appearance that they even confuse Kitty, who at first mistakes Karen for a Gentile. This secondary love story, perhaps created to placate Jewish concerns over the Kitty-Ari pairing, is further undercut by the fact that neither actor was Jewish.

69. Bartov, *The "Jew" in Cinema*, 190.

70. Ibid., 190–191.

71. Moore and Troen, *Divergent Jewish Cultures*, 217–218.

72. Boyarin, *Unheroic Conduct*, 6–7.

73. Cohan, *Masked Men*, 12.

74. Ibid., 13.

75. Benjamin Ivry, "A Jew By Choice: Elizabeth Taylor, 1932–2011," *Forward*, March 23, 2011.

76. Biale, *Eros and the Jews*, 176–177.

77. This link between Israel and sexual potency draws from what Daniel and Jonathan Boyarin describe as the long Jewish tradition that likened scholarly achievement to erotic interplay. See Daniel Boyarin and Jonathan Boyarin, *Carnal Israel: Reading Sex in Talmudic Culture* (Berkeley: University of California Press, 1993), 134–135.

78. Leonard Dinnerstein, *Anti-Semitism in America* (New York: Oxford University Press, 1994), 241.

79. Daniel Boyarin describes Herzlian Zionism as "dueling carried on by other means." Both films embody the notion of Zionist dueling through sexual and physiognomic conflict. See: Boyarin, *Unheroic Conduct*, 295.

80. Marjorie Garber, *Vice Versa: Bisexuality and the Eroticism of Everyday Life* (New York: Touchstone, 1995), 423.

81. Garber notes how gender theorists like Eve Kosofsky Sedgwick have applied Foucauldian readings to these triangles to unpack complex discourses of power, queerness, and bisexuality in which binaries break down under closer critical examination. Ibid., 424–425.

82. The outsider nature of Benjamin is solidified when he enters Carl's quintessential college frat house. Benjamin discovers a number of blond-haired, physically robust men similar to Carl showering together. The frat boys are preening and roughhousing in various states of undress. As in the monkey house sequence, Benjamin is positioned as a disruptive version of alternative masculinity, entering a fully Anglo-Christian world of privilege.

83. The animal motif is also established through Mrs. Robinson's clothing. She wears a fur leopard-print jacket during her initial seduction of Benjamin and is seen in leopard-print underwear during their subsequent bedroom encounters.

CHAPTER 5. PORTNOY'S MONKEY

1. Louis Menand, "Young Saul: The Subject of Bellow's Fiction," *New Yorker*, May 5, 2015.

2. As the *New York Times* noted in its obituary of Henry Roth in 1995, *Call It Sleep* was the only major work Roth ever authored. After the novel initially failed, Roth left writing behind and lived an itinerant life. See Richard Severo, "Henry Roth is Dead at 89; Wrote Novel 'Call It Sleep,'" *New York Times*, October 14, 1995, www.nytimes.com/1995/10/14/nyregion/henry-roth-is-dead-at-89-wrote-novel-call-it-sleep.html.

3. Lev Grossman and Richard Lacayo, "All-Time 100 Novels," *Time*, January 6, 2010.

4. Stanislav Kolar, "Ethnicity and Some Other Aspects of Henry Roth's *Call It Sleep*," *Moravian Journal of Literature and Film* 1, no. 1 (2009): 77–78.

5. Josh Lambert, *Unclean Lips: Obscenity, Jews, and American Culture* (New York: New York University Press, 2014), 62–64, 69–71.

6. Jacobson, *Roots Too*, 130.

7. Gibbs's analysis of Roth's autobiographical extrapolation of Jewish sexuality and Gentile erotic fixation in his work focuses more on Roth's *A Diving Rock on the Hudson* (1995), but similar themes are credited to *Call It Sleep*. See Alan Gibbs, "Ira Stigman's 'Jewish Salami': Sex and Self-Hatred in the Work of Henry Roth," in *Jews & Sex*, ed. Nathan Abrams (Nottingham: Five Leaves Publications, 2008), 141–145.

8. "Nostalgia: 70s Style," *Vintage Traveler*, February 13, 2012, https://thevintage traveler.wordpress.com/2012/02/13/nostalgia-70s-style.

9. Saul Bellow, *Herzog* (New York: Penguin Books, 1991).

10. L. H. Goldman, *Saul Bellow's Moral Vision: A Critical Study of the Jewish Experience* (New York: Irvington Publications, 1984), 137.

11. Pauline Kleingeld, "Romantic Cosmopolitanism: Novalis's Christianity or Europe," *Journal of the History of Philosophy* 46, no. 2 (2008): 269–272.

12. Goldman, *Saul Bellow's Moral Vision*, 144.

13. Saul Bellow, "A Jewish Writer in America," *New York Review of Books*, October 27, 2011, www.nybooks.com/articles/2011/10/27/jewish-writer-america.

14. Ibid.

15. Ibid.

16. Bellow answered by considering the impact of both Benjamin Disraeli and Alfred Dreyfus on his early writing, suggesting that the American Diaspora was an amalgam of these historical figures. The postwar Jew could maintain a perspective aligned with European *métèque* (outsider) writers confronting far more clearly demarcated anti-Semitic cultural boundaries. But the postwar Jew was also distinctly American, relatable and referable for both Jewish and non-Jewish reader alike. Ibid., 9.

17. Scholem saw Benjamin's scholarship on defining the aura of the authentic in the age of mechanical reproduction and his Angel of History as acutely grounded in Kabbalah-inspired critical materialism born directly from Jewish philosophy. Scholem had left Germany (and the Frankfurt School) in 1923 to immigrate to pre-Israel Palestine and found an academic institution focused on Jewish philosophy. His emphasis on Jewish specificity, and exclusivity, rejected Benjamin's argument for a universal accessibility. David Biale, *Gershom Scholem: Kabbalah and Counter-History* (Cambridge, MA: Harvard University Press, 1982), 6–7.

18. In 1982, Woody Allen explored this seen/unseen paradox in *Zelig*. The more the assimilationist Leonard Zelig attempted to blend into the dominant culture, the more he was seen for his Jewish duplicity and outsider status. *Zelig* made this duplicity formal by scrambling the barriers between scripted and documentary aesthetics and even featured an interview with Bellow himself.

19. Boyarin, *Unheroic Conduct*, xvii–xix.

20. Malamud debuted as a novelist in 1952 with *The Natural*, a metaphysical story about baseball as a metaphor for the American dream. The story of Roy Hobbs was steeped in a lyrical and mythic nostalgia. The tale of a fictional baseball player with a traumatic past, who suddenly appears in his late thirties to lead a fictional team in Depression-era New York to the playoffs, was eventually adapted

into a film directed by Barry Levinson in 1984. It "naturally" starred the very un-Jewish and un-Hoffman Robert Redford. Yet, *The Natural* was an outlier to Malamud's career. After this initial success, the young Malamud shifted his lyrical and imaginative writing style toward a series of short stories and novels about explicitly Jewish characters.

21. Bernard Malamud, *The Assistant* (New York: Farrar, Straus and Giroux, 2003), 75.

22. Ibid., 202.

23. Bernard Malamud, *The Magic Barrel* (New York: Farrar, Straus and Giroux, 2003), 212.

24. Ibid., 214.

25. In *The Fixer* (1966), Malamud focused on the story of a European shtetl Jew wrongly accused of child molestation and murder after the body of a young Christian child is discovered. The novel's conceit of a wrong man accused of a crime because of societal paranoia recalled Kafka's *The Trial* and Fritz Lang's film, *M* (1931). Yet, the allegorical tale of sexual paranoia run amok was also a commentary on fears of 1960s youth culture.

26. Roth described his writing process to biographer Claudia Roth Pierpont as a form of revolution meant to reject both "literary education" and "literary seriousness." See Claudia Roth Pierpont, *Roth Unbound: A Writer and His Books* (New York: Farrar, Straus and Giroux, 2013), 52–54.

27. In addition to apple cores and liver, Portnoy begins compulsively masturbating over and over into his sister's bra in the bathroom. With each attempt, he tries to hit the ceiling light with his ejaculation, eventually succeeding. Roth's exuberant description of Portnoy's sperm "sizzling" on the lightbulb broke new ground in explicit literature of the 1960s.

28. Bernard Avishai, *Promiscuous: "Portnoy's Complaint" and Our Doomed Pursuit of Happiness* (New Haven, CT: Yale University Press, 2012), 41.

29. Barry Gross, "Seduction of the Innocent: *Portnoy's Complaint* and Popular Culture," *MELUS* 8, no. 4 (1981): 82–85.

30. David Gooblar, *The Major Phases of Philip Roth* (New York: Continuum Books, 2011), 52.

31. Philip Roth, *Portnoy's Complaint* (New York: First Vintage International, 1994), 235.

32. Portnoy gives her "the Monkey" nickname because she once ate a banana while watching another couple have sex.

33. Josh Greenfeld, "Doctor, this is my only life and I'm living it in the middle of a Jewish joke!" *New York Times*, February 23, 1969.

34. MacGraw's dual star construction as both signifier of the new movie star as well as normative beauty icon of the early 1960s came to its peak in the massively successful *Love Story* (1970) in which MacGraw plays a Catholic opposite Ryan O'Neal's WASP. *Love Story* was set in an ethnic-free, Jewish-free, humor-free, idealized Ivy League world of Anglo-Saxon privilege, making MacGraw's character a thematic, if not literally, "Jewish" interloper.

35. Jewish affects remain in Ben's accent and table manners. They emerge during a scene in which Brenda's family welcomes Neil to dinner at their suburban estate, establishing which side of the divide Neil Klugman falls on.

36. This dialogue did not appear in the novel.

37. Roth, *Portnoy's Complaint*, 121.

38. By 1974, Roth had introduced the character of Nathan Zuckerman in *My Life as a Man*. Zuckerman would continue to represent Roth's alter ego through numerous novels over the next four decades. In *My Life as a Man*, as with so many Roth novels, the Jewish male's pursuit of the Christian female became his singular act of agency.

39. Sanford Pinsker, "Guilt as Comic Idea: Franz Kafka and the Postures of Modern Jewish Writing," in "Franz Kafka," special issue, *Journal of Modern Literature* 6, no. 3 (1977): 466–471. Elaine B. Safer, "The Double, Comic Irony, and Postmodernism in Philip Roth's *Operation Shylock*," in "Ethnic Humor," special issue, *MELUS* 21, no. 4 (1996): 158.

40. Roth made his Kafka connection fully clear in his 1972 short story, "The Breast." The playful reimagining of Kafka's *Metamorphosis* inverts the transformation from his coded Jewish insect into an overtly textual Jew turning into a female breast. That same year Woody Allen used similar imagery in his short sketch depicting a giant female breast as an escaped monster in *Everything You Always Wanted to Know About Sex . . . But Were Afraid to Ask* (1972).

41. Norman Mailer's *The Naked and the Dead*, published to great acclaim in 1948, was one of the first major texts of this period to explore the crisis of postwar identity through Christian-Jewish interplay. Two soldiers, one Jewish (Goldstein) and the other Protestant (Ridges), simultaneously lose their religious faith while developing a powerful homosocial bond as they are forced to transport a dead soldier during the war. But Jonathan Freedman suggests that the link among postwar Jewishness, masculine crisis, sexuality, and American letters actually began a year later with Arthur Miller's triumphant *Death of a Salesman* (1949). Freedman argues that this was confirmed by Miller's subsequent successful seduction of shiksa icon Marilyn Monroe in 1956. See Jonathan Freedman, *Klezmer America: Jewishness, Ethnicity, Modernity* (New York: Columbia University Press, 2008), 96–97. Joel Shatzky and Michael Taub, eds., *Contemporary Jewish-American Novelists: A Bio-Critical Sourcebook* (Westport, CT: Greenwood Press, 1997), 197.

42. Cynthia Ozick, "Judging the World," *New York Times Book Review*, March 16, 2014.

43. Updike's first short story about Bech was "The Bulgarian Poetess." Bech's sexual fixation is a beautiful blonde poetess named Vera Glavanakova. Martin Amis describes Bech as both Updike's appropriation of trendy Jewish protagonists and his expression of anger at the success of Jewish literature. See John Updike, "The Bulgarian Poetess," *New Yorker*, March 15, 1965. Martin Amis, "When Amis Met Updike . . . ," *Guardian*, January 31, 2009, www.theguardian.com/books/2009/feb/01/john-updike-interview-amis-martin.

44. Joyce Carol Oates, "In the Region of Ice," *Atlantic Monthly*, August 1966, 78–85.

45. Jacobson, *Roots Too*, 154.

46. In the summer of 1970, William F. Eich summarized the history of First Amendment protection that had emerged to protect Roth from indecency charges, focusing on three cases in 1966—*Mishkin v. New York, Ginsburg v. United States*, and *A Book Named "John Cleland's Memoirs of a Woman of Pleasure"* (Fanny Hill) *v. Attorney General of Massachusetts*—that each protected the sale of books accused of pornographic content. These cases opened the door for mainstream literature such as *Portnoy's Complaint*. See William F. Eich, "From Ulysses to Portnoy: A Pornography Primer," *Marquette Law Review* 52, no. 2 (1970): 159–162.

47. Peter M. Robinson, *The Dance of the Comedians: The People, The President, and the Performance of Political Standup Comedy in America* (Amherst, MA: University of Massachusetts Press, 2010), 106.

48. Sherman replaced the British professor, Henry Higgins, with a Jewish professor struggling to correct a young British woman's accent by teaching her Yiddish. See Mark Cohen, *Overweight Sensation: The Life and Comedy of Allan Sherman* (Waltham, MA: Brandeis University Press, 2013), 86.

49. Irving Howe, "The Nature of Jewish Laughter," *American Mercury* (1951), 211–212.

50. Michael Gluzman argues that multicultural theorists frequently position Jews as the paradigmatic Diaspora, operating at a unique juncture between modernism and exile. See Michael Gluzman, "Modernism and Exile: A View From the Margins," in *Insider/Outsider: American Jews and Multiculturalism*, eds. David Biale, Michael Galchinsky, and Susannah Heschel (Berkeley: University of California Press, 1998), 231.

51. Lawrence J. Epstein, *The Haunted Smile: The Story of Jewish Comedians in America* (New York: Public Affairs, 2001), xii–xiii.

52. See Vincent Brook, "'Y'all Killed Him, We Didn't!' Jewish Self-Hatred and *The Larry Sanders Show*," in *You Should See Yourself: Jewish Identity in Postmodern American Culture*, ed. Vincent Brook (New Brunswick, NJ: Rutgers University Press, 2006), 312–313.

53. Anthony Gottlieb, "Ruth Hisse Recommends the Best Books on Jewish Humor," *Fivebooks*, September 23, 2013, http://fivebooks.com/interviews/ruth-wisse-on-jewish-humour.

54. Ruth D. Johnston, "Joke-Work: The Construction of Jewish Postmodern Identity in Contemporary Theory and American Film," in *You Should See Yourself: Jewish Identity in Postwar American Culture*, ed. Vincent Brook (New Brunswick, NJ: Rutgers University Press, 2006), 207–209.

55. Andrew Stott, *Comedy: The New Critical Idiom* (New York: Routledge, 2005), 134–135.

56. John Morreall, *Comic Relief: A Comprehensive Philosophy of Humor* (Malden, MA: Wiley-Blackwell, 2009), 6–7.

57. Ibid., 50–51.

58. Joyce Antler describes how Lenny Bruce's impact influenced the Jewish visibility of other performers such as Joan Rivers, who reportedly changed her entire act after seeing Bruce in Greenwich Village in 1961. Bruce encouraged Rivers to speak more honestly and to draw inspiration from the specificity of her Jewish background, her sexual frustrations, and her role as an "urban ethnic." See Joyce Antler, "One Clove Away from a Pomander Ball: The Subversive Tradition of Jewish Female Comedians," in *Jews and Humor: Studies in Jewish Civilization*, vol. 22, ed. Leonard J. Greenspoon (West Lafayette, IN: Purdue University Press, 2011), 162–163.

59. "Jonah and the Whale" was the first sketch the two performed on *The Ed Sullivan Show*. In the sketch, Meara, as journalist Pauline Fredericks, interviewed Mr. Jonah (Stiller), an obnoxious Miami Beach Jew who claimed to have been swallowed by a whale.

60. Jerry Stiller and Anne Meara, interviewed by Gary J. Rutkowski, Archive of American Television, December 12, 2005. Meara described their personas as "the uber-Jewish guy and the uber-Irish girl." See www.emmytvlegends.org /interviews/people/jerry-stiller.

61. Ibid.

62. Gerald Nachman, *Seriously Funny: The Rebel Comedians of the 1950s and 1960s* (New York: Pantheon Books, 2003), 392.

63. For more on Bruce's frequent trials and arrests, see Ronald K. L. Collins and David M. Skover, *The Trials of Lenny Bruce: The Rise and Fall of an American Icon* (Naperville, IL: Sourcebooks, 2002).

64. Sol Saporta argues that Bruce's use of transgressive language is aligned with the work of political activist and linguist Noam Chomsky. Saporta suggests both Bruce and Chomsky located complex language system fractures that challenged the dominant ideological reading strategies and status quo. Sol Saporta, *Society, Language, and the University: From Lenny Bruce to Noam Chomsky* (New York: Vantage Press, 1994).

65. The prosecution cited this routine in Bruce's 1964 obscenity trial over his performance at the Café Au Go Go.

66. Jacques Derrida, "Différance," in *Margins of Philosophy* (Chicago: University of Chicago Press, 1982), 3–27.

67. David E. Kaufman, *Jewhooing the Sixties: American Celebrity and Jewish Identity* (Waltham, MA: Brandeis University, 2012), 128–129.

68. Ibid., 129.

69. Nachman, *Seriously Funny*, 392–394.

70. Steven E. Kercher, *Revel with a Cause: Liberal Satire in Postwar America* (Chicago: University of Chicago Press, 2006), 97.

71. "Nightclubs: The Sickniks," *Time*, July 13, 1959.

72. Kaufman, *Jewhooing the Sixties*, 112–117.

73. Paul Buhle, *From the Lower East Side to Hollywood* (London and New York: Verso, 2004), 184.

74. Roger Bennett and Josh Kun, *And You Shall Know Us By the Trail of Our Vinyl* (New York: Crown Publishers, 2008), 116–118.

75. Musicologist Josh Kun describes an "aurality of Jewish difference" at work in 1950s-era comedy albums in which Yiddishisms ruptured the cohesive framework of the American melting pot. See Josh Kun, "The Yiddish Are Coming: Mickey Katz, Antic-Semitism, and the Sound of Jewish Difference," *American Jewish History* 87, no. 4 (1999): 343–344.

76. Jacobson, among many others, has noted the famous quote from the novel in which Portnoy celebrates his sexual achievement with Monkey: "She puts the id back in Yid, I put the oy back in goy." See Jacobson, *Roots Too*, 155. Roth, *Portnoy's Complaint*, 209, 216–217.

77. Sanford Pinsker, "Shpritzing the Goyim/Shocking the Jews," in *Jewish Wry: Essays on Jewish Humor*, ed. Sarah Blacher Cohen (Detroit: Wayne State University Press, 1990), 89–91.

78. Musicologist Steven Lee Beeber argues that it was Bruce, and not the musical innovators of the 1950s, who was the true progenitor of the counterculture prankster/rock star personas of the 1960s and 1970s such as Bob Dylan, Tuli Kupferberg, and Lou Reed. See Steven Lee Beeber, *The Heebie-Jeebies at CBGB's: A Secret History of Jewish Punk* (Chicago: Chicago Review Press, 2006), 4–5.

79. Kaufman, *Jewhooing the Sixties*, 108–109.

80. Albert Goldman, *Ladies and Gentlemen, Lenny Bruce!!* (New York: Random House, 1974). Via Kaufman, *Jewhooing the Sixties*.

81. Much of this is detailed in Honey Bruce's autobiography, *Honey: The Life and Loves of Lenny's Shady Lady* (Los Angeles: Playboy Press, 1976).

82. Like the 1930s-era movie idols that he idealized and emulated, Hefner expressed a sexual desire that, no matter how libidinal, was untroubled, never neurotic, and fully contained. His act was so archly constructed and obviously performed that it was satirized as early as 1959 by Rock Hudson's unmarried lothario, Brad Allen, in the screwball bedroom farce, *Pillow Talk*.

83. For more on Bruce's frequent trials and arrests, see Collins and Skover, *The Trials of Lenny Bruce*.

84. For more on the history of Jewish radicalism in New York, see Jeffrey S. Gurock, *Jews in Gotham: New York Jews in a Changing City, 1920–2010* (New York: New York University Press, 2012), 57–60.

85. Historian Paul Buhle notes how Abbie Hoffman mimicked the Jewish cadences of Bruce's rebellious jester as part of his late-1960s Yippie persona delivered in the street theater tradition. Paul Buhle, *From the Lower East Side to Hollywood: Jews in American Popular Culture* (New York: Verso, 2004), 185.

86. Nearly a decade after his death, Bruce's life story was adapted into the Bob Fosse-directed *Lenny* (1974). In perhaps a tribute to their already established thematic connection, Dustin Hoffman played the title character. While tracking Bruce's professional career highlights and lowlights, the film primarily focuses on the troubled relationship between Bruce and his "shiksa goddess," Honey Harlow (Valerie Perrine). Editorial techniques such as jump cuts, documentary realist aes-

thetics, and the mixing of black-and-white and color film stock gave *Lenny* a similar French New Wave imprint as that seen seven years earlier in *The Graduate*. The story is fragmented, moving backward and forward in time to explore the early courtship years, blooming love, tragic descent into heroin addiction, and eventual mutual self-destruction.

CHAPTER 6. KATIE'S TYPEWRITER

1. Michel Foucault, *Society Must be Defended: Lectures at the College de France, 1975–1976*, trans. David Macey (New York: St. Martin's Press, 1997).

2. Glenn Linden, "The Historical Profession in Transition: Its Response to the Challenges of the 1960s and 1970s," *History Teacher* 23, no. 3 (May 1990): 293–303.

3. Derrida's examination focused on the contrast between an entrenched European teaching philosophy and the African subaltern in French school systems. Jacques Derrida, *Who's Afraid of Philosophy? Right to Philosophy I*, trans. Jan Plug (Stanford, CA: Stanford University Press, 2002), 102–103.

4. Michel Foucault, *The Order of Things, An Archeology of the Human Sciences* (New York: Vintage Books, 1994), 326–328.

5. Charlotte Kroløkke, "Three Waves of Feminism: From Suffragettes to Grrls," in *Gender Communication: Theories and Analyses: From Silence to Performance*, eds. Charlotte Kroløkke and Ann Scott Sorensen (Thousand Oaks, CA: Sage Publications, 2005). Judith Butler, *Bodies That Matter: On the Discursive Limits of "Sex"* (New York: Routledge, 1993), 167. Carol Hanisch, "The Personal Is Political," in *Notes from the Second Year: Women's Liberation, Major Writings of the Radical Feminist*, ed. Shulamith Firestone and Anne Koedt (New York: Radical Feminism, 1970).

6. Mazursky was fired from directing *I Love You, Alice B. Toklas* by the star, Peter Sellers, who was convinced that Mazursky was interested in Sellers's new wife, Britt Ekland. The film was subsequently directed by Hy Averback. However, for the purposes of this analysis, the film will be considered as part of Mazursky's larger body of work as he was both the screenwriter and the originator of the project.

7. The wedding sequences feature a chuppah (a traditional Jewish wedding canopy), an officiating rabbi, and Harold in a yarmulke, offering some of the most significant and notable imagery of American Jewish life in a major Hollywood release since the 1930s.

8. Sellers's comic masks, from Clare Quilty in *Lolita* (1962) to Dr. Fassbinder in *What's New, Pussycat?* (1965), can be read in the Jewish vaudevillian tradition. But the character of Harold Fine represents the first time the British chameleon Sellers played an explicitly Jewish character. Sellers's Jewish background—in particular, his doting, career-obsessed Jewish mother—was a staple of his star persona in the popular press of the time. His father was not Jewish. But Sellers stated in numerous interviews that he considered himself Jewish growing up and often

suffered anti-Semitic taunts at school in England. See Nathan Abrams, "A Jewish American Monster: Stanley Kubrick, Anti-Semitism and *Lolita* (1962)," *Journal of American Studies* 49, no. 3 (November 12, 2014): 1–16.

9. William Friedkin explored similar themes in his adaptation of the hit off-Broadway play, *The Boys in the Band* (1970). The play depicts the identity struggles of gay men in Stonewall-era 1960s New York by focusing on a birthday party held for Harold (Leonard Frey) and attended by five gay male friends. The party turns aggressive, forcing Harold to confront his self-hatred over his identity as an "ugly, pock-marked, Jew fairy."

10. Eight years earlier, Natalie Wood's breakout role as Maria, the Puerto Rican love interest in *West Side Story* (1961), had emphasized the liberal push to argue against racism and bigotry through interracial romantic coupling.

11. Dialogue via the Internet Movie Database, www.imdb.com/title/tt0064100/quotes?item=qt0171025.

12. The memorial traced this period as beginning in 1965 with Culp's starring role in the TV series *I Spy* (1965–1968), opposite Bill Cosby, and ending with his awkward, stilted performance as a swinger opposite the charming next-generation sexuality of Elliott Gould. The transition from Culp to Gould in 1969 demonstrated how quickly the culture had shifted in just four years. Anthony Giardina, "Robert Culp: The Self-Conscious Hunk," *New York Times Magazine*, December 26, 2010.

13. Gould's first significant role was as Billy Minsky, a Jewish burlesque theater owner, in William Friedkin's 1968 farce, *The Night They Raided Minsky's*. Minsky hires a young Amish woman (Britt Ekland) who accidentally invents the striptease. Gould went on to star in several films in little more than a year, including *Bob & Carol & Ted & Alice* (1969), *M*A*S*H* (1970), *Getting Straight* (1970), and *Little Murders* (1970).

14. Jules Feiffer, "Elliott Gould: Star For an Uptight Age," in *Time*, September 7, 1970.

15. Ibid.

16. Erens, *The Jew in American Cinema*, 258–263.

17. By naming the Gene Wilder character after James Joyce's iconic wandering Jewish schlemiel, Leopold Bloom, in *Ulysses*, writer-director Mel Brooks drew a direct line from the importance of Jewish characters in late modern literature to their self-aware reemergence in the second wave of the late 1960s.

18. Erens, *The Jew in American Cinema*, 308.

19. The location is central to understanding the breakdown of cohesive Jewish life in the early 1970s. The Miami Beach of the 1960s and 1970s was an idealized Jewish nirvana, a proto-Zionist fantasyland of cabanas, pool parties, and canasta games. It was also a favorite destination for Jewish retirees.

20. Sholem Aleichem, *Tevye's Daughters*, trans. Frances Butwin (New York: Sholem Aleichem Family Publications), 1999.

21. Although specific in cultural subject matter, the show was configured to be accessible for both Jewish and non-Jewish audiences. The lead protagonist, Tevye

the Milkman (Zero Mostel on stage, Topol in the film), served as both narrator and interpreter, explaining Jewish terms and rituals to a presumably Gentile audience unfamiliar with such customs.

22. Molly Picon, the young comic star of Yiddish theater and film in the 1920s, appeared in the film version of *Fiddler on the Roof* as Yente the Matchmaker.

23. The play makes numerous references to new philosophical thinking at the turn of the twentieth century. Tevye's use of dream interpretation with his wife Golde, played for comedic effect in the show, invokes Freud. Tevye's playful meta-commentary, often delivered mid-scene, disrupts narrative coherency and suspension of disbelief, echoing the modernist literary frameworks of Joyce, Proust, and Brecht. The irony is comedic. The Jew inherently signifies modernity even when performing a character set in the pre-modern world.

24. Perchik's mix of Jewish ideology and communist politics is presented in contrast to Tevye's apolitical dreamer. This resonated outside the text: Tevye was played on stage by one of the most famous victims of the HUAC blacklist, Zero Mostel.

25. In Aleichem's original story, "Chava," the non-Jew is named Chvedka, not Fyedka. In pleading for Tevye to consider the merits of the non-Jew, Chava compares Chvedka to Maxim Gorky, furthering the alignment between Christian-Jewish coupling and modernist writers of the period. Aleichem, *Tevye's Daughters*, 95–96.

26. Philip Graubart, "From Taboo to Afterthought: A Literary History of Intermarriage," *InterfaithFamily*, www.interfaithfamily.com/arts_and_entertainment /popular_culture/From_Taboo_to_Afterthought.shtml?rd=2.

27. Bial, *Acting Jewish*, 95.

28. Streisand's comment was part of her critique of the removal of political contextualization from the film. In the screenplay, the backdrop of the Hollywood blacklist of the late 1940s directly impacted the love affair between Katie and Hubbell. Katie is informed on by a friend, threatening her husband's career. In the final film, this was removed and replaced by a fight over Hubbell's cheating. See Molly Gregory, *Women Who Run the Show: How a Brilliant and Creative New Generation of Women Stormed Hollywood* (New York: St. Martin's Press, 2002), 141–142.

29. Stacy Wolf argues that Streisand's star persona was defined by disruption and unruliness as early as her breakthrough role in *Funny Girl* (1968). Her performances often broke from character to luxuriate in Streisand's fearlessness as a performer unconstrained by the context of the film. See Stacy Wolf, "Barbra's 'Funny Girl' Body," in *Queer Theory and the Jewish Question*, ed. Daniel Boyarin, Daniel Itzkovitz, and Ann Pellegrini (New York: Columbia University Press, 2003), 253–255.

30. Streisand's breakthrough role as 1920s-era Ziegfeld Follies comedienne Fanny Brice in *Funny Girl* (1968) was infused with a similar sociopolitical corrective. Production on the film began during summer 1967, weeks after the Six-Day War. Egyptian actor Omar Sharif was cast in the role of Fanny's husband, the Jewish gangster Nicky Arnstein. When word got out that Sharif and Streisand would

kiss in the film, the Egyptian press was furious, reportedly trying to get Sharif's citizenship revoked unless he refused. Yet, despite panic among Columbia Pictures over boycott threats, director William Wyler and Streisand refused to make a casting change. See Andrea Passafiume, "Behind the Camera on *Funny Girl*," *Turner Classic Movies*, www.tcm.com/this-month/article/220494%7C0/Behind-the -Camera-Funny-Girl.html.

31. Antler, *The Journey Home*, 260.

32. Daniel Horowitz, *Betty Friedan and the Making of* The Feminine Mystique: *The American Left, the Cold War, and Modern Feminism* (Amherst: University of Massachusetts Press, 1998), 132.

33. Streisand was one of the only Jewish movie stars in the second wave to push back on anxieties of casting her with a Jewish romantic partner. The most notable of her attempts, the box office hit *The Owl and the Pussycat* (1970), paired Streisand with George Segal as neighbors caught up in a screwball bedroom farce. Another effort, not affiliated with Streisand, was *A New Leaf* (1971), written by and starring Elaine May opposite the Jewish actor Walter Matthau. But while both are steeped in Jewish performance codes, neither film made any direct reference to the cultural background of its characters.

34. Mostel's performance was based on and in tribute to the tragic career of Philip Loeb, as discussed in chapter 4.

35. For more on how HUAC began with fears of Jewish global influence in Hollywood, particularly fueled by Congressman John Rankin of Mississippi, see Dinnerstein, *Anti-Semitism in America*, 136.

36. Dialogue via the Internet Movie Database, www.imdb.com/title/tt0074554 /quotes.

37. Howard's moment of empowerment is signified by his ability and decision to speak. However, the twist is that Howard speaks not by "naming" the deceased Hecky Brown as "Herschel Brownstein" (thereby acknowledging Hecky as duplicitous both as a Jew and as a communist), but by telling the committee to go fuck themselves.

38. Kris Kristofferson's role as a rugged, macho, Anglo-masculine version of hippie sexuality was first counterpointed with the neurotic Jewish schlemiel in Paul Mazursky's *Blume in Love* (1973). George Segal's Stephen Blume, a divorced Jewish lawyer dipping a toe into the free love era, finds his insecurities provoked when his ex-wife, Nina Blume (Susan Anspach) begins an affair with Kristofferson's hippie singer-songwriter, Elmo Cole. The contrasting Anglo-Jewish masculinities culminate in a disturbing scene where the insecure Blume proves his "masculinity" by raping his ex-wife as revenge for her affair with Cole.

39. In a twist on the notion that women require men to succeed, Esther's lack of attachment sends Howard into a spiral that culminates in his suicide.

40. For more on my work on Woody Allen's satirical use of Jewish-Christian substitution patterns, see Joshua Louis Moss, "'Woody the Gentile': Christian-Jewish Interplay in Allen's Films from *What's New, Pussycat?* to *Midnight in Paris*," in *Woody on Rye: Jewishness in the Films and Plays of Woody Allen*, ed. Vincent

Brook and Marat Grinberg (Hanover, NH: Brandeis University Press, 2013), 100–121. I have also previously written on Mel Brooks's screen Jewishness as historical renegotiation. See Joshua Louis Moss, "Historiography of the World Part 1: The Jewish Body, Historical Crisis and the Comedic Farce," *Mediascape* (Fall 2009), www.tft.ucla.edu/mediascape/Spring08_HistoriographyOfTheWorld1.pdf.

41. Duddy's motivation is inspired by his grandfather's advice that "a man without land is nobody." The allusion to the Jewish Diaspora is clear in the passing of this generational message.

42. Like *The Graduate*, *Annie Hall* presents an ending that is agnostic about the possibility for Jewish-Christian love to transcend the cultural barriers and gender conflicts of the free love era.

43. The famous split-screen comparison of Allen's Jewish and Keaton's WASP family at the dinner table offers the most obvious example of the comedic mining of this contrast. Later in the same sequence, Allen's nebbish verbosity is also contrasted with the laconic nature of Annie's brother, Dwayne (Christopher Walken), a cliché version of WASP repression and bottled rage.

44. Dialogue via the Internet Movie Database, www.imdb.com/title/tt0075686 /quotes.

45. Lynn Spigel, "From Domestic Space to Outer Space: The 1960s Fantastic Family Sitcom," in *Close Encounters: Film, Feminism, and Science Fiction*, ed. Constance Penley (Minneapolis: University of Minnesota Press, 1991), 206. David Marc, *Comic Visions: Television Comedy and American Culture* (Malden, MA: Blackwell Publishers, 1997), 100–120.

46. For more on the complex relationship of 1960s television to the cultural anxieties of the time, see Lynn Spigel and Michael Curtin's *The Revolution Wasn't Televised: Sixties Television and Social Conflict* (New York: Routledge, 1997).

47. In one of the show's last seasons, after Mike and Gloria had moved to California, the Bunkers adopt Edith's nine-year-old grandniece, Stephanie (Danielle Brisebois), after the death of her father, only to discover that she is Jewish. In Season 9, Episode 20, "Stephanie's Conversion" (1979), Archie attempts to have Stephanie forcibly converted to Protestant Christianity. However, her status as a precocious child and a member of the family forces Archie into introspection regarding his anti-Semitic views. He eventually learns to accept Stephanie's Jewish identity, and the Bunkers help her to join a local temple, Beth Shalom.

48. Litvak, *The Un-Americans*, 153–155.

49. Eric Homberger, "Immigrants, Politics, and the Popular Cultures of Tolerance," in *The Cambridge Companion to the Literature of New York*, ed. Cyrus R. K. Patell and Bryan Waterman (Cambridge, UK: Cambridge University Press, 2010), 136.

50. There is a certain irony to this. The third wave of Christian-Jewish couplings began in the early 1990s, not in cinema but in television, as I argue in chapter 8.

51. For this and other facts on the impact of the broadcast, see Jerryl Brunner, "Surprising Facts about Rhoda Morgenstern's Historic Wedding on *Rhoda*," *Pa-*

rade Magazine, October 27, 2014, http://parade.com/349959/jerylbrunner/surpris
ing-facts-about-rhoda-morgensterns-historic-wedding-on-rhoda.

52. As quoted by Kristen Fermaglich, *Jewish Women's Archive*, http://jwa.org
/encyclopedia/article/arthur-bea.

53. Judith Butler, *Gender Trouble: Feminism and the Subversion of Identity*
(New York: Routledge, 1990), 200.

54. Ibid., 200–201.

55. Biale, *Eros and the Jews*, 206–207.

56. Henry Bial describes this as a distinct form of performance known as
"comic bumbling." It made any sexual transgressions safe through comedic Jewish
self-deprecation. See Bial, *Acting Jewish*, 93.

57. Linda Williams, *Hard Core: Power, Pleasure, and the "Frenzy of the Visible"*
(Berkeley: University of California Press, 1999), 134–135.

58. Al Goldstein, interviewed by Luke Ford at the First Annual Pornography
Conference, University of California, Northridge. Cited in E. Michael Jones, *The
Jewish Revolutionary Spirit: And Its Impact on World History* (South Bend, IN: Fi-
delity Press, 2008).

59. Jay Gertzman, *Bookleggers and Smuthounds: The Trade in Erotica, 1920–1940*
(Philadelphia: University of Pennsylvania Press, 2001). Nathan Abrams, "Triple-
Exnthics," *Jewish Quarterly* 196 (Winter 2004). See also Nathan Abrams, "Kosher
Beefcakes and Kosher Cheesecakes: Jews in Porn—An Overview," in *Jews and Sex*,
ed. Nathan Abrams (Nottingham, UK: Five Leaves Publications, 2008), 177–188.

60. Laura Kipnis, *Bound and Gagged: Pornography and the Politics of Fantasy in
America* (Durham, NC: Duke University Press, 2009), 8–9.

61. Gottfried's quote: "He told me girls in porn were mainly Catholic. And
that there was a higher content of Jews on the male side. He had a whole theory!" See Spencer Morgan, "Porn Star Jamie Gillis Remembered by Non-Porn-Star
Friends," *New York Magazine*, March 15, 2010.

62. Dialogue via the Internet Movie Database, www.imdb.com/title/tt0068612
/quotes.

63. Ibid.

64. Andrea Most, "Re-Imagining the Jew's Body," in *You Should See Yourself:
Jewish Identity in Postmodern American Culture*, ed. Vincent Brook (New Brunswick, NJ: Rutgers University Press, 2006), 22–23.

65. Brian Heater, "Interview: Ralph Bakshi, Pt. 2" *Daily Cross Hatch*, June 30,
2008, http://thedailycrosshatch.com/2008/06/30/interview-ralph-bakshi-pt-2.

66. Most, "Re-Imagining the Jew's Body," 23–24.

67. Bardot was married at the time to the German millionaire Gunter Sachs.

68. A 2010 French biopic directed by Joann Sfar called *Gainsbourg: A Heroic
Life* argues that Gainsbourg's creativity emerged from anxieties provoked in his
childhood as a Jew living in occupied France. The film depicts a series of stylized fantasies in which Gainsbourg (Eric Elmosnino) sees himself haunted by giant anti-Semitic puppets with large noses and beady eyes moving among crowds of
(non-Jewish) French people.

69. As rock music grew more explicit in the period of declining censorship, singers such as Simon and Garfunkel ("Mrs. Robinson"), Leonard Cohen ("Sisters of Mercy"), and Bob Dylan penned ironic, pop-culture-infused love songs to Jesus informed by their Jewish outsider status. Many of these songs were decoded differently by Jewish and Christian listeners. In one famous example, in 1968, the Jewish singer Norman Greenbaum's revival tent preacher parody, "Spirit in the Sky," became an un-ironic hit. Few understood that the intention of the lyrics was to mock Christian religious fervor.

70. Norman Mailer, "The White Negro: Superficial Reflections on the Hipster," *Dissent* (October 1957). Reprinted in Norman Mailer, *Advertisements for Myself* (Cambridge, MA: Harvard University Press, 1992).

71. Andrea Levine, "The (Jewish) White Negro": Norman Mailer's Racial Bodies," *MELUS* 28, no. 2 (Summer 2003): 59–81.

72. Michael Hiltzik, *The New Deal: A Modern History* (New York: Free Press, 2012), 213–236.

73. One of the central industrial changes in the 1980s was the invention of home video and cable markets. Explicit sexuality moved from mainstream crossover films such *Deep Throat* (1972) and *Fritz the Cat* (1972) to the segmented, contained VHS rental market. By 1980, this produced a fissure in American politics, a tension between what Garry Wills describes as the mythic, rogue, by-one's-bootstraps individualist fantasy of the American past and the experiences generated by a rapidly developing technological future. The emancipatory nature of graphic sexuality no longer resonated as either political progressiveness or counterculture manifesto. There was no longer a need for a gender-scrambling, sexually deviant screen "Jew" to embody these destabilizations. See Garry Wills, *Reagan's America: Innocents at Home* (New York: Penguin Books, 1987), 448–450.

74. As Michael Ryan and Douglas Kellner point out, Hollywood feature films had begun to closely mirror political shifts beginning in the mid-1960s. The election of Reagan and rise of the New Right in 1980 brought about a similar shift, even as early examples of this transformation could be detected throughout the previous decade. See Michael Ryan and Douglas Kellner, *Camera Politica: The Politics and Ideology of Contemporary Hollywood Film* (Bloomington: Indiana University Press, 1990), 3–5.

75. Streep's role as the shiksa opposite Jewish leading men would recur throughout her career. As I discuss in chapter 7, Streep first emerged in the television miniseries, *Holocaust* (1978), playing the Polish Inga, who marries the Jewish Karl Weiss (James Woods). In *Manhattan* (1979), Streep played a lesbian whose rejection of Woody Allen satirized Jewish masculinity as flawed and incomplete. By the time of her performance in *Kramer vs. Kramer*, this was a familiar part of her emerging star persona.

76. Jewish stars in the second wave were predominantly male with only Streisand, Madeline Kahn, Carol Kane, and Bette Midler performing in the same comedic romantic space. Goldie Hawn's star persona is harder to pin down. Hawn's

mother was Jewish and her father, Presbyterian, but she was raised Jewish. Her early roles—including her Oscar-winning turn in *Cactus Flower* (1969), *There's a Girl in My Soup* (1970), and *Butterflies Are Free* (1972)—identified her only as the quintessential ditzy, free-love hippie. Jewish associations perhaps belied her blonde hair and blue eyes and were not a visible part of her public persona until *Private Benjamin* in 1980. Like Harrison Ford and a number of other stars of the period with either single- or dual-parent Jewish backgrounds, Hawn did not identify as Jewish in either public profiles or casting choices. Therefore, I am not including her texts prior to *Private Benjamin* in the Jewish New Wave.

PART THREE. THE THIRD WAVE

1. Martin Flanagan, "The Chronotope in Action," in *The Action and Adventure Cinema*, ed. Yvonne Tasker (New York: Routledge, 2004), 112.

2. There were, of course, exceptions. Eddie Murphy and Michael J. Fox, to name just two, were notable exceptions in the emerging star iconography of this period.

3. Susan Jeffords, *Hard Bodies: Hollywood Masculinity in the Reagan Era* (New Brunswick, NJ: Rutgers University Press, 1994), 26–27.

4. Ever-attuned to the role of screen Jewishness in arbitrating issues of sexuality, class, and gender, Paul Mazursky paired the two as an unhappily married couple in *Down and Out in Beverly Hills* (1986), one of the rare Jewish-Jewish couplings of the era. Their waning libidos, as well as their two spoiled Jewish children stereotypes (Tracy Nelson and Evan Richards), become reinvigorated by the unexpected arrival of a large, blond, bearded, homeless man, Jerry Baskin (Nick Nolte). As with *Bob & Carol & Ted & Alice* (1969) and *Blume in Love* (1973), Mazursky plays with intercultural desire. An unhappy Jewish family fixates on Nolte, a laconic, Anglo-beautiful, hyper-masculine stranger. The joke is clear. Even wealthy, successful Jews are so enamored with WASP beauty that they covet it at all costs. This is true even when the WASP is a homeless, suicidal vagrant.

5. One of Gould's last major efforts at mainstream stardom was *Over the Brooklyn Bridge* (1984), a passion project by Israeli director turned Cannon Films executive, Menahem Golan. Gould starred as Alby Sherman, a Jewish diner owner in Brooklyn who dreams of moving to Manhattan. His uncle Benjamin (Sid Caesar) offers to loan him money to open a restaurant in Manhattan provided Alby breaks up with his Catholic girlfriend, Elizabeth Anderson (Margeaux Hemingway) and marries a nice Jewish girl. The film was a significant box-office failure for Cannon Films and one of the clearest signs that second-wave couplings had fallen out of favor in the 1980s.

6. For more on Streisand's navigation of the relationship among gender normativity, Jewishness, and queerness, see Marjorie Garber's "Category Crises: The Way of the Cross and the Jewish Star," in *Queer Theory and the Jewish Question*, ed.

Daniel Boyarin, Daniel Itzkovitz, and Ann Pellegrini (New York: Columbia University Press, 2003), and Eve Kosofsky Sedgwick, *Epistemology of the Closet* (Berkeley: University of California Press, 1990).

7. Joyce Antler, Frank Rich, and Neil Gabler, *Television's Changing Image of American Jews* (New York: American Jewish Committee and Norman Lear Center, 2000), 38.

8. Yvonne Tasker, "Dumb Movies for Dumb People: Masculinity, the Body, and the Voice in Contemporary Action Cinema," in *Screening the Male: Exploring Masculinities in Hollywood Cinema*, ed. Steven Cohan and Ina Rae Hark (New York: Routledge, 1993), 230–231.

9. Examples of metamorph focused on idealized states of highly gendered bodies even outside of the obvious science fiction examples. In the romantic comedy *Splash* (1984), the metamorph of Darryl Hannah's mermaid between fish and human riffed on idealized Anglo-Christian femininity as a mutable state. Susan Siedelman's *Making Mr. Right* (1987) featured a perfect robotic man as played by actor John Malkovich in an exaggerated blond wig. Even a low-budget exploitation sex comedy such as *Hunk* (1987) presented a fantasy in which Bradley Brinkman (Steve Levitt), a scrawny young man with a Jewish-sounding name, is magically metamorphed into a blond-haired, blue-eyed alpha male named Hunk Golden (John Allen Nelson).

10. By the time of *Terminator 3: Rise of the Machines* (2003), this emphasis on Anglo-Christian body types as cyborg ideal was extended to female gender archetypes in the casting of German-Norwegian model Kristanna Loken as the ultimate Terminator, the "Terminatrix."

11. Nathan Abrams argues that President Bill Clinton's emphasis on ethnic visibility played a direct role in restoring the screen "Jew" as an adaptable figural metaphor for this revival. Abrams, *The New Jew in Film*, 80–83.

12. Sander L. Gilman, "We're Not Jews," in *Jewish Frontiers: Essays on Bodies, Histories, and Identities*, ed. Sander L. Gilman (New York: Palgrave Macmillan, 2003), 206.

13. Roland Robertson, "Glocalization: Time-Space and Homogeneity-Heterogeneity," in *Global Modernities*, ed. Mike Featherstone, Scott Lash, and Roland Robertson (London: Sage, 1995), 25–44.

CHAPTER 7. SPIEGELMAN'S FROG

1. Donna J. Haraway, "A Cyborg Manifesto: Science, Technology, and Socialist Feminism in the Late Twentieth Century," in *Simians, Cyborgs, and Women: The Reinvention of Nature*, ed. Donna J. Haraway (New York: Routledge, 1991).

2. Bruce Clark, *Posthuman Metamorphosis: Narrative and Systems* (New York: Fordham University Press, 2008).

3. As Sobchack, Kinder, and others noted, morphing is a storytelling artifact that dates back to ancient folkloric traditions, predating cinema and digital tech-

nologies by thousands of years. From Ovid to William Burroughs, Shakespeare to the Mighty Morphin Power Rangers, the origins of the metamorph located in how it offered the means of exploring fractures, transgressions, and transformations among animal, human, and machine. See Vivian Carol Sobchack, ed., *Meta-Morphing: Visual Transformation and the Culture of Quick-Change* (Minneapolis: University of Minnesota Press, 2000), xxiii–xxiv. Marsha Kinder, "From Mutation to Morphing: Cultural Transformations from Greek Myth to Children's Media Culture," in *Meta-Morphing: Visual Transformation and the Culture of Quick-Change*, ed. Vivian Carol Sobchack (Minneapolis: University of Minnesota Press, 2000), 63.

4. Sobchak, *Meta-Morphing*, 162–163.

5. Litvak, *The Un-Americans*. Bial, *Acting Jewish*.

6. Laurence Baron notes that the value of re-creating the Holocaust in fictional entertainment was primarily measured through the power of genre storytelling techniques rather than through any effort at historical accuracy. See Lawrence Baron, *Projecting the Holocaust into the Present* (Lanham, MD: Rowman & Littlefield Publishers, 2005), 4

7. Ibid., 8–11.

8. Janet Walker, *Trauma Cinema: Documenting Incest and the Holocaust* (Berkeley: University of California Press, 2005), 3–5.

9. Loshitzky defines this period as beginning with the massive success of the NBC miniseries *Holocaust* in 1978 and peaking with the rapturous global reception to Steven Spielberg's *Schindler's List* at the beginning of what this book identifies as the third wave of Christian-Jewish couplings in 1993. See Yosefa Loshitzky, "Introduction," in *Spielberg's Holocaust: Critical Perspectives on* Schindler's List," ed. Yosefa Loshitzky (Bloomington: Indiana University Press, 1997), 5.

10. While Adorno subsequently challenged misunderstandings of this quote, this perspective was the dominant one for much of the 1940s, 1950s, and 1960s. See Theodor Adorno, *Prisms* (Cambridge, MA: MIT Press, 1983), 34. Yvonne Kyriakides, "'Art After Auschwitz is Barbaric': Cultural Ideology of Silence Through the Politics of Representation," *Media, Culture, & Society* 27, no. 3 (2005): 441–450.

11. Arendt described visualizing the Holocaust as beyond comprehension. See Hannah Arendt, "The Image of Hell," in *Essays in Understanding, 1930–1954: Formation, Exile, and Totalitarianism* (New York: Schocken Books, 1994), 198.

12. Subsequent debates over Adorno's proclamation focused on the tension between the Holocaust as unknowable or unrepresentable, or both. See David Bathrick, "Seeing Against the Grain: Re-Visualizing the Holocaust," in *Visualizing the Holocaust: Documents, Aesthetics, Memory*, ed. David Bathrick, Brad Prager, and Michael D. Richardson (Rochester, NY: Camden House, 2008), 12–13.

13. The novel's subtitle, "My Father Bleeds History," made an explicit connection between historical memory and physical violence.

14. Art Spiegelman, *Maus II: A Survivor's Tale: And Here My Troubles Began* (New York: Pantheon Books, 1992), 11–12.

15. Freud's concept of transference inevitably leads to paranoia and schizo-

phrenia, both actions that the self-critical Spiegelman ascribes to himself and his father at various points in the graphic novels. See Richard J. Kosciejew, *The Designing Theory of Transference: Volume I* (Bloomington, IN: Authorhouse, 2012), 475–483.

16. Lippit describes the animal as an intermediary phantom, one caught between this world and another uncanny place. Spiegelman's mouse-human and frog-human hybrids locate this hybrid state at the intersection of memory and presence, Jewishness and Christianness. I also discuss Lippit's animetaphor in chapter 2 in my analysis of the work of Kafka. See Akira Mizuta Lippit, "Magnetic Animal: Derrida, Wildlife, Animetaphor," in "Comparative Literature," special issue, *MLN* 113, no. 5 (1998): 1113–1114. And Lippit, *Electric Animal*, 162–163.

17. This is also parodied when Jews pretending to be Polish Christians are drawn as mice wearing obviously fake pig masks on top of their mouse heads. For an example, see Art Spiegelman, *Maus I: A Survivor's Tale: My Father Bleeds History* (New York: Pantheon Books, 1992), 124–125.

18. That same year, the speculative fiction suspense thriller, *The Boys from Brazil*, played with the idea of cloning Hitler as a plausible way for Nazism to continue in the postwar era. In casting the non-Jewish Laurence Olivier as Jewish Nazi hunter Ezra Lieberman and arguing against punitive genetic punishment on the various children carrying Hitler's DNA, the film continued denaturing the events of the Shoah from any Jewish specificity.

19. There were a number of efforts to tackle the Holocaust in the European cinema of the 1960s and 1970s. Jewish Hungarian filmmaker and Holocaust survivor István Szabó produced a trilogy of films—*Father* (1966), *Lovefilm* (1970), and *25 Fireman Street* (1973)—that each dealt with the lingering, residual traumas of Holocaust postmemory. Yet, as Joshua Hirsch notes, the Jewish background of Szabó's characters is never made explicit. See Joshua Hirsch, "István Szabó: Problems in the Narration of Holocaust Memory," *Journal of Film and Video* 51, no. 1 (1999): 13–14, 17.

20. Anne Morey, "*Holocaust*: U.S. Miniseries," *Museum of Broadcast Communications*, www.museum.tv/eotv/holocaust.htm.

21. Spiegelman described watching *Holocaust* with Robert Crumb in 1978 and feeling disgusted with what he called its glibness. This anger fueled much of his work finishing *Maus* in the early 1980s. See Art Spiegelman, *Meta-Maus: A Look Inside a Modern Classic* (New York: Pantheon Books, 2011), 46.

22. Jeffrey Shandler, *While America Watches: Televising the Holocaust* (New York: Oxford University Press, 1999), 168–169.

23. The Commission issued its report and recommendations on September 27, 1979. The memorial was officially funded and authorized by Congress in 1980 and opened on October 16, 1985.

24. Before *Holocaust*, films such as *Judgment at Nuremberg* (1961), *The Pawnbroker* (1964), and *Marathon Man* (1976) had approached the Holocaust obliquely by depicting residual memory in the survivors. *The Pawnbroker* was the rare film to contain flashback sequences depicting the actual camps. But the imagery was

brief, presented as nightmarish flashbacks experienced by Sol Nazerman (Rod Steiger). European exploitation and art cinema of the mid-1970s—including numerous Nazisploitation quickies and art cinema hybrids such as *The Night Porter* (1974) and *Seven Beauties* (1975)—re-created Holocaust camps, but primarily through the distancing effects of Brechtian theatricality, sadomasochistic taboo, and ironic campiness.

25. Annette Insdorf describes this shift as a movement away from narratives of victims and villains to stories focused on the action-adventure themes of resistance and rescue. See Annette Insdorf, *Indelible Shadows: Film and the Holocaust*, 3rd ed. (Cambridge, UK: Cambridge University Press, 2002), 247.

26. François Truffaut's *The Last Metro* (1980) and Rainer Werner Fassbinder's *Lili Marleen* (1981) each used German-Jewish romantic entanglements to thematize the arbitrary nature of European anti-Semitism. In *The Last Metro*, set in France during the early 1940s, Jewish theater owner Lucas Steiner (Heinz Bennent) is forced to go into hiding in his own theater. While he lives underground, he becomes part of a love triangle with his non-Jewish wife, Marion (Catherine Deneuve), and Bernard (Gérard Depardieu), an actor performing in their latest production. Fassbinder's *Lili Marleen* was a loose adaptation of German cabaret singer Lale Andersen's 1972 autobiography, *The Sky Has Many Colors* (*Der Himmel hat viele Farben*). The film focuses on the illicit love affair between German cabaret singer Willie (Hanna Schygulla) and the talented Jewish composer, David Mendelsson (Mel Ferrer). See Annette Insdorf, "How Truffaut's *The Last Metro* Reflects Occupied Paris," *New York Times*, February 9, 1981, 1.

27. Dialogue via the Internet Movie Database, www.imdb.com/title/tt0084707/trivia?tab=qt&ref_=tt_trv_qu.

28. Streep's performances in *Holocaust* and *Sophie's Choice* form an interesting parallel with her characters in the domestic drama, *Kramer vs. Kramer* (1979), and the Woody Allen comedy, *Manhattan* (1979). In all four films, Streep both exemplifies and resists the projection of an idealized shiksa beauty by her Jewish male counterparts Karl (James Woods) in *Holocaust*, Ted (Dustin Hoffman) in *Kramer vs. Kramer*, Isaac (Woody Allen) in *Manhattan*, and Landau (Kevin Kline) in *Sophie's Choice*.

29. Doneson, *The Holocaust in American Film*, 163.

30. Frank Sanello, "Is TV Trivializing the Holocaust?" *Chicago Tribune*, January 6, 1989.

31. Oscar-nominated films such as Louis Malle's *Au Revoir Les Enfants* (1987) and Agnieszka Holland's *Europa Europa* (1991) visualized Holocaust trauma through forms of sublimation and transference between German and Jewish youth. Paul Mazursky's *Enemies: A Love Story* (1989) explored both sadomasochistic and idealized romantic perspectives in focusing on the postwar marriage of Jewish Holocaust survivor Herman Broder (Ron Silver) and his Polish Catholic former servant turned savior during the war, Yadwiga (Margaret Sophie Stein). In keeping with Mazursky's work in the second wave, the film complicates this crossing when Herman begins an affair with another married Jewish Holocaust survi-

vor, Masha (Lena Olin). See Ruth D. Johnston, "The Jewish Closet in *Europa, Europa*," *Camera Obscura* 18, no. 1 (2003): 1–33. Eve Kosofsky Sedgwick, *Epistemology of the Closet* (Berkeley: University of California Press, 1990).

32. James Chapman notes the film's creative license in introducing Harold's fiancée, Sybil Gordon (Alice Krige). While the real Harold Abrahams married a Sybil Evers in 1934, he did not meet her until nearly a decade after the events depicted in the film. Sybil's invented role in *Chariots of Fire* as a fully British Anglo-Saxon love interest for the Jewish protagonist offers a screen parallel to Benjamin Disraeli's British assimilation via Mary Anne Lewis. See James Chapman, *Past and Present: National Identity and the British Historical Film* (London: I. B. Tauris, 2005), 292–295.

33. Steve Neale, "'Chariots of Fire,' Images of Men: Steve Neale Reflects on an Oedipal Olympics," *Screen* 23, no. 3–4 (1982): 47–53.

34. The inversion of an Anglo-Saxon, female psychoanalyst was an idea previously appearing in Saul Bellow's *Herzog* (1964) and discussed in chapter 5. Bellow himself appears as one of the on-camera testimonials in *Zelig*, issuing the absurdist remark that Zelig's "sickness was also his salvation." The line parodied Bellow's own history in producing paradoxical Jewishness as emblematic of modernist fracture.

35. Roger Ebert, "*An American Tail*," *Chicago Sun-Times*, November 21, 1986, www.rogerebert.com/reviews/an-american-tail-1986.

36. *An American Tail*, Box Office Mojo, www.boxofficemojo.com/movies /?id=americantail.htm.

37. This duality is also communicated by the closing song, the 1980s hit, "(I Had) The Time of My Life." It is one of the only songs on the film's soundtrack that does not fit the period-piece setting. This anachronism reminded its spectators of the film's metaphorical parable.

38. Other 1980s examples include the Neil Diamond remake of *The Jazz Singer* (1980), Woody Allen's *Zelig* (1982), Barry Levinson's *Diner* (1982), and the adaptation of Neil Simon's *Biloxi Blues* (1988). Each paired Jewish characters with Catholic or Protestant love interests but without the confrontational political and cultural critiques offered by the screen couplings of the second wave.

Allen went so far as to actively deconstruct the notion of Christian-Jewish couplings by playing with Jewish conversion themes in *Hannah and Her Sisters* (1986) and Dostoevsky-level nihilism when a Jewish optometrist (Martin Landau) has his non-Jewish mistress (Angelica Houston) murdered in *Crimes and Misdemeanors* (1989).

39. Nora Ephron, Rob Reiner, and Andrew Scheinman, *When Harry Met Sally*, draft script, August 23, 1988, 108, www.dailyscript.com/scripts/whenharrymesally .pdf.

40. Herbert J. Gans, "Symbolic Ethnicity: The Future of Ethnic Groups and Cultures in America," *Ethnic and Racial Studies* 2, no. 1 (1979): 15.

41. Even in *Avalon* (1990), Barry Levinson's patriotic celebration of immigrant Jewish culture in the United States over generations, the words "Jew" and "Jew-

ish" are never mentioned in the text. As Esther Schor notes, the film was received by both critics and audiences as an American immigration narrative with the Jewish specificity of the family intentionally minimalized. See Esther Schor, "Kafka's Ring-Bearer Haunts Barry Levinson's *Avalon* at 25," *Tablet Magazine*, February 22, 2016, www.tabletmag.com/jewish-arts-and-culture/197829/avalon-at-25.

42. Bruce Clarke, *Posthuman Metamorphosis: Narrative and Systems* (New York: Fordham University Press, 2008), 146.

43. Dialogue via the Internet Movie Database, www.imdb.com/title/tt0091064 /quotes.

44. Ibid.

45. *The Fly*, dir. David Cronenberg, Twentieth Century Fox, 1986.

46. Joshua Trachtenberg, *The Devil and the Jews: The Medieval Conception of the Jew and Its Relation to Modern Anti-Semitism* (New York: Jewish Publication Society, 1983), 44–46.

47. Gilman, *The Jew's Body*, 39–40.

48. Five years earlier, in 1981, John Landis's *An American Werewolf in London* had presented the young Jewish male as the unaware inheritor of updated cinematic forms of Gothic monstrosity. The film explicitly identifies David (David Naughton), the werewolf-bitten main character, as Jewish while he's sleeping in the hospital after the initial attack. David's nurse and eventual love interest, Alex (Jenny Agutter) remarks that he looks Jewish and that his circumcision confirmed it. Later, in a nightmare sequence, David dreams that his family is being shot by zombie Nazis during a dinner that implies the Jewish Sabbath. The sequence ends on an image of his family menorah being shot to pieces on a shelf.

49. Halberstam, *Skin Shows*, 97.

50. In Lee Edelman's work on the lack of "queer" reproductive ability, the unseen future child of a presumed pregnancy exists as a critical marker of distinction between normative and deviant polarities. In Edelman's corrective, the future child exists as a perpetual haunting specter across all normative landscapes, an unseen but still present "about-to-be-realized" identity. Edelman locates the future child as an unrealizable abstraction and also an eternally delayed postponement. See Lee Edelman, *No Future: Queer Theory and the Death Drive* (Durham, NC: Duke University Press, 2004), 13.

51. Furthering the notion of dream horror as an extension of cinematic fantasy, the doctor delivering the baby is played by director Cronenberg himself.

52. Sigmund Freud, "Mourning and Melancholia," in *On the History of the Psycho-Analytic Movement: Papers on Metapsychology and Other Works* (London: Hogarth Press, 1925), 243–245.

53. Barbara Creed, "The Untamed Eye and the Dark Side of Surrealism: Hitchcock, Lynch, and Cronenberg," in *The Unsilvered Screen: Surrealism on Film*, ed. Graeme Harper and Rob Stone (London: Wallflower Press, 2007), 120.

54. Murray Forman, "Boys Will Be Boys: David Cronenberg's *Crash* Course in Heavy Mettle," in *Ladies and Gentlemen, Boys and Girls: Gender in Film at the End of the Twentieth Century*, ed. Murray Pomerance (Albany: State University of New

York Press, 2001), 120. Ernest Mathijs, "AIDS References in the Critical Reception of David Cronenberg: 'It May Not Be Such a Bad Disease After All,'" in *Cinema Journal*, Vol. 42, No. 4 (Summer 2003), 29-45.

55. Tim Lewis, "David Cronenberg: 'My Imagination Is Not a Place of Horror,'" *Guardian*, September 13, 2014, www.theguardian.com/film/2014/sep/14/david-cronenberg-interview-my-imagination-not-a-place-of-horror.

56. Michel Chion, *The Voice in Cinema* (New York: Columbia University Press, 1999), 18–28.

57. In *A Dangerous Method* (2011), Cronenberg examined the connection between psychoanalysis and repressed sexual desire in a conceptual origin story about Sigmund Freud (Viggo Mortensen), Carl Jung (Michael Fassbender), and Sabina Spielrein (Keira Knightley). Cronenberg's displaced homosocial/homosexual interest between Freud and Jung is transferred onto the body of their "neurotic" female patient, Sabina Spielrein, a young Russian Jew and aspiring scholar. Her Jewish body becomes the contested landscape for Freud and Jung's competing understandings of psychoanalysis, masculinity, sexuality, and identity. This operates similarly to Spiegelman's transference of postmemory Holocaust trauma onto the Jewish/Christian metamorph of Françoise-Mouse.

CHAPTER 8. SEINFELD'S MAILMAN

1. Tom Gamill and Max Pross, "Cigar Store Indian," December 9, 1993, www.seinfeldscripts.com/TheCigarStoreIndian.htm.

2. Ibid.

3. Stephen Battaglio, "The Biz: The Research Memo that Almost Killed *Seinfeld*," *TV Guide*, June 27, 2014, www.tvguide.com/news/seinfeld-research-memo-1083639.

4. "The Serenity Now" also introduced the neologism "shiksappeal," in which the purportedly non-Jewish Elaine tries to understand why so many Jewish men are romantically fixated on her at a bar mitzvah.

5. Davin Coburn, "'Seinfeld' Debuted 25 Years Ago, Yada Yada Yada, It Remains a Cultural Giant," *Washington Post*, July 3, 2014, www.washingtonpost.com/news/arts-and-entertainment/wp/2014/07/03/seinfeld-debuted-25-years-ago-yada-yada-yada-it-remains-a-cultural-giant.

6. Even *The Cosby Show* (1984–1992) operated as a black version of the fantasy white sitcom family, something television scholar Jason Mittell notes was ultimately overturned by the dysfunctional, cruel relationships depicted on *The Simpsons* (1989–). Jason Mittell, "Cartoon Realism: Genre Mixing and the Cultural Life of *The Simpsons*," *Velvet Light Trap* 58, no. 1 (2006): 29–40.

7. Brook, *Something Ain't Kosher Here*, 10.

8. Vincent Brook cites nine determinants for the rise of Jewish visibility in the 1990s, noting that more than thirty shows had visible Jewish characters by the early to mid-1990s. Ibid., 74.

9. Ibid., 118.

10. Raised a Catholic, Elfman is the only non-Jewish actor in the group. But she made numerous references to her marriage to the Jewish-born Bodhi Elfman during the show's run, giving her public persona at least a quasi-Jewish associative identity.

11. Brook, *Something Ain't Kosher Here*, 74–76, 94.

12. *Seinfeld* featured more than seventy love interests for Jerry, a small number played by Jewish actresses (e.g., Debra Messing, Jamie Gertz, and Marlee Matlin). But these characters were never developed to the point of clarification. They collectively existed in an ethnic-free love interest framework.

13. Joanne Morreale, *Critiquing the Sitcom: A Reader* (Syracuse, NY: Syracuse University Press, 2003), xii–xiii.

14. *Soap* also featured one of the first openly gay characters on television, Jodie Dallas (Billy Crystal). See Jason Mittell, *Genre and Television: From Cop Shows to Cartoons in American Culture* (New York: Routledge, 2004). And Jason Mittell, *Complex Television: The Poetics of Contemporary Television Storytelling* (New York: New York University Press, 2015), 11.

15. This was also influenced by television's increasing deregulation, culminating with the passage of the Telecommunications Act in 1996.

16. Brett Mills, *Television Sitcom* (London: British Film Institute, 2005), 128.

17. As Lawrence J. Epstein points out, it wouldn't be until Shandling's follow-up, *The Larry Sanders Show* (1992–1998) on HBO, that he elevated his Jewish identity to the surface of his neurotic persona. Epstein points out how the show's creation of two personas, the on-camera Larry Sanders and the behind-the-scenes "real" Larry Sanders, thematized the tradition of Jewish doublings and fractured identity that lies at the source of Jewish comedy. Epstein, *The Haunted Smile*, 229–230.

18. Despite the cinema popularity of the star personas of Barbra Streisand and Bette Midler, unapologetically Jewish women had rarely been the lead character of a family sitcom, with the notable exception of Rhoda Morgenstern (Valerie Harper) on *Rhoda* in the 1970s.

19. In Season 8, Episode 4, "The Last Date" (October 24, 1995), Roseanne and Dan decide to crash a bar mitzvah, an event culminating in Dan sampling Jewish food for the first time.

20. Shandling's self-reflexive breakdown of sitcom form, playing both himself and a fictional version of himself and repeatedly breaking the fourth wall, borrowed heavily from the direct address of the genre's origins in the early 1950s on shows such as *The George Burns and Gracie Allen Show* (1950–1958).

21. Jamie Lee Curtis's father was the Jewish movie star Tony Curtis. But her character is clearly identified as Catholic and depicted as completely ignorant of Jewish culture, slotting her into the familiar shiksa role.

22. Zeke Jarvis, *Make 'Em Laugh! American Humorists of the 20th and 21st Centuries* (Santa Barbara: ABC-CLIO, 2015), 206.

23. Some, such as Andrew "Dice" Clay's abrasive misogynist, Paul Reubens's man-child Pee-wee Herman, and Yakov Smirnoff's confused Soviet Union immi-

grant, only performed in character and thus may be excluded from the comedic confessional model of performance.

24. In his breakout film of the period, *Back to School* (1986), Dangerfield plays an uneducated slob turned gauche millionaire who returns to college to complete his bachelor's degree. He falls in love with his highly educated Gentile professor of history, Diane (Sally Kellerman). Dangerfield's unmistakable Jewish persona wins the blonde, erudite, upper-class Diane away from her sexless, uptight aristocratic British boyfriend, Philip (Paxton Whitehead). Yet, Dangerfield's character, Thornton Melon, is identified not as Jewish, but, bizarrely, as Italian, at one point mentioning changing his name from "Meloni."

25. Stephen Holden, "Nine Comedians Appear on Dangerfield Special," *New York Times*, August 2, 1985.

26. Simon Round, "Interview: Rita Rudner," *Jewish Chronicle*, May 12, 2011, www.thejc.com/lifestyle/the-simon-round-interview/48785/interview-rita-rudner.

27. The character of Ross Geller did make references to Hanukkah, explicitly acknowledging his Jewishness late in the series in "The One With the Holiday Armadillo" (December 14, 2000). However, Jewishness circulated much earlier on these shows through casting, performance, and themes. For example, Joyce Antler notes that Ross and Monica, as well as Grace Adler on *Will and Grace*, were identified as Jewish through their stereotypically overbearing Jewish mothers. See Joyce Antler, *You Never Call! You Never Write! A History of the Jewish Mother* (New York: Oxford University Press, 2013), 183–185.

28. Brook, *Something Ain't Kosher Here*, 74–76.

29. Jennifer Holt, *Empires of Entertainment: Media Industries and the Politics of Deregulation, 1980–1996* (New Brunswick, NJ: Rutgers University Press, 2011), 170–177.

30. See Sarah Blacher Cohen, "The Unkosher Comediennes: From Sophie Tucker to Joan Rivers," in *Jewish Rye: Essays on Jewish Humor*, ed. Sarah Blacher Cohen (Detroit: Wayne State University Press, 1990), 105–124.

31. Kathleen Rowe, *The Unruly Woman: Gender and the Genres of Laughter* (Austin: University of Texas Press, 1995), 78–79.

32. Ibid., 79–81.

33. Kevin Abbott and Pat Bullard, "I Pray the Lord My Stove to Keep," May 3, 1994, www.tv.com/shows/roseanne/i-pray-the-lord-my-stove-to-keep-28235.

34. Janet Jakobsen, "Queers Are Like Jews, Aren't They? Analogy and Alliance Politics," in *Queer Theory and the Jewish Question*, ed. Daniel Boyarin, Daniel Itzkovitz, and Ann Pellegrini (New York: Columbia University Press, 2003), 80–84.

35. Helene Myers, *Identity Papers: Contemporary Narratives of American Jewishness* (Albany: State University of New York Press, 2011), 113–114.

36. Roseanne Barr has also repeatedly referenced her Jewishness as a defining element of her identity throughout her post-*Roseanne* career. In 2009, she conflated her satire of postwar domesticity and gender roles with her previously underexplored Jewish identity in a provocative photo spread. Roseanne presented her-

self as a "Nazi Domestic Goddess" in drag as a matronly Adolf Hitler, baking "Jew cookies" in an oven inside a domestic 1950s kitchen. See Oliver Noble, "That Oven Feelin'," *Heeb Magazine*, July 15, 2009.

37. Lynn Spigel, building off David Marc, has observed that domestic and gender critiques on television in the 1960s appeared in coded form on "magical" sitcoms such as *I Dream of Jeannie* and *Bewitched*. Spigel explains how these shows focused on containment of female power, worlds in which supernatural women were forced to repress their potential in exchange for an idealized domestic life within the home. Lynn Spigel, *Welcome to the Dreamhouse: Popular Media and Postwar Suburbs* (Durham, NC: Duke University Press, 2001), 128. Marc, *Comic Visions*.

38. Despite Dharma's dedication to New Age practices, Buddhist meditation, and other satires of neo-counterculture cooption of authentic subcultures, she remains identifiably Jewish. In the 1997 Christmas episode, "Haus Arrest" (Season 1, Episode 12, December 17, 1997), to pick just one example, Dharma and Greg struggle to resolve their religious holiday issues with Dharma at first resisting and then finally agreeing to celebrate Christmas. Comedy is derived from the fact that Dharma's willing embrace of numerous religious cultural practices ends when she's asked to give up Hanukkah in favor of Christmas.

39. The Charlotte-Harry coupling is generationally "validated" in the 2008 film when it is revealed that Charlotte was finally able to conceive a child with Harry.

40. Benjamin Wright argues that while creator and star Larry David clearly continues the Jewish schlemiel tradition, he also problematizes it by performing an uneasy hybridity in which he is "neither comfortably Jewish nor cozily unJewish." See Benjamin Wright, "'Why Would You Do That, Larry?' Identity Formation and Humor in *Curb Your Enthusiasm*," *Journal of Popular Culture* 44, no. 3 (2011): 675.

41. J. Hoberman, "Seinfeld," in *Entertaining America: Jews, Movies, and Broadcasting*, ed. J. Hoberman and Jeffrey Shandler (Princeton, NJ: Princeton University Press, 2004), 251.

42. This choice is even more striking given that David's actual wife at the time, Laurie David, is Jewish and bears little resemblance to the Cheryl character.

43. Echoing (or perhaps stealing from) Woody Allen's nearly identical line in *Deconstructing Harry* (1997), Larry, after being accused of being a self-hating Jew, replies, "I do hate myself, but it has nothing to do with being Jewish" ("Trick or Treat," Season 2, Episode 3, October 7, 2001).

44. Michelle Hilmes, *Only Connect: A Cultural History of Broadcasting in the United States* (Boston: Wadsworth Cengage Learning, 2011), 341–342.

45. Laura Turner Garrison, "The Flashy Girl From La Florida: *The Nanny*'s Global Success," *Mental_floss*, November 3, 2011, http://mentalfloss.com/article /29153/flashy-girl-la-florida-nannys-global-success.

46. Ferrari states that, until she moved to the United States from her native Italy, she did not realize Fran Drescher was Jewish. Her research investigates how

"ventriloquism" across national and transcultural borders can obfuscate specific identity in service of global adaptation. See Chiara Francisca Ferrari, *Since When is Fran Drescher Jewish?* (Austin: University of Texas Press, 2011).

47. Vanna Le, "Jerry Seinfeld Tops Highest-Earning Comedians of 2013 List," *Forbes*, July 11, 2013, www.forbes.com/sites/vannale/2013/07/11/jerry-seinfeld-tops -list-of-the-highest-earning-comedians.

48. Nancy Tartaglione, "*Mad About You* Headed To China; Tom Hiddleston, Gillian Anderson Win UK Theatre Awards," *Deadline*, December 1, 2014, http:// deadline.com/2014/12/mad-about-you-headed-to-china-tom-hiddleston-gillian -anderson-win-uk-theatre-awards-1201304356.

CHAPTER 9. GAYLORD'S TULIP

1. Geoff King, *Film Comedy* (London: Wallflower Press, 2002), 72–75.

2. *Millennium Approaches* usually played in the matinee time slot with *Perestroika* following it a few hours later in the evening. Audiences were free to buy tickets to either show independent of the other.

3. In an interview Kushner gave on the opening night of *Millennium Approaches*, he described his emotions with the Yiddish word *kinnehora*, a nervous feeling of accomplishment. Patrick Pacheco, "How Well Did 'Angels' Fly on Opening Night?" *Los Angeles Times*, May 6, 1993, http://articles.latimes.com/1993-05-06 /entertainment/ca-31954_1_opening-night.

4. Aviva Weingarten, *Jewish Organizations' Response to Communism and to Senator McCarthy*, trans. Ora Cummings (London: Vallentine Mitchell, 2008), 87.

5. Cohn remains in denial about his AIDS, his homosexuality, his Jewishness, and his actions working for McCarthy for the entirety of the play. The gap between the irrefutable truths of Cohn's dying body and the fictive postwar media constructs created by the conservative power structures with which Cohn still identifies offers comment on the crisis of Jewish alienation in the 1950s.

6. Alisa Solomon, "Wrestling with *Angels*: A Jewish Fantasia," in *Approaching the Millennium: Essays on Angels in America*, ed. Deborah R. Geis and Steven F. Kruger (Ann Arbor: University of Michigan Press, 1997), 118–133. James Fisher, "Tony Kushner's Metaphorical Jew," in *You Should See Yourself: Jewish Identity in Postmodern American Culture*, ed. Vincent Brook (New Brunswick, NJ: Rutgers University Press, 2006), 76–77.

7. Furthering the metatextual gender scrambling, a female actor, Miriam Shor, performed the male-identified part of Yitzhak in the initial off-Broadway run.

8. Tom Gunning, building on the seminal theory of laughter introduced by Henri Bergson, argues that malfunctioning bodies were one of the first forms of slapstick in early cinema, using physical chaos to develop a pre-narrative cinematic language built around gag structure. Fluid comedy updated this gag-based structure through the use of graphic body eruptions. See Tom Gunning, "Mechanism

of Laughter: The Devices of Slapstick," in *Slapstick Comedy*, ed. Tom Paulus and Rob King (New York: Routledge, 2010), 137–151.

9. Mary Anne Doane has shown how the technology of screen media began as liberation from chronological space and time in the late nineteenth century. But this was an anxiety-provoking "liberation" that also acted as destabilization. To counter these fears, early cinema introduced structures of narrative temporality as the means of stabilizing and rationalizing the relationship between time and technology in the machine age. See Mary Anne Doane, *The Emergence of Cinematic Time: Modernity, Contingency, the Archive* (Cambridge, MA: Harvard University Press, 2002), 11.

10. One film of note that predated Stiller's emergence was *Defending Your Life* (1991), in which writer-star Albert Brooks plays Daniel Miller, a middle-aged man who tragically dies and is forced to defend his mediocre choices in the afterlife. Brooks's schlemiel shortcomings are counterpointed by the overachieving, ideal life lived by Julia, played by Meryl Streep. The love affair followed many second-wave traditions, but, in keeping with 1980s absences, the character of Miller is never explicitly identified as Jewish.

11. Ryder's father was Jewish, her birth name is Winona Horowitz, and she has stated in various interviews that she identifies as Jewish. But the character of Le-laina Pierce in *Reality Bites* does not read as Jewish. Her parents, Tom (Joe Don Baker) and Louise (Anne Meara), are introduced in an early scene as genteel, culturally Christian southerners.

12. Their performances were part of a reintroduction of a Jewish star persona that Vincent Brook calls the "Super-Nebbish," a familiar Jewish schlemiel informed with supernatural or other exemplary powers. See Vincent Brook, "Boy-Man Schlemiels and Super-Nebbishes: Adam Sandler and Ben Stiller," in *Hollywood's Chosen People: The Jewish Experience in American Cinema*, ed. Daniel Bernardi, Murray Pomerance, and Hava Tirosh-Samuelson (Detroit: Wayne State University Press, 2012), 173–179.

13. Sandler was paired with classic blonde, blue-eyed shiksa love interests in all three films: Veronica Vaughn (Bridget Wilson) in *Billy Madison*, Virginia Vent (Julie Bowen) in *Happy Gilmore*, and Julia Sullivan (Drew Barrymore) in *The Wedding Singer*.

14. Biggs is a notable outlier of the period in that he is Italian and not Jewish. Yet, Jewish identity is so strongly associated with Biggs's star persona that on his Twitter account he describes himself simply as "the Jewiest looking non-Jew."

15. The Jerusalem tulip joke hints at Daniel Boyarin's concept of post-Israeli Diaspora operating as what he calls *"Jewissance,"* an ephemeral identity that circulates outside of fixed locations, geographies, and spaces. Boyarin, *Unheroic Conduct*, xxiii.

16. Boyarin argues that psychoanalysts read circumcision as a "chronic inscription of their own ambivalent gaze on Jewish male difference, an ambivalence recorded in American culture in such mythic figures of Jewish psychoanalytic dis-

course as Alexander Portnoy and Woody Allen." Stiller's zipper castration in *There's Something About Mary* and Speedo moment in *Meet the Parents* draw comedy from this ambivalence about Jewish masculinity. Ibid., 241.

17. *Meet the Parents*, dir. Jay Roach, Universal Pictures, 2000.

18. Numerous bits and jokes throughout the film establish Roz and Bernie as a perverted, sexually adventurous couple, in direct contrast to the repressed relationship of Jack and his wife, Dina. Roz's job, identified only as yoga instructor to Jack by Greg, is revealed to be a sex therapist for senior citizens. When Roz and Bernie greet Harry and Dina at the entrance to their Floridian compound, their dog, Moses, an oversexed Chihuahua, runs up and tries to hump Jack's foot. Riffing on an-imetaphor from Kafka to Philip Roth, Moses's carnal animality embodies Jack's perception of Greg, Roz, and Bernie.

19. In occupying the role of retrograde 1950s-era masculinity, De Niro was also parodying his earlier star persona. The Italian-American De Niro was a staple of the 1970s auteur cinema that focused on violence and angst, with an emphasis on ethnicity.

20. Notable exceptions included the pairing of Streisand and George Segal in *The Owl and the Pussycat* in 1970 and of Streisand and James Caan in *Funny Lady* in 1975, and the marriage of Yankel "Jake" Bogovnik (Steven Keats) and Gitl (Carol Kane) in the immigrant period piece, *Hester Street* (1975). That there were so few Jewish-Jewish couplings was likely due to the fact that, aside from Streisand, there were very few visibly Jewish female movie stars.

21. As Eric A. Goldman notes, Streisand's 1991 film *The Prince of Tides* had previously demonstrated the WASP-Jewish power inversion of the 1990s. Streisand, a psychoanalyst, falls in love with her patient, a repressed WASP played by Nick Nolte, in a fully Jewish New York in which she is the insider and he is the outsider. See Goldman, *The American Jewish Story Through Cinema*, 145–147.

22. Lawrence Baron, "Keeping the Faith: A Multicultural *Jazz Singer*," in *The Modern Jewish Experience in World Cinema*, ed. Lawrence Baron (Waltham, MA: Brandeis University, 2011), 412–413.

23. The conversion solution, as Baron points out, appears to invert the religion-abandoning assimilationism of Jack Robin and Mary Dale in *The Jazz Singer*. Ibid., 418.

24. Biggs completed what can be considered his "Jewish trilogy" in 2003 with his starring role in the Woody Allen–directed *Anything Else*. Biggs's Jerry Falk, a nebbishy but talented comedy writer, was a stand-in for a younger version of the famous Woody Allen persona. As in decades of Allen films, Falk becomes carnally obsessed with the proverbial shiksa, Amanda Chase (Christina Ricci).

25. Marci's eventual barrier-crossing attraction to Dr. S followed the progressive Christian-Jewish pattern of the second wave even as it moved miscegenation from subtext to text. But the film's box-office failure and Kudrow's unusual decision as a Jewish actress to play an obvious Jewish character suggest the limitations of Christian-Jewish couplings even in the seemingly open third-wave era.

26. "Natalie Portman, the Sexy Funny Side of a Hollywood Enigma," *Elle UK*, February 2010.

27. Emma Forrest, "Rachel Weisz," *Index Magazine*, 2001, www.indexmaga zine.com/interviews/rachel_weisz.shtml.

28. *Meet the Fockers* grossed $279,261,160 worldwide on a budget of $80 million. *Knocked Up* grossed $148,768,917 worldwide on a budget of under $30 million. Both films confirmed that specific Jewish subject matter was no hindrance to the global market. *Box Office Mojo*, www.boxofficemojo.com.

29. Dialogue via the Internet Movie Database, www.imdb.com/character /ch0007736/quotes.

30. Apatow had previously directed an updated take on the virgin sex comedy with *The 40-Year-Old Virgin* (2005). Steve Carrell's role as a sexually repressed, genteel Anglo-Saxon virgin gave the film a classic bildungsroman structure built around the notion of delayed adulthood. Apatow surrounded Carrell with an ethnic community made up of black, Arab, and Jewish sidekicks, all of whom exhibited the sexual deviancy that Carrell himself was denied.

31. The film counterpoints Peter's flawed Jewish masculinity with Sarah's subsequent boyfriend, the hyper-masculine rock star Aldous Snow (Russell Brand). The three form a recognizable second-wave love triangle built around competing masculinities.

32. As early as April 1995, the popular children's television cartoon *The Rugrats* was one of the first to depict an interfaith home in "A Rugrats Passover" (Season 3, Episode 26). Tommy (voiced by E. G. Daily) and Angelica Pickles (voiced by Cheryl Chase) hear the story of the exodus from their Grandpa Boris Kropotkin (voiced by Michael Bell).

33. In "The Best Chrismukkah Ever" (Season 1, Episode 13, December 3, 2003), the hyper-verbal Seth explains how he gets around the conflicting faiths of his parents by merging Christmas and Hanukkah into one holiday. Contrast this textual address with the Festivus codes of the Costanza family on *Seinfeld*, and the shift in televisual address of Jewish alterity a decade later is notable. Other examples of sitcom Jews experiencing Christmas in the third wave include "The Christmas Episode" (Season 1, Episode 7, December 22, 1993) on *The Nanny*, in which Fran is confused by the holiday yet actively participating in it and eager to learn. The third season of *Mad About You* establishes that Paul Buchman met and fell in love with Jamie on Christmas Eve ("How to Fall in Love," *Mad About You*, Season 3, Episode 12, December 16, 1992). On a Christmas episode of *Friends* ("The One with the Holiday Armadillo," Season 7, Episode 10, December 14, 2000), Ross (David Schwimmer) goes out of his way to teach his son, Ben (Cole Sprouse), about Hanukkah while still participating in Christmas with the rest of the group. These shows presented Jews on Christmas to explore the negotiable, fluid duality of what Jeffrey Shandler calls the "Crypto-Jew"—characters who are not often identified as Jewish but use Jewish codes and/or are played by Jewish actors. See Jeffrey Shandler, "At Home on the Small Screen: Television's New York Jews," in *Entertaining*

America: Jews, Movies, and Broadcasting, ed. J. Hoberman and J. Shandler (New Jersey: Princeton University Press, 2003), 251.

34. Sound theorist Michael Chion describes how the disembodied voice in screen media contains an uncanny, magical power by virtue of its untethering from the visual realm. Chion calls this affect the *Acousmêtre*. See Chion, *The Voice in Cinema*, 23.

35. One notable dramatic example took place on the long-running family show, *7th Heaven* (1996–2007). One of the few overtly Christian shows of the period, *7th Heaven* was set in small-town America. The hour-long comedic drama followed Reverend Eric Camden (Stephen Collins), his stay-at-home homemaker wife Annie (Catherine Hicks), and their seven cute and precocious children. However, even this show was not immune to the value of the Anglo-Christian-Jewish coupling narrative. Season 6 introduced a love story in which their oldest son, Matt Camden (Barry Watson), becomes engaged to a Jewish girl, Sarah Glass (Sarah Goldberg).

36. *Nick and Norah's Infinite Playlist* connects the creative act of the recording of music to the Jewish Norah (Kat Dennings) experiencing her very first orgasm, brought about by the non-Jewish Nick (Michael Cera) while on mic in her father's recording studio. *Obvious Child*, billed as the very first "abortion comedy," frames the unintended pregnancy and subsequent decision to have an abortion by the Jewish Donna Stern (Jenny Slate) as a step in her early romance with the non-Jewish Ryan (Paul Briganti). Both connect transgressive visuals (female orgasm, abortion) to the female Jewish body as events influenced by unwitting but well-intended non-Jewish males.

37. Two notable exceptions were Ben Stiller's 2007 remake of *The Heartbreak Kid*, opposite Malin Akerman, and his starring role in the independent film, *Greenberg*, opposite Greta Gerwig, in 2010.

38. The breakup offered a similar wave coda as had the divorce of the characters played by Dustin Hoffman and Meryl Streep in *Kramer vs. Kramer* (1979) and the narcissistic boom/bust critique Albert Brooks depicted in *Modern Romance* (1981). Larry's subsequent romance with the African-American Loretta Black (Vivica A. Fox) in Season 7, followed by his attempt to win Cheryl back by offering her a coveted role on a *Seinfeld* reunion in Season 8, both suggest Woody Allen's famous dictum that artists use art to get right what they get wrong in life. Larry's journey to New York to begin dating again in Season 9 marked the cyclical return to *Seinfeld*-esque origins.

CONCLUSION. PLATO'S RETWEET

1. The title of the episode, "Kina Hora," communicates the show's awareness of the problematic nature of emancipation when paired with Jewish neurosis and self-sabotage. A colloquial Jewish expression, *Kina Hora* cautions against bragging

about good fortune, implying that such arrogance will eventually lead to a downfall. The titular warning plays out as Sarah's neurotic insecurities get the best of her. For more on my analysis of the relationship between transgender sexuality and Christian-Jewish interplay on *Transparent*, see my article: Joshua Louis Moss, "'The Woman Thing and the Jew Thing': Transsexuality, Transcomedy, and the Legacy of Subversive Jewishness in *Transparent*," in *From Shtetl to Stardom: Jews and Hollywood: USC Casden Institute for the Study of the Jewish Role in American Life*, ed. Michael Renov and Vincent Brook (West Lafayette, IN: Purdue University Press), 2017.

2. *Transparent* identifies contemporary transgender and transsexual fluidity as a multigenerational renegotiation with the legacy of all three of the transgressive Anglo-Christian-Jewish couplings waves discussed in this book. In Season 2 flashback episodes, set in Weimar-era Berlin, the origins of the Pfefferman's crisis between transgender identification and Jewishness are traced back to the fascist eugenics movement of the 1930s. Sarah's grandmother and great uncle, Rose (Emily Robinson) and Tante Gittel (Hari Nef), attend lectures at the Institute for Sexual Research run by Dr. Magnus Hirschfeld (Bradley Whitford) before Nazi threats force their immigration to the United States. The legacy of the second wave locates in the central protagonist of the show, Sarah's transgender parent, Maura, a retired professor, who offers a reminder of the academic personal-is-political sexual politics of the late 1960s and 1970s. The third wave, embodied by the delayed maturity and gender and sexual confusion of Maura's three Jewish children, reflects the impact of second-wave crisis on third-wave Gen-X Jewish confusion and myopia.

3. Lydia Amir, "Plato's Theory of Love: Rationality as Passion," *Practical Philosophy* (November 2001): 6–7.

4. Plato's philosophy of love, as Amir notes, focuses on the rational mind (logic) struggling to comprehend the primal drives that inform emotion and animality (desire). Ibid., 8–10.

5. James T. Siegel, "Kiblat and the Mediatic Jew," in *Religion and Media*, ed. Hent De Vries and Samuel Weber (Stanford, CA: Stanford University Press, 2001), 302.

6. Ibid.

7. Rieff, *The Jew of Culture*, 95.

Selected Bibliography

Abrams, Nathan. *The New Jew in Film: Exploring Jewishness and Judaism in Contemporary Cinema*. New Brunswick, NJ: Rutgers University Press, 2012.

Alexander, Michael. *Jazz Age Jews*. Princeton, NJ: Princeton University Press, 2001.

Antler, Joyce. *The Journey Home: How Jewish Women Shaped Modern America*. New York: Schocken Books, 1997.

———. *Talking Back: Images of Jewish Women in Popular Culture*. Hanover, NH: Brandeis University Press, 1998.

———. *You Never Call! You Never Write! A History of the Jewish Mother*. New York: Oxford University Press, 2013.

Baron, Lawrence. *Projecting the Holocaust into the Present*. Lanham, MD: Rowman & Littlefield Publishers, 2005.

Bartov, Omer. *The "Jew" in Cinema: From* The Golem *to* Don't Touch My Holocaust. Bloomington: Indiana University Press, 2005.

Baskin, Judith R., ed. *Jewish Women in Historical Perspective*. Detroit, MI: Wayne State University Press, 1998.

Beeber, Steven Lee. *The Heebie-Jeebies at CBGB's: A Secret History of Jewish Punk*. Chicago: Chicago Review Press, 2006.

Beller, Steven. *Vienna and the Jews, 1867-1938: A Cultural History*. New York: Cambridge University Press, 1989.

Bial, Henry. *Acting Jewish: Negotiating Ethnicity on the American Stage and Screen*. Ann Arbor: University of Michigan Press, 2005.

Biale, David. *Eros and the Jews: From Biblical Israel to Contemporary America*. Berkeley: University of California Press, 1997.

———. *Gershom Scholem: Kabbalah and Counter-History*. Cambridge, MA: Harvard University Press, 1982.

Biale, David, Michael Galchinsky, and Susannah Hesche, eds. *Insider/Outsider: American Jews and Multiculturalism*. Berkeley: University of California Press, 1998.

Boyarin, Daniel. *Unheroic Conduct: The Rise of Heterosexuality and the Invention of the Jewish Man*. Berkeley: University of California Press, 1997.

Boyarin, Daniel, and Jonathan Boyarin. *Carnal Israel: Reading Sex in Talmudic Culture.* Berkeley: University of California Press, 1993.

Boyarin, Daniel, Daniel Itzkovitz, and Ann Pellegrini, eds. *Queer Theory and the Jewish Question.* New York: Columbia University Press, 2003.

Bradford, Sarah. *Disraeli.* London: Weidenfeld & Nicolson, 1982.

Bredin, Jean-Denis. *The Affair: The Case of Alfred Dreyfus.* New York: George Braziller, Inc., 1986.

Brodkin, Karen, *How Jews Became White Folks and What That Says About Race in America.* New Brunswick, NJ: Rutgers University Press, 1998.

Brook, Vincent. *Something Ain't Kosher Here: The Rise of the "Jewish" Sitcom.* New Brunswick, NJ: Rutgers University Press, 2003.

———. *You Should See Yourself: Jewish Identity in Postmodern American Culture.* New Brunswick, NJ: Rutgers University Press, 2006.

Buber, Martin. *I and Thou.* New York: Simon & Schuster, 1970.

Buhle, Paul. *From the Lower East Side to Hollywood: Jews in American Popular Culture.* London: Verso, 2004.

Carr, Steven. *Hollywood and Anti-Semitism: A Cultural History up to World War II.* Cambridge, UK: Cambridge University Press, 2001.

Cesarani, David. *Disraeli: The Novel Politician.* New Haven, CT: Yale University Press, 2016.

Cohan, Steve. *Masked Men: Masculinity and the Movies in the Fifties.* Bloomington: Indiana University Press, 1997.

Cohen, Sarah Blacher, ed. *Jewish Rye: Essays on Jewish Humor.* Detroit: Wayne State University Press, 1990.

Davison, Neil R. *James Joyce, Ulysses, and the Construction of Jewish Identity: Culture, Biography, and the "Jew" in Modernist Europe.* Cambridge, UK: Cambridge University Press, 1998.

Desser, David, and Lester D. Friedman. *American Jewish Filmmakers: Traditions and Trends,* 2nd ed. Urbana: University of Illinois Press, 1993.

Diner, Hasia. *In the Almost Promised Land: American Jews and Blacks, 1915-1935.* Baltimore: Johns Hopkins University Press, 1977.

———. *The Jews of the United States: 1654–2000.* Berkeley: University of California Press, 2004.

Diner, Hasia, Shira Kohn, and Rachel Kranson. *A Jewish Feminine Mystique? Jewish Women in Postwar America.* New Brunswick, NJ: Rutgers University Press, 2010.

Dinnerstein, Leonard. *Anti-Semitism in America.* New York: Oxford University Press, 1994.

Doane, Mary Ann. *The Emergence of Cinematic Time: Modernity, Contingency, the Archive.* Cambridge, MA: Harvard University Press, 2002.

Doherty, Thomas. *Cold War, Cool Medium: Television, McCarthyism, and American Culture.* New York: Columbia University Press, 2003.

———. *Hollywood and Hitler: 1933–1939.* New York: Columbia University Press, 2015.

———. *Pre-Code Hollywood: Sex, Immorality, and Insurrection in American Cinema, 1930–1954.* New York: Columbia University Press, 1999.

Doneson, Judith E. *The Holocaust in American Film*. New York: Syracuse University Press, 2002.

Drake, Susanna. *Slandering the Jew: Sexuality and Difference in Early Christian Texts*. Philadelphia: University of Pennsylvania Press, 2013.

Dyer, Richard. *White*. New York: Routledge, 1997.

Epstein, Lawrence J. *The Haunted Smile: The Story of Jewish Comedians in America*. New York: Public Affairs, 2001.

Erens, Patricia, *The Jew in American Cinema*. Bloomington: Indiana University Press, 1984.

Fanon, Frantz. *Black Skin, White Masks*. New York: Grove Press, 1967.

Ferrari, Chiara Francisca. *Since When is Fran Drescher Jewish?* Austin: University of Texas Press, 2011.

Flavin, Michael. *Benjamin Disraeli: The Novel as Political Discourse*. Brighton, UK: Sussex Academic Press, 2005.

Forth, Christopher E. *The Dreyfus Affair and the Crisis of French Manhood*. Baltimore: Johns Hopkins University Press, 2004.

Freedman, Jonathan. *Klezmer America: Jewishness, Ethnicity, Modernity*. New York: Columbia University Press, 2008.

Friedman, Lester. *American Cinema of the 1970s: Themes and Variations*. New Brunswick, NJ: Rutgers University Press, 2007.

Garber, Marjorie. *Vice Versa: Bisexuality and the Eroticism of Everyday Life*. New York: Touchstone, 1995.

Gertzman, Jay. *Bookleggers and Smuthounds: The Trade in Erotica 1920–1940*. Philadelphia: University of Pennsylvania Press, 2002.

Gilman, Sander. *The Case of Sigmund Freud: Medicine and Identity at the Fin De Siècle*. Baltimore: Johns Hopkins University Press, 1993.

———. *Franz Kafka, the Jewish Patient*. London: Routledge, 1995.

———. *Jewish Frontiers: Essays on Bodies, Histories, and Identities*. New York: Palgrave Macmillan, 2004.

———. *The Jew's Body*. New York: Routledge, 1991.

———. *Making the Body Beautiful: A Cultural History of Aesthetic Surgery*. Princeton, NJ: Princeton University Press, 1999.

———. *Smart Jews: The Construction of the Image of Jewish Superior Intelligence*. Lincoln: University of Nebraska Press, 1997.

Goldman, Eric A. *The American Jewish Story through Cinema*. Austin: University of Texas Press, 2013.

Goldstein, Eric L. *The Price of Whiteness: Jews, Race, and American Identity*. Princeton, NJ: Princeton University Press, 2006.

Gruber, Ruth Ellen, *Virtually Jewish: Reinventing Jewish Culture in Europe*. Berkeley: University of California Press, 2002.

Gurock, Jeffrey S. *Jews in Gotham: New York Jews in a Changing City, 1920–2010*. New York: New York University Press, 2012.

Halberstam, Judith. *Skin Shows: Gothic Horror and the Technology of Monsters*. Durham, NC: Duke University Press, 1995.

Hansen, Miriam. *Babel and Babylon: Spectatorship in the American Silent Film.* Cambridge, MA: Harvard University Press, 1991.

Harap, Louis. *The Image of the Jew in American Literature: From Early Republic to Mass Immigration.* Syracuse, NY: Syracuse University Press, 2003.

Harris, Mark. *Pictures at a Revolution: Five Movies and the Birth of a New Hollywood.* New York: Penguin Press, 2008.

Hay, Daisy. *Mr. and Mrs. Disraeli: A Strange Romance.* New York: Farrar, Straus and Giroux, 2015.

Herbrechter, Stefan. *Posthumanism: A Critical Analysis.* London: Bloomsbury Academic Publishing, 2013.

Hibbert, Christopher. *Disraeli: The Victorian Dandy Who Became Prime Minister.* New York: Palgrave Macmillan, 2006.

———. *Queen Victoria in Her Letters and Journals: A Selection.* New York: John Murray Publishers, 1984.

Hilmes, Michele. *The Nation's Voice: Radio in the Shaping of American Culture.* Minneapolis: University of Minnesota Press, 1997.

Hoberman, J. *Bridge of Light: Yiddish Film Between Two Worlds.* Lebanon, NH: Dartmouth College Press, 2010.

Hoberman, J., and Jeffrey Shandler, eds. *Entertaining America: Jews, Movies, and Broadcasting.* Princeton, NJ: Princeton University Press, 2003.

Horowitz, Daniel. *Betty Friedan and the Making of* The Feminine Mystique: *The American Left, the Cold War, and Modern Feminism.* Amherst: University of Massachusetts Press, 1998.

Hughes, Edward J. *Proust, Class, and Nation.* New York: Oxford University Press, 2011.

Jacobson, Matthew Frye. *Whiteness of a Different Color: European Immigrants and the Alchemy of Race.* Cambridge, MA: Harvard University Press, 1998.

Jeffords, Susan. *Hard Bodies: Hollywood Masculinity in the Reagan Era.* New Brunswick, NJ: Rutgers University Press, 1994.

Jones, E. Michael. *The Jewish Revolutionary Spirit And Its Impact on World History.* South Bend, IN: Fidelity Press, 2008.

Kallen, Horace. *Judaism at Bay: Essays Toward the Adjustment of Judaism to Modernity.* New York: Arno Press, 1972.

Kaufman, David E. *Jewhooing the Sixties: American Celebrity and Jewish Identity.* Waltham, MA: Brandeis University Press, 2012.

Kirsch, Adam. *Benjamin Disraeli.* New York: Schocken Books, 2008.

Kleeblatt, Norman L., ed. *The Dreyfus Affair: Art, Truth, and Justice.* Berkeley: University of California Press, 1987.

Lacan, Jacques. *The Four Fundamental Concepts of Psychoanalysis: The Seminar of Jacques Lacan, Book XI.* New York: W. W. Norton, 1981.

Lambert, Josh. *Unclean Lips: Obscenity, Jews, and American Culture.* New York: New York University Press, 2014.

Lippit, Akira Mizuta. *Electric Animal: Toward a Rhetoric of Wildlife.* Minneapolis: University of Minnesota Press, 2000.

Litvak, Joseph. *The Un-Americans: Jews, The Blacklist, and Stoolpigeon Culture.* Durham, NC: Duke University Press, 2009.

Loshitzky, Yosefa. *Identity Politics on the Israeli Screen.* Austin: University of Texas Press, 2001.

———, ed. *Spielberg's Holocaust: Critical Perspectives on* Schindler's List. Bloomington: Indiana University Press, 1997.

May, Lary. *Screening Out the Past: The Birth of Mass Culture and the Motion Picture Industry.* Chicago: University of Chicago Press, 1980.

Moore, Deborah Dash, and S. Ilan Troen, eds. *Divergent Jewish Cultures: Israel and America.* New Haven, CT: Yale University Press, 2001.

Mosse, George L. *Nationalism and Sexuality: Middle-Class Morality and Sexual Norms in Modern Europe.* Madison: University of Wisconsin Press, 1985.

Mufti, Aamir. *Enlightenment in the Colony: The Jewish Question and the Crisis of Postcolonial Culture.* Princeton, NJ: Princeton University Press, 2007.

Mullin, Katherine. *James Joyce, Sexuality, and Social Purity.* New York: Cambridge University Press, 2003.

Nachman, Gerald. *Seriously Funny: The Rebel Comedians of the 1950s and 1960s.* New York: Pantheon Books, 2003.

Navasky, Victor S. *Naming Names.* New York: Hill and Wang, 2003.

Nirenberg, David. *Anti-Judaism: The Western Tradition.* New York: W. W. Norton, 2013.

O'Kell, Robert P. *Disraeli: The Romance of Politics.* Toronto: University of Toronto Press, 2013.

Read, Piers Paul. *The Dreyfus Affair: The Scandal that Tore France in Two.* New York: Bloomsbury Press, 2012.

Rieff, Philip. *The Jew of Culture: Freud, Moses, and Modernity.* Charlottesville: University of Virginia Press, 2008.

Rogin, Michael. *Blackface, White Noise: Jewish Immigrants in the Hollywood Melting Pot.* Berkeley: University of California Press, 1998.

Ross, Steve. *Hollywood Left and Right: How Movie Stars Shaped American Politics.* New York: Oxford University Press, 2011.

Rubenstein, Richard L., and John J. Roth, *Approaches to Auschwitz: The Holocaust and Its Legacy.* Louisville, KY: Westminster John Knox Press, 2003.

Saporta, Sol. *Society, Language, and the University: From Lenny Bruce to Noam Chomsky.* New York: Vantage Press, 1994.

Sarna, Jonathan. *American Judaism: A History.* New Haven, CT: Yale University Press, 2004.

Sartre, Jean-Paul. *Anti-Semite and Jew: An Exploration of the Etiology of Hate.* New York: Schocken Books, 1948.

Scholem, Gershom. *Walter Benjamin: The Story of a Friendship.* New York: New York Review of Books Classics, 2003.

Shandler, Jeffrey. *Jews, God, and Videotape: Religion and Media in America.* New York: New York University Press, 2009.

———. *While America Watches: Televising the Holocaust*. New York: Oxford University Press, 1999.

Sokel, Walter. *The Myth of Power and the Self: Essays on Franz Kafka*. Detroit, MI: Wayne State University Press, 2002.

Spigel, Lynn, and Michael Curtin. *The Revolution Wasn't Televised: Sixties Television and Social Conflict*. New York: Routledge, 1997.

Stern, Sheila. *Proust: Swann's Way*. New York: Cambridge University Press, 1989.

Trachtenberg, Joshua. *The Devil and the Jews: The Medieval Conception of the Jew and Its Relation to Modern Anti-Semitism*. New York: Jewish Publication Society, 1983.

Wenger, Beth S. *New York Jews and the Great Depression: Uncertain Promise*. Syracuse, NY: Syracuse University Press, 1999.

White, Edmund. *Marcel Proust: A Life*. New York: Penguin Books, 1999.

Zivin, Erin Graff. *The Wandering Signifier: Rhetoric of Jewishness in the Latin American Imaginary*. Durham: Duke University Press, 2008.

Zurawik, David. *The Jews of Prime Time*. Hanover, NH: Brandeis University Press, 2000.

Index

Note: Page numbers in italics refer to photos.

animality (*continued*)
  modernist transformation, 50. *See also*
  hybridity; Kafka, Franz; metamorph
Annie Hall (Allen, 1977), 98, 149, 169
Anti-Judaism: The Western Tradition
  (Nirenberg, David), 11–12
anti-Semitism. *See* eugenics; nativism;
  and specific authors and works
"anti-Trinity" (Freud-Marx-Einstein),
  64–65
Antler, Joyce, 76, 164–165, 184, 300n58
Anything But Love (1989–1992), 220
Apatow, Judd, 256–258
Apprenticeship of Duddy Kravitz, The
  (1974), 5, 96, 149, 168
"Are Bolsheviki Mainly Jewish?" (*The
  Literary Digest*, 1918), 64
Arendt, Hannah, 41, 42, 191–192
Arliss, Goerge and Florence, 94
Arthur, Bea, 174, 226
Assistant, The (Malamud, 1957), 130
"At the Suicide of the Last Jew in the
  World in the Last Cinema in the
  World" (Cronenberg, 2007), 211
Avery, Brian, 120
Avishai, Bernard, 132

Bacall, Lauren, 109, 111
Bancroft, Anne, 120
Baron, Lawrence, 254
Barr, Roseanne, 185, 220, 222, 224–226,
  318–319n36
Barton Fink (1991), 13
Bartov, Omar, 9, 78, 117
Baruchel, Jay, 256, 257
Baudelaire, 9
Bauman, Zygmunt, 20, 271–272n6
Baxter, Meredith, 171
Beilis Affair, 63
Being and Time (Heidegger, 1927), 49–50
Bell, Kristin, 257
Bellow, Saul, 5, 123, 127–129, 135, 137,
  296n16

Benjamin, Richard, 6, 99, *134*, 135, 170,
  254
Benjamin, Walter, 9, 19–21, 128; "The
  Last Angel of History," 238, 240–241,
  244, 245; mouse-mountain allegory,
  19, 57, 240, 271n5
Berg, Gertrude, 95–96, 111, 112, 114
Betty Boop (Fleischer, 1921), 78–80, *79*
Bewitched (1964–1972), 226
Bhabha, Homi, 102
Bial, Henry, 10, 99, 109, 163, 190
Biale, David, 116, 119, 174
Bicycle Wheel (Duchamp, 1913), 20
Big Bang Theory, The (2007–), 258
Biggs, Jason, 13, 186, 248, *249*, 254
Billy Madison (1995), 247
Birney, David, 171
Birth of a Nation (Griffith, 1915), 75, 77, 91
Black, Jack, 254
Black, Karen, 134, *134*
"blank page," 26, 31, 40, 42, 43, 50, 57, 61,
  209. *See also* Disraeli, Benjamin
*Bleeding Hearts, The: or Jewish Freedom
  Granted by King Casimir of Poland*
  (Goldin, 1913), 77
Bloomsbury Group, 22, 58–59. *See also*
  Woolf, Leonard; Woolf/Stephen,
  Virginia
Blore, Cathianne, 201
Bob & Carol & Ted & Alice (Mazursky,
  1969), 5, 98, 149, 151, 153–156
Body and Soul (1947), 109
Bonnie and Clyde (1967), 126
Borges, Jorge Luis, 64
Bourdieu, Pierre, 8
Boushel, Joy, 207
Boyarin, Daniel, 11, 65, 115, 118, 129
Braff, Zach, 255
Brey, Philip, 20
Bridget Loves Bernie (Slade, 1972–1973),
  98, 150, 171–172, 218
Brinsley, Richard, 26
Broad City (2013–), 259–260
Brodkin, Karen, 93, 284n19

Miller, Arthur, 118
Miller, Patsy Ruth, 81
Mills, Brett, 219–220
Minnie Moskowitz (Cassavetes, 1971), 157, 177
"Minnie the Moocher" (Calloway, 1932), 79
Mitchell, John Cameron, 243
Mittell, Jason, 219
modernism: as contradictory, 20, 26; and cosmopolitan Jewish identity, 5, 21, 51; and coupling, 41–43, 57, 59; and the emancipated European-Jewish identity, 20–21; and Jewish sexuality, 62; modernist fracture, 10, 11, 21; and the nation-state, 20, 35; and technological development, 19–20, 22, 189. *See also* fracture discourse
Modern Romance (Brooks, 1981), 100, 149, 181, 182
Monroe, Marilyn, 118, 119
Montgomery, Clift, 111
Morreal, John, 141
Mosse, George L., 15
Most, Andrea, 179
Mostel, Zero, 156, 159, 161, 165, 167
"Mourning and Melancholia" (Freud, 1917), 210
Mozzhukhin, Ivan, 85
Mufti, Aamir, 11
multiculturalism, 67, 69, 87–89, 185
Muni, Paul, 95, 105
Murphy, Carolyn, 253
Myers, Helene, 225
My Fairfax Lady (Sherman and Katz), 140

Nachman, Gerald, 139
Naked Lunch (Cronenberg, 1991), 210
Nancy, Jean-Luc, 8
Nanny, The (1993–1999), 6, 185, 218, 226–227, 231–234, 259; adaptations of, 233

nativism, 41, 61–67; and Anglo-Christian-Jewish coupling as decay, 66; as inverted allegory, 61–62, 65; in Latin American literature, 64; literary antecedents to, 65–66; Russian context of, 62–64; US context of, 64, 88, 89–93. *See also* eugenics; Jewishness: as biologically and sexually deviant; Jewishness: as threat to nation-state
Neale, Steve, 199
New Girl (2011–), 258, 259
New Hollywood and counterculture, 98–99, 104, 105, 149–151, 289n2; and stardom, 155–156, 164, 165. *See also* second wave coupling (1967–1980)
Newman, Paul, 3, 5, 116, 117–118, *117*
Nicholas, Thomas Ian, 248
Nichols, Mike, 5, 99, 101, 104–105, 120, 148, 241; and Elaine May, 5, 139, 140, 142
Nick and Norah's Infinite Playlist (2008), 259, 324n36
Nietzsche, Friedrich, 49, 278n16
Nixon, Richard, 97, 98, 183
Nordau, Max, 41, 116
Normal Heart, The (Kramer, 1985), 237
Norris, Kimberly, 215
Norton, Edward, 253

Obvious Child (2014), 259, 324n36
O.C., The (2003–2007), 258, 323–324n33
Odets, Clifford, 110
Odyssey, The (Homer), 55
Office, The (2005–2013), 259
O'Kell, Robert, 30, 32
Oliver Twist (Dickens, 1838), 65
Opening of Misty Beethoven, The (1976), 175
Orbach, Jerry, 202
Origins of Totalitarianism, The (Arendt, 1947), 41
Ozick, Cynthia, 137

Roosevelt, Teddy, 88

Rose, The (1979), 167–168

Roseanne, 185, 220, 222, 223–226, 227

Rosenberg, Ethel, 110, 114, 161, 237, 238, 239, 241, 244

Rosenberg, Julius, 110, 114, 161, 237

Rosenthal, Samuel J., 108

Ross, Katherine, 3, 103, *103*, 104, 136

Roth, Henry, 123–124

Roth, Philip, 5, 96, 132, 135, 138

Roth, Samuel, 89

Rothschild, Lionel de, 29, 32

Rothschilds, the, 26, 27

Rowan, Kelly, 258

Rowe, Kathleen, 224

Rubin-Vega, Daphne, 242

Rudd, Paul, 257

Rudner, Rita, 221–222

Rudnick, Paul, 254

Russell, Rosalind, 114, 115

Ryan, Meg, 1, 184, 201

Ryder, Winona, 246, 321n11

Rylaarsdam, J. Coert, 48

Safer, Elaine B., 137

Sahl, Mort, 5, 139–140, 144

Saint, Eva Marie, 3, 5, 116, *117*

Salmonova, Lyda, 78

Samberg, Joel, 114

Sandler, Adam, 186, 246–247, 259

Sartre, Jean-Paul, 12; *Anti-Semite and Jew*, 12, 41–42

Saturday Night Live (SNL) (1975–), 1, 246–247

Savage, Fred, 204

Saving Silverman (2001), 13, 186, 254

Scholem, Gershom, 21, 128, 129

Schumer, Amy, 259

Schwimmer, David, 222

Schwob, Marcel, 54

Scott, Seann William, 248

Scott, Sherie Rene, 244

second wave coupling (1967–1980), 97–

100, 149, 151; as ambiguous, 120–121, 129, 149, 153, 154, 156; casting patterns of, 104–105, 107, 132, 135, 157, 161; as corrective narrative, 149, 159–167; first wave influence on, 105, 122, 124, 132–133, 153, 155, 159; influence of, on stand-up comedy, 99, 138–147; and masculinity archetype, 99, 102, 104, 120, 132, 155–156, 158–159, 169, 170, 175; in music, 179–180, 308n69; in pornography, 174–179, 308n73; in postwar literature, 123–138; pushback against, 180–183, 184–185; as redemption narrative, 124; and sexual liberalism, 149, 152–155, 162, 177; "shiksa" trope in, 84, 128, 133, 151, 156–158, 162–163, 169, 170; socio-political context of, 109–111, 119, 125–126, 170; on television, 150, 170–174; television prior to, 112–114; as tempering, 100, 151, 161–162. *See also* Anglo-Christian-Jewish coupling; christonormativity; Jewishness: and alienation; Jewishness: and the carnal Jew; New Hollywood and counterculture; sexuality; visibility, Jewish; *and specific actors, directors, and films*

Segal, George, 6, 96, 156

Segel, Jason, 186, 256, 257

Seinfeld (1989–1998), 6, 215–218, 222, 229, 234, 235, 260

Seinfeld, Jerry, 215, 216, 221, 236

Sellers, Peter, 152, *152*, 302n8

Sex and Character (Weininger, 1903), 62, 63

Sex and the City (1998–2004), 227–228

sexuality: and agency, 3, 5, 57, 76, 77; and Jewish masculinity, 85, 115, 118, 119; Jewish, and modernism, 62; Jewish, and sexual desire in literature, 32, 42–43, 51–52, 57; as political, 76, 80, 97, 138; repression of, 15

Shandling, Garry, 220, 317n20

Shaughnessy, Charles, 218

Shawn, Wallace, 204